THE CHORUS IN SOPHOCLES'
TRAGEDIES

THE CHORUS IN SOPHOCLES' TRAGEDIES

BY

R. W. B. BURTON

Emeritus Fellow of Oriel College, Oxford

CLARENDON PRESS, OXFORD
1980

Oxford University Press, Walton Street, Oxford OX2 6DP

OXFORD LONDON GLASGOW
NEW YORK TORONTO MELBOURNE WELLINGTON
KUALA LUMPUR SINGAPORE JAKARTA HONG KONG TOKYO
DELHI BOMBAY CALCUTTA MADRAS KARACHI
NAIROBI DAR ES SALAAM CAPE TOWN

Published in the United States by Oxford University Press
New York

British Library Cataloguing in Publication Data

Burton, Reginald William Boteler
  The chorus in Sophocles' tragedies.
  1. Sophocles—Criticism and interpretation
  2. Drama—Chorus (Greek drama)
  I. Title
  882'.01   PA4417   79-40594
  ISBN 0-19-814374-5

Typeset by CCC, printed and bound in Great Britain by
William Clowes (Beccles) Limited, Beccles and London.

ACKNOWLEDGEMENTS

It gives me great pleasure to recall with gratitude many friends and colleagues who have helped me in various ways, in particular the late Sir Maurice Bowra who, a year before his death, read the first draft of two chapters of this book and encouraged me to continue. I owe much to Professor Lloyd-Jones, Mr G. W. Bond, Mr J. G. Griffith, Mr D. S. Raven, and Mr T. C. W. Stinton, all of whom have read individual chapters in manuscript, made valuable suggestions, and saved me from many errors. All shortcomings which have survived their scrutiny are my own responsibility. I should also like to record the stimulating effect of tutorial discussions with pupils which have enlivened the years of gestation and eased the birth of a book which I hope may be of use both to young students of Sophocles and to those who teach them. My thanks are due finally to the anonymous advisers of the Press for their helpful criticisms, to Mr Richard Robinson for compiling the indexes, to Dr R. C. T. Parker for reading the proofs, and to Mrs Janet Caldwell for her excellent typing of the manuscript.

R.W.B.B.

Kidlington
Oxford

CONTENTS

ABBREVIATIONS FOR PERIODICALS
CITED IN THE FOOTNOTES

AJPh	*American Journal of Philology*
BICS	*Bulletin of the Institute of Classical Studies*, London University
CPh	*Classical Philology*
CQ	*Classical Quarterly*
CR	*Classical Review*
GRBS	*Greek, Roman and Byzantine Studies*
HSPh	*Harvard Studies in Classical Philology*
JHS	*Journal of Hellenic Studies*
LÉC	*Les Études classiques* (Namur)
MH	*Museum Helveticum* (Bâle)
PCPhS	*Proceedings of the Cambridge Philological Society*
RPh	*Revue de philologie* (Paris)
YClS	*Yale Classical Studies*

INTRODUCTION

My intention in this book is to examine Sophocles' handling of the chorus in his seven extant tragedies. I have chosen this aspect of his art for two reasons, first because in many of the most important books on Sophoclean drama his treatment of the chorus has not received the attention it deserves, and secondly because this traditional element in Greek Tragedy strikes modern taste as its strangest and least intelligible feature. Such at any rate is my experience from forty years of discussing the subject with pupils at Oxford, and this may provide an excuse for adding yet another item to the long list of books on this great dramatist.

I have devoted a chapter to each play so that each chapter may be read separately in conjunction with the Greek text. The order in which the plays are listed in the Table of Contents seems to me the most likely order of their composition, though with the production dates of only *Philoctetes* and *Oedipus at Colonus* certainly known, the chronology of Sophocles' *oeuvre* must remain in doubt. In each chapter I have tried to define the personality and status of the chorus chosen by the dramatist, to consider their use both as singers and actors, and to trace the developments in his treatment of their role in so far as this is possible from the evidence of seven plays whose composition appears to have been spread over a period of some forty years.

My method is to analyse the odes with strict regard to their contexts in order to determine their different kinds of relevance, their functions as instruments of dramatic irony, their contribution to our understanding of the intellectual and moral issues that underlie certain of the plays, and their effects upon the minds and emotions of audience and reader as required by the dramatist at each stage in the movement of his plots. I have given attention also to the coryphaeus's interventions in non-choral sections and especially to the chorus's participation in wholly or partly sung dialogue with the actors, because here more than anywhere are to be found the most important developments in dramatic technique. Finally, I have, though with misgivings due to the perils of making subjective judgements, tried to assess the poetic quality of the odes by noting points of style, vocabulary, and imagery; and throughout the book I have done my best to bear in mind that Sophocles regarded the utterances of his choruses, whether sung, recited, or spoken, as an integral part of plays designed for performance before an audience of Athenian citizens.

In discussing textual and linguistic problems I have been deliberately selective, guided sometimes by personal whim, but mainly by a desire to confine such discussions as far as possible to passages of dramatic and stylistic interest. I am conscious that in the chapter on *Trachiniae* I may have overstepped the limits I have elsewhere set myself, but the strange subject-matter of this play, the difficulties of its language and imagery, and the corruptions in its text have seemed to me to require that some passages in it should be examined in greater detail than is needed in any of the other plays. I had thought of relegating some of these textual and linguistic comments to an appendix, but have decided to incorporate them all into the chapter on this play, chiefly in the interests of readability and easy reference.

Since I have concentrated on detailed analysis of the chorus's part in each play and avoided lengthy discussion of general issues in the body of the book, it may be helpful to the reader if I now indicate some points which have been touched upon, perhaps too incidentally, or embedded, perhaps too deeply, in the separate chapters. Much of what I say will be a statement of my *credo* about some aspects of the chorus's relation to the audience as well as to the individual characters in Sophoclean Tragedy. I consider first its role as singers of the odes.

Analysis of each ode in each play must begin by setting it firmly in its dramatic context. The song may be a summary of the preceding act, illuminating by poetical expression certain features in the thought, emotion, and language of the actors' speeches; or it may be a wide-ranging reflection on the deeper issues of the play as a whole. In some cases, both types overlap; and in both, especially when an actor remains on the stage during an ode, we should always be awake to the interaction between the songs and the spoken parts that precede or follow. As to the relevance of the songs to their context, two kinds will be found, an immediate and a remote, sometimes confined to separate odes, sometimes merging into each other or juxtaposed in the same ode. In both kinds the dramatist is using the songs of his chorus to awake definite intellectual, moral, and emotional responses in his audience, and thus to engage their thoughts and feelings for the heroic men and women who act and suffer on the stage and who inhabit a different sphere of being from the ordinary spectator or reader.

In its role as singers the chorus is distinct from the actors. In the Greek theatre this distinction was marked visually by the dance movements which accompanied its songs and by the fact that it occupied a different part of the acting area, perhaps on a lower level than the actors, supposing that the stage was slightly raised. At the same time, it is included in the dramatis personae together with the other characters. Unlike them, however, it is a group, not an individual. It represents, moreover, an average group, sailors, young girls, elders of a city, mature women, guardians of a sanctuary; it expresses the reactions of its group to situations of high tragedy and thus helps to bridge the distance between the characters on the stage and the average audience in the theatre. Further, since the chorus has a group personality, we do not expect from it the same consistency or coherence of character as we expect from an individual; and though Sophocles is careful to make its utterances appropriate to its group and status, he nevertheless manipulates it with great flexibility, different and sometimes conflicting reactions being presented in the same play or the same ode in order to serve a particular dramatic purpose.

There is a further respect in which the chorus is able to reach the audience through its songs. Many of the odes take the form of conventional types of ritual utterance: a hymn to a god, an appeal for a divine presence, a paean raised at a time of fear, a lament for the doomed or the dead. These types of utterance, composed on recognized stylistic principles, but embellished, when transferred from real life to drama, with poetic language and splendid imagery, would strike an immediate chord in an audience who were familiar with them in their daily lives and would help to clarify the structure and pattern of songs such as the parodos of *Oedipus Tyrannus*. Odes cast in these forms also remind us that the performance of Greek Tragedies had a deeply religious significance as an act of public worship.

Before I pass on to the role of the chorus as actors, two further points are to be noted. First, choral odes are on occasions used to mark the passage of time and to take the place of a messenger's speech. Both these functions are performed together by the second stasimon of *Oedipus at Colonus*. Second, and in my view more important, is the extent to which contemporary conditions should be taken into account in interpreting the songs. I have already stated my conviction that the interpretation of every ode must begin by relating it to its context, because it seems to me that Sophocles does not use his songs to express his own views on matters unrelated to the plots of his plays or to warn, exhort, or instruct his fellow-citizens, but to produce certain dramatic effects and to interpret his plays to an audience. Nevertheless, I believe that in some odes, especially of the two great Theban plays and the last play, we should bear in mind the intellectual and political atmosphere of Athens and the dangers that threatened the city from plague, war, and civil strife during the latter part of the fifth century. Odes such as the first stasimon of *Antigone*, the parodos of *Oedipus Tyrannus*, and the first three stasima of *Oedipus at Colonus*, while primarily belonging to the world of dramatic illusion, at the same time speak to the audience with a voice from the real world.

I have said that the chorus as singers are kept distinct from the other dramatis personae and that this distinction is due mainly to their being a group, not an individual. When we consider them as actors, we find that both in the spoken parts and in sung or partly sung dialogues they are drawn into the same dramatic orbit as the great figures on the stage. In the non-singing parts the group is represented by its leader (coryphaeus), who converses with the actors, offering advice, warning, encouragement, instruction, and sympathy, according to the relationship of the group to the individual character. On some occasions, the leader's remarks influence the action, so that a decision is altered and a different turn given to the working out of the plot. In addition to this, he often makes a neutral comment between long speeches in which the actors clash in the heat of debate. These short comments are equally balanced between the speakers and are sometimes surprising when we know that the chorus's sympathies are wholly with one side. Besides reflecting the Greek love of gnomic utterances, they have, though often flat and banal, an important function, in that they represent a norm of ordinary behaviour which points up excesses of passion. Dull comments of this kind also act as a stimulus and a foil to intense speeches in which a character explains his motives and reveals the inmost workings of his heart and mind. This latter function is apparent especially towards the end of a dialogue in which the actor expresses his emotion in song, and the chorus-leader speaks in the calmer tones of iambic trimeters.

It is however in sung dialogue that Sophocles has achieved his most striking effects in making chorus and actors together contribute to the action of his plays on the same level of emotion. In these passages of dialogue, the chorus become actors, no longer commentators, or mediators between stage and audience; and in some plays, notably *Ajax* and *Oedipus at Colonus*, they are so deeply involved in the events on the stage that those who watch or read may feel concerned to an almost equal degree for the chorus as for the characters. I have said enough in the body of this book about Sophocles' development of the technique of lyric dialogue, so I do no more here than emphasize its supreme importance in any account of his use of the chorus.

I close with a few remarks about my treatment of metre. A detailed analysis of metrical usage is obviously out of place in a book of this kind, but I have usually named, without technical discussion, the metres used in the various songs and in the sung parts of dialogue. I have also from time to time speculated on the feel of particular metres and rhythmical patterns, especially sound echoes, repetition of metrical units, and rhyme effects. This is indeed dangerous ground, because so little is known for certain about the impression that would be made upon Greek ears by different metres. There is general agreement for instance that dochmiacs denote increased excitement, both by themselves and in combination with iambics, that sung utterance points to heightened emotion in dialogue where one participant speaks and the other sings, and that a mixture of several different types of metre may indicate mounting intensity of feeling. Beyond that, it is hard to go, and I am conscious that some of my speculations may have exceeded the very little evidence that exists. Nevertheless, as long as its limitations are recognized, an occasional attempt to assess the *ethos* of Greek metres may perhaps be forgiven.

I

AJAX

The chorus of this play consist of men of Salamis, Ajax' native island, who rowed his ship to Troy nearly ten years before the action begins and who are therefore bound to him by the ties of a common fatherland and by the shared experiences of long years of campaigning. Only once in the play are they referred to as warriors (ἄνδρες ἀσπιστῆρες, 565) and there is no hint anywhere that they took part in the actual fighting. Although Ajax himself addresses them as ἑταῖροι in 687, it would not be correct to regard them as his ἐριῆρες ἑταῖροι, his trusty companions in the Homeric sense, who shared with their lord all the perils of warfare. What they share with him are the discomforts of the weary bivouac in a foreign country, the absence from home and the delights of home, and the longing for return to their own land, an emotion of the strongest significance to all Greeks.[1] Throughout the play the sailors are addressed in terms which put their status and function beyond doubt: ναὸς ἀρωγοὶ τῆς Αἴαντος (201), φίλοι ναυβάται (349), γένος ναίας ἀρωγὸν τέχνας, ἄλιον ὃς ἐπέβας ἑλίςςων πλάταν (357 f.), ἐνάλιος λεώς (565), sea-faring men, skilled in the art of rowing, the same type of people who accompanied Neoptolemus to Lemnos in search of Philoctetes. Their dependence on Ajax is absolute: they acquire strength only from him; without him they are defenceless; and when he is shamed and doomed they share his shame and expect a traitor's death by stoning (λιθόλευςτον Ἄρη, 254) unless they can escape by flight from the scene of his ruin.

Ajax in his turn is bound to them by special ties of affection and looks to them as his only friends in his hour of distress:

> φίλοι ναυβάται, μόνοι ἐμῶν φίλων
> μόνοι ἔτ' ἐμμένοντες ὀρθῷ νόμῳ   (349 f.)

---

[1] Cf. esp. 900; 1185–1222.

'Dear sailors, alone of my friends, alone still constant to your loyalty', and

$$c\acute{\epsilon} \ \tau o\iota \ c\acute{\epsilon} \ \tau o\iota \ \mu \acute{o} \nu o\nu \ \delta \acute{\epsilon} \delta o\rho\text{-}$$
$$\kappa a \ \pi \eta \mu o\nu \grave{a}\nu \ \grave{\epsilon} \pi a\rho\kappa \acute{\epsilon} co\nu\tau a \qquad (359 \ f.)$$

'You, you alone I see will be my defence against misery.' These mutual feelings of loyalty and devotion are not made apparent in the relations between the heroes and their subordinates in the *Iliad*, and Sophocles makes them explicit in his play in order to emphasize Ajax' isolation from his equals in the heroic world which he inhabits. The sailors dwell in the same world as he, with its shame-culture values and its exaltation of personal honour, and they have an unshaken confidence in his essential nobility (481 f.). On the other hand, they have little insight into his motives, and to a large extent they find him incomprehensible, a burden to be borne rather than understood.[2] They fail also to acknowledge the problem of his guilt, for he had in full consciousness planned a murderous assault on the Greek chiefs in requital for a slight upon his honour, and yet neither the sailors nor indeed any character in the play comes to grips with this question until Menelaus enters to forbid his burial at 1047. We shall accordingly find no help from the chorus in understanding the moral issues raised by the play. This should not surprise us in Sophocles, who is always concerned to adapt the utterances of his choruses to their status and function.[3] The main function of the chorus in Ajax is to enhance the tragic pathos of the play by contrasting the past glory with the present ruin of their hero and expressing their loyalty and devotion to him in his alienation from his true self and from the fellowship of his equals.

Few if any problems of relevance arise from the odes of *Ajax* or indeed from any of the chorus's sung or spoken utterances, but before entering on a detailed discussion of their role in the play we should define briefly what we mean by the phrase 'dramatic relevance' as applied to the songs or stasima. These songs are to be interpreted primarily as essential parts of a play intended for public performance, so that the first task of interpretation is to relate each one to its precise context. Broadly speaking, we shall find in most of the odes in Sophocles' plays two kinds of relevance,

---

[2] Cf. 609 and their reaction to his speech 646–92.
[3] Cp. e.g. the choruses of *Ant.* and *O.T.* with those of *Aj.*, *Phil.*, and *O.C.*

an immediate and a more remote. In some odes, especially in plays with choruses of important rank, both kinds are found in the same song, a fact which gives such songs great depth and range,[4] but in *Ajax* they are kept distinct. In the first and third stasima (596 and 1185), the chorus stand back from the tensions of the surrounding scenes, and this detachment affords a momentary relief from the emotional strains between the actors and gives these lyrics an air of more generalized reflection. The minds of audience and reader are thus directed away from the immediate context and encouraged to reflect on remoter aspects of the tragedy. On the other hand, the relevance of the second stasimon (693) is immediate: it crystallizes emotions aroused by Ajax' speech and sharpens the impact of the *peripeteia* or crisis-point which follows it. At this stage of our discussion, a mere adumbration of what is meant by dramatic relevance must suffice: details will emerge in clearer definition as we examine the odes of the seven plays.

In form the parodos of *Ajax* resembles those of Aeschylus' *Persae*, *Supplices*, and *Agamemnon*, in which a system of recited anapaests precedes a series of lyrics in strophic corresponsion. The anapaests are recited as the sailors march into the orchestra, and at 172 they sing a single triad when they have taken up their position. Nowhere else in his extant tragedies does Sophocles use this form of parodos, though in *Antigone* he combines the two elements, recitation and song interwoven, thus revealing a half-way stage between the Aeschylean type and the purely lyric type found in *Trachiniae* and *Oedipus Tyrannus*. A further development occurs in *Electra*, *Philoctetes*, and *Oedipus at Colonus*, in which lyrics from the chorus are combined with actors' anapaests or lyrics, so that the parts assigned to actor and chorus are woven closely together in dialogue form. The type of parodos found in *Ajax* may perhaps be used as an argument for dating this play early among Sophocles' extant works, but we should always remember that this form may well have been dictated by dramatic requirements, choice of plot, and the group personality of the chorus. To put it very naïvely, what is more natural than for a body of sailors, subordinate to the chief character, to march into the orchestra in formation? In this connection we may recall the parodos of Aeschylus' *Septem* (467 B.C.) with its chorus of women

[4] Cf. esp. *Ant.* 332 ff. and 583 ff., *O.T.* 863 ff. and 1186 ff.

in a besieged city: instead of marching in with recited anapaests, their role and status demand that for dramatic effect they should enter in a confused and hysterical rush singing a long passage of free dochmiacs before the expected strophic lyrics in which they pray to the gods to save their city.[5] Nine years later, in *Agamemnon*, Aeschylus reverted to what we might consider a less 'advanced' form of parodos. Although *Ajax* is almost certainly to be dated early among the extant plays, arguments used to support such a dating should be based upon grounds of language, style, and metre rather than of dramatic technique. In placing his seven plays in chronological order, Sophocles' own account of his stylistic development as reported by Plutarch is of some importance.[6] Only two of the plays have precise production dates, *Philoctetes* in 409, *Oedipus at Colonus* posthumously in 401. *Antigone* can be assigned reasonably to the end of the decade 450–440, if we may believe the well-known story that Sophocles' election as strategos in 440 was due to the success of that play. The other four plays cannot be precisely dated.

Of more relevance however to the subject of this book is the difference between the recited anapaests in *Ajax* and those of the three plays of Aeschylus mentioned above. In these, the anapaests are predominantly narrative: the chorus introduce themselves and set out the story for the benefit of the audience. In *Persae* and *Supplices* they open the play, so this function is obvious, while in *Agamemnon* they follow the Watchman's brilliant speech which merely hints at hidden menaces but gives little information on the background of the play. The anapaests in *Ajax* on the other hand are in the strictest sense dramatic,[7] because the prologue has made a narrative by the coryphaeus unnecessary. The play begins with a remarkable tableau scene depicting a catastrophe which has already happened. Odysseus is brought by Athena face to face with the great hero, who comes out of his tent at her second summons, all bloody and triumphant (90). Cruelly the goddess taunts the demented Ajax and at the end of the prologue uses him as a warning to Odysseus, who has indeed already drawn the conclusion from what he has seen that men are mere

[5] *Th.* 77–180.
[6] Plu. *Moralia* 79 b. For a discussion see Bowra, *Problems in Greek Poetry*, ch. 7 and Lloyd-Jones, *JHS* 75 (1955), 158 f.
[7] See Nestle, *Die Struktur des Eingangs in der Attischen Tragödie*, 52–8, for a discussion of parodoi.

shadows (125 f.). We are left with the impression of a malignant
and spiteful goddess contrasted with a humane and sympathetic
mortal whose reactions to the spectacle of a mighty foe laid low
mark him as inhabiting a world vastly different from that of the
Homeric hero. Earlier in the prologue, Athena had told Odysseus
what Ajax had done to the cattle and had then revealed the full
horror to him, as she says (67):

$$ὡc \ πᾶcιν \ Ἀργείοιcιν \ εἰcιδὼν \ θροῇc$$

'so that you may look upon him and report to all the Greeks', a
line which prepares us for what we are to expect when the chorus
enter. Odysseus reports as instructed, between the end of the
prologue and the entry of the chorus, because it is clear from the
anapaests that the sailors have heard what they call Odysseus'
whispered slanders (λόγουc ψιθύρουc, 148). We need not however
assume a time-break of any length between prologue and
parodos, because as we learn from 28, rumour has already
attached to Ajax the responsibility for slaughtering the cattle,
and Odysseus' task is to spread the rumour with circumstantial
detail. We may also assume that the action of the play, as in
Antigone, Trachiniae, and *Electra*, opens at dawn with Odysseus
tracking Ajax, and that when the chorus enter day is not very far
advanced.[8]

Two important consequences result from the way in which
Sophocles has opened his play. In the first place, the coryphaeus
can dispense with a narrative, as noted above, so that the whole
of the parodos, including the anapaests, which are, like the lyric
triad, addressed to Ajax, is an essential part of the plot and
therefore dramatic, and also vital to the revelation of character.
Secondly, *Ajax*, like *Trachiniae, Antigone*, and *Oedipus Tyrannus*,
gives the impression of a second start: the prologue is a scene
apart, essential indeed to the structure of the play, and the
parodos, though normally prepared for by a line or two in the
prologue,[9] follows as a juxtaposition instead of flowing naturally
out of it as in Sophocles' last three plays. As to the revelation of
character, the prologue has shown Odysseus in a favourable
light: he ignores Athena's challenge to laugh in Homeric fashion
over a stricken foe (74 f.); on the contrary, he pities him, aware

---

[8] Cf. νυκτὸc τῆcδε (21), νύκτωρ (47), τῆc νῦν φθιμένηc νυκτόc (141).
[9] *Aj.* 67; *Ant.* 33 f.; *O.T.* 144.

that his condition is due to an ἄτη to which he is bound; and his conduct and remarks show that he has learnt the lesson of cωφροcύνη. The picture of Ajax in the prologue is of course a distortion produced by madness: nevertheless when his sanity is restored, we discover a character of exactly opposite type to Odysseus': unaware of cωφροcύνη, at any rate to begin with, unconscious of guilt, savage in reaction, yet heroic, formidable, and grand, to his devoted sailors he is the great one who dwarfs the rest of mankind, the tower of strength, the eagle.[10] Odysseus on the other hand is the villainous teller of tales. Sympathy with his character, aroused in the prologue, is suspended during his absence throughout the main part of the play and only returns at the end when he persuades Agamemnon to allow Ajax' burial. The contrasting pictures of character in prologue and parodos suggest that the play is concerned among other things with a conflict between two worlds, the world of the Homeric warrior and a more compassionate and humane world to which Odysseus belongs, and in which Ajax is an alien.

In the parodos, both in the anapaests and in the sung triad, the chorus, as we have seen, address Ajax in the second person, even though he is not present on the stage, because he dominates their thoughts and because they urgently need his presence. The whole parodos is in effect a challenge to him to show himself. In particular, the last 14 lines of the anapaestic system suggest this theme of challenge by underlining certain features of the relationship between the sailors and their hero: their need of each other, their ineffectualness when apart (χωρίc being repeated at 158 and 166), and their power when united to confound the meaner sort of people. The sailors' urgent wish for his presence gathers in intensity from the second part of the anapaests until it reaches its climax in the antistrophe and epode of the triad. The recurrent use of μέγαc in 154–71 well illustrates the impression made upon them by Ajax. This greatness denotes physical stature and strength, and the qualities that accompany it are familiar from the Homeric world: prowess in battle, inborn quality (φύcιc) inherited from a heroic ancestry, and a high sense of personal honour expressed in uninhibited boasting. Sophocles further explains the bonds between the sailors and their hero in

[10] See *Thompson's Glossary of Greek Birds*, s.vv. αἰγυπιόc and αἰετόc. It is not apparent that the Greek poets distinguished the two species.

the curiously intricate lines 158–61 with their antithesis between great and small and their latent imagery from building, suggested by the metaphor in πύργου ῥῦμα and elaborated in the four following lines:

καίτοι cμικροὶ μεγάλων χωρὶc
cφαλερὸν πύργου ῥῦμα πέλονται·
μετὰ γὰρ μεγάλων βαιὸc ἄριcτ᾿ ἂν
καὶ μέγαc ὀρθοῖθ᾿ ὑπὸ μικροτέρων

'The small apart from the great are an unsafe tower of defence: for with the great the weakling will best be sustained upright, just as the great will be by the help of the lesser.' These words aptly convey the interdependence of the great Ajax and the lesser mortals who serve him and form the chorus: together they build a strong tower: apart they have no strength (165 f.). We may recall that Ajax is himself a tower in the *Odyssey*[11] and that his shield is, uniquely, like a tower throughout the *Iliad*. The Homeric world has generated further epic phrases and images in these anapaests: the dove as a symbol of fright, αἴθωνι cιδήρῳ (147), and the extended simile of the eagle and the small birds at the end (167–71).[12]

The gnomic comment on envy (φθόνοc) at 154–7 needs a brief discussion because it reflects a view of life which long persisted in Greek thought. These lines recalled to the writer of the ancient scholium on this passage a sentence from Pindar's *Nemean* 8.21 f. (?459 B.C.), which indeed he quotes in his note:

ὄψον δὲ λόγοι φθονεροῖcιν,
ἅπτεται δ᾿ ἐcλῶν ἀεί, χειρόνεccι δ᾿ οὐκ ἐρίζει

'rumours are a relish to the envious; envy always attacks the noble, but never fights with the mean.' Pindar illustrates this sentiment by the story of Ajax, in which he depicts Odysseus as a deceitful rogue whose lies deluded the Greeks into awarding him, instead of Ajax, the arms of Achilles.[13] The sailors use the same maxim about envy in their first reaction to Odysseus' tales, and precisely because it is a frequent commonplace throughout Greek literature, it would be wrong to assume any connection

[11] *Od.* 11. 556.
[12] Cf. *Il.* 4. 485 (αἴθωνι cιδήρῳ); *Od.* 22. 302.
[13] The story appears also in *N*. 7. 20–30. φθόνοc is indeed a familiar Pindaric theme.

between Sophocles and Pindar. Envy explains satisfactorily enough for the chorus the quick spread of rumour, the ease with which Odysseus persuades his hearers of its truth, and the delight with which it is received.

The lyric triad which follows, while developing the theme of the anapaestic system and echoing much of its language and content, provides a powerful quickening of emotion with its excited double question about the cause of Ajax' behaviour. Such openings are usual in Sophocles' parodoi:[14] appeals to the sun for information or in thanksgiving (*Trachiniae* and *Antigone*), urgent questions arising from facts revealed in the prologue and not yet imparted to the chorus (*Ajax*, *O.T.*, and *Electra*), and the thrill of a search (*Philoctetes* and *O.C.*). In *Ajax* alternative questions introduced in dactylic rhythms soon merging into dactylo-epitrites raise the tension after the recited anapaests. Doubt and wonder occupy the first stanza, and the rapid run of the metre reflects the singers' emotion. The thought of this strophe is rooted in the Homeric world where men are punished for failure to offer sacrifice and thanksgiving for services rendered by gods in war or the chase.[15] Artemis was prone to anger especially when men were cruel to animals; and that, rather than any explicit reference to the Attic cult of Artemis Tauropolos, determines the choice of her epithet here. Nevertheless there are evocative associations in the word Ταυροπόλα (172) which may be explored in order to elicit the emotional overtones in this part of the song. Ajax has destroyed bulls, which were under Artemis' protection. On one coin from Amphipolis she rides a bull, a torch in either hand;[16] on another, inscribed Ταυρόπολος, she is depicted with a bull's horns springing from her shoulders. The chorus conceive her here as a power who can drive men to violence, even as Ares can, and it is therefore appropriate that we should think of her also as Artemis Ταυρική, goddess of a wild and orgiastic cult imported by Orestes and Iphigeneia from the Tauric Chersonnese to Brauron in Attica, where, Euripides tells us,[17] she was worshipped as the Ταυρόπολος θεά. Under this aspect she symbolizes the frenzy of destruction, which the chorus think she inspired in Ajax, the ἄτη οὐρανία of 195. The word ἐλαφαβολίαις

---

[14] Jens-Uwe Schmidt, *Sophokles, Philoktet* (1973), 55–9, has some good remarks on Sophocles' parodoi.

[15] Cf. e.g. *Il.* 9. 537 ff.   [16] Cf. ἀμφίπυρον *Trach.* 214.   [17] *I.T.* 1454–7.

in 178 reminds us also of Artemis Ἀγροτέρα, the huntress-deity
worshipped at the Elaphebolia. Thus does Sophocles give life to
the opening of the song by calling to the mind of his audience
contemporary Attic festivals with which they were familiar.[18]
The answer to the chorus's question is, as we know, Athena, but,
ironically, they remain in ignorance until the messenger's speech
reporting Calchas' instructions and the reasons for Athena's
anger (756 f. and 770–7).

The antistrophe, opening with γάρ, gives the reasons for the
questions: the chorus are certain that it was not of his own
intention that Ajax attacked the cattle, and they infer that a
sickness may have come on him from the gods: ἥκοι γὰρ ἂν θεία
νόcοc (185). At 186 ἀλλά breaks off the speculations and
introduces a prayer to Zeus and Apollo based on the assumption
that the rumour (ὦ μεγάλα φάτιc 172) is true, in which case the
gods alone can avert the evil. If however the stories are false,
Ajax must not hide his face in his tent but come out and confront
his revilers (187–95). The thought of the antistrophe is thus
carried over into the epode, which continues with a striking
image, suggested by φλέγων in 195, of the insolence of Ajax' foes
spreading undeterred like wild fire in the windy glens amid
shrieks of mocking laughter:

> ἐχθρῶν δ' ὕβριc ὧδ' ἀτάρβητα
> ὁρμᾶται ἐν εὐανέμοιc βάccαιc,
> πάντων καχαζόντων
> γλώccαιc βαρυάλγητα·
> ἐμοὶ δ' ἄχοc ἕcτακεν.

The closing line with the emphatically placed personal pronoun
breaks off the ode abruptly as the sailors draw attention to the
permanence of their own distress.

The whole of this song is composed as a unit in triad form
rather than as a strophic pair with summarizing epode, as for
instance *Oedipus at Colonus* 1239–48[19]. Its structure is simple, and
apart from 182–5, so are its thought and expression. The
threefold repetition of φάτιc indicates what impinges most on the
sailors' thoughts: the rumour of Ajax' deeds is at first personified
as the mother of their shame in a bold metaphor (μᾶτερ αἰcχύναc

---

[18] For these festivals see Deubner, *Attische Feste*, 204–9.
[19] The parodos of *Trach.* has a summarizing epode 132–40.

ἐμᾶc) (173 f.); it next stands (187) in a near rhyme with χάριν at the corresponding place in the strophe (176=186) for the concrete evil which it purveys, and finally (191) in a sense restricted to Ajax himself, the slander on his character. It is μεγάλη and twice κακή. All these repetitions recall phrases in the anapaests, ζαμενὴc λόγοc κακόθρουc (137), μεγάλοι θόρυβοι (142), λόγουc ψιθύρουc (148). The words πάντων καχαζόντων (198) with their vivid *onomatopoeia* echo the theme of laughter at a stricken foe which is first heard in the prologue (79) and recurs throughout the play,[20] emphasizing that mockery over the mighty when fallen is another important aspect of the tragedy in addition to the conflict between two worlds. Thus, after the excited questions of the opening strophe, the content and thought of the remaining two stanzas are in the main amplifications of ideas in the anapaests, culminating in the challenge to Ajax to show himself and confound his enemies like the eagle in the simile at the end of the anapaests. The song is strictly confined to the immediate dramatic context and does not range over a vast field of contemplation in the manner of Aeschylus. In the whole parodos, recitative and lyric parts alike, gnomic reflection is confined to the four lines on φθόνοc. Sophocles, while employing the Aeschylean form, has adapted it with skill to his own purpose, shortening it, simplifying it, and giving it great dramatic intensity.

The parodos illustrates an important feature in Sophocles' delineation of his chief characters. After the horrifying glimpse of madness in the prologue, the chorus reveal the true greatness of a typical Sophoclean hero as he appears to the average man. All these chief figures in his plays, male or female, are great and in their greatness, formidable and to some extent incomprehensible to their fellows: such are Ajax, Antigone, Heracles in *Trachiniae*, Oedipus in both the Oedipus plays, Electra, Philoctetes. They transcend the norms of ordinary behaviour, they stand outside human jurisdiction, they come into conflict with the societies to which they belong, and they threaten by their very greatness the established order of things human and divine which the Greeks called Δίκη. Hence, vulnerable alike to men and gods, they are doomed to disaster. In some cases they are rehabilitated after long years of suffering at the end of their lives

[20] For the γέλωc theme cf. 367, 382, 957, 961, 969, 1043.

(Oedipus and Philoctetes); in others, not until after death (Ajax by the rite of burial, Antigone by Teiresias and the gods, Heracles by deification); with Electra, a character ruined by her circumstances, the issue is left open. In the case of Ajax the formidable greatness of his character involves defects equally formidable, all of them suggested by the portrait in the prologue and parodos and brought into stronger relief in subsequent scenes of the play; self-glorification, indifference to divine aid, a temperament savage, hard-hearted, and impatient, remorseless cruelty in revenge, and a complete absence of any sense of guilt.[21] Such a character, while alive, is incompatible not only with Odysseus' world but also from the enormity of his vengeance for slighted honour, with his own Homeric world; incompatible, finally, with divinely established order. He is therefore destroyed and must wait until after death for rehabilitation. *Ajax* differs from the other extant plays in that the revelation of the hero's character takes place in the parodos, so that when he appears we know all about his personality and the reasons for his actions. The following scenes strengthen features already apparent instead of portraying their emergence and development, as in the later plays, in the self-revelation of spoken utterance or against a background of ordinary or lesser characters.[22]

At the end of the parodos, the mood is one of suspense, due partly to the sailors' incomplete knowledge and partly to the excitement aroused by their appeal to Ajax. His appearance, expected in answer to the challenge

$$\dot{\alpha}\lambda\lambda' \, \ddot{\alpha}\nu\alpha \, \dot{\epsilon}\xi \, \dot{\epsilon}\delta\rho\dot{\alpha}\nu\omega\nu \qquad (192)$$

is however delayed, and this delay greatly increases the tension throughout the earlier part of the first epeisodion, which begins at 201 with Tecmessa's entry. The matter-of-fact comment in the ancient scholia may be quoted:

ἔξεισι Τέκμηςςα καὶ διδάςκει τὸν χορὸν ὅτι Αἴας ἐςτίν ὁ ςφάξας τὰ ποίμνια, πυνθάνεται δὲ παρὰ τοῦ χοροῦ ὅτι Ἑλληνικὰ ἦν τὰ ςφαγέντα· ἑκάτερος οὖν παρ' ἑκατέρου τὸ ἀγνοούμενον μανθάνει.

Tecmessa comes out of Ajax' tent and informs the chorus that it is Ajax who slaughtered the cattle, whereas she discovers from them that the slaughtered

---

[21] For the epithets applied to him by the chorus and Tecmessa, who are devoted to him, cf. ὁ δεινὸς μέγας ὠμοκρατής (205), θούριος (212, 1213), αἴθων (221), δυςθεράπευτος (609), ςτερεόφρων, ὠμόφρων (926, 930); and cf. 368 f., 421–6, 548 ff., 586–95, 758–75.

[22] Cf. e.g. Antigone and Ismene; Oedipus and Creon in *O.T.*; Electra and Chrysothemis.

animals belonged to the Greeks: they therefore learn from one another what each does not know.

This exchange of information takes place in an epirrhematic conversation between actor and chorus, beginning with anapaests during which Tecmessa enlightens the sailors, and continuing with a single strophic pair sung by the chorus, the two stanzas being divided and closed by further anapaests from the actor. The lyrics begin at the precise moment of Tecmessa's revelation, when what was φάτιc ('rumour') in the parodos becomes ἀγγελία ('news', 224), and all conjectures as to what happened are turned into certainties. Hence the quickened emotion of the sung strophe after the formal question in the sailors' anapaests (208–13).

The main functions of epirrhematic scenes, in which originally the actor spoke trimeters interspersed with the chorus's lyrics in strophic corresponsion, are to advance the dramatic movement by giving necessary information and to heighten tension by depicting a clash of views or personalities.[23] The former function is seen very clearly in Aeschylus' *Persae* 256–80, where the messenger reveals, during the chorus's sung lamentations, the full extent of the Persian disaster. By way of variation from spoken trimeters, the actor on occasions recites anapaests, as Tecmessa does in this scene from *Ajax*. The epirrhematic form is here used to reveal facts which were before in doubt, for there is no conflict of personalities between Tecmessa and the sailors. In scenes such as these we may perhaps regret more than in any other parts of Greek Tragedy our ignorance of the music and dance movements which accompanied the lyrics of the chorus. It is however certain that in passages of dialogue between actor and chorus singing is a mark of high emotion, while speech or recitative denote a calmer state of mind. This is apparent especially when the roles of actor and chorus are reversed, so that lyrics are given to the actor, and the coryphaeus, representing the chorus, has trimeters in order to calm the actor's passion, as in the commos of *Ajax* 348–429.

At 208 the chorus, having learnt from Tecmessa that Ajax lies sick in confusion of mind (θολερῷ χειμῶνι νοcήcαc, 206 f.), ask if the night just past has brought any relief. In answer she reports that he was indeed seized with madness and slaughtered the

---

[23] For this second function cf. Aesch. *Th.* 203–44, 686–711; *A.* 1407–61.

cattle. The sequence of events must be made clear. The play, as
we have seen, opens at dawn, when Odysseus is tracking Ajax.
The onslaught on the herds and herdsmen was made during the
night, and we may presume that Ajax had spent the previous day
or days, since the award of Achilles' arms to Odysseus, meditating
revenge in his tent: if the manuscripts' reading ἡμερίας can be
kept in 208,[24] the reference may then be to this period, described
in the epode of the parodos as μακραίων ἄδε ἀγώνιος σχολά (193):
this rest from the battle which lasted for a long time; in other
words, he took time off from the fighting in order to plan his
revenge, which 'seemed like an age'.[25] Although the correct
interpretation of the sailors' question in 208 must remain in
doubt since the text is uncertain, it is a good example of inflated
language used to express what could have been put quite simply.
The ὄγκος of this sentence (to use Sophocles' own word in the
passage from Plutarch referred to above) is paralleled in 397 ff.,
where a simple remark such as οὐκ ἐστ' ἐμοὶ ζῆν κέρδος is inflated
into an extremely tortured form of words. Such instances of
stylistic ὄγκος may be a more reliable indication than anything
else of an early date for this play.[26]

As the truth bursts upon the chorus with Tecmessa's reply
214–20, they break into lyric. The image of fire, used in the
parodos (195), is repeated in ἀνδρὸς αἴθονος (221), and we hear
again of the μέγας μῦθος, now confirmed as an ἀγγελία. The
sailors' first reaction is fear that Ajax will die (θανεῖται 229), and
later, in the corresponding place in the antistrophe, that they
themselves will suffer death by stoning (λιθόλευστον Ἄρη, 254),
the special punishment for those who commit crimes against a
whole community. Although the verb θανεῖται is ambiguous,
meaning either 'he will die' or 'he will be put to death', the
balance of these sentences at the ends of the two stanzas suggests
that it is, on the chorus's lips, a true passive: Ajax will be stoned
to death, and his sailors with him, μετὰ τοῦδε τυπείς (255). This
is the view in the ancient scholium, where the writer of the note
explains θανεῖται by ὑπὸ τῶν Ἑλλήνων. While in a flash of insight
the chorus foretell what will actually happen, at this stage of the
play they envisage death by stoning, not suicide. They admit

---

[24] See R. D. Dawe, *Studies on the Text of Sophocles* i. 134 ff., for a discussion of this
doubtful text.

[25] See Stanford's edition of *Aj.* ad loc.   [26] Cf. also 869–75.

moreover that his murderous assault on the herds and herdsmen
(βοτὰ καὶ βοτῆρας, 231) will be visited by the appropriate
punishment, but we may note again that they do not at this or
any other stage of the play acknowledge the guilt of his intention
to kill the Greek chiefs.

This epirrhematic scene closes, as it began, with anapaests
from Tecmessa in which she corrects the chorus's epithet ἄπλατος
(256) of Ajax' condition: he is no longer unapproachable because
the storm of frenzy has subsided, and now his return to sanity
brings a fresh woe,

$$\text{καὶ νῦν φρόνιμος νέον ἄλγος ἔχει·} \qquad (259)$$

he gradually regains contact with the real world, and as he looks
at the evidence of what he has done, the agony is appalling, both
for him and for those who watch. Tecmessa explains the point to
the chorus in the dialogue in which she corrects their naive
assumption that with the fury of madness gone, things are in a
happier state (263 f.). She has witnessed Ajax' recovery: the
process of self-recognition (a kind of ἀναγνώρισις) has taken place
inside the tent, not, as with Heracles and Agave in Euripides'
plays, on the stage,[27] so that she must explain to the sailors the
whole course of his νόσος from the initial onset to the return to
sanity. This she does in the long speech 284–327. At the end of
it, the chorus's knowledge of what has happened is complete: no
detail either of Ajax' recent actions or of his present despair has
been omitted, but doubts still remain in their minds. They
confirm the conjecture, made in the parodos, that he must have
been the victim of a θεία νόσος (185):

$$\text{Τέκμηςςα δεινὰ παῖ Τελεύταντος λέγεις}$$
$$\text{ἡμῖν τὸν ἄνδρα διαπεφοιβάςθαι κακοῖς} \qquad \text{(331 f.)}$$

'You tell a terrible story—that he has been driven mad by his
troubles' (i.e. the award of Achilles' arms to Odysseus), but when
they hear his first inarticulate cries ἰώ μοί μοι they wonder
whether he is still mad or whether his pain is due to the sight of
the shambles round him as evidence of his madness (337 f.). This
doubt is resolved when they hear his first articulate utterance in
the cry for Teucer, and they conclude that he is sane, ἀνὴρ

[27] *H.F.* 1089–1162; *Ba.* 1216–1300.

φρονεῖν ἔοικεν (344), where the verb φρονεῖν recalls Tecmessa's φρόνιμος at 259. They feel that though in an agony of despair he may now be rational enough to be influenced by the sight of his sailors. Hence when the tent is opened and they see the full horror, they try to communicate with him at intervals during his lyrics in the ensuing commos, as indeed she had asked them to do at the end of her speech (328 ff.).

The gradual build-up of tension and expectation, retarded but never broken, culminates in the protagonist's appearance heralded by cries off stage, which punctuate the final brief conversation between Tecmessa and the sailors. Throughout the whole powerful scene from the opening words of the parodos until this moment of revelation, the chorus have played their part, not as a commentator, but as an actor participating with the utmost dramatic effect in its development from doubt to horrified discovery of the truth. With Ajax's appearance at 347, their role becomes less active as they retire into the background, and the coryphaeus speaks his comments, often trite and banal, on the hero's predicament. It is important to note that throughout the parodos and much of the first epeisodion of this early play, Sophocles uses his chorus as one of the actors[28] to a greater extent than in *Trachiniae*, *Antigone*, and *Oedipus Tyrannus*, and that in *Ajax*, both in the first part of the play and again in the second parodos, when the chorus re-enter after leaving the orchestra (866 ff.), we have a foretaste of developments which reappear in the parodos of *Electra* and reach their full perfection in his last two plays.

The commos (349–429) consists of three strophic pairs each of increasing length, in the first of which Ajax sings dochmiacs leading to iambic dimeters with a choriambic clausula, and the coryphaeus closes each stanza with two recited or spoken trimeters. The lyrics of the second pair are again a mixture of dochmiacs and iambics in the first half of each strophe ending with a trimeter just before the two-line interventions, and iambic and aeolic in the second half. Tecmessa shares with the coryphaeus the trimeters which divide Ajax' lyrics. In the last pair the sung part predominates, as each stanza is closed with a couple of trimeters from Tecmessa and the coryphaeus respectively. This formal structure is careful and symmetrical: the

---

[28] Arist. *Po.* 1456ᵃ 25 f.

mixture of dochmiacs and iambics in the sung parts is a sign of high emotion, and the effect is enhanced by the echoing ἰώ and αἰαῖ from Ajax.

We may trace a gradual development of tension in Ajax' lyrics. In the first two stanzas he appeals to the sailors as his only loyal friends to kill him, ἀλλά με cυνδάιξον (361). The second pair points the contrast between what he was and what he now is, and the theme of mockery is heard across the two stanzas (367 = 382). There is a sudden burst of anger in the strophe at 368 f., when Tecmessa's voice is first heard appealing to him. Though he ignored her presence at the beginning of the commos when he addressed the sailors exclusively, here he answers her with a quick impatient retort, ordering her out of his sight,

οὐκ ἐκτός; οὐκ ἄψορρον ἐκνεμῇ πόδα;

The line is probably spoken, not sung, in order to pair with her trimeter. This stanza closes with a sentence that illustrates more than anything else Ajax' view of his abortive assault on the Greeks: there is no sense of guilt, only an exclamation against his bad luck in letting them escape and slaughtering the cattle instead (372–6). Thus does he explain what he meant by

οἴμοι γέλωτος, οἷον ὑβρίcθην ἄρα

in 367: the mocking laughter and insults directed against the intrepid and formidable warrior who has shown his prowess against harmless animals.

Most of the antistrophe of the second pair of stanzas (379–93) is an impassioned attack on Odysseus in language derived from the market-place, more frequent in Old Comedy and Attic Oratory than in the lyrics of Tragedy: κακοπινέcτατον ἄλημα (381), τὸν αἰμυλώτατον, ἐχθρὸν ἄλημα (388 f.). In the third pair Ajax' language regains the dignity momentarily lost as he appeals in highly figurative and moving terms:

ἰώ,
cκότος, ἐμὸν φάος,
ἔρεβος ὦ φαεννότατον, ὡς ἐμοί,
ἔλεcθ᾽ ἔλεcθέ μ᾽ οἰκήτορα,
ἔλεcθέ με

'Come, darkness, my light, depth of gloom for me most brilliant, take me, take me to dwell below with you'. The confusion of darkness and light reflects the turmoil in his mind as he realizes that death can be the only end for him. Finally, in the last antistrophe he calls upon the familiar places round Troy as witnesses of his quality as a warrior the like of whom was never seen. His closing words τανῦν δ' ἄτιμος ὧδε πρόκειμαι proclaim with stark emphasis his present dishonour, and if we press one of the common meanings of the verb, after uttering them he falls amid the carnage like a cast out corpse.[29] After a pause he recovers sufficient self-control to set forth his arguments for death in a long and closely reasoned speech.

This commos (348–429) is a powerfully tragic scene between Ajax, Tecmessa, and the coryphaeus, representing the chorus. The mixture of song and speech, with the protagonist singing and the other two never abandoning spoken utterance, raises him to the highest level of emotional intensity and isolates him in his sense of mockery and dishonour. The sailors' attempt to establish communication with him has failed in spite of his affection for them acknowledged in his opening words; and his only positive reaction is to Tecmessa, a brutal and impatient rebuff. The coryphaeus's trimeters offer conventional commonplaces of consolation and advice, appropriate to a body of men faced with a horror they only partly understand, and their remarks fail to move him. We may contrast the different effect of the commos in *Antigone* (806–82), where a much closer communication is established between actor and chorus, and the cut and thrust of argument reflects the conflict of views, though the protagonist's utter desolation is exactly the same as in *Ajax*.

The most important effect of this scene on the movement of the play is that it gradually confirms beyond doubt that death is the only solution for Ajax, and that he has made up his mind himself that this is so. He first asks his devoted sailors to kill him. Next, after abusing Odysseus, he wishes he could kill him and the Atreidae and then die himself, τέλος θάνοιμι καὐτός (391): though ambiguous as in 229 above, the verb, used here in the personal wish, suggests that the thought of suicide has entered his mind. This concept strengthens in the appeal to σκότος and ἔρεβος to

---

[29] Cf. e.g. *Aj.* 1059 of corpses awaiting burial; *Ant.* 1101 of Polyneices' corpse; Eur. *Alc.* 1012, of Alcestis'.

receive him, and in the reason he gives that he can in the future
expect no benefit from gods or men. He then envisages a violent
death at the hands of all the Greek host,

$$\pi\hat{a}c\ \delta\grave{\epsilon}\ c\tau\rho\alpha\tau\grave{o}c\ \delta\acute{\iota}\pi\alpha\lambda\tau oc\ \mathring{a}\nu\ \mu\epsilon\ \chi\epsilon\iota\rho\grave{\iota}\ \varphi o\nu\epsilon\acute{\upsilon} o\iota\quad (408\ \text{f.})$$

whether by the sword or by ritual stoning, is not certain. His last
utterance (412 ff.) is in the form of a conventional farewell
speech to the familiar scenes of life from one about to die,[30] and
his closing words, symbolic of what he feels may happen to his
corpse, set the seal on his certainty of death. In their final
comment the chorus are non-committal: the flat words reflect
helpless doubt and bewilderment. It is however dramatically
necessary that at the end of the scene (595) their doubts should
be replaced by a conviction that Ajax is determined to die and
that when he and Tecmessa withdraw into the tent, they do not
expect to see him alive again. This certainty of his death is
impressed upon those who listen by the speech in which he
addresses his son, arranges for his future up-bringing, and invests
him with his famous shield (545–77). This speech must be taken
as a farewell from one who has decided to die. He himself clinches
the matter after ordering Tecmessa to close the tent: 'a skilful
doctor does not wail incantations over a wound that needs the
knife' (579), a remark whose implications are not lost upon her
and the sailors, as is clear from the tense exchanges that close the
scene (583–95). The chorus's conviction that Ajax intends to use
the knife upon himself inside his tent explains the dirge as for one
dead in the first stasimon. This conviction must be shared also by
the audience, who of course know that he must kill himself but
do not expect the startling innovation of a death on stage which
Sophocles has in store for them. His reappearance at the end of
the song is thus one of the most striking examples in extant Greek
Tragedy of dramatic surprise, a stroke of genius from a master
of theatrical effect.

The stasimon, 596 ff., sung to an empty stage and therefore
designed to awake its own mood in the audience, is straightforward in structure and consists of two strophic pairs mainly in
aeolic metres. The first stanza, opening with a salute to Salamis,
the common home of Ajax and his sailors, introduces the themes
of homesickness and of the prospect of death for men wearied by

[30] Cf. also 856–65.

long years in a foreign land, set against the background of their island abiding happy and famous amid the waves that beat upon it. These themes are repeated and amplified in the third stasimon (1185–1222) which affords a close parallel to the first, so that the two together provide a unity of lyric reflection across the central section of the play. The simplest form of contrasting statements leads from Salamis to the chorus's own lot: cὺ μέν ... ναίειc ... εὐδαίμων ... ἐγὼ δ᾿ ὁ τλάμων ...

The antistrophe (609–20) turns to the particular trouble which now confronts the chorus. Ajax, θεία μανία ξύναυλος 'dwelling with madness from the gods', is there with his sailors, suffering from a disease hard to cure, an additional adversary for them to wrestle with (ἔφεδρος). The language of this first sentence is highly concentrated, each word making its special effect as they review Ajax' sickness in broadest terms, ignoring Tecmessa's distinction between the frenzy of his bewitchment and the pain of his return to sanity. The interjection ὤμοι μοι (610) lends to the whole utterance an emotional tone which is renewed at the end of the stanza by the double repetitions ἄφιλα παρ᾿ ἀφίλοιc and ἔπεc᾿ ἔπεcε, a device of style used only sparingly by Sophocles. The unique and remarkable phrase φρενὸς οἰοβώτας (614),[31] 'lonely pasturer of thought', conveys the all-important sense of isolation which is a hallmark of the Sophoclean tragic hero.

In the second strophe a theme is taken from Tecmessa's speech 506 ff. where she appealed to Ajax to respect the feelings of his aged father and mother. This is developed into a dirge as though for one dead, a vivid and moving scene of mourning with the sounds of lamentation, the beating of breasts, and the tearing of hair. Tecmessa's phrase μητέρα πολλῶν ἐτῶν κληροῦχον (507 f.), 'your mother with her heritage of many years', is amplified into the double phrase παλαιᾷ μὲν cύντροφος ἀμέρα, λευκῷ τε γήρᾳ μάτηρ, and the poet's imagination works throughout the strophe on the figure here visualized until a climax of sound is reached in the alliteration of the final period:

> χερόπλακτοι δ᾿
> ἐν cτέρνοιcι πεcοῦνται
> δοῦποι καὶ πολιᾶc ἄμυγμα χαίταc   (632–4)

'the sound of hands striking the breast and the tearing of grey

---

[31] Cf. the metaphorical uses of βουκολεῖν, Aesch. *A.* 669 and *Eu.* 78.

hair.' The accumulated phrases for the rituals of mourning are a feature of this stanza. Heard first in the repeated αἴλινον αἴλινον in 627, they increase in poetic intensity and feeling and create the impression that Ajax' sailors, though describing the actions of his parents, are in fact uttering their own θρῆνος for him, so strongly do their words point to a scene of death.

The opening line of the antistrophe explains the direction of their thoughts:

κρείccων γὰρ Ἅιδᾳ κεύθων ὁ νοcῶν μάταν   (635)

'far better hidden in Hades is he in his sickness'. This is not a general statement, as the following relative clause shows, but refers to Ajax and emphasizes what is essential for the interpretation of the song, that the sailors are convinced that he must die. They also amplify what they consider to be the fact and nature of his θεία μανία:

οὐκέτι cυντρόφοιc
ὀργαῖc ἔμπεδοc, ἀλλ' ἐκτὸc ὁμιλεῖ.   (639 f.)

He is no longer true to the impulses which he owes to his birth and nurture, but dwells outside them: the words epitomize his alienation from his heritage. The chorus are fully aware of his condition, and to them, death is the only cure for his δύcφοροc ἄτα. The ode closes with an acknowledgement of his father's grief, complementary to the scene of his mother's lamentations in the strophe.

In this song the chorus stand back from the tensions apparent at the end of the preceding scene. There is no comment on Ajax' bitter words or Tecmessa's appeals, no expression of hope that she may prevail upon him. Its relevance extends to the whole play as it has progressed instead of being limited, like that of the next stasimon, to the immediate context. It creates a mood of resignation to a death that seemed imminent as soon as the tent doors closed on him and Tecmessa; and it introduces a pause for reflection on certain issues raised hitherto at intervals in the tragedy: longing for home, weariness of war, the intolerable burden of Ajax' madness, the contrast between past prowess and present desolation, and in the last two stanzas a gathering despair for his life strengthening into a certainty of death as the sailors dwell on a mother's mourning and foretell a father's grief. As

they hear the closing words of the song this certainty must have
been impressed upon the minds of an audience. Then, at its end,
against all expectation, Ajax reappears with Tecmessa and
makes his great speech. Despair gives place to an ecstasy of joy in
the first line of the following ode (693):

$$\text{ἔφριξ' ἔρωτι, περιχαρὴς δ' ἀνεπτάμαν}$$

'I thrill with rapture and soar on the wings of joy.' The two songs
together, separated by a single speech of forty-seven lines, are a
striking example of Sophocles' use of song to awake contrasting
emotions within a brief period of time.

At the end of the first stasimon (645), Ajax, accompanied by
Tecmessa, comes out of his tent with Hector's sword in his hand.
We are to assume that while the chorus were singing their ode,
she has been urging him to alter his hard, embittered attitude
towards her. Her last words to him were πρὸς θεῶν, μαλάccου, 'for
love of the gods, be softened' (594), and in 650 ff. he says

$$\text{κἀγὼ γάρ, ὃc τὰ δείν' ἐκαρτέρουν τότε}$$
$$\text{βαφῇ cίδηρος ὥc, ἐθηλύνθην cτόμα}$$
$$\text{πρὸς τῆcδε τῆc γυναικόc}$$

'For I, who was so terribly hardened like steel by dipping, have
had my speech's sharp edge[32] softened by this woman'. So far as
she is concerned, the process of persuasion behind the scenes has
been successful:[33] he now feels pity and expresses it in his next
words: οἰκτίρω δέ νιν χήραν παρ' ἐχθροῖc ... λιπεῖν, a highly
ambiguous statement which could mean either that he intends to
commit suicide and feels pity at leaving her a widow, or that pity
at the thought of leaving her has led him to change his decision
to end his life. The psychology of this speech has been discussed
by every scholar who has edited the play but it is no concern of
ours here.[34] We are concerned solely with its effect on the chorus
at the most dramatic moment in the play. Although Ajax almost
certainly does not intend to deceive either Tecmessa or his sailors
about his decision to kill himself, Sophocles has worded his speech
with such ambiguity of language that they are both completely

[32] Cf. γλῶccά cου τεθηγμένη, 584.

[33] See Tycho Wilamowitz, *Dramatische Technik des Sophokles*, 55 ff. and E. Fraenkel, *MH*,
24 (1967), 79 ff.

[34] See, as well as the editions, Reinhardt, *Sophokles*, 31 ff., B. M. W. Knox, *HSPh*. 65
(1961), 1–37, and M. Sicherl, *Die Tragik des Aias*, *Hermes*, 98 (1970), 14–37.

deluded.[35] Despair at the thought of Ajax' death changes to joy
in the confidence that he will live. This emotion is in turn
shattered in the scene following the second stasimon. A double
peripeteia (μεταβολὴ εἰς τὸ ἐναντίον τῶν πραττομένων (Arist. *Poetics*
1452ᵃ22)) is thus effected within 160 lines. At the climax of joy
comes the song at 692, immediately relevant, springing directly
out of a deluded interpretation of the speech, and expressing a
new and wild emotion. With the arrival of the messenger from
the army to report Calchas' instructions that Ajax must be closely
guarded for this one day, and with the revelation of 735 ff. and
794 that he has left his tent, hope and joy are banished.

The ode, sung like the previous one to an empty stage and
therefore intended to awake a specific response in the audience,
consists of one strophic pair in the form of a prayer-hymn (ὕμνος
κλητικός) to Pan and the Delian Apollo. Each stanza opens with
a single-sentence lyric iambic trimeter of exactly parallel
rhythmical form with identical resolutions at the caesura. The
metrical pattern of the first words of the song thus echoes the last
words of Ajax' speech, and there is no rhythmic break in the
change from spoken to sung utterance. The close connection of
the song with the speech is emphasized also by the two
instantaneous aorists ἔφριξα and ἀνεπτάμαν. The use of this idiom,
frequent in the quick interchanges of spoken conversation, here
suggests that the lyric is an immediate reaction to the speech,
leaving no time for reflection on the ambiguities of its language.
Emotion finds spontaneous expression, the *frisson* of ἔφριξ' ἔρωτι,
'I thrill with rapture',[36] being accompanied by excited physical
movement (ἀνεπτάμαν). The hymn begins with the repeated ἰὼ
ἰὼ and the fourfold Πάν, followed by the 'epiphany' imperative
φάνηθι (697), the first two repetitions of the god's name being
especially marked by double syncopation of the iambic metron;[37]
and after the slow emphatic start the rhythm gathers momentum
with glyconics and other aeolic lengths. We thus have, after the
opening statement in the iambic trimeter, a crescendo of speed
and urgency. The corresponding repetitions

> ἰὼ ἰώ, νῦν αὖ,
> νῦν ὦ Ζεῦ

---

[35] Cf., as well as 652 ff., 654–60 and 687–92.   [36] Cf. ἀείρομαι, *Trach.* 216.
[37] Cf., for the same effect, *Trach.* 221.

in the antistrophe are a striking example of Sophocles' fondness
for word and rhythm echoes in the structure of his lyrics.

Pan is here invoked, with the usual attributes of the hymn
formula, as a being whose dances are the self-taught expression
of ecstasy (ὀρχήματ' αὐτοδαῆ, 700). Pindar called him χορευτὴν
τελεώτατον,[38] 'dancer most consummate', and to the Athenians
he was especially familiar from the time of the Persian Wars, for
he met Philippides on the mountain above Tegea as he ran from
Athens to Sparta to ask for aid;[39] he haunted the island of
Psyttaleia off Salamis as φιλόχορος, lover of the dance;[40] and he
is addressed as ὀρχηστά, βρομίαις ὀπαδὲ νύμφαις in the fourth Attic
Skolion. In this ode he is summoned from the heights of Cyllene,
a being from rocky, snow-beaten wilds, in order to help Ajax'
sailors express their joy in dancing. These dances are called
Μύσια, Κνώσια (699), epithets that conjure up a vision of the
place where danced the wild votaries of the Great Mother, Rhea
Cybele, whose companion was Pan, and Crete, a famous home of
dancing[41] and scene of the ecstatic rites of the Curetes with their
clashing cymbals. We can only read Sophocles' words, but we
must imagine the physical movements, the gestures and the music
that accompanied them, in order to grasp the full effect of the
line which states the reason for the prayer at the end of the
invocation:

$$νῦν γὰρ ἐμοὶ μέλει χορεῦσαι \qquad (701)$$

'Now, I have a mind to dance.' References to the act of dancing
are not common in the lyrics of Greek Tragedy,[42] and when they
occur they remind us that the dance was not only an act of
worship, as for instance in *O.T.* 896, but also an essential part of
dramatic lyric in which voice, musical accompaniment, and
rhythmic movements combined to express a wide range of
emotion. The strophe closes with an appeal to the Delian Apollo,
also associated with dancing.[43] We may notice the same features
as in the invocation to Pan: the words μολών and ξυνείη (703,
705) echoing φάνηθι and ξυνών, and the localized references,
Ἰκαρίων ὑπὲρ πελαγέων and Δάλιος, which are essential elements
in ritual songs.

---

[38] Fr. 89 B.   [39] Hdt. vi. 105–6.   [40] Aesch. *Pers.* 448 f.
[41] *Il.* 18. 590.   [42] Cf. e.g. *Trach.* 216–20; *O.T.* 896; Eur. *H.F.* 763.
[43] Pi. Fr. 135 B.

In the antistrophe the chorus give their interpretation of Ajax' speech: the bright day may come again to the ships since he has forgotten his troubles and performed the sacrifices demanded by the act of purification described at 655 ff. He has also, they believe, repented of his anger with the sons of Atreus: the words

$$Aἴαc μετανεγνώcθη$$
$$θυμοῦ τ' 'Ατρείδαιc μεγάλων τε νεικέων \quad (717 f.)$$

recall μαθηcόμεcθα δ' 'Ατρείδαc cέβειν in 667. In 714 is a brief summary of the opening of his speech, as the writer of the note in the ancient scholia perceived: τὰ ὑπὸ τοῦ Aἴαντος διὰ πολλῶν εἰρημένα διὰ βραχέων διεξῆλθεν, 'the chorus expounds in a few words what Ajax said in many.' The manuscripts give this line as πάνθ' ὁ μέγας χρόνος μαραίνει τε καὶ φλέγει 'great time both quenches and kindles all things'. If this were to be accepted, metrical correspondence would require the assumption of a lacuna to complete 701 with an iambic metron, but nothing could be added to the emphatic statement, νῦν γὰρ ἐμοὶ μέλει χορεῦcαι, without ruining its effect.[44]

What is certain about the lines 714 to the end of the song is that they stress the concept of impermanence and change in men's states of mind as well as in their circumstances. This is indeed a frequent theme in Greek thought from Homer onwards in all genres of literature, and it plays an important part in Sophocles' tragedies.[45] It is often expressed in imagery drawn from the processes of nature, the movement of the heavenly bodies, the contrasts between day and night, light and dark, growth and decay as well as in matter-of-fact language like οὐδὲν ἀναύδατον φατίcαιμ' ἄν and ἐξ ἀέλπτων μετανεγνώcθη (715 f.), which stress the sense of sudden shock at unexpected change. This final sentence sums up the whole song against the background of mutability in Ajax' affairs which he expressed himself in some immortal lines of his speech; and apart from the echo of its opening in the chorus's 714, we may note especially 669–77, with its imagery from the changing pageant of nature, and 679–83 with its comment on the impermanence of human relationships. This last point, together with his enigmatic lines

---

[44] For an opposing view see the editions of Lobeck, Kamerbeek, and Stanford ad loc.

[45] Cf. e.g. *Trach.* 132–40; *O.T.* 1186–1206; *O.C.* 609–20. This last passage especially recalls parts of Ajax' speech 646–92.

about the Atreidae (667 f.) and his apparent resolve to learn the
lesson of cωφροcύνη (667), is concentrated in the single word,
μετανεγνώcθη 'he has changed his mind, repented of', a double
compound found only here in extant Greek literature.

The sentence structure of this ode is uncomplicated and reveals
a close parallelism between strophe and antistrophe with strong
pauses at the same places (693 = 706; 700 = 713; 701 = 714), so
that rhythmical and grammatical correspondences are carefully
adjusted one to the other. The language of the strophe conveys
a vivid sense of movement and of geographical range from snow-
beaten Cyllene in Arcadia to Mysia and Crete, then from Delos
over the Icarian Sea as Pan and Apollo are summoned from their
haunts to be with the sailors in their dances. There is little place
for metaphor and the more subtle forms of imagery in the
invocations of prayer-hymns: what is required is the single
epithet or brief phrase to evoke in concrete terms a scene and a
deity with his birthplace, powers, and functions. Such effects are
produced here by the description of Pan's Arcadian home in 695
ff., his functions in 698 ff., and Apollo's range and birth-place in
703 ff. By contrast, the first half of the antistrophe is metaphorical
in language, reintroducing in its first line the theme of a cloud of
darkness heard in Ajax' lyrics at 394 f. Ares symbolizes violence
and destruction whether by war, pestilence, or, as in this play,
the act of a soul in frenzy; and the same power who darkens the
eyes with the cloud can also dispel it.[46] The image of the change
from dark to light, prominent in Ajax' lament at 394, where in
his distraught condition the two are for him confused and
indistinguishable, is sustained throughout the first half of the
stanza from the opening words through λευκὸν εὐάμερον φάος to
μαραίνει. The ode closes in language free from metaphor which
reveals beyond all doubt how well Ajax' speech has achieved its
dramatic function of misleading those who heard it.

Sophocles employs songs of this type in most of his extant
plays. They express joy, or confidence in a happy issue, just
before the revelation of a terrible truth and are thus a powerful
instrument of dramatic irony. Delusions, misjudgements, and
false conclusions are the very stuff of such odes. An emotion
voiced by the chorus in a song sometimes ecstatic in mood and
language, sometimes more measured in tone is shown in the

[46] Cf. *Trach.* 653 f., also of Ares.

following scene to have been deluded, and this delusion is shared between chorus, actors, and audience. Thus in *Ajax*, the truth is revealed and the delusion shattered, as far as the chorus are concerned, in the conversation that begins with the messenger's despairing cry ἰοὺ ἰού at 737; and Tecmessa's eyes are opened in the passage 787–803. In the subsequent plays the same technique appears with subtle variations and always with great theatrical effect. There are no examples of it in extant Aeschylus and perhaps only one in Euripides, the ode χοροὶ χοροί at *Hercules Furens* 763, just before the entry of Iris and Lyssa. The evidence of only seven plays is too scanty for any dogmatic assertion, but the fact that five of these[47] contain instances of this use of song suggests that it may have been an invention of Sophocles himself.

In the scene following the ode the chorus summon Tecmessa (784 f.) who arranges the details of the search for Ajax. In answer to her call for action they leave the orchestra in two groups, one to the east, the other to the west (805). She also goes out in order to take part in the search, so that stage and orchestra are left empty. Ajax' final speech and suicide are set against a different background, a deserted part of the shore with some bushy scrub behind which his body may fall so that it is not immediately visible to the chorus upon their re-entry at 866.[48] This emptying of the orchestra and change of scene,[49] unique in extant Sophocles, is a bold theatrical stroke, which effectively concentrates attention on the hero's isolation. It is in no way contrived or artificial but arises naturally from the requirements of the plot and from the way in which the dramatist has prepared for it in the last dozen lines of the scene, during which the sailors are caught up in the action with its urgency and excitement:

> χωρεῖν ἑτοῖμος, κοὐ λόγῳ δείξω μόνον·
> τάχος γὰρ ἔργου καὶ ποδῶν ἅμ᾽ ἕψεται   (813 f.)

'I am ready to go and will show it not only in word—speed of act and foot shall follow together.'

At 866 the chorus resume their role as actors, their re-entry

---

[47] *Trach.* 633; *Ant.* 1115; *O.T.* 1086; *Phil.* 719.
[48] See P. D. Arnott, *Greek Scenic Conventions*, 131–3.
[49] For examples of exit and re-entry of the chorus, cf. Aesch. *Eu.* 231–44; Eur. *Alc.* 746–861; *Hel.* 374–515; *Rh.* 564–674. For *Aj.* see Taplin, *The Stagecraft of Aeschylus*, 384 f.

being in effect a second parodos, the type of 'search' parodos
which Sophocles employs in *Philoctetes* and *Oedipus at Colonus* and
which demands the lively participation of both actor and chorus
in order to exploit to the full its inherent possibilities of suspense
and excitement.[50] The dramatic situation at this moment of the
play provides a striking parallel with its opening. In the prologue
we saw Odysseus tracking the footprints of the living Ajax, and
now we see the two groups of sailors entering from opposite sides,
one before the other, searching, but for one who is dead. Clearly
they have had a laborious and fruitless task, as their first words
show, with their threefold repetition and alliterations:

πόνος πόνῳ πόνον φέρει·
πᾷ πᾷ
πᾷ γὰρ οὐκ ἔβαν ἐγώ;   (866–8)

'toil brings toil upon toil: where, where have I not been?' The
insistent π sound is heard again in the second group's replies at
874 and 876. The third searcher is not visible to the chorus until
after her cry at 891, as is proved by the sailors' question 892 and
the two trimeters at 894 f. The climax of the scene is Tecmessa's
discovery of Ajax' body at 891. From the sailors' re-entry up to
this moment the tension has been mounting in stages as the
audience wonder which of the searchers will find it. The words

ἰδοὺ ἰδού,
δοῦπον αὖ κλύω τινά[51]

announce the approach of the second group, and as the two
converse the suspense continues until a moment of retardation is
provided by the passage of continuous lyric which opens the long
strophic utterances 879–914 = 925–60. In this passage the chorus
question the gods of sea and river as to Ajax' whereabouts. The
answer is given by Tecmessa's agonized cry

ἰώ μοί μοι.   (891)

The brief dialogue 870–8 is conducted in a curious mixture of

---

[50] Cp. also the search parodos of Eur. *Heracl.*

[51] Dawe, op. cit. 155, supports the conjecture οὐ, with the line as an interrogative,
'Listen! don't I hear a sound?' This is preferable to αὖ, for there hasn't been a previous
δοῦπος.

colloquial speech and stilted periphrases, ἰδοὺ ἰδού ... τί οὖν δή; ἔχεις οὖν; being interlaced with formal trimeters at 872, 874 and 876–8. It is as if two styles were in competition with each other, the Aeschylean solemnity of ναὸς κοινόπλουν ὁμιλίαν and

$$\pi\hat{\alpha}\nu \ \dot{\epsilon}\sigma\tau\acute{\iota}\beta\eta\tau\alpha\iota \ \pi\lambda\epsilon\upsilon\rho\grave{o}\nu \ \ddot{\epsilon}\sigma\pi\epsilon\rho o\nu \ \nu\epsilon\hat{\omega}\nu$$

with the naturalism of the urgent bacchiac questions at 873 and 875. When the sailors turn to lyrics at 879, they sing principally dochmiacs until 890 when the coryphaeus converses with Tecmessa in trimeters. Lyrics reappear when she tells them that Ajax is dead (898 f.). This alternation of iambic conversation with lyrics continues throughout the whole of this highly formalized scene. Tecmessa is a non-singing character, and apart from her exclamations she must therefore speak in trimeters. The coryphaeus, when asking questions and communicating closely with her, also speaks or recites, song being reserved for more intensified, personal emotion as in 900 ff. = 946 ff., and 909 ff. = 955 ff.

The strophe and antistrophe are separated and rounded off by two iambic speeches from Tecmessa, each of which picks up and develops a theme she has just heard from the chorus. Thus, at 915, in answer to the question where Ajax' body lies, she says οὗτοι θεατός, and gives an exact description of its appearance, which prepares us for the moment at 1003 f., when Teucer orders it to be revealed for all to see. At 961, when the sailors have introduced the theme of mockery, γελᾷ δὲ ... πολὺν γέλωτα (958 f.) which dominates much of the earlier part of the play, she speaks her views on the subject, ending with two lines that emphasise most poignantly her sorrow and desolation and form a fitting close to the whole dialogue.[52]

The commos from 866 to 973 is a carefully integrated piece of writing in which communication is established first between the two halves of the chorus and then between them and Tecmessa. The noteworthy correspondences in echoing exclamations and word groups[53] and the alternations of song and speech reflect and sustain the tensions inherent in a scene which leads up to the discovery of a death on the stage and depicts its emotional

[52] See Dawe, op. cit. 158–61, on the question of corruption and interpolation in her speech. We certainly expect her two speeches to be of equal length.

[53] Cf. e.g. 891 ff. = 938 ff.; 900 = 946; 912 = 959.

aftermath. More light is also thrown on the character of the chorus by their reaction to Ajax' death. Their language at the beginning expresses weariness, even boredom. Then the shock of Tecmessa's announcement at 898 f. wrings from them a lament for the loss of their νόςτιμον ἦμαρ which is indeed a death-blow:

ὤμοι ἐμῶν νόςτων·
ὤμοι κατέπεφνες ἅμ᾽, ὦναξ,
τόνδε cυνναύταν, ὦ τάλαc

'Alas for my return home! Alas, you have killed me, who shared your voyage!' Their words recall the antistrophe at 253 ff.:

πεφόβημαι
λιθόλευcτον Ἄρη
ξυναλγεῖν μετὰ τοῦδε τυπείc

'I am afraid to share the pain of a death by stoning by his side', and the opening of the first stasimon, especially 606 f.; and they foreshadow the lament for the lost delights of home which forms the central theme of the last. A little further on the sailors are tortured by feelings of guilt that Ajax should have died in the absence of friends to protect him, ἄφαρκτοc φίλων, and they blame themselves for the stupidity and lack of perception which led them to neglect him (910 f.), thus showing again how well his last speech to them has done its work. In the lyric opening to the antistrophe (925–35) this theme is developed, and the repeated imperfect tenses ἔμελλεc ἔμελλεc and ἄρ᾽ ἦν express bitter regret at knowledge revealed too late: disaster can have been the only end for a man of such a character, ὠμόθυμοc (885), δυcτράπελοc (914), cτερεόφρων (926), ὠμόφρων (930). Finally we may repeat the point already made, that the structure and to some extent the language of this commos hint at further developments in the use of the chorus as an actor which reach their fulfilment in Sophocles' last two plays.

At the end of the commos the coryphaeus introduces Teucer and informs him of Ajax' death. The conversation between them leads up to his long lament (992–1039). A noteworthy feature of this dialogue is the use of broken lines (ἀντιλαβή) at the beginning instead of the end or climax of a scene, involving not only interruption of the trimeters but also, at 981 f., a break in the grammatical structure. The emotional state of the participants accounts for these broken lines. Subsequent plays reveal a further development into what may be called lyric stichomythia, in which both grammatical and metrical units are interrupted in passionate or excited sung dialogue between actor and chorus.[54]

At 1040, the coryphaeus, on seeing Menelaus approaching, interrupts Teucer's speech to urge the speedy burial of Ajax, thus raising the subject that dominates the rest of the play. Although Tecmessa had incidentally referred to his burial in the commos at 922, it was not then envisaged as a problem owing to the immediate shock of sorrow. Now it naturally comes to the fore, and the brief exchange at 1040–6 prepares the mind for the angry scene between Teucer and Menelaus. Menelaus has a good case for disallowing the burial on the grounds of Ajax' guilty intention in planning the massacre of the Greek chiefs, but his character and manner are so offensive that he forfeits all sympathy. The conflict between the two is depicted in a scene of mounting anger which reaches its peak in heated stichomythia (1120–42) and then subsides into cold and calculated insult as the contestants pose riddles to each other in short speeches of parallel structure (1142–58). The chorus's function here, as often in such debates, is to make a balancing two-line comment after each main speech in order to provide a pause and preserve impartiality. It is a convention in Greek Tragedy that a group of people whose sympathies are known to be wholly devoted to one contestant should step out of character for a moment and make a detached, even censorious reflection on both. The question of Ajax' guilt, first raised by Menelaus, is however ignored in the coryphaeus' remarks in this scene, just as it has been throughout the first half of the play, when the hero was alive. On Menelaus' departure the sailors resume their role for five lines of anapaests (1163–7), in which they again press the need to hasten the funeral rites. The tension of the quarrel is completely relaxed by Teucer, who stations Tecmessa, henceforward a silent character, and her child beside the body. Ajax' son is to offer locks of hair and keep watch as he embraces it. The group thus forms a tableau of infinite pathos, of a type depicted on many a funerary urn and grave-relief. If need should arise, the sailors are to defend the corpse. Teucer then leaves the stage.

[54] Cf. *Trach.* 871–95, where however the nurse doesn't sing; *O. T.* 646–96; *El.* 824–70; *Phil.* and *O.C. passim.*

Against this scene of mother and child sitting in supplication and in the calm of sorrow that pervades it, the chorus sing the third and final stasimon (1185). The first strophe, consisting of a single sentence with double interrogative, springs from the general predicament of the sailors and reverts to the theme of war-weariness heard in the opening stanza of the first stasimon. The antistrophe is a curse on the inventor of war as the destroyer of men,[55] and its final sentence, following the alliterative exclamation

$$\dot{\omega} \ \pi\acute{o}\nu o\iota \ \pi\rho\acute{o}\gamma o\nu o\iota \ \pi\acute{o}\nu\omega\nu \qquad (1197)$$

gives intense feeling to the imprecation. There is no hint here of the glories to be won in heroic battles, no echo from this aspect of the Homeric world. Ajax has left his sailors no legacy of remembered honours but merely an infinite weariness and an impassioned yearning for the joys of home characteristic of the man on active service in every age and country. In this lie the pathos and the power of the song, apparent especially in the second strophe (1199 ff.) with its review of τὰ τερπνά, the garlands, the wine-cups, and the music, that mark the familiar symposia of home; and the whole is summed up with great emotional effect in the repeated ἐρώτων ἐρώτων (1205 f.). The scholiast is unlikely to be right in referring this word especially to τὰ ἐρωτικά and in accusing Sophocles of lack of taste (ἀκαιρία): it has a wider significance here and includes all the delights, as well as those of love, mentioned in the preceding lines and here remembered the more poignantly at a time of woe as the objects of passionate desire which the inventor of war has forever banished from the sailors' lives. The realistic tone of this strophe is sustained into its last sentence where the words ἀεὶ πυκιναῖς δρόσοις τεγγόμενος κόμας (1208 f.), 'my hair drenched by heavy dews', recall parts of the herald's speech in *Agamemnon*,[56] though Aeschylus describes the discomforts of camp life in earthier detail.

In the final antistrophe the sailors point the contrast between Ajax as their bulwark against the terror and the weapons and Ajax as he is now, victim of a malignant fate. Their thoughts thus move to him quite late in the ode, and immediately afterwards

[55] For the πρῶτος εὑρετής topic, see Kleingünther, *Philologus*, supp. 26 (1933), 95 ff.
[56] *A.* 558–67.

they turn again to the theme of lost delight, marked here by a significant verbal and rhythmic echo with the corresponding strophic line, τέρψιν ἰαύειν = τέρψις ἐπέσται (1204 = 1216). The word in fact occurs thrice in the song, each time in the same rhythmic context, and in two of these it is followed by an infinitive, so that in the strophe τέρψιν ὁμιλεῖν (1201) and τέρψιν ἰαύειν (1204) are rhymes, and the effect is to mark this word as essential to the structure and thought of the whole stasimon.[57] The last sentence comprises a wish for the wooded promontory of Sunium, past which the sailors' ship would sail on the return from Troy and whence they would greet the island of Salamis with a cry of welcome. This is no conventional escape wish, but as the detailed description shows, a longing for a particular spot where many an Athenian voyager in the audience would make landfall on his return home.

The movement of this song is circular: the opening and closing stanzas reflect the feelings of the chorus in their predicament, while the central two are linked closely in content and range over thoughts suggested by the topic of war's first inventor. This unity of structure helps to make it the most poetically satisfying lyric in the play. A comment in the ancient scholia is apt and perceptive: ὁ χορὸς πάλιν καθ᾽ ἑαυτὸν γενόμενος ἐν ἀναλογισμῷ γίνεται, the sailors are left alone with the silent tableau of the mother and child watching beside the body, and they reflect. As in the first stasimon, they stand back from the tension of the scene they have just witnessed and move out of the immediate orbit of the play's action. They make no comment on the quarrel between Teucer and Menelaus or on the moral issue raised by Ajax' guilt, nor do they refer to the conflict that is to come when Agamemnon arrives, though they are well aware of its imminence: as they say at 1163,

ἔσται μεγάλης ἔριδός τις ἀγών

'there will be a great trial of strength.' Sophocles has with consummate art chosen the interval between two scenes of strife for a reflective song whose content gives it a certain quality of timelessness and universality.

[57] Cf. the fourfold occurrence of ἄτα in the second stasimon of *Ant.*, 582–625.

No doubt the ode is intelligible out of context as a meditation, even perhaps a lyric cry of distress,[58] about the sorrows of war, and as such it can be given a relevance to the dramatist's own times, with their conflicts between Greek and Greek, campaigns in distant parts, and yearnings for the comforts of home. Thus at 1195 we can sense the expletive force of the epithet στυγερῶν and the overtones of the juxtaposition "Ελλασιν κοινὸν "Αρη and regard the words as an outcry against war in general. Nevertheless we must remember that Sophocles does not use his songs to express his own views on the contemporary scene, though no doubt it may on occasion colour them.[59] The rhythm of the play at this stage requires a quiet ode that contrasts both with the two angry scenes that surround it and with the wild ecstasy of the previous lyric. Further, this last stasimon clearly resembles the first in mood and content: both, while relevant to their dramatic setting and consistent with the sailors' role and status, bring out some of the tragedy's deeper implications. This resemblance provides in the person of the chorus a link between the two 'halves' of the play, thus mitigating what some critics have felt to be a fault in its structure.[60]

At the conclusion of the ode there is little left for the chorus to do. Agamemnon's approach is announced not by the coryphaeus but by Teucer,[61] who having caught sight of him enters in haste in order to protect Ajax' body, and the mother and child, from molestation. Two lines from the coryphaeus after Agamemnon's speech urge self-control on both parties (1264 f.), and two after Teucer's herald Odysseus' timely appearance, 1316 f. A final two lines record the opinion that Odysseus, who has argued Agamemnon into allowing the burial, is γνώμῃ σοφός (1374), wise in judgement, thus confirming the view of his character presented in the prologue and reinstating him in the chorus's eyes after their bitter attacks on him. The play ends with the conventional anapaestic coda, which is in this case not particularly appropriate as it is for example in *Antigone* and *Trachiniae*. Doubts have been expressed about the authenticity of

---

[58] G. M. Kirkwood, *A Study of Sophoclean Drama*, 199.

[59] As in the first stasimon of *Ant.* and the first three of *O.C.*

[60] On the 'diptych' form, see T. B. L. Webster, *Sophocles*, 102 ff., 172 ff., 176 f.

[61] See however Dawe, op. cit. 168 f., who, following Morstadt, gives the announcement to the coryphaeus, with a lacuna before Teucer's line 1223.

the anapaests from 1402 to 1420,[62] but it is certain that the final scene presented a funeral procession conducted with due solemnity on Teucer's instructions.

The chorus in *Ajax* are handled with masterly skill. The anapaests of the parodos merge into a lyric triad much of which reflects and amplifies ideas from the recitative on a higher level of emotion. There follows an epirrhematic scene which advances the action of the play by an exchange of necessary information between Tecmessa and the sailors. In the first commos the coryphaeus is given trimeters, leaving the lyrics to Ajax, so that his passion and despair stand out against a background of calmer utterance. The first stasimon is reflective in contrast to the tension at the end of the previous scene. Then comes a striking reversal of mood for the next song which follows quick upon Ajax' speech and expresses an ecstasy of joy. This ode is the pivot of the *peripeteia* and marks the supreme dramatic moment of the play, the high point of irony and delusion. When the chorus have left the orchestra so that the suicide may take place in a changed scene, a second parodos is necessary, and this leads naturally to a second commos when Tecmessa finds the body. The active participation of the sailors in the search and the passion of the commos are followed by a return to reflection in the third and final stasimon. This perfect ABA pattern in the mood and content of the three odes helps to bind the play together in the person of the chorus. We may note also the flexibility in Sophocles' use of lyric as he seeks to express and awake emotions appropriate to different stages of the action. Contrast and variety are evident both in the combination of spoken and sung utterance within individual scenes and in the alternation of moods in the three songs.

The lyrics are also a mirror in which we see reflected the characters of Ajax and of his sailors, and their mutual relationship of devotion and interdependence. The chorus's expressions of loyalty and affection and their meditations on the life of men at war in foreign lands are moreover a powerful means of revealing the pathos inherent in the story and the setting of the play. This pathos increases after his death, and their desolation, all hope of home banished, gives to the last song a tragic significance of universal appeal. In none of these odes is there the slightest hint

[62] See Dawe, op. cit. 173 ff.

of irrelevance; and the chorus's utterances are in the truest sense ἠθικαί, expressive of their character as sailors from Salamis, and this explains the absence from them of the moral and intellectual content which informs the songs of the Theban Elders in *Antigone* and *Oedipus Tyrannus*.

II

TRACHINIAE

The title of this play might at first sight suggest that the maidens of Trachis played a dominant part. It is the only extant tragedy of Sophocles to be named after the chorus, and there is insufficient evidence from the fragments of tragedies so named for any judgement to be formed about the role sustained in them by the chorus. Since however in *Trachiniae* the chorus is not dominant, as it is for instance in Aeschylus' *Supplices* and *Eumenides* and Euripides' *Troades* and *Bacchae,* we may ask why the play was given this title, whether by Sophocles himself or by the compilers of the *didascaliae*.[1] The maidens are not deeply involved in the fortunes of the characters; they do not belong to the household of Deianira, who has been lodging for fifteen months in Trachis as a guest of the king (39), but are local girls whose interest is stimulated by anything that concerns the great hero whose family is residing in their town. Their arrival in the orchestra is incidental,[2] without any preparation in the prologue, for they are drawn by a natural curiosity to discover more about Heracles' absence and by a desire to comfort Deianira in her anxiety (πυν-θάνομαι 103). Their main task is to form a sympathetic audience for her changing moods. After her suicide their role is finished. They also reveal what Heracles meant to them and to the Greek world: a symbol of mighty heroism whose ruin is a disaster for Greece. Such indeed is the view also of the characters in the play, for the nearest approach to criticism of him occurs in Deianira's speech at 540 ff., lines wrung from her in a moment of anger and jealousy. Sophocles himself may well have intended his audience to think of him both as a hero and as a monster of savagery, if we give full weight not only to the chorus's sentiments about him, but also to Lichas' account of the murder of Iphitus (269–73), and above all to the brutal language in which Hyllus describes

---

[1] On the titling of plays see Taplin, *JHS* 95 (1975), 184.
[2] Cp. the arrival of the chorus in Eur. *Med.* and *Hipp.*

the destruction of Lichas (779–84). Finally, in their odes especially, the chorus emphasize at intervals the power of Ἔρως, a theme which runs throughout and gives an underlying unity to the whole tragedy.

Such in briefest outline is the role of the maidens of Trachis, and the play may have been named after them because their presence and certain of their utterances bind together a plot which is so constructed that neither of the two main characters could have provided a satisfactory title. Heracles' presence is felt from first to last, but he is not seen until some 300 lines from the end (971 ff.), on the brink of death, asleep at first and then in agony. The play could hardly have been named after a character whose role is limited in this way. Nor would *Deianira* have been an appropriate title, not because her part is finished by suicide before the end, but because she is no Antigone or Electra, a dominating and formidable personality. On the contrary, she is not a typical Sophoclean protagonist who initiates action and quells opposition by sheer will power. Her greatness is of a completely different kind, and in her the dramatist has created perhaps the gentlest and most compassionate character in the whole of extant Greek Tragedy.

Her qualities are revealed in her contacts with the chorus as well as with the actors. We may note especially the opening of her first speech to them after the parodos (141–52) in which as an older woman she displays her sympathetic understanding of their inexperience of trouble; the frankness with which she explains to them her attitude towards Heracles after the first stasimon (536–54) and suggests her misgivings about using the love-charm (582–98); and the way in which she seeks their comfort and advice after her horrifying experience with the tuft of wool which she used to anoint the shirt of Nessus (672–730). These passages emphasize the rapport established between her and the chorus at their first meeting and continued until her final exit (812). They illustrate also the sympathy, common sense, and understanding of the young women. This relationship between middle age and youth, the one first torn with anxiety and then confronted with her husband's young and beautiful mistress, the other sheltered from the storms of life (144 ff.), is deeply moving and forms an impressive contrast to the agonies of Heracles' destruction. After Deianira's suicide, the chorus's part is limited to a dramatic preparation for the Nurse's account of her death, the only occasion on which they desert their role of confidante and contribute actively to the movement of the play by helping to create tension at a tragic climax (863–95). Their last remark to Deianira (813 f.) is an attempt to get her to speak in her own defence as she leaves the stage after Hyllus has described Heracles' agony and cursed his mother. It is curious that they do not warn him of her intention to kill herself if the love-charm proves fatal, for they have known of it since 719 f. At similar places in *Antigone* (1251 f.) and *Oedipus Tyrannus* (1073 ff.) the chorus hint at the probable tragic end of a wife and mother who leaves the stage suddenly after a recital of disaster and a revelation of truth, but in *Trachiniae* there is no warning from the chorus, possibly because it would lessen the impact of Hyllus' amazement and grief in the Nurse's account of Deianira's death (936–42).

We may now turn to the lyrics which are among the most difficult of any in Sophocles' plays. This is due not only to insoluble textual corruptions, especially in the second and third stasima (633–62 and 821–62), but to a boldness of language and imagery which derives largely from the subject-matter of the play: supernatural events such as the wrestling match between Heracles and the river Achelous, the centaur Nessus who assaulted Deianira and gave her his blood to use as a love-charm, the charm itself and its effects described by the actors in long speeches full of imagery designed to evoke a sense of horror and corruption, and marked by similes which are among the most remarkable in the speeches of Greek Tragedy;[3] these are some of the elements from a fairy-tale world which form the stuff of the choral odes. Not only is the language of the speeches reflected in the lyrics but the atmosphere of the whole play has communicated itself to the songs and given rise to problems of interpretation and textual analysis which will require more detailed discussion than will be found in the other chapters of this book. Difficulties of relevance do not however arise, because all the odes in *Trachiniae* are closely related to their dramatic context.

In the prologue action has been initiated by the Nurse (54 ff.), and Hyllus is despatched to search for his father (92 f.). Certain information essential to the plot has also been given. In her

---

[3] Cf. e.g. 676 f., 695–704, 767–71, 777–82; and for a discussion of the play's subject-matter and its effect on the imagery, see Charles Segal, *YClS* 25 (1977), 99 ff.

opening speech (1–48), Deianira explains the reason for her anxiety over Heracles' absence, recalls in outline the oracle that foretold his return, now overdue, and mentions the tablet (δέλτος 47) which he left with her on his last departure. Hyllus reveals that his father is now invading Euboea (74 ff.) and learns from her that the oracle foretold either his death or the termination of his troubles in a life of peace (79 ff.). At the end of the prologue Hyllus leaves the stage, and the maidens of Trachis appear by chance (94). All they know is that Heracles is overdue and that Deianira is anxious. It is doubtful whether Deianira remains on stage after Hyllus' exit.[4] More probably she leaves because in her speech after the parodos (141) she does not answer the chorus's opening question πόθι μοι . . . ναίει, 'Where is he?' (98), which she could have done had she heard it. Further, in the antistrophe, they refer to her in the third person (104), and it is not until the second antistrophe that they address her directly (χρῆναί ϲε 126). Hence it is likely that she does not appear until the end of the second strophe (121), and if ἐπιμεμφομέναϲ (122) is read,[5] the reference of the feminine participle will be immediately clear. All she hears of the song will then be the last two stanzas. Had she heard the opening, Sophocles would probably have made her answer the appeal to the sun (αἰτῶ) by telling them what she had learnt from Hyllus in the prologue. Her absence during the first part of the parodos seems to be further confirmed by her opening words at its close: πεπυϲμένη μὲν, ὡϲ ἀπεικάϲαι, πάρει πάθημα τοὐμὸν, which would not be very natural had she heard the chorus's πυνθάνομαι in 103. Finally, there is an obvious dramatic effect in keeping them in ignorance of Heracles' whereabouts until the messenger arrives with the good news at 180.

The structure of the parodos is straightforward, each stanza being a self-contained unit. The first is formalized on the principles of a traditional ὕμνος κλητικός (prayer-hymn) to the sun. The limits chosen to define its journey are the πόντιαι αὐλῶνες, the narrow sea-straits at the eastern exit of the Mediterranean, and the pillars of Hercules at the western, the straits of Gibraltar separating the two continents of Europe and

[4] See Tycho Wilamowitz, *Dramatische Technik des Sophokles*, 125. I follow his view, though there is indeed no firm evidence in Greek Tragedy that a character enters during an ode. See Taplin, *The Stagecraft of Aeschylus*, 248, 263.

[5] So Kamerbeek in his edition ad loc., probably rightly.

Africa (δικκαῖκιν ἀπείροικ).[6] The language is highly coloured, especially at the opening: the relative clause, a type of extended attribute conventional in such prayers, is a development of a metaphor whereby night and day are seen as parent and offspring.[7] Sophocles appears to be using ἐναριζομένα here to mean despoiled, rather than slain:[8] night is despoiled of her glinting splendour of stars in the growing light of dawn. Apart from the intrinsic power of this image, the use of this mainly epic verb almost certainly in its commoner epic sense[9] and of κτεροπά[10] in 99 for the flame of a sunbeam, an echo of Homer's usage to describe the gleam of weapons, gives the opening of the song an epic colouring which appears again in the simile at the beginning of the second strophe (113 ff.) and in the expansion of Homer's description of the Bear at 130 f.[11] Interspersed amid the attributes of the power addressed are the terms of the request, which comes after the chiastic opening period (94 f.) in shorter cola "Ἅλιον "Ἅλιον αἰτῶ ... παῖς followed by a longer dactylo-epitrite line (99) which repeats both in content (a further attribute, ὦ λαμπρᾷ κτεροπᾷ φλεγέθων) and rhythm the opening of the stanza. Then at 100, where the dactyls disappear, we have a continuation of the construction begun at πόθι ... ναίει, and the stanza closes with a further attribute, dynamic, not purely descriptive: ὦ κρατικτεύων κατ' ὄμμα suggests that the sun has eyesight powerful enough to see Heracles.[12] This strophe well illustrates Sophocles' skill in taking the traditional elements of a prayer-hymn and combining them into a whole in which thought, expression, and rhythm are perfectly integrated. It also creates dramatic excitement by the urgency of its emotion, and its description of the gathering light of sunrise contrasts with Deianira's account of her anxious nights in the prologue (27–30) and with the chorus's echo of this in the second stanza (106 ff.).

The antistrophe (103–11) gives the grounds for the prayer

[6] See Lloyd-Jones, *CQ* n.s. 4 (1954), 91 ff.

[7] Cf. e.g. Aesch. *A.* 279.

[8] As in the active ἐνάριξον, *O.C.* 1733.

[9] ἐναρίζειν and ἐξεναρίζειν in Homer more often mean to strip bare of armour than to kill.

[10] Cf. *Il.* 11. 83; *Od.* 4. 72.

[11] *Il.* 18. 487 ff.

[12] This point is made explicit by T.C.W. Stinton's attractive suggestion κρυφείς for κλιθείς in 101. See *JHS* 96 (1976), 127 ff.

and the reason for the chorus's presence (ποθουμένᾳ γὰρ φρενὶ πυνθάνομαι). Sophocles concentrates into a brief compass the impression Deianira conveyed in her opening speech of her life and circumstances. For instance the epithet ἀμφινεικῆ (104) gathers into one word the whole of the passage 9–27 and points forward to the phrase at the end of the first stasimon,

> τὸ δ' ἀμφινείκητον ὄμμα νύμφας
> ἐλεινὸν ἀμμένει   (527)

and the longings, the fears, the sleepless nights, and the forebodings described in 106–11 are an amplification of her own lines 27–30. Purely linguistic echoes are however faint, though perhaps Deianira's ἐκ φόβου φόβον τρέφω (28) may incline us to accept Casaubon's τρέφουσαν for φέρουσαν to govern δεῖμα in 108.

In the second strophe (112–21), the chorus allow their imaginations to play freely on the picture of Heracles battling with the stormy seas of his life. The extended simile with which it opens, the dactylic rhythm, and such turns of language as ἀκάμαντος ἢ νότου ἢ βορέα κύματα, whereby waves are regarded as belonging to winds, give a strong epic tone to the first sentence.[13] Recognition of the Homeric character of this passage may win support for Erfurdt's suggestions for healing the corruption in 114 f.[14] Most modern editors accept Wakefield's and Porson's κύματ' ἂν εὑρέι πόντῳ, but a potential ἄν in this position in a clause is doubtful, since it is normally placed either after the first word or next to the verb.[15] If it is accepted, ἴδοι may be retained as a Homeric potential optative without ἄν or κε. Alternatively, Erfurdt's ἴδη may be substituted for ἴδοι, an example of the epic subjunctive in similes. True enough, in Attic tragedy the potential optative without ἄν is confined to negative sentences or to questions expecting a negative answer,[16] and the subjunctive in a simile is doubtfully paralleled by the corrupt line 1026 of Euripides' *Hecuba*. There is however reason to think that the anomalous syntax may have been generated by the epic expressions and rhythms of the first four lines. In the apodosis to

[13] For Homeric originals of Soph.'s language cf. *Il.* 2. 396 ff.; 11. 307; 15. 620 f.; *Od.* 3. 290.

[14] κύματ' ἐν for κύματ' and κύματα, and ἴδη for ἴδοι.

[15] Mr Stinton suggests to me that πολλὰ ... κύματα might count as one word.

[16] Cf. e.g. *Ant.* 604 f.

the simile, οὕτω δὲ τὸν Καδμογενῆ ... Κρήϲιον (116–19), there are serious doubts both as to the reading and the word-arrangement. In view of the appearance in Homer of τρόφι and τροφόεντα in connection with the swell of waves and of Euripides' ὦ πόνοι τρέφοντεϲ βροτούϲ ('troubles, the food of mortal men'),[17] τρέφει in 117 should not be lightly abandoned in favour of Reiske's ϲτρέφει, 'turns aside', or 'overturns'; and as to punctuation, one inclines to delete the comma at πολύπονον, taking ⟨τὸ μὲν⟩ ... τὸ δὲ as subject of the verbs (one wave and then another) and to combine βιότου ... Κρήϲιον as a single word-group in apposition to the sentence: 'even so does one wave sustain him, another raise him up, so as to make for him as it were a troubled Cretan sea of life'. This is probably the best that can be done for the manuscript tradition. There remains however the lack of the contrast between τρέφει and αὔξει demanded by the ellipse of τὸ μὲν before the first verb to balance τὸ δὲ before the second. It may perhaps be possible to force such a contrast by stressing the physical sense of αὔξει, 'raises him up', and taking τρέφει of a less turbulent motion, 'supports'. We may then imagine ourselves on the shore watching a swimmer now in a trough, now on the crest, as the waves follow one another in unending succession. At one moment he may be almost invisible, at another he seems to grow in size as he rides the sea. Alternatively, we may consider the suggestion that αὔξει may be a gloss on τρέφει, in which case τὸ δ' should be read as τόδ' and perhaps αἰεὶ for αὔξει, 'this troubled Cretan sea of life always sustains him'.[18] The stanza ends with a confident statement introduced by ἀλλά: 'but (in spite of this) some god always keeps him from death, and he strays not from his course.'

The function of this second strophe in the structure of the ode depends to a large extent on the reference of ὧν at the beginning of its antistrophe (122). If the word ἐπιμεμφομέναϲ is divided as ἐπιμεμφομένα ϲ', ὧν must refer not to the preceding stanza but to the first antistrophe (103–11), because what the chorus blame Deianira for is not the perils of Heracles but her own attitude of mind. The text with ἐπιμεμφομένα ϲ' forces us to take the second strophe as an extended parenthesis. This reference of ὧν over an intervening stanza is undoubtedly difficult but perhaps not

---

[17] *Hipp.* 367.
[18] So Stinton, *JHS*, loc. cit. 129 f.

impossible. The difficulty should certainly not be dealt with by transposing the second strophe and antistrophe, as Nauck proposed, because this would ruin the close connection of the epode with 129 ff. A further objection to ἐπιμεμφομένα ϲ' is that this verb is found only with the dative of the person in Greek of this period. We should therefore read ἐπιμεμφομέναϲ, genitive absolute, referring to Deianira, who, as suggested above, reappears on the stage at this moment. ὧν will then sum up the preceding stanza: 'as you (or she) complain because of Heracles' perils, I offer . . .'. The second strophe is thus the centre piece of the whole song.

In the next stanza (122) the chorus turn directly to Deianira with advice based upon a traditional Greek way of looking at human life. The lesson of this stanza and of the epode is that while pain is ordained for mankind by Zeus, it is nevertheless not unremitting because by the same natural laws that govern the movements of the constellations and the passing of night into day, the impermanence of any state is guaranteed by an unending cycle of change.[19] The simile in 130 f. is a development of Homer's phrase for the constellation of the Bear in *Iliad* 18.488, ἥ τ' αὐτοῦ ϲτρέφεται: the Bear turns in the sky round the pole, never vanishing below the horizon, a symbol of circling movement eternally visible. The point was hinted at in the visualization of Heracles in the third stanza battling with his sea of troubles, sustained by the perpetual movement of waves, yet never diverted from his course. The words

$$\text{ἀλλ' ἐπὶ πῆμα καὶ χαρὰ}$$
$$\text{πᾶϲι κυκλοῦϲιν}$$

'pain and joy circle for all men' (129) and their echo in the epode 134 f.

$$\text{χαίρειν τε καὶ ϲτέρεϲθαι}$$

are appropriate not only to Heracles' condition and his life of labours but also to the way in which the play depicts a series of changing states in Deianira's mind: anxious fear in the prologue and in her speech after the parodos turns to joy when the messenger brings his news (180 ff.); in the central scene joy gives

---

[19] For further examples of this idea in Soph. cf. *Aj.* 670–82 and 1359, and *O.C.* 610–15. Further on this image, see John Jones, *Aristotle and Greek Tragedy*, 174–7.

way to misgiving; the use of the love-charm suggests the renewal of hope; and finally comes despair, leading to suicide.

The epode opens with a paratactic simile (132) in which the words of the first line of the song, αἰόλα νύξ, are repeated. This repetition, besides imposing a formal unity on the ode, reaffirms the points made in the opening stanza and in the advice given to Deianira in the second antistrophe: the alternation of darkness and light, the cycle of joy and sorrow, and the mutability of men's fortunes, all of which constitute a major theme in the play. The epode moreover, marked off from the preceding stanzas by its wholly iambic rhythms, acts as a coda, with the final emphasis on Zeus' care for his children, as a climax to the whole structure:

$$\text{ἐπεὶ τίς ὧδε}$$
$$\text{τέκνοιϲι Ζῆν' ἄβουλον εἶδεν;}$$

'Who has ever seen Zeus thus careless of his children?' This is the thought which the chorus wish to leave with Deianira as the ultimate guarantee of Heracles' safety and of her grounds for hope.

This parodos is a fine example of a song directed towards definite ends, the establishment of sympathy between the chorus and Deianira and the attempt to banish her anxiety and encourage her to hope. The first two stanzas comprise a prayer-hymn and the grounds for it and while composed in accordance with traditional formulae, display at the beginning a brilliance of language and an intricacy of pattern which arrest attention and awake excitement. The second strophe visualizes the life of Heracles in a highly pictorial form with imagery derived from Homeric sources and acts as a high-light of the ode, concentrating for a space on the figure who is the focus of everyone's thoughts. The last two stanzas are addressed to Deianira with a message of hope and comfort. Communication is thus established between her and the maidens of Trachis, and the way is open for the following scene in which, clearly moved by their concern, she explains the reasons for her anxiety, adding necessary details about the tablet and the oracle which were merely hinted at in the prologue. The transition from song to speech is thus perfectly natural both psychologically and dramatically.

At 180 a messenger arrives with the news of Heracles' safety and approaching return crowned with victory over Oechalia.

Deianira's anxiety is banished and at 202 ff. she bids the women raise the ὀλολυγή:

> φωνήσατ', ὦ γυναῖκες, αἵ τ' εἴcω cτέγηc
> αἵ τ' ἐκτὸς αὐλῆς

'Raise your voices, women, both you inside the house and you outside'. This ritual cry from women is as old as Homer, where it marks the utterance of prayers and thanksgiving or accompanies the supreme moment of sacrifice when the animal's neck is struck by the axe. Examples from classical times indicate that it was a regular feature of Greek domestic life, a cry of good omen associated mostly with joyful occasions.[20] Thus at 205 Deianira's command is expanded into a lyric in which the young women of the chorus catch her mood and begin their song with the ritual word ἀνολολυξάτω. They are absorbed in the joy of the whole household and share completely in the emotion generated on the stage and in the activity that arises from it. The effect is intensely dramatic after the mood of anxious doubt and fear which pervades the opening of the play.

The ode may be conveniently labelled a *hyporchema*, a song accompanied by dancing, in view of the note in the ancient scholia on 216: τὸ μελιδάριον οὐκ ἔcτι cτάcιμον, ἀλλ' ὑπὸ τῆς ἡδονῆς ὀρχοῦνται, 'the little song is not a stasimon, but they dance for joy.' We should however remember that all stasima in Greek Tragedy were accompanied by rhythmic movements of some kind, so there is probably no difference in kind between what Aristotle called cτάcιμα and the Byzantine Tzetzes ὑπορχήματα.[21] The note in the scholia was prompted by the explicit reference in 216 and 218 ff. to the physical movements of a dance (ἀείρομαι and ἀναταράccει ... ἅμιλλαν). There is a similar indication of excited dancing by the chorus at *Ajax* 693 and 699 ff. What makes this lyric remarkable in extant Sophocles is that it is astrophic. There are indeed other ἄcτροφα, but in the surviving plays they are confined to utterances shared between actor and chorus.[22] The metre of this little song is iambic, at times highly resolved and syncopated, with a dactylic run at 213 f.

[20] For ὀλολυγμός, ὀλολυγή and ὀλολύζειν cf. e.g. *Il.* 6. 301; *Od.* 3. 450; 4. 767; Aesch. *Th.* 268; *A.* 28, 587, 595; Eur. *Med.* 1176; Ar. *Eq.* 1327; *Pax* 97; *Lys.* 240.

[21] Arist. *Po.* 1452^b 23. See A. M. Dale, *The Lyric Metres of Greek Drama*^{2}, 210, and *Collected Papers*, 34–41.

[22] Cf. *Trach.* 871–95; *Phil.* 1169–1217; *O.C.* 207–36. In the two latter instances, the ἄcτροφα are in fact extended epodes to preceding strophic pairs.

The ode is normally divided into three periods but there is no evidence to support Christ's theory, followed by Jebb, that the first two are to be assigned to the two semi-choruses, and the third to the coryphaeus.[23] The mainly iambic metre running through the whole song is against such a division; the imperative ἀνάγετε in 211 does not prove that this section is a command given to another group, and had the coryphaeus alone announced Lichas' approach (221–4), he would instead of singing have made his announcement in spoken trimeters or recited anapaests. We should almost certainly regard the whole ode as sung by the complete chorus, and the three sections as differentiated by content and mood, not by division between singers.

The first 'stanza' (205–15) opens with the ritual word. The third person imperative is Burges's suggestion for the unmetrical readings of the manuscripts. δόμος, also from the same scholar, should probably be accepted for δόμοις in view of the scholiast's paraphrase ὁ πᾶς οἶκος Ἡρακλέους and of Euripides' words in a similar context (*Electra* 691), where a whole household is to raise a cry of joy, ὀλολύξεται πᾶν δῶμα. This latter passage inclines one also to accept Elmsley's ἀνολολύξεται for the opening word. The main problem however in the first sentence is the interpretation of ὁ μελλόνυμφος as a definition of δόμος used here of a household and its members, like the Latin *familia*. The word normally means a girl intending to marry, and δόμος ὁ μελλόνυμφος may be a bold phrase for αἱ ἐν τῷ δόμῳ μελλόνυμφοι, the girls in the house, an amplification of Deianira's αἱ εἴσω στέγης in 202. This interpretation satisfies the careful division of functions in the first section of the song: the girls of the household are to raise the ὀλολυγή, the men are to call on Apollo, and the chorus (αἱ ἐκτὸς αὐλῆς, 203), the local girls who do not belong to the *familia*, are to lift up a paean to Artemis. The voices of all are thus united in thanksgiving for Heracles' victory, and the unison is emphasized by ἐν δὲ κοινὸς ἀρσένων κλαγγά and ὁμοῦ δὲ παιᾶνα (207 and 210). A more subtle interpretation, though equally difficult linguistically, runs as follows.[24] One notes the emphasis ὁ μελλόνυμφος acquires from its position at the end of the sentence with a strong break at the caesura of the iambic trimeter (207) as if Sophocles

---

[23] This view is refuted by Wilamowitz, *Griechische Verskunst*, 526 ff.
[24] See T.B.L. Webster in *Greek Poetry and Life*, 167. The difficulty lies in taking δόμος ὁ μελλόνυμφος to mean δόμος ὁ νύμφην δέξεσθαι μέλλων.

were aiming at a special effect; and if the phrase can mean the household which is expecting a bride, or which is ready for a marriage, it will refer on the face of it to the reunion of Deianira with Heracles after his long absence. Beneath the surface there may well be a sinister meaning intended by the dramatist but hidden at this stage from the chorus, for the household is indeed about to receive a bride, Iole, who will bring ruin upon it; and the irony begins to emerge when Deianira speaks to her in the next scene (307), gathering in intensity as the play advances and becoming fully apparent in the chorus's words after the suicide: 'this new bride has given birth to a great Ἐρινύς for this house':

> ἔτεκ᾽, ἔτεκε μεγάλαν ἁ
> νέορτος ἅδε νύμφα
> δόμοισι τοῖςδ᾽ Ἐρινύν.   (893–5)[25]

In the second section (216–20) we must visualize the leaping into the air (ἀείρομαι) as the maidens of the chorus submit to the music of the αὐλός. ὦ τύραννε τᾶς ἐμᾶς φρενός, 'lord of my soul', is probably addressed to Dionysus, though Jebb's suggestion that it refers to the music is attractive. The ivy, whether wreathed round the head or bunched on the thyrsus, is a symbol of ecstasy and excites the dancers to utter the ritual cry εὐοῖ and strain every effort in the motions of the Bacchic dance (βακχίαν ἅμιλλαν). In 220 the participle ὑποστρέφων, read by all the manuscripts, should not be altered, because it describes the dance, a circling movement in which the dancers return to the starting-point. This is a regular meaning of ὑποστρέφειν in Homer.[26] The pronoun μ᾽ in 218 is the direct object of both ἀναταράσσει and ὑποστρέφων, and the second μ᾽ in 219 should perhaps be omitted, so that εὐοῖ is *extra metrum*. ἅμιλλαν will then be an internal accusative defining the action of the verb: 'the ivy rouses me to ecstasy, εὐοῖ, whirling me round in the effort of the Bacchic dance.' The virtual personification of the ivy (ὁ κισσός), so that it actually sets the dancers in frenzied motion and controls their movements, is a bold and remarkable use of language, and

---

[25] Thus Pearson's text, but the colometry is much discussed; see Stinton, *BICS* 22 (1975), 96.

[26] Cf. e.g. *Il.* 5. 581, ὁ δ᾽ ὑπέστρεφε μώνυχας ἵππους, 'he was turning his chariot round to bring it back'; also Eur. *H.F.* 736, of Heracles bringing himself back from Hades. See further on this passage Lloyd-Jones in *YCIS* 22 (1972), 264.

the brief five line passage highlights the overmastering compulsion imposed upon the chorus by the music of the αὐλός and the ivy as a vehicle of the god Dionysus.[27]

In the last section (221–4), beginning with the refrain of the Paean which they were asked to raise in the first, the chorus announce the arrival of Lichas with the captives from Oechalia, and in order to sweep Deianira into the orbit of their own emotion (ἴδε ἴδ' ὦ φίλα γύναι), they fuse the announcement into the rhythmic and ecstatic mood of the whole song.

The astrophic form of this ode contributes much to its dramatic effect. There is no need at this juncture for a formal stasimon with corresponsion of metre and symmetry of thought, though one should note the echo in Παιάν (221) of παιᾶνα παιᾶν' ἀνάγετε (210 f.) which secures a balanced circular structure. Sophocles has provided a quick-moving song to express an immediate reaction of joy mounting to a climax in excited dancing and closing with an equally excited announcement of a new character. The tension is relaxed by Deianira's opening words, calm and dignified, and especially by her characteristic reservation χαρτὸν εἴ τι καὶ φέρεις, 'if you really do bring joyful news' (228); and the piteous spectacle of the captives from Oechalia, Iole conspicuous among them (298–313), casts a shadow of foreboding against which the chorus's brief ecstasy shines in bright relief. We may stress the irony inherent in this song and note how it points forward to the more formalized ode of welcome in the second stasimon (633–62), where we shall again meet Artemis and the music of the αὐλός.

In the following scene Deianira and the chorus discover from the messenger that it was for love of Iole that Heracles sacked Oechalia (351–65). They hear her characterize Ἔρως as an invincible power against which it is folly to fight (441 ff.): even gods are ruled by it, and she would be mad to blame her husband or Iole for falling victims to this disease. Finally the chorus hear Lichas' conclusion after he has admitted the truth of the messenger's account of Heracles' motive: that the great hero was no match for the power that caused his passion for the captive (488 f.). Deianira takes up the same theme again after the song: ἔρως is a νόσος (544), and we become aware of the efforts she is

---

[27] For the significance of κισσός in Bacchic worship, see Dodds's edition of Eur. *Ba.* pp. 77 and 208 (on 81 and 1054 f.).

Trachiniae

making, in spite of her bitterness and jealousy, to fight down her anger with Heracles (543 and 552). Such a view of ἔρως appears to be normal in Greek of this period, and any attempt to romanticize it in this play would be mistaken.[28] On the contrary, we must never forget that it is a force for destruction, a disease that is to bring ruin and death; and that in her jealousy Deianira, as well as Heracles, is in its grip.

It is therefore not surprising that the theme of the first stasimon (497–530) should be the power of Cypris. The example chosen to illustrate it is the battle long ago between Heracles and the river Achelous for Deianira's hand. Despite the leap back over the years to a distant past the relevance of the ode to its dramatic context is complete. Not only does it arise naturally from the preceding scene, but its theme is continued into the later stages of the play where it grows in importance with the progress of the tragedy and supplies the chorus with some of their most powerful utterances.[29] Further, the lyric narrative which forms the centre-piece of the song has been expected ever since the prologue, where Deianira described the metamorphoses of her monstrous suitor (11–14) and hinted at the conflict between him and Heracles, saying that she could not recount the details herself for she sat there distraught with fear, but would leave the task to another:

ἀλλ' ὅστις ἦν
θακῶν ἀταρβὴς τῆς θέας, ὅδ' ἂν λέγοι

'but if there was anyone sitting there and watching the sight without fear, he might tell the story' (22 ff.). The task is fulfilled in this song, not however by an eye-witness but by the young girls of Trachis who must have been, like all Greeks, familiar with the saga of the great Dorian hero from their early childhood. Finally, the last four lines of the ode are exactly applicable to Deianira's situation in the play.

The song opens with a statement of its theme:[30] most of the rest is illustration. Examples of Cypris' victories over the gods, suggested perhaps by Deianira's words in 443 (οὗτος γὰρ ἄρχει

---

[28] For Ἔρως in Soph. cf. *Ant.* 781–801 and Fr. 941P.

[29] Cf. e.g. 860 f. and 893 f.

[30] For a discussion of the grammatical structure of the first line, see Stinton, *JHS*, loc. cit. 136 ff.

καὶ θεῶν ὅπως θέλει) are rejected (παρέβαν 499) in favour of one which is supremely relevant to the play. Introduced at 503 by a question-formula familiar from epic and found in varied forms throughout choral lyric narrative,[31] the story begins in the antistrophe. It has been remarked that this type of 'lyrical ballad' is rare, perhaps unique in extant Sophocles.[32] There are indeed examples in Euripides, where we can see how easily they may develop into what Aristotle called ἐμβόλιμα,[33] choral intermezzos of little relevance to the dramatic context. Lyric narratives of this kind are seen at their best in Pindar and Bacchylides, and it is of value to bear their poems in mind when reading Sophocles' song and to note his use of parataxis and vivid highlights which recall the style of the myths in the Epinician Odes.

The scene and the combatants are presented here with the clarity of a work of art.[34] The three figures in the antistrophe, Achelous, Heracles, and Cypris, are grouped to form a spectacle that must have been familiar to those among the audience who had watched the wrestling or the *pancratium* at any Greek athletic festival. The two clauses describing the wrestlers in answer to the question at the end of the strophe sound like the official announcement by the herald of the competitors' names and home towns[35] and are wrought with conscious artistry in chiastic form. The identity of the combatants is held back until the last words, 'one ... Achelous from Oeniadae, and the other from Bacchus' Thebes ... the son of Zeus' (507–13). Their figures are drawn with great economy: Achelous, ποταμοῦ cθένος, appears in the form of a bull, one of the three shapes in which he wooed Deianira (11 ff.), and Heracles enters the lists armed with bow and arrows, spears, and a club. After a short sentence (513) corresponding in sense and rhyming at the end with its strophic equivalent (504), the picture is completed with the third figure between the two principals, Cypris, staff in hand, in her role as sole umpire of the fight:

---

[31] Cp. the familiar question formula at the beginning of Homeric ἀριcτεῖα in the *Iliad*, τίνα δὴ πρῶτον, τίνα δ᾽ ὕcτατον and e.g. Pi. *P.* 4. 70 f.; also the long list of questions suggesting various possible mythical themes which the poet rejects, at the beginning of *I.* 7.

[32] Kranz, *Stasimon*, 254; Reinhardt, *Sophokles*, 253.

[33] *Po.* 1456ᵃ 29.

[34] The scene is indeed depicted on vase-paintings, cf. Philostratus Jun. *Imagines* 4.

[35] The point is well made by Stinton in *JHS*, loc. cit. 126, with refs. to Soph. *El.* 701–8, εἷc ἀπὸ Cπάρτηc and ἔνατοc Ἀθηνῶν... ἄπο.

μόνα δ' εὔλεκτρος ἐν μέcῳ Κύπρις
ῥαβδονόμει ξύνουcα.   (515)

In the epode (516–22) the scene comes to life. The four clauses, each introduced by the most naked of verbs (ἦν) with words chosen for their alliterative and onomatopoeic effect, give an impression of energy powerfully controlled: such simplicity of style and structure is a product of the highest art. The violence and noise cease at 522 (cτόνοc ἀμφοῖν), suspended at their height, the issue of the contest undisclosed. With a striking change of rhythm from dactylo-epitrite to a most unusual type of colon, twice repeated, we are made aware of the fourth figure:

ἁ δ' εὐῶπιc ἁβρὰ
τηλαυγεῖ παρ' ὄχθῳ
ἧcτο, τὸν ὃν προcμένουc' ἀκοίταν

'She, fair of face, delicate, on a slope visible from afar, sat awaiting him who was to be her husband' (523 ff.). The rest of the song is concentrated upon her. Wilamowitz[36] well draws attention to the significance of the tense-change to the primary (ἀμμένει, 528) and to the effect of the closing simile. The calf gone from its mother is a traditional image of forlornness, and this, together with the sentence at 527, brings the ode in its last lines into immediate relation to Deianira's patient and lonely waiting in the play, as she described herself in the prologue and as the chorus depicted her in the second stanza of the parodos.

A few details of language and interpretation require further comment. There are bold uses of individual words. ἀμφίγυοι (504), a stock epithet of ἔγχοc in Homer, is here applied to the two combatants in a sense that eludes exact definition, and as there are no parallels to help, I can do little more than acquiesce in the scholiast's paraphrases, ἀντίπαλοι ἢ ἰcχυροὶ ἐν τοῖc γυίοιc, μαχεcάμενοι χερcὶ καὶ ποcίν, 'adversaries, or strong in their limbs, fighting with hands and feet'. It seems that Sophocles intended to convey the impression of a balanced strength on both sides (ἀμφί), Heracles matching his weapons and the techniques of human skill against the natural equipment of the bull. The adjective is at any rate unique outside epic, and here uniquely employed. Likewise τετράοροc (508) and ἀολλεῖc (513) both

---

[36] *Griechische Verskunst*, 529 ff.

appear in unparalleled usages, the former, elsewhere only of a four-horse chariot team, here meaning four-legged, and the latter, normally of a crowd, here limited to two, but suggesting perhaps a full complement of arms, legs, and weapons filling the scene as the combatants rush to meet each other. The word certainly conveys much more than ὅμοϲε, the usual adverb with ἰέναι in the sense of fighting at close quarters. Finally the phrase ἀμφίπλεκτοι κλίμακες[37] (520) introduces into the description of the fight a technical term of wrestling which has the effect of momentarily normalizing what would otherwise be fantastic, for though κλίμακες is unparalleled in this scene in a literary text,[38] there can be little doubt, in view of Hesychius' gloss εἶδος πάληϲ, that the hold it describes would be familiar to wrestling fans among the audience, just as devotees of modern all-in wrestling would appreciate at once what is meant by 'the scissors'.

As to the much discussed

$$\text{ἐγὼ δὲ μάτηρ μὲν οἷα φράζω} \qquad (526)$$

no solution has yet been found. There are no variants in the manuscripts. On the face of it the words mean 'I am telling the story as a mother would', which is absurd on the lips of young girls half Deianira's age. Attempts to translate the sentence 'as my mother told me' force too much out of the Greek.[39] The suggestions for altering μάτηρ are unsatisfactory, Zielinski's θατήρ, a spectator, perhaps least so in view of Deianira's hint at a possible eye-witness in the prologue (22 f.), because all single-word substitutes fail to account for the difficult μὲν following close on ἐγὼ δὲ and with no satisfactory contrast in the next sentence. These considerations suggest that the corruption includes μάτηρ μὲν at least and possibly the next word also. The scholia contain a paraphrase παρεῖϲα τὰ πολλά, τὰ τέλη λέγω τῶν πραγμάτων, 'omitting many details, I am telling the main points of the story', which may indicate a reading now lost. There is however little doubt that whatever else in the line is corrupt ἐγὼ δὲ is sound for the following reason. The function of this sentence is to break off the narrative of the wrestling match and to bring

---

[37] Pearson's ἀμφίπλικτοι seems unnecessary, though it perhaps makes the epithet a technical term, cf. Hesychius s.v. πλίγμα ἀπὸ τῶν παλαιόντων.

[38] The verb κλιμακίζειν appears as a wrestling term in Ar. Fr. 4 D.

[39] So Kamerbeek ad loc.

the song at its close back into the dramatic context. This use of the first person pronoun is a recognized device in choral lyric where poet or chorus intrude at the end of a myth to stay the narrative and return to the occasion of the poem. ἐγὼ δέ is used here in precisely this way, and to emend it out of the text would destroy this important sign of a coda or a transition to another theme.[40]

As to the form into which Sophocles has cast this ode, the general similarity of the rhythm all through into the first half of the epode (522) suggests that we should regard the whole as a single triad rather than as two strophes and an epode, just as we think of Pindar's epinicians as composed in triads. The rhythms are a perfect vehicle for the subject: the speed of the anapaests and dactylo-epitrites recalls the movement of a narrative from choral lyric, and the change at 523 to a slower metre as the chorus bring Deianira into focus marks the return of the pathos inherent in her situation. As a piece of poetic description the song has few equals in extant Sophocles. It displays a remarkable clarity of vision and energy of movement. Nothing is blurred or imprecise either in the tranquil setting of the scene or in the burst of sound and fury at the beginning of the epode. Such is the combined effect of stirring rhythms, vivid phraseology, and verbal assonance that we not only visualize the fight as if we were spectators but also hear the thudding of the blows and the groans of the combatants. In addition to the impact of its poetry on the senses, the song makes a strong dramatic point by its emphasis at the beginning and at the end of the antistrophe on the power and authority of Cypris. Her influence was felt as soon as her silent symbol Iole appeared on the stage in the preceding scene. In this ode she is seen herself as umpire of the wrestling match, and from this moment onwards her control over the action becomes ever more apparent as the tragedy moves towards its end.

In the next scene (531–632), Deianira recounts the incident which led to Nessus' death. She tells of his gift to her of the supposed love-charm, and announces her decision to use it in order to win back Heracles. At 588–93 the exchange between Deianira and the coryphaeus is important in that it emphasizes

---

[40] Cf. e.g. Pi. *O.* 1.100; 8.54; 9.21; 10.97; *N.* 1.33; *I.* 1.14. See Schadewaldt, *Der Aufbau des Pindarischen Epinikion*, 300 n. 6.

her misgivings about using the love-charm. Her doubts are however allayed, and the scene ends with the dispatch of Lichas with the fatal robe. Her apprehensions, momentarily quietened by the coryphaeus' reasoning, reappear in her last lines, another characteristic and moving reservation:

δέδοικα γὰρ
μὴ πρῷ λέγοις ἂν τὸν πόθον τὸν ἐξ ἐμοῦ
πρὶν εἰδέναι τἀκεῖθεν εἰ ποθούμεθα

'I fear you may perhaps be too soon in speaking of my longing for him, before I know whether my longing is returned by him' (630 ff.). The following song reflects none of her doubts. It comes at the moment of suspense when all is poised for the *peripeteia*: the chorus, mistaken as to what will shortly happen, express sentiments which are to be violently belied in the next scene. Lyric thus crystallizes the irony inherent in such situations, establishing a deluded emotion just before the revelation of truth.[41] In *Trachiniae* the confidence expressed in the second stasimon echoes less ecstatically and more formally the mood of the *hyporchema* (205), to which it constitutes a parallel: the irony faintly perceptible in the earlier song is here strengthened to an almost intolerable degree as the inhabitants of the whole region round the Malian Gulf are asked to join in a song of welcome[42] to Heracles on his return to what the chorus believe is a scene of triumph but is soon to be revealed as one of agony and death.

The first strophe (633–9) presents this scene in precise geographical detail, thus creating a powerful atmosphere of place. Thermopylae, the hot springs made according to legend by Athena for Heracles after his labours and renowned in the Persian Wars; Mount Oeta which saw his apotheosis in fire; the Malian Gulf, a celebrated land-locked harbour; the rocky coast which contained the original seat of the immemorially old Amphictyonic League, an important element in the life of Greek city states during the classical period: all these are drawn into the opening appeal. Sophocles could hardly have chosen a more impressive way of stressing Heracles' significance not only to the

---

[41] Cp. *Aj.* 693; *Ant.* 1115; *O.T.* 1086.

[42] Such songs were classed by Menander Rhetor (3rd cent. A.D.) as προσφωνήτικα and followed a definite pattern. For this genre see Francis Cairns, *Generic Composition in Greek and Roman Poetry* (Edinburgh 1972), 21–6.

persons in the play but also as an abiding figure of Greek life and
thought than by describing a region so rich in historical and
legendary associations and including a reference to the ἀγοραὶ
Πυλάτιδες (638), the Πυλαῖαι cύνοδοι, a contemporary focus of
Panhellenic aspirations. At 637 we again meet Artemis to whom
the maidens appealed in the *hyporchema* and at 641 again the
αὐλός which shall sound no dissonant strain of mourning, but
heavenly music in answer to the lyre. After the extended vocative
of the strophe the antistrophe completes the construction and
gives the grounds for the appeal in three impressive lines at its
close: 'for the son born of Alcmena to Zeus is hastening
homewards with the spoils of all prowess' (644 ff.). The irony in
the confident statements of this stanza will soon be terribly
revealed, for instead of the music of flute and lyre there will be
nothing but the sound of lamentation, and the great Heracles
will come home robed not in the spoils of victory but in the shirt
of Nessus.

The mood of the second strophe is in sharp contrast until the
last sentence where νῦν δέ (653) marks a return of confidence
after the imperfect tenses εἴχομεν (647) and ὤλλυτο (652).
Protracted waiting amid tears for the return of a longed-for
husband has up to now been a dominant feature of Deianira's
life, and the opening sentences of this stanza concentrate it into
a few key words: ἀπόπτολιν, δυοκαιδεκάμηνον ἀμμένουcαι χρόνον,
πελάγιον, πάγκλαυτος all echo substantial parts of previous
trimeters and lyrics. ἀπόπτολιν, 'away from our city of Trachis',
recalls much of the prologue and first epeisodion, while πελάγιον,
'on the open sea', picks up the extended image in the second
strophe of the parodos (112–21). There is a discrepancy in the
time-reference of δυοκαιδεκάμηνον which all critics have noticed:
fifteen months, not twelve, has been the period mentioned
previously in precise detail, not only in the prologue 44 f. (where
of course the chorus were not present), but explicitly in front of
them at 164 f. The inconsistency however is of little importance
and may well be a slip on the dramatist's part. Finally the
picture of Deianira's past wretchedness and tears (650 ff.), with
the repeated τάλαινα δυcτάλαινα and the powerful word ὤλλυτο
suggesting a gradual mental and physical decline, is an effective
contrast with the relief of pain heralded in the closing lines of the
stanza:

νῦν δ' "Αρης οἰcτρηθεὶc
ἐξέλυc' ἐπιπόνων ἀμεράν⁴³   (653 f.)

'but now the god of war, stung to fury, has delivered her from
her days of trouble.' We may here recall the second antistrophe
of the parodos with its image of alternating joy and sorrow in
terms of the wheeling paths of the Bear and its continuation into
the epode of the same song (133 ff.)

ἀλλ' ἄφαρ
βέβακε, τῷ δ' ἐπέρχεται
χαίρειν τε καὶ cτέρεcθαι.

In the present stasimon (633–62), pain has given way to joy:
soon, after the moment of joy, comes its loss, and pain recurs.

After the reflective mood of the second strophe, the antistrophe,
opening with the excited repetition of ἀφίκοιτο, concludes the
song on a note of eager hope. A reference to the love-charm
which formed the central theme of the preceding scene is
reserved to an emphatic place at the end (661 f.). In contrast to
the clarity of language which marks the rest of the ode, the last
three lines are corrupt and hard to interpret. It would be rash to
dogmatize over a passage which has so far defied solution, but a
few tentative remarks may be made.

In the first place πανάμεροc of the manuscripts in its obvious
derivation from ἡμέρα with the normal sense 'all day long' is
difficult with the aorist μόλοι, 'may he arrive': one would have to
understand a participle, e.g. πορευθείc, 'having travelled all day'.
Alternatively, the word may be translated 'completely gentle',
παν- reinforcing the adjective ἥμεροc in its Doric form ἄμεροc. A
scholiast's paraphrase may support this: εὐμενὴc ἐν τῇ αὐτῇ ἡμέρᾳ
ἔλθοι, 'may he come kindly disposed', though indeed it includes
an impossible sense of πανάμεροc from ἡμέρα. This interpretation makes a good point: the chorus pray that the fierce warrior
who has sacked Oechalia may return to his wife in a gentle mood
after the frenzy of destruction (cf. "Αρης οἰcτρηθείc, 653).⁴⁴
Finally, we may take refuge in Zachariah Mudge's πανίμεροc
along with Jebb, who prints it in his text. 'Full of desire' well suits

---

⁴³ Erfurdt's suggestion, genitive plural for the accusative of the manuscripts (ἐπίπονον
ἀμέραν), corrects both grammar and metre.
⁴⁴ So Kamerbeek in his edition, pp. 148 f.

the erotic tone of the following lines describing the love-charm. The second point concerns the participle in 662. Although cυγκραθεὶc of the manuscripts is metrically possible, a molossus answering the cretic in 654, there is much to be said for Blaydes's cυντακεὶc (which would secure exact corresponsion), because compounds of τήκειν occur in the play with sinister effect. Deianira uses ἐντακείη in an erotic sense of the relationship between Heracles and Iole in 463 ('melted or absorbed in loving him'); the chorus use προcτήκειν twice in the next stasimon (833 and 836) of Heracles and the poisoned robe ('fused or melted to'); and cυντακεὶc if introduced into the text at 662 would combine the erotic sense of ἐντακείη in 463 with a foretaste of the literal sense in the next ode.

These are however minor details compared with the problem of τᾶc πειθοῦc παγχρίcτῳ ... ἐπὶ προφάcει θηρόc which the manuscripts offer with no variant in 661 f. The phrase τᾶc Πειθοῦc[45] πάγχριcτοc πρόφαcιc is of a type familiar in Aeschylus[46]. The abstract noun is qualified by an epithet applicable only to something concrete, and the whole phrase must therefore describe a concrete object. πρόφαcιc means a motive or a pretext, presumably for Heracles to return home full of love for Deianira, and it may be possible to regard τᾶc Πειθοῦc πάγχριcτοc πρόφαcιc, 'Persuasion's well-anointed pretext' as an Aeschylean-type description of the robe. Two points however arouse misgivings: first, if the phrase describes the robe, it should be governed directly by the participle cυγκραθεὶc or cυντακεὶc, and the preposition ἐπὶ should be removed; and secondly, πρόφαcιc is not natural in the phrase thus produced, 'fused to the well-anointed pretext'. We need a word meaning allurement, which is provided by Paley's παρφάcει, admitted into the Oxford text by Pearson. πάρφαcιc, from παραφάναι,[47] appears in *Iliad* 14. 217 along with φιλότηc and ἵμεροc as one of the contents of Aphrodite's girdle and is therefore singularly appropriate to denote a robe smeared

[45] The word should probably be written with a capital Π. The article personifies it and should not be altered. In Hes. *Th.* 349 Πειθώ is a goddess; she also has a cult, see Deubner, *Roscher* iii. 2138–9.

[46] Cp. e.g. Aesch.'s phrase for lamp oil at *A.* 93 ff., χρίματοc ἁγνοῦ μαλακαῖc ἀδόλοιcι παραγορίαιc.

[47] The verb in Homer means 'persuade, appease', and in Pindar carries the notion of deceit, *O.* 1. 66; *P.* 9. 43; *N.* 5. 32, the two latter examples being in erotic contexts. The noun πάρφαcιc, both in *Il.* 14. 217 and in Pi. *N.* 8. 32, implies deception.

with an unguent purporting to win Heracles' love. The erotic sense is further assisted by the word Πειθώ (661), which appears in similar contexts as a preliminary to seduction.[48] Accordingly παρφάcει has a great deal to commend it: the robe, so far as the chorus know at this stage of the play, is precisely 'Persuasion's well-anointed allurement' to which they hope he will be fused, the charm melting him with desire. The deception, inherent in the word, is not yet apparent but is soon revealed when Heracles is indeed fused or melted to it in a horrible manner (768 ff. and 831–40). This is the last and most powerful stroke of irony in a song which is remarkable throughout for its exploitation of this peculiarly Sophoclean feature. Having argued for παρφάcει, an uncommon word which could easily be corrupted into the familiar προφάcει, we may perhaps conclude that Sophocles wrote

> τὰc Πειθοῦc παγχρίcτῳ
> cυγκραθεὶc (or cυντακεὶc) . . . παρφάcει.

As to ἐπὶ and θηρόc, they look very much like part of a glossator's attempt to define this periphrasis for the robe. Closer definition would however weaken the effect of closing the song with what amounts to an enigma or kenning. If an intrusive gloss is likely, it may have ousted a word, perhaps an adverb qualifying the participle, of the metrical form ∪ ∪ ∪ – or – ∪ – to secure corresponsion with ἐπιπόνων in 654.[49]

Apart from the last few lines the language is clear and straightforward. In common with some of the other lyrics in this play the ode has its share of epic words or forms of words: ναύλοχα (633), παραναιετάοντεc (635), χρυcαλακάτου (637), κλέονται (639). It is moreover completely integrated into the context of the play where it occurs, and its themes are clearly defined. The first strophic pair embraces a wide appeal to the whole neighbourhood to join in welcoming Heracles. The second strophe relates this to the immediate circumstances of the play, pausing for reflection on past anxieties before returning to the reason for present hope. At the end we are left with a description of the magic robe, mysterious, elusive, and evocative of that

---

[48] e.g. Aesch. *Supp.* 1040; Pi. *P.* 9. 39; Fr. 108. 9 B. In Hes. *Op.* 73 she is one of the goddesses adorning the sinister Pandora.

[49] Perhaps δυcλύτωc might do as a stop-gap.

hope. For all its confidence and its echoes of the joyful mood of
the *hyporchema*, the general effect of the song is deeply sinister in
the irony of its contrast with what swiftly follows.

In the next scene Deianira describes what happened to the tuft
of wool which she used to anoint the robe with Nessus' blood.
Sophocles heightens the impact of her description by the detail
he puts into her mouth, and her words suggest horror of the most
acute physical kind, culminating in two striking similes (699–
704). The passage 693–704, particularly 702, ἀναζέουςι θρομβώδ-
εις ἀφροί, 'clots of foam bubble up', contributes much to the
second stanza of the following stasimon (831–40). Further, the
chorus hear her state what, if only she had reflected, she should
have realized at the time when the dying Nessus gave her his
blood: that he must have been planning revenge on Heracles
(705–10). She acted in ignorance and discovery has come too
late:

$$\mathring{\omega}\nu \; \mathring{\epsilon}\gamma\mathring{\omega} \; \mu\epsilon\theta\acute{\upsilon}\varsigma\tau\epsilon\rho\sigma\nu$$
$$\mathring{\sigma}\tau' \; \sigma\mathring{\upsilon}\kappa\acute{\epsilon}\tau' \; \mathring{\alpha}\rho\kappa\epsilon\mathring{\iota}, \; \tau\mathring{\eta}\nu \; \mu\acute{\alpha}\theta\eta\varsigma\iota\nu \; \mathring{\alpha}\rho\nu\upsilon\mu\alpha\iota$$

'I am gaining knowledge of these things too late when it is no
longer of any use.' Obsessed by her love for Heracles and her
jealousy of Iole (536–49 and 1138 f.), she resorted to the supposed
love-charm without due thought, assuredly one of the best
instances of the Aristotelian ἁμαρτία in Greek Tragedy.[50] This
hasty act of hers gives rise to the reflections in the second strophe
of the next ode (841–50). The chorus also listen to Hyllus'
account of the effect of the poisoned robe on his father (765–
806), which prompts them to concentrate into the second
antistrophe the full horror of what they have heard in the actor's
speech. Finally, they see Deianira, deaf to their appeal that she
should speak in her own defence, leave the stage in silence with
her son's curse in her ears (807–16). Although they fail to warn
him that she may be about to kill herself they probably suspect
it, and they voice their suspicion in the last sentence of the second
strophe after they have envisaged her lamenting her act in tears:

$$\mathring{\alpha} \; \delta' \; \mathring{\epsilon}\rho\chi\sigma\mu\acute{\epsilon}\nu\alpha \; \mu\sigma\mathring{\iota}\rho\alpha \; \pi\rho\sigma-$$
$$\phi\alpha\acute{\iota}\nu\epsilon\iota \; \delta\sigma\lambda\acute{\iota}\alpha\nu \; \kappa\alpha\mathring{\iota} \; \mu\epsilon\gamma\acute{\alpha}\lambda\alpha\nu \; \mathring{\alpha}\tau\alpha\nu, \qquad (849 \; f.)$$

[50] Stinton, *CQ* N.s. 25 (1975), 237, points out that her act is not merely a ἁμαρτία in the
sense 'mistake of fact', but more precisely an act done in ignorance through passion
(πάθος).

'The coming fate (of Heracles) foreshadows a great disaster, planned by cunning.' The ode however does not confine itself to echoes from the preceding scene. It ranges also over the whole play and its antecedents, the fateful oracle, the encounter with Nessus, the sack of Oechalia, the bringing home of Iole; and at the end, just as Cypris sat as umpire at the fight between Heracles and Achelous in the first stasimon (515), so here she is revealed as the silent agent of doom:

> ἁ δ' ἀμφίπολος Κύπρις ἄ-
> ναυδος φανερὰ τῶνδ' ἐφάνη πράκτωρ.   (861 f.)

The word ἀμφίπολος reminds us however that she is the minister of a greater power, and we should remember that throughout the play Zeus is supreme.[51]

The ode (821–62) is the most difficult linguistically of all the lyrics in the play. We may start from the comment in the ancient scholia on 821: ὁ χορὸς πρὸς ἀλλήλας διαλέγεται περὶ τοῦ δεδομένου μαντείου τῷ Ἡρακλεῖ ἐν τῇ Δωδώνῃ ὅτι νῦν ἀπέβη, 'the chorus discuss with each other the outcome of the oracle given to Heracles at Dodona.' This sentence pinpoints an initial difficulty. In 166–72 Deianira told the chorus of the contents of this oracle with its ambiguous prophecy that at the end of fifteen months Heracles would either die or live happily ever afterwards. In the second stasimon they referred to a period of twelve, not fifteen, months:[52] in the first stanza of the present ode they say that the oracle had mentioned twelve years, at the end of which his succession of labours would cease (824–7). Further, the way in which they speak of the prophecy shows that they are not thinking of it in the terms in which Deianira described it to them in 166 ff. There, she gave alternatives, either death or a life free from pain; here, there is no mention of alternatives, only the one issue, release from his labours, just as there is in Heracles' own account of the same oracle in 1165–72.

Two points may be made here. First, the inconsistency in the time-references must simply be accepted. Attempts to make τελεόμηνος δωδέκατος ἄροτος mean twelve months,[53] in order to

---

[51] Cf. e.g. for Zeus' connection with Heracles' story in the play, 26, 140, 251, 275, 825, 995 f., 1001 f., 1159–68, and above all the last line.

[52] Cf. 648.

[53] As e.g. by Kühner-Gerth 1. 262.

bring the phrase into line with δυοκαιδεκάμηνον χρόνον in 648, are bound to fail because the words can only mean the twelfth ploughing season with its full tally of months, i.e. the twelfth year. When Heracles refers to this oracle in 1165 ff. he does not say how long ago he received it but calls the contents of it μαντεῖα καινά, recent, that is, in relation to the much older one from his father (1159 f.), which foretold that he would not be slain by any living creature, but by one already dead. It is however a reasonable assumption that he received the oracle at Dodona at the beginning of his enslavement to Eurystheus to perform the twelve labours, each taking a year, and that the chorus supply this information in the third stasimon, even though they have not received it during the play. This oracle, given to Heracles at the outset of his labours, was probably a well-known item in the hero's saga[54] with which the maidens of Trachis would be as familiar as they were with the wrestling match described in the first stasimon.

The second point concerns the way in which Deianira, the chorus, and Heracles respectively refer to the oracle. In 166 f. she gave alternative issues, death or a life free from pain, because Sophocles wished to portray her suspense between hope and despair, and also because the audience must, early in the play, be told exactly what the alternatives are. When the third stasimon is sung her part is finished, and the truth is known so there is no further dramatic need for alternatives, and the chorus conclude, rightly, that a rest from labours signifies death. This looks forward to Heracles' outburst in 1143 ff., where the word Nessus on Hyllus' lips gives him a sudden revelation of inevitable death. He grasps the connection between the older oracle (1159–61) and the one he received at Dodona, and comes to the same conclusion as the chorus in this song:

> τὸ δ᾽ ἦν ἄρ᾽ οὐδὲν ἄλλο πλὴν θανεῖν ἐμέ.
> τοῖς γὰρ θανοῦcι μόχθος οὐ προcγίγνεται

'So the meaning, it seems, was nothing but that I should die, for the dead have no troubles' (1172 f.). Sophocles has used the theme of the oracles in this play with great subtlety and above all as a means of creating dramatic suspense. He reveals only what

[54] Cf. Apollodorus ii. 4. 12, where however the oracle is said to have been given to Heracles by the Pythian prophetess.

is necessary for the situation at any one given moment, with the result that we are not, as in *Oedipus Tyrannus*, made continually aware of the working out of an oracle, but that we sense the theme running through the play as it were below the surface and emerging at intervals to serve dramatic requirements.[55] Here, in their words at 826 f.

> καὶ τάδ' ὀρθῶς
> ἔμπεδα κατουρίζει

the chorus clarify the issue that has been in doubt ever since Deianira first hinted at the contents of the δέλτος in the prologue (46 f.) in vague and inexplicit terms; and from this moment in the song we wait for the stricken Heracles to appear as a fulfilment of their imaginings.

The antistrophe (831–40) is a lyric summary of Hyllus' account of his father's agony (765–71) with echoes of Deianira's speech (693–704). It consists of one long grammatical period carefully constructed on the ABA pattern, with the main sentence (835) in the middle flanked by dependent clauses containing words which amplify and repeat each other across the central question

> πῶς ὅδ' ἂν ἀέλιον ἕτερον ἢ τανῦν ἴδοι;

'how can he look upon tomorrow's sun?' Exact symmetry is avoided in the second half of the stanza by the substitution of a finite verb αἰκίζει (838) for a participle parallel with προστετακώς (836). This change in construction does not interrupt the flow of the period, and accordingly the stanza should be punctuated with the question-mark at the end and a comma before μελαγχαίτα.[56] As to the amplifications, we may note how the first three lines are echoed in the last clause with verbal repetitions, προστακέντος, προστετακώς, φονία, φόνια, δολοποιός, δολιόμυθα, and the expansion of χρίει πλευρά (832) into κέντρ' ἐπιζέσαντα at the end. The antistrophe thus opens with the Centaur, then alludes to the Hydra (αἰόλος δράκων) before reaching the main sentence, and unwinds again, closing with the Centaur with which it began. Attention to this careful structure

---

[55] Compare the treatment of the oracle theme in *Phil.* and *O.C.*

[56] So Radermacher (edition of 1914) and Dain–Mazon (Budé 1955) but not Jebb and Pearson.

may possibly throw a little light on the obscurities of the text. An exhaustive examination of all the difficulties is inappropriate here, but a few words on selected points may not be out of place.

First we may consider the grouping and interpretation of the phrases in the opening clause. It seems likely that Κενταύρου φονίᾳ νεφέλᾳ should be taken together,[57] and that the phrase is a metaphorical description of the shirt of Nessus, 'in the Centaur's murderous cloud'. The association of νεφέλη and νέφος with death may be seen in such Homeric expressions as θανάτου μέλαν νέφος and νεφέλη δέ μιν ἀμφεκάλυψε κυανέη (*Iliad* 16. 350 and 20. 417). Closer to our passage is Pindar's use of φόνου νεφέλαν in *Nemean* 9. 38 to describe the cloud of bloody carnage on a battlefield.[58] So far we may say that Sophocles here envisages the robe as a cloud of death enveloping Heracles and that he had in mind these Homeric metaphors. In addition there is evidence going back perhaps to Homer that νεφέλη and νέφος could also mean a net for snaring birds. At *Odyssey* 22. 304 a Scholiast interprets νέφεα in this sense. More appropriate to the chorus's φονίᾳ νεφέλᾳ is the Hoopoe's oath in *Birds* 194, μὰ παγίδας, μὰ νεφέλας, μὰ δίκτυα, where the context shows that νεφέλας must be some kind of trapping nets; Callimachus in *Aetia* 75. 37 mentions λίνεαι νεφέλαι ('clouds', i.e. nets of linen thread) for catching quails; and Hesychius and Suidas explain νέφεα and νεφέλη as λίνα θηρατικά and εἶδος δικτύου θηρατικοῦ, 'nets for hunting'. This usage, confirmed for the fifth century by the Hoopoe's oath, should be borne in mind for the interpretation of the phrase in *Trachiniae*,[59] nor is it out of place to recall that in 1051 f. Sophocles, in what may be a conscious echo of *Agamemnon* 1382 and *Choephoroe* 492, calls the shirt of Nessus Ἐρινύων ὑφαντὸν ἀμφίβληςτρον 'the Furies' woven net', thus equating the fatal garment with a net used in hunting.[60] We may now clarify the meaning of Κενταύρου φονίᾳ νεφέλᾳ beyond reasonable doubt: it is the shirt of Nessus in which Heracles is ensnared, and it

---

[57] So Kamerbeek, following Dain–Mazon. Word order is against taking Κενταύρου with ἀνάγκα.

[58] Cf. also *I.* 7. 27.

[59] Wakefield interpreted it in this way.

[60] For further examples of nets as an image for doom and death, cf. also Aesch. *A.* 358–361, 1115 f.; *Cho.* 998 ff. (δίκτυον and ἄρκυς); *Pr.* 1078. See Stinton, *PCPhS* 201 (1975), 90 ff.

envelops him in a cloud of death. The image is thus double, both net and cloud being ideas essential to its comprehension.

The next passage requiring comment is 836 f., δεινοτάτῳ μὲν ὕδρας προστετακὼς φάϲματι (so the manuscripts, with no variants), 'fused to the Hydra's most terrible shape'. Editors have been quick to point out that Heracles was not fused to the Hydra but either to the poison (προϲτακέντος ἰοῦ in 834) or to the robe, and they have accordingly sought to introduce into the text in place of φάϲματι a word meaning poison or a word meaning robe.[61] None of these suggestions is satisfactory as they do not account for the supposedly corrupt φάϲματι; and Pearson's νήματι (a robe spun from yarn), which he says was ousted from the text by the gloss ὑφάϲματι, itself corrupted to φάϲματι, is, for all its ingenuity, flawed because the robe belongs to Nessus, not the Hydra.[62] We are then left with φάϲματι, which is almost certainly what Sophocles wrote. This word cannot mean either 'robe' or 'poison', but only 'shape' as in φάϲμα ταύρου of Achelous in 509, a periphrasis for the river god, physically present. Since then ὕδρας φάϲματι must be a periphrasis for the Hydra, and since that monster was not present when Heracles donned the robe, we must either remove ὕδρας from the text or alter δεινοτάτῳ to δεινοτέρῳ. The first suggestion is due to Hermann who proposed ἄρθρα for ὕδρας, assuming that ὕδρας was a gloss intended to define φάϲματι. The resulting phrase 'fused as to his limbs to a most terrible shape', recalls with some precision Hyllus' simile at 767 f.:

$$προϲπτύϲϲεται$$
$$πλευραῖϲιν ἀρτίκολλος ὥϲτε τέκτονος$$
$$χιτὼν ἅπαν κατ' ἄρθρον$$

'the robe clings to his sides as by a craftsman's art close-moulded to every contour of his limbs'. Since however a mention of the Hydra is perhaps required here to balance its appearance in 834, Professor Lloyd-Jones's δεινοτέρῳ has much to commend it: 'fused to a shape more terrible than the Hydra'.[63]

Lastly, the problem in 839, where all the manuscripts give νέϲϲου (νέου) θ' ὕπο φοίνια or ὑποφοίνια, centres on the question

---

[61] For a list of suggestions see Jebb's edition, 195.
[62] Cf. *CR* 39 (1925), 4.
[63] *YClS* 22 (1972), 265 ff.

whether μελαγχαίτα alone is sufficient to identify Nessus. To call him 'Black Hair' is certainly menacing and enigmatic;[64] further, the epithet is used of the Centaur Mimas in *Scut. Her.* 186 and appears as the name of a Centaur on the François vase. Alternatively, it might be a kenning for Hades or Death.[65] This however is unlikely, because the whole stanza is about the Centaur. If we think that μελαγχαίτα need not be defined more specifically, Νέccου will be a gloss, though it is difficult to see how θ' ὕπο got in as well. If, with Jebb, we agree that Νέccου is essential, doubts must remain whether ὑποφόνια[66] is a possible epithet for κέντρα, and we should regard the word or words between Νέcου and φόνια as corrupt. The balance is in favour of omitting the proper name and θ' ὕπο, and leaving the sinister μελαγχαίτα by itself as in Pearson's text.

This difficult stanza is noteworthy for the concentration of its phraseology and the concreteness of its imagery. Not only has Sophocles compressed into its single period salient features from the previous scene, but the accumulation of phrases to describe the poisoned robe and its effect produces a sense of physical horror and corruption which sharpens the irony in the last lines of the preceding ode and prepares us for the spectacle of Heracles' torments in the final scene of the play. Sophocles knew well how to exploit scenes of anguish and cruelty not only by the skill of his dramatic technique but also by his choice of language, and this antistrophe is a good example among many in his plays of the way in which he uses words to create shock and horror.[67]

The transition to the second strophic pair is effected by a relative pronoun in the genitive (ὧν 841), as in the last antistrophe of the parodos (122). In both cases the chorus turn from reflecting on Heracles' fate to Deianira, in this song ἅδ' ἁ τλάμων, who left the stage towards the end of the previous scene (813). The opening lines of the stanza present problems: the construction and meaning of ἄοκνος, if this suggestion of Musgrove be accepted for the manuscripts' ἄοκνον, and the doubt

---

[64] 'A sort of kenning for Centaur', Kamerbeek's edition, 182.

[65] Hades is called ὁ μελαγχαίτης θεός at Eur. *Alc.* 439. See Stinton, *PCPhS* loc. cit. 91 f.

[66] A pupil of mine, M.N. Mahony, once suggested that ὑποφόνια κέντρα might mean that the goads of poison were Heracles' payment to Nessus for killing him; cp. τὰ ὑποφόνια as a term of Attic law, 'blood-money'.

[67] Cf. e.g. *Trach.* 777–82 (iambics); *Ant.* 972–6 (lyrics); *O.T.* 1276–9 (iambics).

whether αὐτά should replace οὔτι of the manuscripts in 843. The strongest arguments in favour of ἄοκνος are first, that it is a comment on Deianira's ἁμαρτία, and second, probably decisive, that it provides a construction for ὧν, which must otherwise be taken as a partitive with the widely separated τὰ μὲν in 843. The word must however be correctly translated. It cannot mean 'resolute', as it usually does, because it could not then govern ὧν. Applied to Deianira it means 'not shrinking from' and can govern ὧν,[68] the antecedent to which is the description in the preceding stanza of what happened to Heracles as a result of her hasty resort to the supposed love-charm. The opening lines of the second strophe (841 ff.) thus make the point that she acted precipitately when she saw in his liaison with Iole the swift ruin of her own family life,

> μεγάλαν προσορῶσα δόμοιϲι βλάβαν . . .
> ἀίϲϲουϲαν γάμων[69] . . .

Instead, as she realized herself in 707–18, she should have stopped to think what Nessus had in mind when he gave her instructions for the use of his blood (569–77).

The final problem is in 843 f., where the manuscripts read τὰ μὲν οὔτι προϲέβαλεν. In trying to decide whether οὔτι can be retained or Blaydes's suggestion αὐτά (αὐτή Nauck) should be accepted, we may begin with two assumptions, first, that this sentence echoes 580 f., where Deianira stated that she followed Nessus' instructions when applying the supposed love-charm to the robe, προϲβαλοῦϲ' ὅϲα ζῶν κεῖνοϲ εἶπε, so that we should translate the verb in the same way in both passages; and secondly, that there is a strong contrast in 843 f. between τὰ μὲν and τὰ δέ, τὰ μὲν being ὅϲα ζῶν κεῖνοϲ εἶπε (580), 'all the details he prescribed while still alive', and τὰ δ' ἀπ' ἀλλοθρου γνώμαϲ μολόντα being his intentions, which she did not realize at the time. That this is the essential contrast between τὰ μὲν and τὰ δέ is further confirmed first by 680–8, where after her experience with the tuft of wool she is at great pains to impress on the chorus how she obeyed Nessus' prescription to the letter (παρῆκα θεϲμῶν

---

[68] For a similar genitive with ἄοκνος cf. *Aj.* 563, τροφῆϲ ἄοκνον, 'not shrinking from his care for you'.

[69] One inclines to Nauck's ἀίϲϲουϲαν for ἀιϲϲόντων because the verb goes better with βλάβαν, equivalent to ἄτην or Ἐρινύν, than with γάμων.

οὐδέν᾽, ἀλλ᾽ ἐcῳζόμην, 682), and then by 705–18, where later in the same speech she explains how she has just realized that he said one thing and meant another. This necessary distinction between what he said and what he meant, an extension of the familiar λόγῳ μὲν ... ἔργῳ δὲ antithesis, can only be made apparent if we accept αὐτὰ for οὔτι and take προcέβαλεν here and προcβαλοῦca in 580 to mean the physical act of applying the love-charm to the robe. Further confirmation that this is what the verb means is provided by 1138, cτέργημα γὰρ δοκοῦca προcβαλεῖν, 'thinking to apply a love-charm'.

Those who would keep οὔτι of the manuscripts[70] (in the adverbial sense 'not at all') point to the Scholiast's gloss on 843, οὐκ ἔγνω, οὐ cυνῆκεν, 'she did not know, she did not understand'. For this meaning of προcέβαλεν they cite for a possible analogy *Iliad* 5. 879 where the middle ποτιβάλλεcθαι is found in a negative sentence with an accusative object, 'pay no attention to'. There is however no parallel for taking the active προcβάλλειν governing τὰ μὲν as equivalent to προcέχειν τι 'pay no attention to', a variant of the common προcέχειν [τὸν νοῦν] τινι, found once in Greek in the fifth century.[71] In addition to this linguistic anomaly, it will be seen that the translation 'she paid no attention at all to what Nessus said' contradicts Deianira's statements in 580 and 680–8 that she did in fact follow his instructions; and it also destroys the antithesis between τὰ μὲν and τὰ δὲ. Further, the chorus in 843 clarify for us the irony in her earlier remarks about applying the love-charm: it is precisely because she obeyed his verbal instructions without stopping to think what he meant that she causes the death in agony of the husband she loves. We may then paraphrase 841–8 as follows, accepting αὐτὰ for οὔτι: with no shrinking from the consequences (or, as Jebb, no foreboding), this unhappy woman, seeing a great ruin swooping upon her household from the new marriage, with her own hand applied the prescription (ὅca ζῶν κεῖνος εἶπε 580), but the results of what he had in mind she laments in tears. In the last two lines of the strophe the chorus hint at the imminent death of Heracles and see in it the manifestation of ἄτη. In order to bring out the full force of this word here we may note the line of thought running from μεγάλαν δόμοιcι βλάβαν in 842 through μεγάλαν ἄταν in 850

---

[70] See Kamerbeek's eloquent defence of οὔτι in his commentary, 182 ff.

[71] Critias 25. 19 DK, προcέχων ταῦτα, 'paying attention to these things'.

to μεγάλαν δόμοιcι τοῖcδ' 'Ερινύν in 893 f., where the repetitions of μεγάλαν and δόμοιcι point to an identity of meaning in the three keywords βλάβη, ἄτη, and 'Ερινύc and emphasize the impending doom of a house and its family life.

The final stanza needs little comment as its interpretation does not require a discussion of the corruption in 853 f. The tears of the chorus match the tears of Deianira as they think of Heracles' agony and lament the feat of arms which sacked Oechalia and brought Iole to Trachis. The last sentence, 860, as in the strophe, is separated grammatically from the rest. The chorus concentrate into these words much that has been stated earlier in the play, especially in the first stasimon 497 and 515. The single word ἄναυδοc, applied to Cypris, reminds us of her instrument Iole, uttering no word throughout her journey to Trachis, and silent also when Deianira questioned her.[72] The parallelism of verbal and grammatical shape in the closing sentences of the last two stanzas is noteworthy:

ἁ δ' ἐρχομένα μοῖρα προφαίνει δολίαν καὶ μεγάλαν ἄταν.

ἁ δ' ἀμφίπολοc Κύπριc ἄναυδοc φανερὰ τῶνδ' ἐφάνη πράκτωρ.

These lines proclaim in an impressive and formal manner a dominant theme of the tragedy.

In contrast to the difficulty of its language this song is straightforward in structure. The two strophic pairs are distinguished by a difference of content, the link between them being forged as in the parodos, 122, by the vague connecting relative ὧν where the chorus turn from Heracles to Deianira. The first pair is dominated by the oracle and the highly wrought visualization of Heracles' agony derived from Deianira's account of the dissolution of the tuft of wool and Hyllus' description of what happened when his father donned the fatal robe. The second ranges widely over the events of the play and its antecedents and ends by revealing the cause of the tragedy. The ode is strictly relevant to the dramatic context. Combining comment on previous events with foreboding for the future, it discloses the true meaning of the oracle; it creates a sense of physical horror; it defines the nature of Deianira's ἁμαρτία; it prepares the mind for the appearance of the stricken Heracles and lays upon Cypris the responsibility for disaster.

[72] Cf. 307 ff. and 322 ff.

In the dialogue which follows (863–95) Sophocles uses the members of the chorus as actors in order to create tension and lead the Nurse step by step to the tale she has to tell. At the end of the previous ode we were left in suspense, the last words ἁ δ᾽ ἀμφίπολος Κύπρις ἄναυδος (861 f.) suggesting a moment of silence, soon broken by the cry of woe within the house (κωκυτός, 867), as the Nurse finds Deianira's body. An instinct for symmetry has led most scholars to divide the trimeters 863–70 into three groups, the first two spoken by the leaders of each semi-chorus and the last, announcing the actor's entry, by the coryphaeus. At 871 the exchanges open with spoken trimeters in complete lines until 876, when they are interrupted, the divisions between speakers coming at the weak caesura. Finally, as they ply the Nurse with excited questions, the chorus's utterances change to lyrics, beginning with the dochmiac at 880. She, for her part, is used here as an ἐξάγγελος deeply involved in the horror, so that she has none of the conventional messenger's detachment and objectivity. Her shocked bewilderment is marked by the imprecision of her replies, and tension increases as she holds back details on which curiosity cries out to be satisfied. For instance, at 879, in reply to the question how Deianira died she says cχετλίῳ τὰ πρός γε πρᾶξιν.[73] This naturally evokes a further question, εἰπὲ τῷ μόρῳ, γύναι, cυντρέχει, the dochmiac denoting heightened emotion. To this she answers 'Suicide' (αὑτὴν διηίcτωcε, 881), but says nothing of the means; and in the end it is not she but a member of the chorus who, in a further question, τίc θυμός, ἢ τίνεc νόcοι ... cιδάρου (882–7), reveals the precise method of suicide, jumping to a conclusion about a fact which the Nurse's state of dither (ὦ ματαία, 888) prevents her from stating herself.

As to the last point, Maas has shown beyond doubt that the whole passage from 882–8, being in lyric metres, should be assigned to members of the chorus, since the Nurse, both in her character as a humble person and in her role as messenger, cannot be given sung lines.[74] Accordingly, in this dialogue her utterances are confined to spoken trimeters or portions of them,

---

[73] So Hermann for the unmetrical cχετλιώτατα πρός γε πρᾶξιν, but τὰ πρός πρᾶξιν is a dubious phrase. L.D.J. Henderson in *Maia* (1976) 19–24 suggests cχετλιώταθ᾽ ἅπερ ἔπραξεν.

[74] *Greek Metre*, § 76, p. 53.

and we must not only follow the manuscript L in assigning to the chorus everything from τίс θυμόc at 882 to μόνα at 886, but also take away from the Nurse the words cτονόεντοc ἐν τομᾷ cιδάρου. The sung passage will then consist of two questions τίс θυμόc ... ξυνεῖλε;[75] and πῶc ἐμήcατο ... cιδάρου; There is nothing to prevent us from assigning each to a separate singer. In fact such a division of the questions from 873 to 892 adds greatly to the growing excitement as the distraught old woman faces a barrage from individual members of the chorus. A difficulty may be felt in the singers' assumption that Deianira killed herself with a sword (αἰχμᾷ βέλεοc κακοῦ 883) when no hint of the means has been given by the Nurse beyond what can be conveyed by the very strong word cχετλιώτατα in 879. There were two conventional methods of suicide in Greek Tragedy, the noose and the sword,[76] and it is just possible that an excited and impatient questioner, failing to extract the full details at once and receiving them bit by bit, should in the end himself suggest one of these alternatives. The violent passion of Deianira's suicide is emphasized by the Nurse at 891 in answer to the questions τίc ἦν; πῶc; She did the deed with her own hand, i.e. without anyone to hold the sword:

αὐτὴ πρὸc αὐτῆc χειροποιεῖται τάδε.

The closing lines from the chorus in the dialogue (893–5) are an impressive last statement of the Cypris theme. As noted already, the words recall especially the opening of the third and the end of the fourth stanza of the preceding song (841–3 and 857–62). The final result of Cypris' work is seen in the birth of a great Ἐρινύc to her instrument Iole. The epithet μεγάλαν acquires a strong emphasis through its wide separation from Ἐρινύν, just as in 842 the same adjective is separated from βλάβαν; and ἁ νέορτοc ἅδε νύμφα echoes both νεῶν ἀίccουcαν γάμων (842) and νύμφαν ... τάνδε (857 ff.).

The above analysis of the dialogue follows Jebb's text, except that it assumes, correctly, that all the sung lines belong to

---

[75] Read Hermann's αἰχμᾷ and translate as Jebb.

[76] Besides Deianira, Eurydice in *Ant.* and Iocasta in Eur.'s *Ph.* use a sword: in *O. T.* she uses the noose. In Eur. *Supp.* 1070 f. Evadne leaps from a rock into Capaneus' funeral pyre, and Menoeceus throws himself into the dragon's lair at *Ph.* 1018. On suicide in Greek Drama, see E. Fraenkel, *Philologus* 87 (1932), 470 ff.

members of the chorus. If however it seems unlikely that they could, without any explicit statement from the Nurse, conclude that Deianira's weapon was the sword, we may suppose a lacuna after διηΐϲτωϲε in 881. The supplements φαϲγάνου τομῇ and ἀμφήκει ξίφει have been suggested.[77] The first is preferable, because the chorus's ἐν τομᾷ ϲιδάρου (887) will echo the Nurse's word. This solution has a great deal to recommend it: though it perhaps involves the loss of some of the incoherence appropriate to the participants' state of mind, it banishes the need to assume a guess by a member of the chorus, provides a reference for αἰχμᾷ βέλεοϲ (883), answers precisely the question in 879, and gives the Nurse a complete trimeter to match her lines 889 and 891.

The effect of this dialogue is achieved more by its rhythmic form and sentence structure than by a choice of evocative poetical expressions. In the opening passage, after the Nurse's entry, the lines are complete, the rhythm of the trimeters slow and measured, the language plain and yet impressive. Especially moving in its solemnity is the announcement of Deianira's death, 874 f.:

βέβηκε Δηάνειρα τὴν πανυϲτάτην
ὁδῶν ἁπαϲῶν ἐξ ἀκινήτου ποδόϲ

'Deianira has gone on the last of all her travels, without movement of foot.' At this moment the trimeters are interrupted as the chorus's questions begin first in speech, and then at 880 they sing. The resulting mixture of speech and song, here maintained until 895, is a sign of gathering excitement and a favourite device of Sophocles both in the utterances of actors and in lyric stichomythia between actor and chorus. We should note also that this dialogue is astrophic, as at the opening of the second parodos of _Ajax_ (866 ff.), where a short 'free' lyric passage soon turns into spoken trimeters interrupted by bacchiacs.

The language reveals little change in character as song intrudes upon speech. The bold use of ξυνεῖλε (884) with the subject τίϲ θυμόϲ ... in the sense 'destroy' ('What passion ... caused her destruction by the edge of the sword?') may be an echo of the Homeric ἀμφοτέραϲ δ' ὀφρῦϲ ϲύνελεν λίθοϲ (_Iliad_ 16.

---

[77] By L.D.J. Henderson in _Maia_ 1976, loc. cit. A more complicated solution, involving further lacunae and transpositions, is A.M. Dale's published posthumously in _BICS_ Suppl. 21. 1 (1971), 32 f.

740), but the word should more probably, in view of its appearance in later prose[78] with the meaning 'annihilate', be regarded in a less violently physical sense than in Homer's line, which suggests a stone smashing the front of the skull and obliterating the features. It is interesting that there should be two other noteworthy words in the dialogue, καινοποιηθέν (873) and χειροποιεῖται (891), the first recurring only in late prose,[79] the second unique. Both of these are formed from elements common in everyday speech so that their effect lies not in any poetic quality but in the solemnity of sound and rhythm which they give to the lines in which they appear.

The immediate consequence of the Nurse's speech as ἐξάγγελος (900–46) is a lament in ritual form. Stunned by what they have heard and full of apprehension at Heracles' imminent appearance, the chorus express their dismay at the horrors they have to lament in two three-line stanzas (947–52) in which repetition, assonance, alliteration, and rhyme, both external and internal, all combine not only to convey the deadening effect of disaster upon themselves but to crystallize for the audience a sense of overwhelming shock. The technical devices here used are best illustrated by the two three-line stanzas from the chorus in Aeschylus' *Persae* 694–6 and 700–2 on the appearance of Dareius' ghost in answer to their invocations. Similar also are the repetitions in the preceding stasimon of the same play 550 ff. = 560 ff., where the chorus bewail Xerxes' disastrous leadership and the loss of the ships. In this passage of *Trachiniae* metre assists formal and verbal artifice in the dragged close of the choriambic dimeter which acts as a clausula to the two highly resolved iambic lines. The strophe (947–9) exploits assonance of π and τ to the utmost, but this hardly supports the manuscript reading τέλεα in 948 with the sense 'complete': nothing can be added to complete the sum of woes.[80] Musgrave's μέλεα is to be rejected as it would substitute a commonplace word.

In the second strophic pair (953–70) there is a striking change of mood, rhythm, and style. Stunned shock yields to a passionate

---

[78] e.g. D.S. 15. 44; D.C. 40. 23 and Plu. *Lys.* 11.

[79] In Polybius and Lucian. Note the other καινο-compound, καινοπαγῆ or καινοπαθῆ, unique in extant Greek literature, at *Trach.* 1277.

[80] Cp. τέλεος of disease in Hipp. *Prorrh.* 2. 30 and Plato's use of it with ἀδικία, 'absolute injustice', *Rep.* 348 b. τέλεα περαιτέρω is a strange phrase and may be corrupt.

desire to escape from the situation on the stage, and the contrast
is marked by a greater variety in the metrical units, including an
anapaestic line at 959 = 968. Such 'escape' lyrics are found
notably in Euripides,[81] but this is the only example in extant
Sophocles apart from *O.C.* 1044, whose dramatic purpose is
entirely different, and it is especially appropriate here to the
character and role of the chorus: the young girls long to escape
from the scene for fear that they may die of fright on seeing
Heracles in his agony (955–8). However, the report (λέγουϲιν,
960) of the procession bearing him recalls them quickly to the
happenings on the stage, so that the second antistrophe (962–70)
prepares us step by step for his entry. At the opening of the
stanza the inferential ἄρα points to his proximity as the litter-
bearers come into the chorus's view,

ξένων γὰρ ἐξόμιλοϲ ἥδε τιϲ βάϲιϲ

an abstract expression equivalent to ξένοι γὰρ ἐκτὸϲ τῆϲ ἡμετέραϲ
ὁμιλίαϲ οἵδε οἱ βαίνοντεϲ, 'those who are coming are strangers, not
of our community'. The deictic ἥδε and the early placing in the
sentence of ξένων and ἐξόμιλοϲ emphasize both the moment of
their appearance 'in the wings' and their physical aspect. δ' αὖ at
965 introduces a new concern: aware of the solemn, noiseless
tread of the procession the chorus ask how they are carrying him.
Finally at

αἰαῖ, ὅδ' ἀναύδατοϲ φέρεται

they see Heracles himself. There is no sound from him, and we
are left with the question 'Is he dead or asleep?' followed by the
laments of the waiting Hyllus[82] and the command of the old man

ϲίγα, τέκνον, μὴ κινήϲῃϲ
ἀγρίαν ὀδύνην πατρὸϲ ὠμόφρονοϲ.
ζῇ γὰρ προπετήϲ

'Silence, my son, lest you wake the fierce pain that ravages your
father. He is alive, though prostrate' (974 ff.).

This lyric comment on events happening off stage prepares
the mind for what the eyes are soon to see. A further function of

---

[81] e.g. *Hipp.* 732; *Andr.* 862; *Hel.* 1478.
[82] On Hyllus' part in this scene, see Winnington-Ingram, *BICS* 16 (1969), 44 f.

this stasimon is to connect Deianira's suicide with Heracles' agony, the link being forged by the first antistrophe, 950–2:

τάδε μὲν ἔχομεν ὁρᾶν δόμοις,
τάδε δὲ μελόμεν' ἐπ' ἐλπίϲιν·
κοινὰ δ' ἔχειν τε καὶ μέλλειν

'One sorrow we can see in the house, another is our concern with foreboding; present and future woes are one and the same.'[83] This point must be clearly grasped because in some discussions of the play, so much emphasis has been laid upon its so-called diptych structure[84] that the impression has been given of a lack of dramatic unity, with the climax occurring at Deianira's suicide and the last scene, showing Heracles' anguish, regarded as an appendix to what is already complete. The unifying role of the chorus has been referred to before, and this ode reveals how naturally Sophocles has bridged the gap between the two main characters, ensuring that without the appearance on stage of the mighty figure who has dominated the thoughts of everybody from the prologue onwards the play would indeed be felt as incomplete. Finally, the song, like the previous one, again shows up the irony inherent in earlier odes which expressed joy and confidence at his victorious return.

With Deianira dead, the chorus's task is done. They take no part in the anapaests or the lyrics which open the final scene. It would be inappropriate for these young girls to do so, overwhelmed as they are by her death and the sight of Heracles. This is one example among many of Sophocles' strict attention to *vraisemblance* in the treatment of his choruses. Accordingly, the remaining problem that confronts us is the attribution of the last four lines of the play.

The scholia and the medieval manuscripts testify to ancient doubts whether they should be assigned to the chorus or to Hyllus, and it is worth speculating why these doubts should have arisen. So far as our evidence goes, it was the custom of tragedians in the second half of the fifth century to close their plays with a few anapaestic lines recited by the coryphaeus representing the whole chorus. This is the normal practice of Sophocles, except in

---

[83] μένομεν (Erfurdt) is attractive, more so than Hermann's μελόμεν', for the unmetrical μέλλομεν in 951: 'other sorrows we await with foreboding'.

[84] See e.g. Webster, *Sophocles*, 172.

Oedipus Tyrannus, where the final trochaic tetrameters may have replaced a lost anapaestic coda, and except in *Ion* and *Troades,*[85] of Euripides, whose 'curtain lines' are often a fossilized formula. In *Trachiniae,* the lines of dismissal are unusual in form: instead of λειπώμεθα or λείπεσθε, which might have been expected on the analogy of the endings of *Philoctetes* and *Oedipus at Colonus,*[86] we have λείπου μηδὲ σύ, παρθένε (1275). The second person singular together with the vocative παρθένε was bound to cause difficulties, because when the coryphaeus addresses his chorus as their leader he normally uses the plural.[87] Hence probably arose the idea that the lines should be given to Hyllus, who could as an actor address the coryphaeus in the singular. If they can be assigned to him, he is here dismissing the maidens of Trachis from the scene of disaster, and in the last line,

$$κοὐδὲν \ τούτων \ ὅτι \ μὴ \ Ζεύς$$

he reaffirms the bitter judgement on the gods' unconcern for the sufferings of their offspring expressed in 1266–74, lines which recall Philoetius' reproach to Zeus at *Odyssey* 20. 201 ff. This would end the play on a strong note of defiance with no hint of acquiescence and no resolution to the problem of what we are intended to think about Zeus' part in Heracles' story. If however the four lines are given to the coryphaeus, the last words are an affirmation of Zeus' omnipotence, and they modify Hyllus' verdict on the gods' ingratitude. This interpretation of the line assumes that the pyre on Mount Oeta implies Heracles' deification. Hyllus' charges of ingratitude against the gods will then be unjustified, for at the end of the play Zeus' son is admitted to their company, and the chorus's confidence in Zeus' continuing concern for his children, expressed at the end of the parodos (139 f.), finds confirmation in their final utterance. The sombre simplicity of this line is very powerful: it closes the play with a proclamation of the supreme god's power made manifest in the apotheosis of his son after the troubles of his life. The words οὐδὲν τούτων ὅ τι μὴ Ζεύς, 'the hand of Zeus is in all things', recall the

---

[85] *Ion* ends with four trochaic tetrameters, *Troades* with sung iambics closing a strophic lament from Hecuba and the chorus.

[86] Cp. also the final anapaests of Eur. *Her., Hec., Supp.,* and *H.F.*

[87] See Maarit Kaimio, *The Chorus of Greek Drama within the light of the Person and Number used* (Helsinki 1970), 190 f.

lines of the chorus at *Agamemnon* 1485 ff., when they realize that
a mighty δαίμων is at work destroying the House of Atreus:

ἰὼ ἰή, διαὶ Διὸc
παναιτίου, πανεργέτα.
τί γὰρ βροτοῖc ἄνευ Διὸc τελεῖται;
τί τῶνδ' οὐ θεόκραντόν ἐcτιν;

'Woe, woe, it is the work of Zeus, cause of all, doer of all; what
is fulfilled for man without Zeus? What of these things is not
ordained by the gods?'[88]

If, as seems probable, the coryphaeus, not Hyllus, recites the
final anapaests,[89] we still have to explain the first line (1275).
Most scholars who have given the passage to the coryphaeus
have, on the whole, not squarely faced the difficulty of the
singular παρθένε emphasized by μηδὲ cύ. The pronoun suggests
that a single individual is being addressed with pointed emphasis,
and that παρθένε is not a collective singular for παρθένοι, as it
must be if the coryphaeus is speaking to members of the chorus.
Some modern scholars have accordingly identified the maiden as
Iole.[90] This suggestion has been described as a fantasy not to be
taken seriously.[91] On the contrary, it has much to commend it.
True enough, Iole left the stage at 334, and there is no firm
evidence in the text that she ever reappears. She is moreover a
silent character, but in her very silence lies her power as a
symbol of Κύπρις ἄναυδος at the end of the third stasimon, and
not only while she is on the stage 229–334, but even more after
she has left it she personifies the disease of Ἔρως which causes the
tragedy.[92] As the chorus put it at 893, she has brought forth a
great Ἐρινύc. In this passage we should note the force of the
pronoun ἅδε (894) which, while of course not implying her
physical presence, indicates that she is present in the forefront of
the singers' mind. This presence is felt increasingly during the
final scene of the play and becomes almost visible when Heracles
orders Hyllus to take her as his own (1222–7): ταύτην... προcθοῦ

---

[88] Fraenkel quotes the last line of *Trach.* in his note on Aesch. *A.* 1488.
[89] So Kranz, *Stasimon*, 205.
[90] e.g. Radermacher (edition of 1914); Bowra, *Sophoclean Tragedy*, 158; Webster in
Greek Poetry and Life, 175.
[91] So Mazon, *RPh* 25 (1951), 11.
[92] Cf. e.g. 441–67; 536–51.

δάμαρτα... τοῦτο κήδευϲον λέχοϲ.[93] In these lines the emphatically placed ταύτην at the beginning of 1222 may suggest that she appears on the stage at this moment. At any rate, present or not, she dominates the action and the actors' emotions for some thirty lines, almost precipitating a violent quarrel between father and son. Heracles' command to Hyllus to take her and look after her as his concubine (τοῦτο κήδευϲον λέχοϲ) and the effect of this command upon him form the final dramatic situation with which the chorus are faced, and it seems likely that the coryphaeus should in the last lines of the play urge her to leave the house of death and suffering so that she may enter upon her life with Hyllus. It would be a nice point for a producer to decide whether the effect of the play's ending, thus interpreted, would be enhanced if Iole was visible on the stage, having entered at some moment when father and son were talking about her.

The choral lyrics of *Trachiniae* display interesting formal features which may be briefly summarised. First is the persistence of dactylo-epitrites which occur more frequently than in any other of Sophocles' extant plays.[94] They are dominant in the first strophic pair of the parodos and appear in the epode of the first stasimon and in the opening lines of the third, though in the two latter cases they are mixed with or merge into different metrical elements. Secondly, we should note the two astrophic passages, first the dance-song 205–26, where the 'free' rhythm suggests the chorus's abandonment to the music of the αὐλόϲ and the challenge of the Bacchic ecstasy. No other extant play of Sophocles contains an astrophic song complete in itself, and we may recall that in *Ajax* 693–718, an ode similar in mood and movement to this passage of *Trachiniae*, the poet adhered to the usual strophic form. The second astrophic passage is the dialogue between the chorus and the Nurse which leads up to her account of Deianira's suicide (871–95). This is noteworthy in that it does not, like the astrophic dialogues in the last two plays, conclude a series of lyrics in strophic form, but stands by itself as a prelude to a tale of death. Finally, this passage is the only instance of partially sung dialogue between chorus and actor in the play. All the other

---

[93] J.K. MacKinnon, *CQ* n.s. 21 (1971) 33, argues convincingly that δάμαρτα and κήδευϲον here imply concubinage, not marriage; cf. 428 f., where δάμαρτα cannot mean 'legal wife'.

[94] For the details see A.M. Dale, *BICS* Suppl. 21.: (1971), 14–41.

plays exploit the use of song or song and speech in exchanges between the two, first in more formal commoi and then, beginning with *Oedipus Tyrannus* 649 ff., in the quick interchange of lyric stichomythia. None of these features provides any firm evidence for the relative dating of *Trachiniae*, and since a detailed linguistic and metrical examination lies outside the scope of this book, all I can do is to record an impression that it is to be placed early, if not first, among the seven extant tragedies.[95]

As to the general treatment of the chorus's role in this play, perhaps the most interesting feature is the extent to which Sophocles has used their songs as a vehicle for sustained dramatic irony. His choice of young maidens as his singers has greatly helped him in this respect, for their naïveté, their limited experience, and their straightforward, unsophisticated attitude to the predicament of Deianira and Heracles make it natural for them to feel and express immediate emotions and to indulge in confident forecasts which we know are to be contradicted by the facts. Instead of being concentrated in a single ode immediately before the revelation of the truth, as in *Ajax*, in *Trachiniae* irony is present in the optimism of the parodos, in the ecstatic joy of the *hyporchema*, and in the more sober confidence of the song of welcome for Heracles; and the contrast between illusion and reality, between ignorance in the chorus and knowledge in audience or reader, creates an almost intolerable suspense as we wait for the truth to be revealed. Not until the last two songs, when all the chorus's illusions have been shattered, can we fully appreciate the linguistic subtleties in the earlier odes by which Sophocles has achieved this gradual building up of irony.

It is also in keeping with the youthful character of the chorus that their songs, in spite of difficulties of language, are simple in thought and structure. Apart from the judgement towards the end of the parodos on the transience of joy and sorrow and the affirmation of Cypris' power at the beginning of the first stasimon, there is a complete absence in the odes of gnomic reflection, nor is any attempt made to range outside the play or its antecedents in order to extend the scope of thought and feeling by the use of moral or intellectual comment, as in some of

---

[95] Reinhardt, *Sophokles*, dates it between *Aj.* and *Ant.*; Dain–Mazon (Budé, 1955) p. 9, Kamerbeek, pp. 27–9 and E.-R. Schwinge, *Die Stelle der Trachinierinnen im Werk des Sophokles*, 70–3, put it first; so also Stinton, *CQ* N.S. 27 (1977), 70, on metrical grounds.

the great songs of *Antigone* and *Oedipus Tyrannus*. The chorus never lose sight of their main task, which is to comfort Deianira. They become absorbed in her reactions; they offer advice both in song and in spoken interventions which are impressive for quiet sympathy and commonsense, and they stress at intervals the power of Ἔρως which motivates and unifies the plot. This concentration upon Deianira sharpens the impact upon us of her changing moods, anxiety, joy, hope, horror, and despair, precisely because it allows no merging of her personal tragedy in a wider background.

III

ANTIGONE

In the two great Theban plays, *Antigone* and *Oedipus Tyrannus*, an important change comes over Sophocles' choice of chorus. They are no longer attached to one individual, either, as in *Ajax*, by ties of personal devotion and shared experience, or as in *Trachiniae*, by a natural sympathy of sex generated within the play. Their loyalties embrace a whole community, with the result that in *Antigone* especially they are independent of personal attachment. Moreover in this play alone among Sophocles' extant works they are of a different sex from the main character: this has the important effect of isolating her from their sympathy and understanding. They are elders of their city, committed to its interests, representative spokesmen of its opinions. It is as elders who have experienced the horrors of the Labdacid house with its tale of murder, incest, invasion, slaughter of brother by brother, and threatened anarchy that they react to the events of the play, and as elders that they take part in the action and sing their odes. Their utterances are therefore wider ranging and clothed in greater poetry than those of more limited choruses, and at the same time they are completely appropriate to their characters as mature and responsible citizens of Thebes. Our task, especially with the first two stasima, is to interpret them first within their immediate context and then seek for a wider relevance to the whole story of the house to which the principal character belongs, and to the problems raised by the central conflict of the plot. We may also, as occasion requires, take into account the effect upon the dramatist of contemporary ideas and of the literary heritage at his disposal. Naturally, a poet and prominent citizen living in the intellectual atmosphere of Periclean Athens colours his work with reflections from current thought. Sophocles has certainly done this in the first stasimon of *Antigone*, but it would be a great mistake to regard this ode as a *parabasis* in which the chorus lay aside their role so that the dramatist may address the spectators in his own person.[1] This famous song (332–75) is an integral part of a play and must be interpreted as such, but if its full intellectual and political significance is not revealed by relating it solely to its context, and it is likely that it will not be, then we must attempt to trace the sources of its inspiration and the origins of its ideas in contemporary thought and the utterances of earlier poets and writers. Such an attempt may give us a deeper insight into the quality of the dramatist's vision; and so far from disproving, it may enhance the relevance of the song to the play for which he composed it. But this is to anticipate. We must first gain from the text of the play as precise an impression as we can of the chorus's role and personality. The iambic parts furnish most of the clues, and when we have constructed a picture from them, we can then turn to an examination of the lyrics.

At the end of the parodos the chorus give the reason for their presence in the orchestra: they have been summoned by Creon's command delivered to each one of them to attend a meeting convened for a particular purpose (160 ff.). The audience had been prepared in the prologue for their appearance (31–6), where Antigone tells Ismene that Creon is coming in person to announce his proclamation of the death sentence on anyone who should bury Polyneices. The new king, who has just assumed the throne on the death of his nephews during a night of battle, enters after the parodos and makes a highly reasonable speech of statesman-like quality,[2] in which he commends the elders for maintaining their loyalty and their respect for Laius' throne ever since the days of Oedipus. The state of Thebes at this moment of victory suggests that the threat of anarchy was very real when Creon took command, and much of his speech confirms this. The first need is accordingly the restoration of law and order, and both he and the chorus are deeply aware of it. Consequently, when he has published his decree forbidding the burial of Polyneices as a traitor (his crimes from a patriotic Theban point of view were enormous, 198–202), the chorus's first reaction is one of acquiescence. It is difficult to see in the lines coì ταῦτ'

---

[1] Wilamowitz, *Griechische Verskunst*, 517, speaks of the poet as warning and instructing his contemporaries.

[2] Demosthenes quotes 175–90 of this speech in 19. 247 (περὶ τῆς παραπρεϲβείαϲ) as an example to Aeschines of statesmanlike eloquence.

ἀρέσκει ... (211 ff.) any hint of misgiving or doubt, as so many critics have done. True enough, there is no positive statement of approval, but there is an admission from these elders that Creon has the power to enforce the rigour of the law in respect of both the living and the dead. This respect for authority, attributed to the chorus by him in his opening speech and implicit in their reaction to his decree, is vitally important if we are to understand their role in the play. It is moreover not respect so much for the individual who exercises it as for authority itself in whomsoever it may be vested. This is apparent at intervals throughout the action, nowhere perhaps more strikingly than in their solemn words to Antigone in the commos:

$$\text{κράτος δ' ὅτῳ κράτος μέλει}$$
$$\text{παραβατὸν οὐδαμᾷ πέλει} \qquad \text{(873 f.)}$$

'authority in whomsoever vested must on no account be transgressed'. Creon himself, well aware of their loyalty and position in the city, places upon them the responsibility of acting as guardians of his decree; and it is the chorus who conclude that the penalty of disobedience is death (220), even though he had not mentioned this sentence in his speech to them.

Another equally important characteristic of these elders is revealed after the guard's account of the rites paid to Polyneices' body. They suggest, as a result of reflection (ἡ ξύννοια βουλεύει πάλαι, 279), that the burial may have been instigated by the gods, θεήλατον: even so had they attributed the defeat of the Argives to the supreme god Zeus (128–33 and 143). Such a belief in divine sanction and intervention is the other corner-stone of their creed, and at the conclusion of the first stasimon the two tenets of their belief are stated together as necessary for a man who would be high in his city:

$$\text{νόμους περαίνων}^3 \text{ χθονὸς}$$
$$\text{θεῶν τ' ἔνορκον δίκαν,}$$
$$\text{ὑψίπολις} \qquad \text{(368 f.)}$$

'if a man honours the laws of the land and the justice of the gods by whom he swears, high is he in his city'. Creon's reaction to the chorus's suggestion is an outburst of anger (280 ff.). He cannot

---

³ Thus Pearson's text in OCT, but see p. 97 n. 17 on the reading and punctuation of 367 ff. I translate Reiske's γεραίρων.

that the gods can have had a hand in the burial of one who came to commit sacrilege. Not unnaturally for a new ruler who has inherited a state of near-anarchy, he is obsessed with the fear of ϲτάϲιϲ, and he regards the act of defiance as proving the existence of a pro-Polyneices party plotting under the inducement of bribery to usurp his power (289–303). The chorus are silenced by his wrath and take no further part in the scene. The importance of his long speech is that it allows us a glimpse of what his mind will in the sequel prove to be: closed to any opinion but his own, its standards of judgement purely political.

The elders' words at the end of the first stasimon on seeing Antigone led on to the stage are precisely what one would expect (376 ff.). They regard the sight as a portent sent by the gods (δαιμόνιον τέραϲ), and for all the pathos of the repeated δύϲτηνοϲ ... δυϲτήνου,[4] their final comment is unequivocal: disobedience to the king's laws is an act of folly, and that she, Antigone, should have disobeyed them is almost past belief. They maintain this view of her act and of the speech in which she defends it (450 ff.) in the great lyric of the second stasimon, where they conclude that folly of words and a madness in the brain have destroyed the last roots of the house:

λόγου τ' ἄνοια καὶ φρενῶν Ἐρινύϲ. (603)

Their immediate comment on her defence (471 f.) points forward to the theme of heredity which appears in the first half of that ode and in the commos (856 ff.): Antigone is truculent (ὠμὸν γέννημα) like her father and does not know how to submit to her troubles. She herself is convinced that she has the chorus's support in defying Creon and believes that their silence in her defence is due to fear and subservience (504–9). How wrong she is becomes poignantly clear in the commos and in her speech that follows it (906–28). On the other hand the scenes of confrontation first between her and Creon and then between her and Ismene, and above all, his rejection of Ismene's appeal for her sister's life produce a measure of surprise, even shock, in their question

ἦ γὰρ ϲτερήϲειϲ τῆϲδε τὸν ϲαυτοῦ γόνον;

'Are you really going to take this girl from your own son?' They

---

[4] Although δύϲτηνοϲ usually expresses pity, it can also express condemnation, e.g. of Clytaemnestra in *El.* 121 and 806.

do not however either question or approve his decision but receive his reply with resignation:

δεδογμέν', ὡς ἔοικε, τήνδε κατθανεῖν   (574–6)

'The decision, so it seems, is that she must die'.

The coryphaeus's comments (681 f. and 724 f.) on the two long speeches in the quarrel between father and son commend the arguments of both for their good sense, and we are not disposed to disagree when he says that each can learn something from the other, though we should note the word μαθεῖν in 725: the idea of learning, and of learning too late, is a recurrent theme not only in many of Sophocles' plays but throughout the whole field of tragedy, and is brought home to Creon in the final scene of the play (1270) and in the anapaests at its close. At the end of the quarrel the elders make a suggestion that influences the action, and he accepts with approval of its good sense the hint that Ismene should be spared (771). From this moment, as Creon moves unwittingly ever nearer to the brink of disaster, they become bolder in their advice to him. After Teiresias' speech, their expression of confidence in the seer's infallibility throws him into consternation, ταράccομαι φρένας (1095), and it is they who assume control and advise the practical steps which he must take, first to release Antigone and then to bury Polyneices. The requirements of the plot make it necessary for him to perform these two actions in the reverse order, so that nothing can prevent the deaths of Antigone and Haemon. Apart from their commos with her (806–82) and certain of their lyrics, which will be considered in detail later, there is nothing further in the play indicative of their role and personality. A few conventional commonplaces help to complete the rhythmic and formal structure of the second commos (1261–1346), though the anapaestic coda is of importance in summing up the play, being something more than a formula of dismissal.

Such then is the group personality of the chorus as they present themselves in the iambic scenes: men of long standing prestige and proven loyalty throughout the turbulent story of Thebes; committed to their city and not to any individual; rescued by a new unproven ruler from war and threatened anarchy; full of respect for authority and established religion; and when confronted by a fresh threat in the act of disobedience to the new king's first proclamation, resigned at first to accept his exercise of power; then, when the tragedy gathers momentum, assuming some measure of influence over him, giving him advice, issuing precise instructions; confused and shocked by Antigone's deed, clinging for support to the twin pillars of the state's laws and a tradition of belief in divine sanctions, yet unwilling to make up their minds in the crisis of conflict between the two. More knowledge of what they think and what they are can be gleaned from their lyrics, but this is in brief the context of status and character in which these lyrics must be studied.

The parodos (100), as in *Ajax, Trachiniae,* and *Oedipus Tyrannus,* constitutes a fresh start to the play. The two sisters have met during the night, after the defeat of the Argives (ἐν νυκτὶ τῇ νῦν, 16), Antigone having heard rumours of Creon's proclamation. In spite of Ismene's arguments, she determines to bury Polyneices and at the end of the prologue leaves to perform her task. The whole scene is a masterpiece of construction. Its principal effect is to show the rending apart of the sisters, the change of love and community of feeling in ὦ κοινὸν αὐτάδελφον Ἰσμήνης κάρα into a future of bitter hatred on Antigone's part:

$$\text{εἰ ταῦτα λέξεις, ἐχθαρῇ μὲν ἐξ ἐμοῦ,}$$
$$\text{ἐχθρὰ δὲ τῷ θανόντι προσκείσῃ δίκη}\qquad\text{(93 f.)}$$

'if these are your words, you will earn my hatred and the lasting hatred of the dead—justly so'. After the sisters have left the stage, we must postulate an interval, allowing time for Antigone to scatter dust on the body where it lies on the battlefield, a task she must perform while it is still dark, and for the sun to rise, so that when the chorus enter the orchestra they can salute its first rays. They know nothing of Creon's decree, nothing of what has happened or been planned to happen in the prologue; only, as they explain at the end of their song, that they have been especially summoned. The parodos is thus a complete contrast in mood and setting; darkness has yielded to sunrise, passion to joy and thanksgiving for victory, secret plotting to public jubilation.

In structure the ode marks a transitional stage. It consists of two strophic pairs sung by the whole chorus, each stanza separated by seven lines of anapaests recited by the coryphaeus.[5]

---

[5] Dindorf may be right in replacing the Doric forms γᾶν and γᾷ etc. in these anapaests by the Ionic/Attic forms γῆν and γῇ.

Sophocles has thus combined the *Ajax*-type of parodos with the purely lyric type used in *Trachiniae* and *Oedipus Tyrannus*. Recitative parodoi as employed by Aeschylus in *Persae, Supplices*, and *Agamemnon* normally give place to sung strophes, so that a factual statement of the situation in even-toned narrative is succeeded by a quickened emotion. It is natural therefore to expect that in the parodos of *Antigone* Sophocles should match his combination of sung and recited utterance by a combination also of different contents and moods. This is in fact what he has done. The first strophe, mainly glyconic, salutes the newly risen sun with apostrophes and appositional clauses that suggest a ritual song, possibly a paean, if we may recall the opening words, ἀκτὶς ἀελίου, of Pindar's ninth *Paean* on the eclipse of the sun in April 463 B.C.[6] This stanza gives a glimpse of the Argive panoply with their white shields, retreating under the sharp constraint of flight. The language is highly coloured, the mood exalted as the singers greet the dawn, their long awaited deliverer from the night of battle. The seven-line anapaestic system (110–16) which divides strophe from antistrophe gives an essential explanation in narrative form, introducing Polyneices and his quarrel with his brother as the cause of the invasion and expanding the single epithet λεύκασπιν (106) into a lengthened description of the white-plumaged eagle. In the antistrophe, while the first seven lines pick up the image of the eagle flying on high into the land of Thebes (113), a single peak of tension is stressed, the moment of suspense before the invaders are put to flight. The end of the antistrophe recalls the end of the strophe, as both emphasize the fact of retreat.

With the anapaests at 128 comes a pause for reflection with a conventional gnomic comment on Zeus' hatred of the loud-tongued boast and the clang of gold. This comment merges in the last three lines (131 ff.) into a single conspicuous example of vaulting insolence destroyed by a thunderbolt in the moment of triumph. The same scene is continued into the lyric of the second strophe (134) with an equal vigour of description enhanced by further alliteration, mainly of π and τ, bold imagery and language, and the repeated dactyls of the opening two lines. Though he is not mentioned by name, no doubt ancient scholars

[6] Fr. 44 B. *Paean* 9 is apotropaic, while Sophocles' ode is a victory-song. The echo is therefore purely verbal.

were correct in detecting in this passage the braggart Capaneus, the most colourful of the Argive leaders, whose shield bore the device of a man with a flaming torch in his hand ($\pi\upsilon\rho\phi\acute{o}\rho\text{o}\text{c}$, 135), proclaiming in letters of gold $\pi\rho\acute{\eta}\text{c}\omega$ $\pi\acute{o}\lambda\iota\nu$.[7] The strophe ends with a more generalized description of the blows dealt by Ares to the other invaders. Thus the second system of anapaests and the second strophe are woven together, as is the first with the first antistrophe, by unity of content: statement of the maxim is followed by an example ($\pi\alpha\rho\acute{\alpha}\delta\epsilon\iota\gamma\mu\alpha$). The change from recitative to song occurs at the moment of the *peripeteia*, when Capaneus' shout of victory is stopped by Zeus' thunderbolt, so that the opening lines of the lyric point the contrast between his plunge to earth and the frenzy of his assault. The whole passage is a miniature of so much Greek choral lyric: the poet states a maxim and illustrates it by a myth, though here the illustration is no myth to the chorus but an incident from immediate experience.

At 141 the anapaests again take up the narrative style with a factual account of the seven invading groups against the seven gates of Thebes, and they end on a note of pathos with the death of the two brothers, thus forming a strong contrast to the mood of exaltation which inspires the rest of the ode. The language, too, of this system is on a restrained level of poetry, free of metaphor, striking words, and brilliant effects, and the tale is told in a single flowing period. We may perhaps imagine a slight pause at 146 after the recitative before the chorus attack the song of the final antistrophe with $\dot{\alpha}\lambda\lambda\grave{\alpha}$ $\gamma\grave{\alpha}\rho$ dismissing thoughts of sadness as they turn again to the main theme of the parodos, Victory. The ode closes with an appeal to forget war and visit the temples of the gods with companies of dancers led by Bacchus. The last system of anapaests (155) is not a part of the emotion and content of the parodos at all. Its function is to announce Creon's arrival and account for the chorus's presence. It also communicates to the audience the elders' own wonder as to the tone of the new king's first statement, thus leading naturally into the main action of the play.

The chief poetical image in the parodos is the conflict between the eagle of Argos and the snake of Thebes, occupying the central place. Eagle and snake are traditional enemies, as is evident from

[7] Aesch. *Th.* 423–34.

many a simile and omen in Epic and later poetry.[8] If we accept the manuscripts' reading ὃν ... Πολυνείκης with a lacuna at 112 containing a verb,[9] and if we agree with Hermann to delete ὡς in 113 as an insertion to mark the simile, we gain two advantages. First, we have two practically rhyming paroemiacs, αἰετὸς ἐς γᾶν ὑπερέπτα = χρυσοῦ καναχῆς ὑπερόπτας (130), and secondly, Polyneices as leader of the Argive invaders is himself the eagle, just as in *O.T.* 478 the unknown fugitive is himself the bull, πετραῖος ὁ ταῦρος.[10] The text thus produced, as printed by Pearson, is satisfactory: the leader is introduced in the nominative case and controls the whole sentence, while the assumed lacuna secures the desired rhythmic balance between 112 and 129. The eagle Polyneices is further individualized from 114 to 121, his plumage white as snow, his beak agape as he hovers ready to swoop on his victim. It is noteworthy how the poet interweaves words and phrases applicable only to a vividly envisaged bird of prey (ὀξέα κλάζων, πτέρυγι ... στὰς ὑπὲρ μελάθρων ... ἀμφιχανών, γένυσιν) with words descriptive of an attacking army (πολλῶν μεθ' ὅπλων ξύν θ' ἱπποκόμοις κορύθεσσι, φονώσαισι ... λόγχαις) so that image and original merge into one instead of being kept apart as in the conventional simile. The snake does not appear until the end of the antistrophe, and then with none of the splendid imagery that heralds the eagle and in a difficult appositional phrase where the text is uncertain. Sophocles has indeed coined a word δυσχείρωμα to be the opposite of εὐμαρὲς χείρωμα, a thing easy to overcome.[11] The asyndeton at 125 shows that this sentence explains why the eagle Polyneices and his host were routed: such a din of battle, difficult for the snake's enemy to overcome, was raised at his back. Jebb's text, ἀντιπάλῳ δράκοντος, which would easily be corrupted by assimilation of case endings, gives the most satisfactory sense.

A few further linguistic features may be briefly noted. In the first stanza both the literal dawn and the metaphorical dawn of salvation (φάος) from the dark night of battle are marvellously suggested by an accumulation of words signifying light, ἀκτὶς ἀελίου, φανέν, φάος, ἐφάνθης, χρυσέας ἁμέρας βλέφαρον. Moreover

---

[8] e.g. *Il.* 12. 200 ff.

[9] Nauck's ἤγαγεν· ἐχθρὸς δ' is very prosaic.

[10] The ὡς-less simile appears early in Greek poetry, cf. Alcm. *Parth.* 85 f., Thgn. 347; and later, Pi. *P.* 4. 289; Aesch. *Pr.* 857; Hor. *Odes* ii. 20. 15.

[11] Aesch. *A.* 1326, where see Fraenkel's note ad loc. on the derivation of χείρωμα.

the sun's ray is itself the agent of the enemy's rout, stirring the Argive host to headlong flight. In the last lines of this strophe, ὀξυτόρῳ of the manuscripts LA must be kept, and χαλινῷ is a metaphor for ἀνάγκη, 'necessity's sharp contraint', as in Aesch. *Pr.* 672, ἐπηνάγκαζέ νιν Διὸς χαλινός, 'the constraint of Zeus forced him'.[12] Other images are conveyed by single words, the unique τανταλωθείς in the second strophe (134) of Capaneus swung or suspended in the air between rampart and ground, cτυφελίζων (139) from the vocabulary of epic, δεξιόcειρος, also a unique coinage, a conflation of δεξιὸς cειραῖος (*Electra* 722), the right-hand trace-horse whose effort is decisive at the critical turn round the stele in a chariot-race, implying that Ares acted as a trace-horse at the crisis of battle. The ode of course contains other examples of metaphorical language, but they are less striking because conventional; and the instances chosen are enough to indicate the poetic intensity, higher perhaps in the lyric stanzas than in the anapaests, which distinguishes the parodos as a whole.

Unquestionably the most striking technical feature of this opening ode is its combination of song and recitative in the chorus's utterances, unique in the parodoi of extant Greek tragedy.[13] Sophocles has exploited at the entry of his chorus in the play the possibilities inherent in the different moods of these two elements, a technique seen elsewhere principally in those scenes between actor and chorus where one recites and the other sings in order to mark different levels of emotion. Thus, to sum up the effect of this fusion of both in the parodos of *Antigone*, the excitement of the lyric opening with its greeting to the sunrise gives place to the quieter narrative anapaests. These are followed by a sung antistrophe of vivid description fused to the anapaests by identity of image and content. The next anapaestic system, reflective in mood at the start, introduces a gnomic comment illustrated by the example of Capaneus which continues into the second strophe. The last system, like the first, is a narrative, simple in language, pathetic in mood and content, while the final antistrophe, a strong contrast, resumes the feeling of joy and thanksgiving with which the song opened. This feeling inspires

[12] See Lloyd-Jones, *CQ* N.S. 7 (1957), 12 ff.

[13] The parodos of *Pr.* consists of song and recitative, but the two are shared between chorus and actor.

the whole ode. The sunrise welcomed in the opening words is symbolic of its dramatic setting in the bright dawn after the darkness and the passion of the prologue. At this stage the chorus raise no far-ranging issues and give no hint of the tensions to come. Their sole task is to represent the mood of a community on the morning of its deliverance.

Before discussing the first stasimon (332) we must set it as precisely as possible in its dramatic context. In the scene that precedes it the following points deserve particular emphasis. First is Creon's insistence, apparent especially in 182 f. and 187–191, on the need for the individual citizen to govern his personal relationships by reference to his πάτρα, his fatherland. It follows then that respect for the state's laws as a condition of the state's safety, above all in time of danger, is of supreme importance, and that the ties of kinship and friendship must be subordinate. This view of man's duty as a citizen finds an echo at the end of the song (368). Secondly, Creon twice dwells on the crimes of Polyneices (199 ff. and 285 ff.), so that there can be no doubt of their enormity and of the terrors (τὰ δεινά) from which Thebes has just been saved. Thirdly, the guard, in a state of high alarm, has reported the burial with a detailed description intended to awake a sense of mystery as to the performance of the deed (249–258). He was one of the night-watch ordered to guard the body (217), and the first day-watch (ὁ πρῶτος ἡμεροσκόπος 253) on taking over at dawn had pointed out that it had been covered with a layer of dust while the night-watch were on duty. Hence the guard's panic: he realizes that he and his companions have failed at their post. Hence also Creon's threat that unless they find the culprit they will be put to death (305 ff.). The important point here is the cleverness of the culprit in eluding the watch and burying the body under cover of darkness,[14] a signal act of δεινότης both in itself and in its defiance of the laws of the state. Finally there is that passage of Creon's speech (289–303) in which he expresses his conviction that the burial is a symptom of ϲτάϲιϲ, of something involving bribery that may destroy the state whose security he is trying to restore after the recent turmoil; and there is also, earlier in the same speech (288 f.), his angry rejection of the chorus's suggestion that the gods may have had a hand in the deed. This last point is however incidental at this

[14] See A. T. von S. Bradshaw, *CQ* N.S. 12 (1962), 201–4.

stage of the play, for the religious problem does not arise in an acute form until Antigone introduces it in her speech at 450 ff. In addition to these particular points, which concern mainly the political background of the ode, we should remember also what the chorus have experienced in the recent history of Thebes. We can thus assess with some accuracy their state of mind when they sing their lyric. Their confidence in the re-establishment of order has been shaken by an act of defiance cleverly carried out. The state's security is their interest as much as Creon's, and as guarantees thereof they rely on the laws of the land and the sanctions of religion. Enough has been done and said within the play and experienced by the chorus before it begins to give a very real meaning to the opening words of the song:

πολλὰ τὰ δεινὰ κοὐδὲν ἀν-
θρώπου δεινότερον πέλει

'Many are the things that are formidable, and nothing is more formidable than man.'

Before pursuing the argument further it will be convenient at this stage to give an outline of the ode. The first sentence is a fairly close echo of the second stasimon of Aeschylus' *Choephoroe* (585 f.)

πολλὰ μὲν γᾶ τρέφει
δεινὰ δειμάτων ἄχη

'Many are the formidable pains of terrors that earth breeds', in which the etymological connection of δεινός, δέος, δεῖμα is made clear by juxtaposition.[15] Sophocles has no doubt chosen the Aeschylean phrase as a theme for his own song, and this justifies the translation 'formidable' rather than 'strange', 'wonderful', or 'clever'.[16] However different the content and intention of Sophocles' ode from Aeschylus', it may be admitted that at its outset, when its connection with the dramatic context is closest, this rendering is highly appropriate both to that context and to the chorus's state of mind. Man is formidable, and when clever, he is so in a formidable way. Moreover, there is intrinsically nothing moral about his δεινότης, as the last antistrophe will show.

[15] The relation of δέος to δεινός is similar to that between κλέος and κλεινός.
[16] See P. Friedländer, *Hermes* 69 (1934), 56–63.

The statement of man's surpassing δεινότηc is followed by a series of examples showing what this creature (τοῦτο, 334) has achieved. At the beginning he is introduced in the neuter, as if dehumanized, a sort of portent, a τέραc or *monstrum*, and he acquires a human personality with the change to the masculine participle at the end of the strophe (πολεύων, 341). The examples chosen depict a range of different skills of a type familiar in ancient literature. There is the skill of the sailor in his quest for the fruits of commerce and of the farmer ploughing his land. These occupy the first stanza and represent man's struggle with the inanimate elements, water and earth. There follow in the antistrophe (342) the skills of the huntsman, the fisherman, and the subduer of wild animals to the service of mankind. Here man is shown in successful combat with animate nature. The list in the first strophic pair comprises the acquisitive and mainly self-interested skills by which he earns his living in conflict with the sea and the earth and bends wild nature to his purposes. In the second strophe (354) are the less selfish, more social and intellectual skills: speech, the basis of communication; thought, swift as the wind; the impulse to live in cities, possible only when he has built himself houses for shelter against the frosts and the rains; and the art of healing. In fact he has found a resource for everything; in no direction is he resourceless except one: he cannot escape death. While there is in this account no chronological order of development, it displays nevertheless an inner logic of its own, a movement from the less to the more sophisticated; and it indicates precisely the one frontier which man shall never cross:

> "Αιδα μόνον
> φεῦξιν οὐκ ἐπάξεται.					(361 f.)

In the last antistrophe (365) comes the conclusion to which the whole song is directed: man with his incredible skill moves now towards evil, now towards good.[17] In other words, his moral direction is neither assured not consistent in spite of his achievements in technology (τέχνη). He requires two conditions if his path is to be towards good, respect for the laws of the land,

[17] The text of 367–70 should be punctuated with a colon at ἕρπει and a comma at δίκαν. παρείρων of the manuscripts in 368 is corrupt. γεραίρων (Reiske), 'honouring', gives better sense than περαίνων (Pflugk), 'accomplishing', printed in the OCT.

and for the justice of the gods. If he chooses to accept them, he is high in his city, ὑψίπολις.[18] If however his choice as a companion is τὸ μὴ καλόν, he is ἄπολις, without a city, an outcast disfranchised from his community (367–71). The ode ends with a personal wish from the elders, that he who does these things may never share hearth or thoughts with them. By a superb dramatic stroke, immediately after the clause ὃς τάδ᾽ ἔρδοι with its masculine relative pronoun, the guard brings in the woman, Antigone.

Analysed in this way, the song has a very close relevance. It opens with a judgement that arises naturally out of the dramatic context of the play at the moment at which it occurs, and it closes with a personal utterance which clarifies beyond doubt the attitude of the chorus. Its thesis is developed unambiguously to its conclusion: the absolute importance for man of respect for the laws of the land and the sanction of divine justice if he is to reach the high end of his existence as a member of a πόλις. Now in the eyes of the chorus the unknown person who buried Polyneices has defied the laws, respect for which is one of the two conditions that make civilised society possible. The other condition, respect for divine justice, is not yet in question: no one within the play has, so far as concerns the plot at this stage, been represented as violating that condition, and we must await the sequel in order to have Creon's impiety brought to light. But at the moment, the fact is that the laws of the land have been broken, and in the context of this ode the culprit is on one count ἄπολις. There can then be no question of any reference to Creon, who has himself made the law whose transgression is seen as a threat to the safety of the state. In fact the conclusion reached in the final stanza is in no respect inconsistent with Creon's own views as expressed in his speeches during the first scene.

So far we have tried to consider this ode solely in its limited context, bearing in mind the status and experiences of the chorus. It has however a wider significance as a work of extraordinary beauty and power, so that some attempt must now be made to trace its deeper implications. Sophocles has in the first three stanzas drawn initially upon two types of source. First, there can be detected a view of man's development diametrically opposed to the theory found in Hesiod's *Works and Days* (109–201), that

---

[18] ὑψίπολις, not found elsewhere, can be translated 'he has a proud or high city', but this does not pair so well with ἄπολις, 'citiless'.

human life has progressively deteriorated through four ages corresponding to four metals, gold, silver, bronze, and iron, with a fifth race, the heroic, inserted incidentally between the last two under the influence of Homeric epic. In this ode however the poet describes a gradual improvement towards a peak of achievement, life in a city. The most interesting feature of this improvement is that it is due entirely to man's own efforts, unaided either by divine intervention or by a superhuman teacher of skills like Prometheus. Such an idea of progress unassisted is to be found in a fragment of the Ionian philosopher-poet Xenophanes (Fr. 18 DK), who lived probably into the first thirty years of the fifth century: 'not from the beginning did the gods reveal everything to mankind, but in time, by research, men discover a better way', χρόνῳ ζητοῦντες ἐφευρίσκουσιν ἄμεινον. Sophocles has developed this idea in his song, using certain keywords to make his point: περιφραδὴς ἀνήρ (347), ἐδιδάξατο (356), παντοπόρος (360), ξυμπέφρασται (364), with their emphasis on surpassing skill, self-teaching, resourcefulness, and inventive thought. As to other famous Greek texts on man's development, Aeschylus in *Pr.* 442–506 puts into Prometheus' mouth a speech recording man's advance from a drifting, dream-like life to be a lord of creation, an intellectual being of the highest order, with the help of the great teacher Prometheus, while Euripides in *Supplices* 195 (*c.* 421 B.C.) makes Theseus give a rather similar account of human progress which he attributes to a god, θεοῦ κατασκευὴν βίῳ δόντος τοιαύτην (214 f.). Sophocles' man however has achieved his end without either a Prometheus or a god to help him. From this point of view πολλὰ τὰ δεινά is of considerable importance in any discussion of Greek ideas on progress.[19]

As to the second kind of source, Sophocles selects, in order to illustrate man's δεινότης, certain instances of different types of lives. The literary precedents for this begin probably with Solon 1. 43 ff., σπεύδει δ' ἄλλοθεν ἄλλος, with its list of careers: trading over the sea, agriculture, craftsmanship, poetry, soothsaying, medicine.[20] Neither of these sources will however by itself prove adequate, for while they give the stages of man's development and a list of skills and careers which help him in the business of

---

[19] See E. R. Dodds, *The Ancient Concept of Progress*, esp. 4–13.
[20] For similar lists, cf. Pi. Fr. 208 B. and Horace's adaptation in *Odes* i. 1.

living, they contain no hint of what gives Sophocles' ode its
unique interest: man's impulse to live in cities (355 f.) and his
emergence as a being faced with a moral choice which if made
correctly will ensure his successful life as a citizen (367–70). To
account for this we must turn to a third source, important
especially in interpreting the last antistrophe. This lies in the
contemporary intellectual atmosphere of Athens.

It is known that Protagoras spent the ten years from 454 to 444
teaching in Athens; that he exercised a great influence on the
intellectual life of the city; and that he was chosen to draw up a
code of laws for the colony of Thurii where he may have gone at
its foundation in 443 B.C. [21] Sophocles must unquestionably have
been aware of the ideas of this remarkable man, and we may
now turn to the myth put into his mouth by Plato in the dialogue
bearing his name, for though we have no right to say that it
represents with strict accuracy what Protagoras said, we are
justified in taking it as evidence for ideas current at Athens when
Sophocles was writing his play.

The relevant passage of the myth is at *Protagoras* 321 c, which
may be paraphrased as follows. Man first acquired, with the gift
of fire stolen by Prometheus, skill in the arts of daily life, but not
the art of living in cities (πολιτικὴ τέχνη). He was enabled by his
cleverness to articulate speech and to invent dwellings, clothes,
sandals, beds, and to get food from the earth, but since he had no
cities, he was destroyed by wild beasts. Men accordingly sought
to bind themselves together and achieve security by founding
cities, but because they lacked this 'political art', they did wrong
to one another, and their first political associations came to grief.
To prevent man's destruction, Zeus told Hermes to apportion
Δίκη and Αἰδώc (Justice and a feeling of Respect) to all men so
that they could live in communities, and any man who could not
partake of these two was to die the death as a disease of his city
(νόcoc πόλεωc). Now let us look at Sophocles' ode. Various stages
of man's advancement are given in the first three stanzas. The
goal towards which he is moving is the πόλιc, his teaching of
himself ἀcτυνόμουc ὀργάc is the impulse; and the belief that the
πόλιc represents the highest achievement of man's ingenuity is
fundamental to Greek thought in the Periclean age. Indeed

[21] See J. S. Morrison, *Protagoras in Athenian Public Life*, *CQ* 35 (1941), 1–16, and
W. K. C. Guthrie, *History of Greek Philosophy* iii. 63–8.

Aristotle's dry, biological description of man as a 'political animal' (πολιτικὸν ζῷον, *Pol.* 1253ᵃ3) is foreshadowed perhaps here for the first time in this song. By the end of its third stanza we have reached the stage when man has taught himself the value of political association. He has achieved all that technical skill can accomplish:

$$\pi\alpha\nu\tau o\pi\acute{o}\rho o c\cdot\ \breve{\alpha}\pi o\rho o c\ \dot{\epsilon}\pi\ \check{}\ o\dot{v}\delta\grave{\epsilon}\nu\ \breve{\epsilon}\rho\chi\epsilon\tau\alpha\iota$$
$$\tau\grave{o}\ \mu\acute{\epsilon}\lambda\lambda o\nu. \hspace{3cm} (360\ f.)$$

He has what Plato's Protagoras calls τὴν περὶ τὸν βίον coφίαν, skill in the business of living, in Sophocles' words

$$coφ\acute{o}\nu\ \tau\iota\ \tau\grave{o}\ \mu\alpha\chi\alpha\nu\acute{o}\epsilon\nu$$
$$\tau\acute{\epsilon}\chi\nu\alpha c\ \dot{v}\pi\grave{\epsilon}\rho\ \dot{\epsilon}\lambda\pi\acute{\iota}\delta\ \check{}\ \breve{\epsilon}\chi\omega\nu$$

which mean that his technical ingenuity is skilful or clever beyond belief (365 f.). The poet's conclusion is the same as the philosopher's: both have perceived the problem that confronts all technical and scientific progress, that in itself man's ingenuity is non-moral. Protagoras tells us that Δίκη and Αἰδώc were allotted to men so that they could live in communities without doing wrong to each other, and Sophocles' chorus conclude that in order to give a moral direction to man's τέχνη, to save it from evil ways and turn it towards good, man must honour the laws of the land and the justice which he has sworn by the gods to uphold, νόμους χθονὸς θεῶν τ' ἔνορκον δίκαν (368 f.). These two sanctions will ensure that he is ὑψίπολιc, high in his city. Neither of them alone is enough. Without them he is truly δεινόc, formidable in skill but non-moral, and as such, ἄπολιc. Protagoras puts it as follows: ὡς παντὶ προcῆκον τῆς πολιτικῆς ἀρετῆς μετέχειν ἢ μὴ εἶναι πολεῖc, 'it being necessary for everyone to share in political virtue, otherwise there will be no cities.' The two expressions in Sophocles' ode (368 f.) together cover both the laws of the particular city of which Creon's decree is an example and the unwritten laws (ἄγραπτα νόμιμα, 454) to which Antigone will later appeal.

Such an interpretation, without in any way diminishing its strict dramatic relevance, enables us to relate the song to the intellectual climate in which Sophocles and his audience lived, gives us an insight into its sources, and helps us to perceive in it a wider relevance to the whole problem of the play. *Antigone* is concerned with a conflict between νόμοι χθονόc and θεῶν δίκη. In presenting these together as the two conditions of moral life in a city, the chorus are stating that neither can be dispensed with if a citizen is to be ὑψίπολιc and implying, one feels, that in an ideal state of society they should not be in conflict. In this play they conflict, though at this moment the Theban elders, ironically, do not realize that they might. The clash however becomes ever clearer as act follows act, and the characters and positions of the two contestants emerge from the heat of argument. Creon, we shall see, is a stupid and short-sighted man who allows the claims of the gods no validity beyond the immediate and limited scope of his own political principles; and Antigone rejects the laws of the state when they clash with the laws of the gods. The ode thus affords a fitting background against which the tale of conflict and disaster is to be played out.

Before we consider some of the linguistic and rhythmical features of the song a few further observations may be made, most of which have been hinted at already. It should not be regarded as an ἐμβόλιμον, a 'fill-in',[22] or as a παράβαcιc in which the poet addresses the audience in his own person through the chorus. Naturally a dramatist of Sophocles' quality reflects some of the facets of contemporary thought, but he is in no sense warning, exhorting, or preaching to the audience. Nor must we forget that there is nothing in the ode inconsistent with the status of the people who sing it. Sophocles is very particular in this respect. He would never have put these sentiments into the mouths of a chorus of women or young girls because they would have been out of character, but Θήβηc οἱ κοιρανίδαι 'members of the ruling class', as Antigone calls them in 940, can utter them with perfect propriety. Next, we must grasp the dramatist's intention here to put the audience in the frame of mind in which he wants them to be at this stage of the play. They are made aware of an ideal state of affairs in a city, described in the second antistrophe; they have in the earlier stanzas listened to an account of man's progress towards it, and they know that defiance of the law is impeding his achievement of it. The chorus present them with certain standards by which to judge the impending conflict between Antigone and Creon. It is thus essential to stress the very important contribution made by the

[22] Arist. *Po.* 1456ª 29.

ode to our understanding of the moral, intellectual, and political ideas that lie at the root of this great play. Finally, this ode, like so many in Sophocles' plays, is a powerful instrument of dramatic irony. For instance, the chorus's fierce condemnation of the unknown miscreant ὃc τάδ᾽ ἔρδοι at the end of the second antistrophe is followed by Antigone's appearance under guard, a reversal of expectation as ironical as it is dramatic. Looking further ahead into the play, it becomes apparent that what is said in the last stanza will later be seen as more appropriate to Creon than to her, if not by the chorus, at any rate by the audience. Such instances of judgements based on ignorance or limited evidence and subsequently proved wrong by a revelation of truth are to be found in the songs of the chorus as well as in the speeches of the actors.

We may now attempt to assess the poetical quality of this remarkable ode, for it is not merely a résumé of arts and skills, nor a lesson in political philosophy, nor a sermon for the times but first and foremost a song composed for a play. The impression it gives is one of lucidity of thought matched by clarity of language. It has a single theme and moves to a single conclusion. No irrelevances, digressions, or subsidiary motifs break its tension or impede its flow. The highly practical nature of its contents has generated an objective and practical style marked by great economy of language and a striking absence of simile and metaphor. The vocabulary is sparing in its use of purely decorative epithets, which are confined mostly to the first antistrophe (342–52), κουφονόων, δικτυοκλώcτοιc (a unique word), ὀρεccιβάτα, perhaps tautological with οὐρεῖον just below, λαcιαύχενα, ἀκμῆτα; and there are no unnecessary circumlocutions. The sentences in which it is composed are simple and paratactic: main verbs preponderate, their action defined by a few subordinate participles; and there are only two dependent clauses, both relative and at the end of the final antistrophe (370 and 375). The whole ode is carefully paragraphed between its separate stanzas, each self-contained in content and grammatical structure. The first three give examples of man's δεινότηc grouped within the confines of strophic discipline by the logic of poetry, and the last presents the conclusion to which all else is directed.

Sophocles has employed certain effects which contribute most subtly to the rhythmic pattern of the song. The first strophe and antistrophe show in their opening sentences an exactly similar word division across the choriambic dimeters and a rhyme at the end (κοὐδὲν ἀν/θρώπου and φῦλον ὀρ/νίθων and πέλει = ἄγει);[23] the enjambment between the iambic diameters at 337 f. is answered by a similar one at 348 f. (θεῶν τε = κρατεῖ δὲ); and there are three examples of word and rhythmic echo, πόντου in 335 and 345, ἀνεμόεν = μαχανόεν (354 = 365), and a more remarkable one at the climax points of the last two stanzas, involving also a pause-echo, παντοπόρος· ἄπορος = ὑψίπολις· ἄπολις (360 = 370). The actual metres used are simple to grasp. In the first strophic pair the opening major period is choriambic, its clausula an eight-syllable line with a pendent close (336 = 346). Then come two iambic diameters merging into a couple of dactylic tetrameters[24] with a syncopated iambic trimeter for clausula. The three types of rhythm are clearly defined. The second pair contains only two types, choriambic enoplian (354–6 = 365–7), and iambic to the end.

It is not surprising that an ode which exhibits such perfection of structure, such lucidity of thought, and such clarity of language should have been regarded as Sophocles' most celebrated song or that it should have been given high-sounding titles: a Hymn to Man's Greatness, a Triumph-song of Culture,[25] a Speculation on the Tragic Essential in Man.[26] These titles may serve as appropriate headings for it when wrested from its context and placed in an Anthology, but they tend to cloud judgement and to distract attention from what we must assume to have been Sophocles' purpose in putting it where he did in a tragedy intended for performance before an audience of Athenian citizens.

The dramatic relevance of the second stasimon (583–626) is far more obvious than that of the first. The chorus have listened to Antigone's defence of her act and heard Creon condemn both her and Ismene to death. They know also of Ismene's willingness to share the blame and die with her sister, and they are left in no doubt of the finality of the sentence, which they accept with resignation:

[23] The MSS. ἄγει should be kept in 343.

[24] ζυγόν must be kept in 351, because the dactyl must be open at the end. ζυγῶν, accepted by Jebb, is therefore impossible.

[25] Weinstock, *Sophokles*, 161.

[26] C. H. Whitman, *Sophocles*, 91.

Χο. δεδογμέν᾽, ὡς ἔοικε, τήνδε κατθανεῖν.
Κρ. καὶ σοί γε κἀμοί   (576 f.)

'*Ch.* It is decided, so it seems, that this girl must die. *Creon.* Yes, by both you and me.' This means the end of the house of Labdacus. The ode which follows, sung in front of Creon[27] after the sisters have been taken away to prison, offers an Aeschylean interpretation of the disaster, seeing in it the last act in the working out of the inherited doom that has held each generation in its grip. Stress is laid on the destruction of the family by the will of the gods, θεόθεν (584), and the first strophic pair is in effect a dirge for the doomed house. The thought of the ode is drawn from ancient tradition: it expresses beliefs dominant throughout ancient literature and heard intermittently well into the second half of the fifth century.[28] In the commos (802 ff.) the chorus offer Antigone the same explanation of her plight,

πατρῷον δ᾽ ἐκτίνεις τιν᾽ ἆθλον

'You are paying for an ordeal inherited from your fathers' (856), and she takes the point by acknowledging that they have touched the source of her most poignant woe. On this theory it is not so much the acts of individuals that are to blame as the inherited curse that pursues a whole family over a period of time. Antigone herself is not mentioned in the ode as a personality, her existence being merely hinted at in the imagery of 600 ff. What matters is the destruction of a house and its breed, a point made clear in the first strophic pair in the words δόμος (584 and 600), γένος and γενεά (585 and 596) and Λαβδακιδᾶν οἴκων (594). Such a theory of course raises important problems of free will, just as it does in the great scene between Clytaemnestra and the chorus in *Agamemnon* after the king has been murdered (1407–15) and as it will do in the first commos of *Antigone*, but this problem is not at issue in the present ode.

The song begins with an impressive definition of εὐδαιμονία, a condition of godlike bliss persisting throughout the lifetime of succeeding generations. This conception of εὐδαιμονία is a

---

[27] This is clear from 626–34.

[28] See Dodds, *The Greeks and the Irrational*, 49 f., for Sophocles as the last exponent of the archaic world-view, with a fine translation of this ode. Mrs. Easterling's fine study of this ode in *Dionysiaca, Nine Studies in Greek Poetry presented to Sir Denys Page* (Cambridge, 1978), 141–58, appeared too late for me to take it into account.

commonplace of popular wisdom, for in *Agamemnon* 553 the
herald asks

$$\tau i c \ \delta \grave{\epsilon} \ \pi \lambda \mathring{\eta} \nu \ \theta \epsilon \hat{\omega} \nu$$
$$\mathring{\alpha} \pi \alpha \nu \tau' \ \mathring{\alpha} \pi \mathring{\eta} \mu \omega \nu \ \tau \grave{o} \nu \ \delta \iota' \ \alpha \mathring{\iota} \hat{\omega} \nu o c \ \chi \rho \acute{o} \nu o \nu;$$

'Who but the gods is free from woe throughout the whole period
of his life?' As a contrast to this opening statement, the main
theme of ἄτη is introduced immediately, and the word itself tolls
like a knell four times in the ode, twice at exactly similar places
and in identical phrases at the end of the last two stanzas.[29]
There is significance also in the fivefold repetition of θεός in
different forms beginning with the adverb θεόθεν in 584, and in
the echo of γενεᾶc and γενεὰν γένος in the same places in the first
strophic pair (585 = 596). These repeated keywords are essential
to the thought and structure of the ode. Ἄτη here means the
physical fact of ruin or destruction, not the infatuation or
perverted state of mind which precedes, induces, or accompanies
it. So much is apparent from 620–4 where the state of mind and
its disastrous consequences are kept apart. Moreover, the ἄτη
which is ruin is the result of a god's will bent upon harming
generation after generation until the whole race is in the end
destroyed. Not only is the thought Aeschylean but in the forms
of expression there are strong echoes of part of a chorus in
Aeschylus' *Seven against Thebes* (720–61), where the subject is, as
here, the hereditary curse on the descendants of Laius operating
against Oedipus and his sons. There we meet, as in Sophocles'
ode, the Ἐρινύc described as ὠλεcίοικοc, the Fury that destroys
a house; the recent woes mingled with the ancient; the metaphor
of the root-stock; the φρενώλης παράνοια, the madness that ruins
the brain; and the simile of the waves of doom. Sophocles
introduces this simile at 586 with a change of rhythm from
dactylo-epitrite to iambic, amplifying the brief Aeschylean
phrase so that it extends over the rest of the strophe, where it is
remarkable for the assonance and alliteration of its language and
its observation of visual details chosen to create a sustained
impression of storm, darkness, and depth as a contrast to the
enduring light on Olympus that illuminates the second strophe
(609 f.).

[29] 584, 624, and 614 = 625.

The antistrophe (594) refers the opening general statement to the particular instance. ἀρχαῖα is emphatic by position, and we may think of the woes of the Labdacid house over the generations: Laius' rape of Pelops' son Chrysippus and his neglect of the oracle warning him against the peril of begetting a child; Oedipus' murder of his father and marriage with his mother; his curse upon his sons and their slaughter of each other. Such are the successive strokes of doom, which allow no release to the race. The choice of language,

$$\pi\acute{\eta}\mu\alpha\tau\alpha\ \varphi\theta\iota\mu\acute{\epsilon}\nu\omega\nu\ \grave{\epsilon}\pi\grave{\iota}\ \pi\acute{\eta}\mu\alpha\sigma\iota\ \pi\acute{\iota}\pi\tau\nu\tau\alpha$$

'woes falling upon woes of the dead' (595) and the alliterative words continue the effect of the simile across the strophe and antistrophe; and the connection of the two stanzas is further assisted by an echo of thought and word in 585 and 596 f. With νῦν γάρ in 599 we reach the present situation of the play. Antigone and her projected marriage with Haemon represented a light of hope (φάος) for the continuance of the family; now in its turn it is extinguished.

This is not the place for an exhaustive discussion of the problem of κόνις, given by all manuscripts in 602 and accepted without question until the Reverend Dr John Jortin (1698–1770) proposed κοπίς, a meat-chopper, cleaver, or a Thessalian curved knife, a word which may therefore be thought out of place in high poetry, though it does appear in an iambic fragment of Sophocles in a simile describing an old man's temper as a μαλθακὴ κοπίς, quickly sharpened, quickly blunted.[30] The controversy between κόνις and κοπίς has continued for two centuries and is unlikely to be settled, though at the moment κοπίς is in the ascendant.[31] If κόνις is kept it must mean the dust scattered by Antigone on Polyneices' corpse, or perhaps, by a brachylogy for κόνις σκεδασθεῖσα, the act of scattering it, a rite due to the gods below. This dust mows down the last root (καταμᾷ, 601), a somewhat bizarre phrase, but perhaps not impossible in Greek metaphorical speech. If however the language is felt to be too forced, refuge may be taken in the alternative paraphrase of καταμᾷ in the ancient scholia, καλύπτει (conceals, buries), based no doubt on the epic use of the middle καταμήσασθαι, to heap up

[30] Fr. 894 P. Though the second line is corrupt, this appears to be the sense.
[31] See the editions, *passim*.

so as to cover (*Iliad* 24. 165). In this case the dust thrown over the
body smothers the light, νιν referring to φάος not ῥίζας. The most
formidable objection to κόνις lies in the fact that it has

$$λόγου \ τ' \ ἄνοια \ καὶ \ φρενῶν \ 'Ερινύς$$

in apposition to it, for dust could hardly be defined as folly in
speech and madness in the brain,[32] though if we can translate
κόνις 'the act of scattering', this objection largely disappears.
More readily intelligible sense is certainly provided by κοπίς:
the chthonic powers use a φοινία κοπίς, a murderous chopper, to
obliterate the last root-stock in the house of Oedipus, and this
instrument is defined by the apposition λόγου τ' ἄνοια καὶ φρενῶν
'Ερινύς, Antigone's mad act of burying her brother and her
justification of it in a foolish speech. Such is the unambiguous
judgement of the chorus, and their words echo Creon's description
of the sisters in 533 as δύ' ἄτα and his remark at 561:

$$τὼ \ παῖδέ \ φημι \ τώδε \ τὴν \ μὲν \ ἀρτίως$$
$$ἄνουν \ πεφάνθαι, \ τὴν \ δ' \ ἀφ' \ οὗ \ τὰ \ πρῶτ' \ ἔφυ$$

'As to these two girls, one of them has been proved a fool just
now, and the other from the moment she was born.' We may also
recall the coryphaeus's reaction to Antigone's appearance under
guard at the end of the first stasimon, especially ἐν ἀφροσύνῃ
καθελόντες, 'having caught you in act of folly' (383).

   The second strophic pair, composed in choriambic metres,
moves away from the particular instance and opens with an
acclamation of Zeus' power and its invincibility. The last
sentence (611 ff.) give an example of one of his laws, for the
asyndeton at 613 shows that νόμος ὅδε is defined by what follows.
The last line of the stanza is corrupt, but it is highly probable
that Sophocles wrote βίοτος πάμπολυς, 'abundant means of
livelihood',[33] in one word ὄλβος, as in Aeschylus' phrase at
Agamemnon 750 ff., μέγαν τελεσθέντα φωτὸς ὄλβον, 'man's prosperity grown great'.[34] This law reflects a traditional view that
excessive prosperity automatically involves ruin, a belief based
upon a primitive conception of φθόνος θεῶν, familiar enough in
earlier Greek literature, though refined somewhat by poets of the

---

[32] See Lloyd-Jones, *CQ* n.s. 7 (1957), 17 ff., for powerful arguments supporting κοπίς.
[33] Thus Lloyd-Jones, loc. cit. 19.
[34] Cf. ὄλβος ἄγαν παχυνθείς, Aesch. *Th.* 771.

fifth century who emphasized the importance of ὕβρις as a stage on the path to destruction, as Aeschylus does in the passage just quoted. The refinement of the crude idea of φθόνος θεῶν is indeed hinted at by the chorus in the word πάμπολυς, suggesting an excess which predisposes a man to sin. The aim of the strophe is certainly to contrast man's vulnerability with Zeus' unassailable power.

The final antistrophe amplifies in general terms the chorus's view of the act which has brought destruction on the house, and defines at the close in language bare of imagery the state of mind induced by the gods in a person whom they are driving to ruin; his judgement is so perverted that evil seems to him good (τὸ κακὸν δοκεῖν ποτ' ἐсθλόν, 622). The process is clearly described by Theognis, 402–6:

πολλάκι δ' εἰς ἀρετὴν
cπεύδει ἀνὴρ κέρδος διζήμενος, ὅντινα δαίμων
πρόφρων εἰς μεγάλην ἀμπλακίην παράγει
καὶ οἱ ἔθηκε δοκεῖν ἃ μὲν ᾖ κακά, ταῦτ' ἀγάθ' εἶναι
εὐμαρέως, ἃ δ' ἂν ᾖ χρήсιμα, ταῦτα κακά

'Often does a man in the search for profit pursue excellence and then willingly a god leads him astray into a great error, having easily made evil seem to him good and good evil.' These lines, like much of Theognis' advice to Cyrnus, represent a distillation of ancient wisdom, and form the best commentary on the anonymous κλεινὸν ἔπος with which Sophocles ends his ode. The association of ἐλπίς with ἀπάτη, apparent in the definition of hope as both a blessing and a delusion of light-headed desires (615 ff.) also has a long tradition behind it, for Hope in Hesiod's story of Pandora's box is without doubt sinister and treacherous.[35] Aeschylus associates the two with Ἄτη in the parodos of *Persae* (94–100), and as a final illustration of the impressive opening of this stanza we may quote some words from one of the more sophisticated writers of antiquity. Thucydides makes Diodotus say in the debate on Mytilene (iii. 45. 5–9):

ἥ τε ἐλπὶς καὶ ὁ ἔρως ἐπὶ παντί, ὁ μὲν ἡγούμενος, ἡ δ' ἐφεπομένη, καὶ ὁ μὲν τὴν ἐπιβουλὴν ἐκφροντίζων, ἡ δὲ τὴν εὐπορίαν τῆς τύχης ὑποτιθεῖcα, πλεῖcτα βλάπτουcι, καὶ ὄντα ἀφανῆ κρείccω ἐcτὶ τῶν ὁρωμένων δεινῶν,

[35] *Op.* 94 ff.

hope and desire in every case, desire leading, hope in attendance, desire thinking out the plan, hope suggesting that luck will provide the means, do most harm, and because they are unseen they are more powerful than dangers that can be seen.

The logic of Sophocles' ode requires us to relate its last stanza closely to the whole. The instrument used by the gods to obliterate the house of Oedipus and his fathers was described in the first antistrophe as

$$\lambda \acute{o} \gamma o \upsilon \ \tau\ ' \ \ddot{a} \nu o \iota a \ \kappa a \grave{\iota} \ \phi \rho \epsilon \nu \hat{\omega} \nu \ ' E \rho \iota \nu \acute{\upsilon} \varsigma.$$

In the final antistrophe the chorus present us with a generalized account of the advance to destruction of a mind thus afflicted. We see the deception of its hopes by thoughtless desires, its unawareness of the unseen fire beneath the ashes, and its blindness to a proper sense of moral judgements. Its doom within a short time is assured.

It may seem strange to us that Antigone's act, undertaken in high confidence with such deliberation and defended with such clarity of argument, should be regarded by the chorus as evidence of a mind impaired. Sophocles has however chosen to make the Theban elders in this ode the mouthpiece of views persistent in Greek thought from Homer well into his own times, and likely to be held by the older generation of Athenian citizens. There is nothing therefore in what the chorus say inconsistent with their role and status as old men. Further, as we have seen, Aeschylus had thus interpreted the doom of the house of Labdacus in a song which may well have been in Sophocles' mind. We should not however be induced by romantic conceptions of what Antigone has done into believing that the ode cannot possibly refer to her and must therefore refer to Creon.[36] He has not yet done or said anything that these elders could interpret as folly in words and madness in the brain, though in the sequel it is he who is going to be shown as the possessor of a mind deeply and irrevocably impaired. Therein lies the irony which is inherent to a greater or lesser extent in so many of Sophocles' odes. At this stage of the play however our thoughts are riveted upon Antigone and her deed; and the audience expects that the song will offer some reflections on the extinction of the house which that deed has

---

[36] See Gerhard Müller, *Sophokles, Antigone*, 135 ff.

ensured. The result is a magnificent ode which brings us close to the very heart of much of Sophoclean tragedy: man, for all his confidence and his high hopes, is deluded by his passions and doomed to suffer, while the 'President of the Immortals'[37] occupies the radiance of Olympus, omnipotent, ageless, and merciless.

There are striking contrasts in style, structure, and thought between this stasimon and the first. This song, while displaying a similar economy of language, glows with a richness and splendour of imagery absent from πολλὰ τὰ δεινά. The darkness and depth of the detailed simile in the first strophe has its foil in the φάος that hung above the last root of the house (600) and to a greater degree in the blaze of light which surrounds Zeus on Olympus (609). There is an exploitation also of the effect of sound contrasts: in the simile the alliterations and the clash of sibilants suggest the tumult of the seas beating upon the headlands, while in the second strophe the sound of the long vowels, especially ω and η, and the echo in παντογήρως and ἀγήρως indicate the ageless tranquillity of Zeus' abode. Further, in the structure of its thought πολλὰ τὰ δεινά is dynamic in its development, moving to a climax at the end, whereas εὐδαίμονες οἷσι κακῶν is static, composed mainly of amplifications of a theme stated at the beginning: the advance of ἄτη is illustrated by a simile, the general statement of the first strophe by the particular reference in the antistrophe; the law of Zeus is carefully defined at the end of the second strophe, and the last antistrophe clarifies λόγου τ' ἄνοια καὶ φρενῶν Ἐρινύς. Neither the changing pattern of light and shade nor the development of themes already stated has any counterpart in the mounting tension of the previous ode.

As to the content of thought in the two songs, Sophocles draws for the main idea in the first upon contemporary opinion in an endeavour to show how man can achieve the high end of his existence as a successful member of a city, so that the mood of the audience at the end is one of confidence for his future. In the second, the dramatist is concerned rather with ancient beliefs and the doctrine of the hereditary curse, potent in each generation until it has worked itself out in its last victim. The

---

[37] μακάρων πρύτανις, Aesch. *Pr.* 169, is thus translated by Thomas Hardy on the last page of *Tess of the d'Urbervilles*.

emphasis is on θεός intent upon destroying a family in dark, irrational ways which may seem to us morally repugnant, and the pessimism thus generated contradicts the confidence of the earlier song. The two odes thus guide the audience's emotions in contrasting directions at critical stages in the play, and taken together, present two conflicting views of man's destiny, one depicting his advance towards civilised life, the other revealing his inherent vulnerability.

The third stasimon (781–800) is sung to an empty stage, Creon having left at 780 to arrange for Antigone's entombment. He re-enters at the end of the commos in time to hear her closing words (880 ff.), as is clear from his opening lines at 883 f. In the song the chorus comment on the quarrel between father and son, τόδε νεῖκος ἀνδρῶν ξύναιμον (793), ascribing it to the power of "Ἔρως, whose effect is to drive its victims mad, ὁ δ᾽ ἔχων μέμηνεν (790). They say nothing at all about Haemon's main point, that public opinion is wholly on Antigone's side, or about his sole expressed motive, concern for his father's interests; nor do they refer to Creon's reactions to his son's speech, which reveal a mind so limited, bigoted, and tyrannical as to forfeit all respect. Their remark at 791

> cὺ καὶ δικαίων ἀδίκους
> φρένας παρασπᾷς ἐπὶ λώβᾳ

'It is you ("Ἔρως) who drag the minds of even just men into injustice to their ruin', records their views of love's perverting effect on just men. Shocked by the violent turn the quarrel had taken after the two opening speeches which they themselves had commended (681 f. and 724 f.), they can think of no other explanation than that it is the work of "Ἔρως. Haemon himself, even when taunted by Creon as μιαρὸν ἦθος καὶ γυναικὸς ὕστερον (746) and γυναικὸς δούλευμα (756), taunts which imply that in his father's opinion he was enslaved to his passion for Antigone, says nothing of his love for her, and this has led to the suggestion that love has nothing to do with his motive.[38] It is however not easy to account for his threat in 751 or for his behaviour in the cave, described by the messenger (1223–37), unless this love, alluded to by Ismene in 570, was in fact among his motives.

---

[38] See K. von Fritz, *Antike und Moderne Tragödie*, 227 ff. and 234 ff.

Whether the chorus are right or wrong in ascribing the quarrel to "Ερως (cὺ καὶ τόδε νεῖκος ἀνδρῶν ξύναιμον ἔχεις ταράξας, 793 f.), the fact remains that they have ignored the whole moral basis of Haemon's arguments. Sophocles' purpose, one suspects, was twofold: first, to make the chorus suggest the motive which he had been careful to exclude from Haemon's own arguments in order not to weaken his moral position in the conflict with his father, and secondly, to bring out the irony latent in implying at 791 that he has been driven into injustice by "Ερως when it will be shown later that his advice to his father was in fact just and correct. Moreover, the relegation of this motive to the song ensures that attention is not distracted from the main issues by the introduction of a subsidiary theme into the quarrel scene.

The ode, consisting of a single strophic pair in choriambic metres, is composed in the traditional form of a hymn. The subject of such hymns, whether a god or an abstract power, is addressed at the beginning, diversified by attributes in apposition or in a series of relative clauses giving instances of its functions and emphasizing their range. Another famous hymn to "Ερως, at Euripides' *Hippolytus* 525, has, in addition to these features, a prayer after the address and two examples from myth to illustrate Love at work. Sophocles' song however contains neither prayer nor myth; like Euripides' second hymn to Love in *Hippolytus* (1268 ff.), it is all predication, and as in that hymn, the subject shifts between "Ερως and 'Αφροδίτη without any appreciable difference in meaning. It is the habit also of such hymns to end with a return to the power apostrophized at the start, often, as in Sophocles' ode, with a verbal echo: "Ερως ἀνίκατε μάχαν and ἄμαχος... 'Αφροδίτα. The absence in this hymn of an imperative, optative, or infinitive of request affects its grammatical structure: the vocative, defined by two relative clauses, is left suspended at 786 and succeeded by statements in which the repeated second-person pronouns are prominent, so that we have a type of anacoluthon, as in the splendid hymn to the lyre which opens Pindar's first *Pythian Ode*.

The instances selected to illustrate the domination of "Ερως occupy the whole of the first strophe and are a commonplace of all poetry. At the beginning of the Homeric Hymn to Aphrodite (probably seventh century B.C.), in addition to the control she exercises over gods and men, we are told how she subdues

οἰωνούς τε διπετέας καὶ θηρία πάντα
ἠμὲν ὅς' ἤπειρος πολλὰ τρέφει ἠδ' ὅσα πόντος,

'birds that fly in the air, and all the many creatures that live on dry land and in the sea'. The same theme appears throughout Greek poetry of every type, notably in the iambic fragment 941 P of Sophocles. In Latin it occurs in extended form in the great hymn which opens Lucretius' *De Rerum Natura*, where Venus is described as coming first upon birds, then upon wild beasts and cattle, *ferae, pecudes*, and finally advancing her sway over all creation. Most of these passages have one feature in common: they give a more or less stereotyped list of creatures that feel the power of love and that inhabit the three elements of earth, sea, and air: gods, men, and animals wild and tame; fish; and birds, though in Sophocles' ode birds are missing and fish are represented solely by the sea over which love ranges (φοιτᾷς ὑπερπόντιος, 785). This feature may help us to interpret κτήμασι, given by all the manuscripts in 782. ὃς ἐν κτήμασι πίπτεις has caused a lot of trouble. Both the immediate context and the convention illustrated by the examples quoted suggest that the reference is to something living and that such translations as 'make havoc of wealth or possessions' in an inanimate sense may be wrong. This view led Brunck to suggest κτήνεσι, cattle, which Pearson accepts, because the examples[39] quoted for κτήματα meaning cattle hardly support such a translation. We may finally note how Sophocles has in this strophe imposed his own poetic imagination on the catalogue in the detail of 783 f.

ὃς ἐν μαλακαῖς παρειαῖς
νεάνιδος ἐννυχεύεις

'you who sleep upon a maiden's soft cheeks', echoing a phrase of Phrynichus[40] admired by Sophocles who has transformed it into an original *lumen ingenii* by the verb ἐννυχεύεις.[41] Moreover its beauty is enhanced by its setting between the violence of ἐν κτήνεσι πίπτεις and the more general terms that follow it. The climax is reached in the last line with the emphatic statement ὁ δ' ἔχων μέμηνεν.

---

[39] Pl. *Grg.* 484 c and *Phd.* 62 b. See Chantraine, *RPh* 20 (1946), 1–11.

[40] λάμπει δ' ἐπὶ πορφυρέαις παρῇσι φῶς ἔρωτος Fr. 13 N.

[41] Cf. Horace's echo, *Odes*, iv. 13. 8, 'pulchris excubat in genis' of Cupid.

In the antistrophe the particular application of the general apostrophe of Ἔρως is introduced by two parallel statements that continue the hymn formula in the repeated pronouns cὺ καὶ ... cὺ καὶ ... The quarrel, all the more deplorable in the Greek view when between men of the same blood, father and son, is the work of Ἔρως (793 f.). The rest of the ode amplifies the point in a sentence beginning emphatically with the word νικᾷ which has as its subjects ἵμερος, desire visible in the maiden's eyes: the direct sensual impulse of sex is victorious.[42] The appositional phrase τῶν μεγάλων πάρεδρος ἐν ἀρχαῖς θεcμῶν imparts a certain magisterial quality to ἵμερος, who is seated beside οἱ μεγάλοι θεcμοί, the great laws or ordinances, like a partner in office, as in Euripides' phrase at *Andromache* 699,

cεμνοὶ δ᾽ ἐν ἀρχαῖς ἥμενοι κατὰ πτόλιν

used literally of magistrates. This metaphor, from officials sitting either as equal partners (cύνεδροι, cύνθακοι) or as assessors to a supreme magistrate (πάρεδροι), is common in Greek and found in exalted contexts to describe the mutual relationships of gods and abstract powers. For instance, in Sophocles, apart from this passage in *Antigone*, it appears twice in *Oedipus at Colonus*. Αἰδώς, compassion, is Ζηνὶ cύνθακος θρόνων, a partner of Zeus' throne at 1267, and at 1382 Δίκη is ξύνεδρος Ζηνὸς ἀρχαίοις νόμοις, enthroned with Zeus' ancient laws. The frequency of this type of phrase is enough of itself to confirm the manuscript tradition in 799 of this ode against all attempts to alter it.[43] The famous passage in Euripides' *Medea* (843) is close to Sophocles, in that Ἔρωτας are there described as τᾷ Cοφίᾳ παρέδρους παντοίας ἀρετᾶς ξυνέργους, desires, partners of Cοφίᾳ working together to create every type of excellence, a remarkable phrase which looks forward to the Platonic sublimation of sex into every kind of creative activity.[44] Sophocles however limits his use of Ἔρως/ἵμερος to sexual desire, acknowledges its power, and applies to it a familiar metaphor: τῶν μεγάλων πάρεδρος ἐν ἀρχαῖς θεcμῶν, 'seated in office beside the great θεcμοί'. Some light may be thrown on the association of ἵμερος with the μεγάλοι θεcμοί by

[42] For the eyes as a source of love, cf. Aesch. *Pr.* 654; Soph. *Trach.* 107, Frs. 157, 474, 801 P.; Eur. *Hipp.* 525.
[43] For πάρεδρος, cf. also Pi. *O.* 2. 76 (of Rhadamanthys); *O.* 8. 22 (of Themis); Ar. *Av.* 1753.
[44] Cf. e.g. *Smp.* 210–12. See Pearson, *CQ* 22 (1928), 184.

the difficult and possibly corrupt passage in Aeschylus' *Supplices*, 1034 ff.[45] where marriage is described as Κύπριδος θεςμὸς ὅδ' εὔφρων, 'this kindly law of Cypris', which with Hera wields power very close to Zeus. If θεςμός can be kept here,[46] love and marriage are one of the θεςμοί, as indeed in *Odyssey* 23. 296 of Odysseus and Penelope, λέκτροιο παλαιοῦ θεςμὸν ἵκοντο. In a more general sense, the word θεςμός covers both divine and human law in Greek usage, not of course only the institutions of love and marriage, and the definite article τῶν at 799 of Sophocles' ode suggests that they are here something perfectly well known and understood. Ordinances, interpreted in conflicting ways, play an important part in *Antigone*: for Creon they are such principles of conduct as loyalty to the ruler and the laws of the state, and in the quarrel scene which precedes this ode we find also the rule of obedience to parents to which Haemon as well as his father subscribes. In the last sentence of the song the chorus are asserting that ἵμερος is a πάρεδρος of the great rules of conduct and in Haemon's case has gained the victory over its partners in the conflict between father and son. The final words

$$\text{ἄμαχος γὰρ ἐμπαί-}$$
$$\text{ζει θεὸς 'Αφροδίτα}$$

sum up the point of the whole ode: Aphrodite is invincible, ἄμαχος reinforcing ἀνίκατε μάχαν, ςε . . . φεύξιμος οὐδείς, and νικᾷ, and she makes sport among her victims. There may be felt in the verb ἐμπαίζει an almost playful tone which corrects the solemnity of the phrase in the preceding lines and lightens the mood of the whole song at the end. The mockery of Aphrodite is a theme of Greek poetry from Sappho's hymn to the conceits of the Alexandrians.

The view taken of love in this ode is traditional throughout archaic and classical Greek literature, and Sophocles is no exception. To him "Ερως was an all-subduing force, as we may see from the iambic fragment 941 P, where he describes it as ἄφθιτος βία, λύςςα μανιάς, ἵμερος ἄκρατος, οἰμωγμός, indestructible force, raging madness, desire untempered, lamentation, whose influence permeates the whole of living creation:

---

[45] I owe this ref. to Professor Lloyd-Jones.
[46] Page prints Scaliger's ἔςμος in the OCT of 1972.

εἰςέρχεται μὲν ἰχθύων πλωτῷ γένει,
χέρςου δ᾽ ἔνεςτιν ἐν τετραςκελεῖ γονῇ,
νωμᾷ δ᾽ ἐν οἰωνοῖςι τοὐκείνης πτερόν,
ἐν θηρςίν, ἐν βροτοῖςιν, ἐν θεοῖς ἄνω.

In *Trachiniae*, Heracles' love for Iole and by implication for all
the other women he had had is called by Deianira a νόςος (445
and 544), and she also says (441 f.) that whoever fights against
"Ερως is a fool. There is therefore nothing romantic or chivalrous
about the concept of Love presented in this ode, nor do the
chorus, although their song is in the form of a hymn, praise it in
any way. They regard it quite objectively; they give it a certain
solemnity, they note its invincible power and its mockery, and in
implying that it is a madness (790) and saying that it forces the
minds of just men into injustice, they deny that it has any ethical
content whatsoever.

The hymn to "Ερως has little to do with the main issue of the
play, though Sophocles' emphasis on Love as a force that leads to
madness and ruinous action may remind us of λόγου τ᾽ ἄνοια καὶ
φρενῶν Ἐρινύς in the previous ode. The relevance of the song is
in fact strictly limited, for it touches on a theme which occupies
a very subordinate place, emerging for a moment in the exchange
between Creon and Ismene at 568–73,[47] in the coryphaeus's
anapaests announcing Haemon's entry at 628–30, in some of
Creon's taunts as the quarrel reaches its climax (740, 746, 756),
and finally in the messenger's account of Haemon's behaviour on
finding Antigone's body in the cave (1223 ff.). Unlike the two
preceding songs, it does not comment on any problem essential
to the plot, for it ignores all the ethical implications of what
Creon and Haemon said to each other in their set speeches.
Instead, it fastens upon one aspect of the previous scene, the
violence of the quarrel, and offers an explanation for it. The
contribution made by the song to dramatic irony has already
been mentioned. Apart from that its interest is mainly
psychological, for it allows us a glimpse of the conflict within
Haemon between his duty to his father and his love for Antigone.
It also affords a moment of relief from profound issues as the
tragedy advances. It is a work of great beauty composed in the
easily grasped form of a hymn to a familiar human instinct and

[47] The manuscripts are right in assigning 572 to Ismene.

set by Sophocles with consummate art between the tension of the
quarrel scene and the moving pathos of the following commos.

Immediately upon the end of the ode Antigone enters under
guard, and on seeing her the chorus give way to tears. The close
connection between the song and the anapaests is made clear by
the repetition of θεcμῶν in 802. As in Haemon's case it was ἵμεροc
which overruled the principles of behaviour, so in theirs it is an
upsurge of pity at the sight of Antigone, a pity which is however,
in order to emphasize her isolation, suppressed when the commos
begins. In form the scene is epirrhematic: anapaests from the
coryphaeus introduce Antigone, interrupt her lyrics between the
strophe and antistrophe, and close the first strophic pair. In the
second pair the chorus change to lyric iambics, so that this part
is wholly sung, and there is no contrast between sung and recited
utterance. The scene ends with an epode from Antigone. Her
lyrics become more varied and complicated in metre as the
commos progresses: the first pair is purely choriambic, the second
combines choriambic and iambic rhythms, and the epode
contains a dactylic line in the middle (879), the rest being iambic
and choriambic. Communication between the participants is
quick and complete at all stages and especially in Antigone's
immediate responses οἴμοι γελῶμαι and ἔψαυcαc at 839 and 857;
and her epode is a summing up of the whole. While there is no
appreciable difference in the language used by her and by the
chorus, her lyrics naturally attain to a higher degree of emotion,
especially in the second strophic pair with its echo of the
exclamations ἰώ twice in the same places (844 = 863, 850 = 869).
The two sung iambic utterances of the chorus (853–6 = 872–5)
are noteworthy for the alliteration of π in the first and the
rhyming ends of the two central cola (μέλει, πέλει) in the second.
Together they give an effect of solemnity and calm authority in
contrast with her distress.

In order to clarify the chorus's view of Antigone's predicament
in this scene, certain of their statements must be considered in
some detail. She is on her way to imprisonment in the cave,
leaving the light of the sun, her hopes of marriage gone; and she
appeals to the chorus to look upon her as she goes. Instead of
joining in her lamentations, they remark on the fame and praise
she will get for having died no ordinary death by disease or in
battle, but because while still alive (ζῶcα in 821 echoes her ζῶcαν

in 811), and thus unique among mortals, she will go down to Hades αὐτόνομος. This word, emphatic by position at the beginning of the clause, is usually translated 'of your own free will', but this is not adequate. True enough, at her last appearance she had insisted to Ismene that she had chosen death:

$$cὺ \ μὲν \ γὰρ \ εἵλου \ ζῆν, \ ἐγὼ \ δὲ \ κατθανεῖν \qquad (555)$$

'You chose to live, but I to die', so with this translation the word has a plausible reference back. The normal usage of αὐτόνομος however suggests that the chorus regard Antigone as making her own laws independently of the laws of the state in which she lives, as if she were a sort of state within a state. They will then be thinking especially of the speech in which she defended herself in front of Creon (450–57), where she explicitly rejected the state's laws in favour of the unwritten laws of the gods which alone she obeys. Antigone herself refers again to the state's laws in 847 (οἵοις νόμοις) as responsible for her punishment, and the chorus's final words to her in 875 repeat in αὐτόγνωτος ὀργά, 'a temper which makes its own decisions', the idea inherent in αὐτόνομος. The theme of a conflict between laws which is fundamental to the play is thus made as explicit in the commos as it has been in previous scenes.

In the antistrophe (823) Antigone compares herself to Niobe in the manner of her death.[48] In reply the chorus (834), not without a hint of reproof (τοι), point out that she, a mortal, is likening herself to an immortal, but offer her the assurance of posthumous fame. She reacts to this with a bitter outburst οἴμοι γελῶμαι (839): she regards the promise of renown after death as a mockery, even an insult (ὑβρίζεις, 841). What she is looking for is not only sympathy for her present predicament but also an acknowledgement from the chorus that what she has done is right. Towards the end of her scene with Creon (504 ff.), she expressed confidence that the Theban elders approved of her act but dared not say so through fear. She has not heard Haemon tell his father that public opinion is on her side, so she is in fact unaware that the people of Thebes think her deserving of honour instead of death for what she has done (692–700), and she dies

---

[48] For the Niobe paradeigma cf. *El.* 150 f. Sophocles wrote a *Niobe*, Frs. 442–5 P. See W. S. Barrett in *The Papyrus Fragments of Sophocles*, ed. Richard Carden (Berlin and New York, 1974).

believing that she has acted βίᾳ πολιτῶν ('despite the citizens', 907). By such means does Sophocles emphasizes the irony, the loneliness, and the bitter pathos of her position. She next appeals with heightened emotion to her city and its elders:

> ὦ πόλις, ὦ πόλεως
> πολυκτήμονες ἄνδρες.

Then, convinced that they have no word of comfort for her, she calls upon inanimate things, the springs of Dirce and Thebe's grove, for additional witness to her lack of friends to mourn her and to the sort of laws that have condemned her, ἰὼ ... ξυμμάρτυρας ὔμμ᾽ ἐπικτῶμαι (844–9). ἰώ here, as so often in Greek tragedy, is a call for support from one in need or distress. Her strophe closes with an elaboration of the concept of the living death, a theme which appears at intervals throughout the commos.

The chorus's reply, 852 ff., has been interpreted in two completely different ways. According to the majority of scholars it means that Antigone has advanced to the limit of audacity and stumbled against the lofty pedestal of Justice (ὑψηλὸν ἐς Δίκας βάθρον, 854), which stops the march of the transgressor. On this view the chorus are condemning her for what they consider is a bold trespass against Dike, here equated perhaps with the laws of the state which she has disobeyed. Elsewhere in the play however Dike is separated from these laws by the chorus themselves in 368 f., by Antigone in 451, and by the chorus again in their remark to Creon at 1270,

> οἴμ᾽ ὡς ἔοικας ὀψὲ τὴν δίκην ἰδεῖν

'Alas! too late it seems you have seen the right.' Further, in 872 ff. they acknowledge Antigone's piety, and it is perhaps strange that they could at such a short interval describe her behaviour both as a transgression and as an act of piety. Moreover, linguistic objections have been raised against taking προσέπεσες ἐς in the sense 'stumble against', for elsewhere the verb is found, with the dative, of a suppliant falling at an altar or at the knees of the person to whom he appeals.[49] These considerations have suggested an alternative interpretation, that

---

[49] Cf. *Trach.* 904; *O.C.* 1157.

Antigone has boldly advanced and prostrated herself as a
suppliant before the altar of Dike and that the chorus are
thinking in particular of

$$\dot{\eta} \ \xi\dot{\nu}\nu o\iota\kappa o\varsigma \ \tau\hat{\omega}\nu \ \kappa\acute{\alpha}\tau\omega \ \theta\epsilon\hat{\omega}\nu \ \varDelta\acute{\iota}\kappa\eta$$

to which she referred in 451.[50] If this interpretation can be
accepted, the chorus's reply will mean that the Theban elders do
in fact recognise the justice of her act. The advantage of this view
is that it gives a pertinent reference back to Antigone's own
words in 451 and removes the apparent inconsistency in the
chorus's ascription to her of a trespass and an act of piety.

Lesky's interpretation is however unlikely to be right for the
following reasons. First, on the linguistic point, the translation
'fall as a suppliant at the altar' fails to do justice to the
combination of πρoς and ἐς which strongly suggests a rush
towards an object ending in a collision. More important is that
similar passages in Aeschylus indicate that the chorus are indeed
regarding Antigone's act as a trespass. At *Agamemnon* 381–4 there
is a reference to the man who has kicked into oblivion the great
altar of Dike, μέγαν Δίκας βωμόν; at *Eumenides* 539 f. the chorus
proclaim the commandment

$$\beta\omega\mu\grave{o}\nu \ \alpha\grave{\iota}\delta\acute{\epsilon}\sigma\alpha\iota \ \varDelta\acute{\iota}\kappa\alpha\varsigma$$

and state that punishment will fall upon him who spurns it with
impious foot, ἀθέῳ ποδί. Later in the same ode (564) with a
change of metaphor, destruction awaits the man who has
wrecked his prosperity on the reef of Dike,

$$\tau\grave{o}\nu \ \pi\rho\grave{\iota}\nu \ \acute{o}\lambda\beta o\nu$$
$$\acute{\epsilon}\rho\mu\alpha\tau\iota \ \pi\rho o\sigma\beta\alpha\lambda\grave{\omega}\nu \ \varDelta\acute{\iota}\kappa\alpha\varsigma \ldots$$

Whether the metaphor in these passages is from an altar which
demands reverence or a reef which sets a limit to the transgressor's
career, the point is the same: Dike is not a power at whose feet
men fall in suppliance but a power who stops a trespasser to his
hurt. So in our passage of *Antigone* the ὑψηλὸν Δίκας βάθρον may
be envisaged as a pedestal upon which stands the figure of Dike.
She stops Antigone in her wild career as she runs against it with
her foot. Taking a cue from Aeschylus' ἀθέῳ ποδί, we should

[50] Lesky, *Hermes* 80 (1952), 98 = *Ges. Schriften*, 176 ff.

accept ποδί for πολύ in 855 and keep the manuscripts' order, reading the line thus:

$$προcέπεcεc \ \overset{\circ}{ω} \ τεκνον \ ποδί.^{51}$$

Another point in favour of the 'trespass' interpretation is that it suits better the phrase

$$προβᾶc᾽ ἐπ᾽ ἔcχατον \ θράcουc$$

which, with θράcοc in its usual sense of rash audacity, is more appropriate to a bold trespasser running against a barrier in his path than to a suppliant approaching an altar. Finally, this interpretation is in keeping with the chorus's clearly expressed judgements on Antigone's character in 821 (αὐτόνομος), and 875 (cὲ δ᾽ αὐτόγνωτος ὤλεc᾽ ὀργά), and further back in the play ὠμὸν γέννημα in 471 f. The image of a suppliant falling in an act of worship before an altar would not suit one who is described in the commos as making her own laws and as destroyed by a self-willed temperament defying the state's authority.

It remains to consider as precisely as possible what the chorus mean here by Δίκη. At first sight it appears that they are equating it with the laws of the state, the νόμοι χθονός which Antigone has disobeyed. However, the grandiloquence of the phrase ὑψηλὸν Δίκας βάθρον and the Aeschylean contexts in which similar ideas are expressed suggest the larger concept of a cosmic order[52] embracing the laws of the state and the unwritten laws of the gods, both of which must be observed if disorder and anarchy are not to result. Such indeed was the chorus' conclusion at the end of the first stasimon which presented the ideal of a non-conflicting society as man's supreme achievement. In this play this order or harmony has been upset as much by Antigone as it will be shown to have been by Creon. In fact much of the tragic power of Sophoclean drama arises from the tendency of his characters to disturb a balanced order of things; and this applies as much to the heroic and the righteous as to the weak, the wrong-headed, and the wicked. Both types pay for their acts of disturbance, and Dike is restored at a terrible cost. The ultimate identity of the

---

[51] ποδί was suggested by Bruhn in his edition of 1913. See also J. U. Powell, *CQ* 21 (1927), 176.

[52] See H. D. F. Kitto, *Sophocles, Dramatist and Philosopher*, 47 ff. on this aspect of Δίκη; also Lloyd-Jones, *The Justice of Zeus*, 128, in reference to Sophocles. For Δίκη as the Order of the Universe, cf. Anaximander Fr. 1 DK.

moral and the cosmic aspects of Dike is not revealed in this play until Antigone, the righteous, has been removed by death, and Creon, the wrong-headed, broken by suffering. Perhaps the most impressive description of Dike in Sophocles is to be found at *O.C.* 1381 f.:

$$ἡ παλαίφατος$$
$$Δίκη, ξύνεδρος Ζηνὸς ἀρχαίοις νόμοις.$$

These words stress the antiquity of her tradition in Greek thought (παλαίφατος), and her close association with Zeus' ancient laws.

In her reply (857 ff.) Antigone accepts the point just made by the chorus, that she is atoning for her act with an ordeal transmitted from her forefathers, and reviews the woes that have fallen on the generations of the Labdacid house down to herself and Polyneices, acknowledging that she is going to her death under a curse, ἀραῖος (867). This word shows the extent to which she feels herself to be the victim of the family curse described with such power in the second stasimon. At 872 ff. the chorus state in unequivocal terms the central conflict of the play: to honour the dead (cέβειν has this specific meaning here) is an act of piety of a sort (εὐcέβειά τις), but authority, in whomsoever vested, is not to be transgressed. κράτος is here not regarded as vested in a particular person, so that no approval of Creon is implied. The proposition, put in the most general terms possible, is not a moral judgement but a statement of fact: when authority is transgressed, punishment follows. In this particular case, Antigone has transgressed it; the decision to do so was her own; she has this kind of temperament, and it has destroyed her. αὐτόγνωτος echoes αὐτόνομος in 821. The two words together sum up the formidable quality of her character,[53] and on the evidence of the play so far the summing up is correct. Again, no moral judgement is implied either of approval or of disapproval: the facts are stated as they appear to the chorus. Their final remark makes it clear that even though, as they stated in the second stasimon and in 856 above, she is the victim of the family curse, they do not regard her as an involuntary agent: the decision to act as she did in an individual case is her own responsibility. Such is the normal view of the Greek tragedians

---

[53] 'Questa terribile eroina', Perrotta, *Sofocle*, 113.

on the subject of free choice: even when the individual is admittedly an instrument of the family curse, his personal initiative is stressed when he takes action that furthers its operation. The concluding epode (876–82), sung by Antigone when she sees the guards making ready to take her away, leaves us with an abiding sense of her desolation.

This desolation is in fact the outstanding tragic effect achieved by Sophocles in this scene. It is moreover a culmination to which previous scenes from the beginning of the play have contributed. Antigone has from her initial appearance been shown as sundered from those with whom she is in contact: first from Ismene, both in the prologue and in the scene in which she rejects her sister's offer to share her death (536–60), then from Creon, especially at 499–501, and finally from the chorus, whose support we must believe her to have counted on (504–9). The one person whose comfort she might have accepted, Haemon, is not shown with her on the stage, and we can judge of her relationship with him only from Ismene's incidental remarks (570 and 572) and from her own lamentations over the loss of marriage (813–16; 867; 876). These are however in purely general terms of regret that she cannot fulfil her womanhood in marriage, and they express no personal feeling for him. The expression of such emotions by her would have been alien to the mood of the play. The sense of Antigone's desolation must not be diminished in any way at her last appearance. Sophocles has been most careful to provide for this in the commos: the chorus neither join in her lamentations nor express sympathy for her point of view; those of her kin who would have mourned for her are dead; the living whom she has met in the play either do not understand her or are rejected by her; and Haemon, who could have assured her of the support of public opinion, is kept apart from her. These points she makes in the epode, a powerful concentration of expressions she has used earlier in the scene. She repeats some of these thoughts in her final iambic speech (891–928), especially those which draw attention to her loneliness: loss of fulfilment in marriage, lack of friends to mourn her, and the living death she faces (916–20), so that in any discussion of the authenticity of this speech account must be taken of its close connection with the commos and of the state of mind her lyrics there reveal as well as of her character and principles of conduct as shown earlier in the play. Nor must we forget that, for all her distress, she remains on the brink of death still formidable and heroic.[54]

When we turn to the chorus's part in the commos we find that, detached as they are from Antigone by age, sex, and status, they express views on what she has done that are consistent with what we have learned of their role in the play and with Sophocles' dramatic purpose in this scene. We might have expected them to have made use of Haemon's speech in which they had heard him record popular support for her, but that would have lessened the isolation, irony, and pathos of her situation. In judging her act, they state, if the interpretation given above of 854 ff. is correct, that she has advanced to the limit of audacity and stumbled to her hurt against the pedestal of Dike; and after admitting, perhaps grudgingly, that in honouring the dead she has shown piety of a sort, they then proclaim in solemn and impressive terms that authority is not to be transgressed. This is a belief held sincerely by them and no doubt acceptable to most of the Athenians who saw the play. They attribute her destruction first to the family curse to which she owes a debt of suffering and then to a temperament which induces her to make her own decision. The first cause recalls the explanation given in the second stasimon, the second, together with αὐτόνομος (821), is a true account, by people in the chorus's position, of the character she has presented of herself in the play. In thus combining these two explanations of her conduct the chorus reflect the Aeschylean view that when the gods have afflicted a house with a curse that must eventually destroy it, the individual is nevertheless responsible for his choice of action at each stage in the chain of destruction. The attitude of the chorus to Antigone may appear cold, even cruel, in its objective statement of the facts: we, no less than she herself, may have been looking for a warmer sympathy, a more unqualified acknowledgement that she is right, but Sophocles is not ready for that yet. The tension of the play requires final judgement to be postponed and to emerge, not in the chorus's words in this scene, but from the subsequent action, when Teiresias has revealed the full horror of Creon's impiety, and Antigone, Haemon, and Eurydice are dead. The maintenance of this tension is essential to the unity of the play, and to

---

[54] Compare the epode of the commos and 916–20 of her speech with its closing words (927 f.), the coryphaeus's remark (929) and her own final anapaests, 940–43.

keep it alive is an important function of the chorus in the commos. In addition, any relaxation of it by a display of sympathy with Antigone would diminish her sense of loneliness and weaken the scene's tragic impact. Finally, like the first two stasima, the commos, especially in its statement of the central conflict (853–875), forces concentration on the moral and intellectual content of the tragedy.

In the brief anapaestic conversation that separates Antigone's speech from the fourth stasimon, the coryphaeus, impressed by the tone of her last two lines (927 f.), realizes that there is no change in her defiant attitude. Distress has not weakened her spirit. Her doom is ratified beyond hope of reprieve (935). While there can be no doubt that this sentence must be given to Creon, not the coryphaeus, to whom an ancient scholium suggests it can be assigned, it is strange to find that 933 f. has been given by some scholars, including Pearson, to the coryphaeus. After Creon's threat to the guards for their reluctance to take her away, it must be Antigone who cries out at the imminence of her death, because a cry of distress ($οἴμοι$) from the coryphaeus would be inconsistent with the chorus' attitude in the commos. Moreover, if the words are given to the coryphaeus, we should miss the final sharp contrast between her distress and her defiance which is a strongly marked feature of the commos and of her last speech.

The ode which follows at 944 is a direct reply to Antigone's appeal to the Theban elders to witness the sufferings that await her at the hands of Creon and his guards ($οἷα πρὸς οἵων ἀνδρῶν πάσχω$, 942) in return for her act of piety,

$$τὴν εὐσεβίαν σεβίσασα.$$

They do not answer her call in the way she might expect, whether by a sustained expression of sympathy in the form of a lament, or by confirming her own belief that she is right and Creon wrong. Instead, they offer her three examples, $παραδείγ$-$ματα$, by way of encouraging her to submit to her fate. The opening words of the song, $ἔτλα καί$, are a formula and indicate at the outset the type to which it belongs. The three examples chosen, Danae, Lycurgus, and Cleopatra, are all of noble birth, like Antigone, who referred to herself in 941 as

$$τὴν βασιλειδᾶν μούνην λοιπήν$$

a point taken up by the chorus in each of the examples: καίτοι καὶ
γενεᾷ τίμιος (948), Ἠδωνῶν βασιλεύς (956), and ἃ δὲ σπέρμα ...
Ἐρεχθειδᾶν (981).[55] Gnomic comment is confined to one
conventional thought, the inevitability of fate, stated twice,
elaborately at the end of the first strophe, and succinctly, with a
word echo, in the last sentence of the song:

> ἀλλ᾽ ἁ μοιριδία τις
> δύνασις δεινά   (951 f.)

and

> ἀλλὰ κἀπ᾽ ἐκείνᾳ
> Μοῖραι μακραίωνες ἔσχον   (986 f.)

The presence of this one maxim, twice repeated, and the absence
of all other comment show that the ode has a single purpose: to
exhort Antigone to submit to her fate by the example of three
persons of high birth who also had to submit. That it is addressed
solely and personally to Antigone is proved by the repeated ὦ
παῖ παῖ in 948 and by ὦ παῖ as its last words (987).

Exhortations of this type, supported by examples, are a fixed
element in Greek literature from the earliest times, beginning
with Dione's speech to her daughter Aphrodite who had
complained to her mother when wounded by Diomedes.[56] Three
examples, Ares, Hera, and Hades, of wounded deities, each
introduced by the word τλῆ, are presented to Aphrodite with the
implication that she should take courage from being in such
company. Similarly, Clytaemnestra attempts to reconcile Cassandra to slavery by pointing out that even Heracles endured to
be sold as a slave (πραθέντα τλῆναι).[57] An important feature of
this use of myth for exhortation is the often very tenuous point
of contact between the examples chosen and the detailed stories
and personalities of the people exhorted. Only a very general
similarity at one or two points is required. Thus in the Homeric
passage there is nothing in common between Aphrodite and the
other three deities except the facts of divinity and of physical

---

[55] Danae was a daughter of Acrisius, son of Abas, King of Argos, and Cleopatra was
an Athenian princess, a granddaughter of Erectheus, King of Athens. For Lycurgus, cf.
Il. 6. 130 ff. Aeschylus wrote a trilogy about his story.
[56] *Il.* 5. 384 ff.
[57] Aesch. *A.* 1041.

hurt, and nothing at all shared by Cassandra and Heracles except slavery. We would therefore be wrong to seek for precise points of contact at every stage between Antigone and Danae, Lycurgus and Cleopatra. All of these are royal personages, but only the first two, according to Sophocles' account in this ode, were, like her, imprisoned.

Another feature of this hortatory use of myth is that there is little need for the Greek poets to be precise in the identification of mythical personages or in the details they select. If myth is to be used for instruction, the poets must assume their audiences' familiarity with the stories. So in this ode of *Antigone*, while Danae is identified by name and Lycurgus, not so clearly, by his father's name and that of the people over whom he ruled as king, Cleopatra is to begin with not mentioned or identified at all, but emerges gradually towards the end of the song as descended from Erectheus and as a daughter of Boreas the North Wind (981–6); and the references to the other persons in this third tale are so allusive and the particulars so obscure that we accept with wonder the knowledge of detail expected by the poet from his audience. We may however recall that all three stories supplied the plots of plays no longer extant composed by the three tragedians and presented in Athens. We know that Sophocles himself wrote two if not three plays about Phineus and his children as well as plays on Danae and Acrisius,[58] but whether this ode is a résumé of tragedies already produced or a forecast of future productions, there is no evidence to show.

Apart from noble birth, the only other fact in common between Antigone and the examples is imprisonment; and that, according to this song, she shares only with the first two, for there is no allusion in it to imprisonment as part of Cleopatra's fate; and in fact it may be doubtful whether she was in any version of the story imprisoned at all. The important point is that she too, like Antigone, was the victim of fate. Nor do we know from the chorus's account what form her disaster took, for Sophocles lavishes his descriptive powers not upon her but on the cruelty of Phineus' second wife in blinding her stepsons with a shuttle (970–6). Cleopatra's part in the story is kept in the background, and no conclusion can be drawn from 979 ff. as to any further

[58] For the Phineus plays see Pearson, *Fragments* ii. 311–20; and for those on Acrisius and Danae, i. 38–46 and 115–17.

resemblance, besides high birth, between her and Antigone. Consequently it may be going too far to see in this ode three different ways in which the chorus are regarding Antigone's fate: whether her imprisonment will be, like Danae's, a prelude to good fortune, or a deserved punishment for impiety, like Lycurgus', or an act of horrible cruelty against an innocent person.[59] While such an interpretation gives the ode a close relevance to the dramatic context and may reflect, for those who believe that the chorus are in a state of doubt, their conflicting emotions, it is not at all clear that this is what Sophocles intended. If it had been, he would probably have indicated it in the course of the ode, perhaps by a series of alternative questions indicating a dilemma or by more explicit gnomic comment on the ethical problems involved or at any rate by bringing the fate of his third example into a closer relation with that of the other two, so that we could have seen Antigone's fate mirrored in all three. It is more likely that his intention was to compose a set of variations on the theme of fate's inevitability, choosing three stories to illustrate it and indulging both his own gift for lyric narrative and his audience's delight in listening after the time-honoured fashion of choral lyric. The chorus thus exhort Antigone just before her punishment but do not invite us either to trace exact parallels or to ponder over conflicting interpretations. The first point was well made by the writer of a comment in the ancient scholia on 955:

μὴ οὕτω δὲ αὐτὸ λαβῶμεν ὅτι καὶ ἡ Ἀντιγόνη ἀcεβὴc οὖca πέπονθεν ὅπερ ὁ ἀcεβὴc Λυκοῦργοc, ἀλλ᾽ ἁπλῶc τῇ παραθέcει τῶν ὁμοίων δυcτυχιῶν παραμυθεῖται τὴν κόρην,

let us not take the story to mean that Antigone also has suffered punishment for impiety like the impious Lycurgus, but the chorus are simply trying to give her encouragement by the parallel of similar misfortunes.

There is nothing like this elsewhere in *Antigone*, nor indeed are mythical parallels a common feature of Sophocles' extant choral odes, which are as a rule too closely connected with the dramatic context to indulge in extended narrative. This ode is the only one in his extant plays consisting wholly of myth,[60] and in that lies its main interest: we are made aware of a fresh facet of his poetic

---

[59] See Bowra, *Sophoclean Tragedy*, 105.

[60] The Ixion example in *Phil.* 676 ff. is little more than a simile. Other examples are all in lyric dialogue, e.g. the Niobe parallels in *Ant.* 823 and *El.* 149 f., and the Amphiaraus one in *El.* 837-45.

versatility, his skill in concentrating into two strophic pairs three
stories of diverse type, each, as we know, the subject of whole
plays and each told with subtle differences of language, style,
and structure.

On this last point we may notice a growing intensity of
language and elaboration of detail as the three stories follow one
another. The first is briefly told, with great economy and
simplicity, a striking metaphor in

$$καὶ \ Ζηνὸς \ ταμιεύε-$$
$$cκε \ γονὰς \ χρυσορύτους$$

'she stored the treasure of Zeus' seed, falling in golden rain'
(950), and a moment of personal sympathy for Antigone in the
repeated vocative, ὦ παῖ παῖ. No reason is given for Danae's
imprisonment: merely the bare fact is stated. The second half of
the stanza announces the maxim and elaborates it with traditional
polarity of expression. The formal connection of the antistrophe
with the strophe is established by the word ζεύχθη (955),
emphatically placed as the opening word, so that the fact of
Lycurgus' imprisonment, like Danae's, is stated at the beginning.
Here however the resemblance ceases, for both the result and the
reason are given: his punishment saw the cure of his ebullient
frenzy and taught him to know the god whom he had insulted.
In spite of the obvious opportunity offered by the myth, there is
nevertheless no moralization on the subject of impiety and its
punishment, a fact which suggests that Sophocles was not
concerned with this aspect of the story.

Two stanzas are devoted to the last example. The style is more
highly wrought, especially in the strophe, which consists of one
long, complicated sentence describing first the wild and rugged
setting and then the act of cruelty in a clause with a closely
woven texture of interlocked adjectives and participles each
uniquely effective in conveying the violence, even the sound, of
the shuttle's blows by a skilful use of assonance and alliteration.[61]
Not until the antistrophe do we meet Cleopatra, and she seems
a remote figure, connected with the deed of horror only through
her children. The language at the end of the song returns to a

---

[61] For the textual difficulties in 966–77, see, besides the editions, Jackson, *Marginalia
Scaenica*, 22 ff., and Lloyd-Jones, *CQ* N.S. 7 (1957), 23.

simpler form as the emotion subsides in intensity and the scene recedes further into the past. Sophocles reserves his identification of her to the closing lines of the antistrophe (984 ff.), where he describes her up-bringing in distant caves among her father Boreas' storm-winds and the horses in whose shape Greek mythology envisaged them.[62] The last sentence restates the maxim which all three myths illustrate, and the final words ensure that our thoughts are brought back to Antigone after the mythological excursion. The ode presents a clear formal pattern, with each stanza self-contained in subject-matter. Between two stories of undeserved suffering is set one of merited punishment, guilt framed by innocence. Fate's inevitability, valid for guilty and innocent alike, is the unifying theme of the whole, and the appearance of this motif in the first and last stanzas gives the song a circular structure.

Finally it is to be noted that while the ode consists of three illustrations of a conventional theme, Sophocles has been careful throughout to adapt its tone to the mood of his play. Danae, like Antigone, leaves the bright day for the darkness of a prison: the words οὐράνιον φῶς ἀλλάξαι . . . κατεζεύχθη (944–7) re-echo what Antigone said of herself in the commos,

$$\text{νέατον δὲ φέγ-}$$
$$\text{γος λεύσσουσαν ἀελίου} \qquad \text{(808 ff.)}$$

But unlike hers, Danae's prison was illuminated by the golden rain. Similarly Lycurgus was imprisoned in bonds of rock, visited with madness for attempting like Pentheus to suppress the worship of Dionysus. Though he shares nothing with Antigone except royal birth and imprisonment, in the stanza that tells his story we meet with angry passions, attacks of madness, and the language of scorn and abuse (ὀξύχολος, κερτομίοις ὀργαῖς, μανία and μανίαι, κερτομίοις γλώσσαις, the words describing them repeated and echoed for emphasis), all of which have occurred or been referred to in the play. In the last story the outstanding feature is cruelty, horrible and violent; and there is cruelty in Creon's punishment of Antigone, and there will be violence in the cave where she is to be entombed.

None the less, this song, in spite of its points of contact with

---

[62] See Lloyd-Jones, loc. cit. 24 ff.

Antigone and its consonance with the mood of the play, looks
forward to what is so familiar in Euripides, the use of ballad-like
lyrics in which there is at times only a very tenuous connection
with the plot. It could indeed with very little alteration be made
relevant to any character in any tragedy who is under sentence
of death and who stands in need of exhortation before the stroke
falls. In this play it is set precisely where Antigone's story ends
and the revelation of Creon's impiety is about to begin. At such
a juncture a song of this type performs its task of creating a pause,
providing a contrast of subject-matter with the serious issues
raised in the first two stasima and the commos, and diverting the
audience with mythical parallels just before Teiresias' revelations
force their attention again on the quickening movement of the
tragedy.

The fifth and final stasimon (1115–52) reflects two aspects of
the scene between Teiresias and Creon. First there is the prophet's
dire warning of pollution from Polyneices' unburied corpse
infecting not only the citizens of Thebes but spreading its
influence over neighbouring cities (1080–3). Secondly, for its
mood, the song seizes upon the urgency of Creon's final speech in
which he issues orders for carrying out his decision to release
Antigone and bury the body (1108–14). The result is a brilliant
hymn (ὕμνος κλητικός) to Bacchus appealing for his presence to
cleanse the city from the infection which grips it (1140–4), and
conveying a mixture of apprehension and excitement, even of
exaltation, at the thought of urgent action. Bacchus, the god of
Thebes, already invoked in the parodos (153) to lead the dances
in celebration of victory, is an appropriate deity to receive the
Theban elders' prayers at this crisis of the tragedy. Their ode
consists of two strophic pairs. The first stanza contains the
apostrophe to the god, addressed in the first word by the all-
embracing title πολυώνυμε which is defined by further attributes
suggesting his power and wide geographical range. Here we
may again recognize certain formal features: apostrophe, relative
clauses, pendent participle, each evoking a new association of
cult and place. First comes his birth to Zeus and Semele, Theban
Cadmus' daughter; then his range to southern Italy, famous for
the vine and scene of the recently founded colony of Thurii; then
his association with Demeter and the mysteries of Eleusis; and
finally his special abode of Thebes, the waters of Ismenus, and

the myth of the Thebans' birth from the dragon's teeth: all these add to the sense of the god's all-pervading power, ranging from myth to the living, contemporary world.

In the antistrophe comes the predication with repeated second person pronouns at the front of the two sentences that compose it. This stanza presents a vivid picture of the Bacchic rout (θίασος) and is remarkable for its further, detailed evocation of a sense of place, the twin peaks of Parnassus,[63] the Corycian cave, the Castalian spring, and the ivy-clad slopes of Euboea. Though the θίασος here described is supernatural, its participants nymphs and immortal revellers (1129 and 1134), it mirrors nevertheless contemporary human revels[64] in honour of the god who watches over the streets of Thebes. The second strophe completes the grammatical structure and contains the prayer and its grounds in simplest form, the single word μολεῖν (1144) and the clause introduced by ὡς. A paraphrase will bring out the logic of the stanza: 'Seeing that you honour Thebes above all cities, come now, if ever before, with footstep that cleanses, since our city with all its people is in the grip of disease . . .' The climax of the whole ode is concentrated in the final four lines. Here the chorus pray as the mouthpiece of all the people, πάνδαμος πόλις (1141), just as they did in the parodos. In the words βιαίας ἐπὶ νόσου they have in mind Teiresias' warning to Creon on the consequences of leaving a dead body unburied and burying a living one (1064–1083).

The second antistrophe (1146), as if to counteract the feeling of imminent doom conveyed by the grounds of the prayer, reverts to the apostrophic style in which the ode began. The excitement breaks out afresh in the renewed invocation to Bacchus as leader of the dance of the stars which move in sympathy with the revellers' torches. We hear again the cries in the night (cf. 1134 and νυχίων φθεγμάτων 1148), and feel the ecstasy of the θίασος in the presence of the Thyiads who represent the frenzy of the nocturnal worshippers. In the middle of the stanza comes the ritual word προφάνηθι, 'appear in person'. The answer to the cry is not Bacchus but the messenger with his tale of death.

---

[63] For Dionysus at Delphi, see G. W. Bond's edition of Eur. *Hypsipyle*, p. 53.
[64] For the Bacchic θίασος, see Dodds's note on Eur. *Ba.* 306.

In structure the song displays a careful division of its hymn elements, apostrophe, predication, prayer, and grounds, between the first three stanzas, and at the same time maintains an uninterrupted flow towards the climax in the second strophe. Not until then are sense and grammar complete, and the climax is all the more powerful for being delayed. The impetus of the stream of poetry is then checked, and the cry to the god with which it began is repeated in the final stanza so that the demands of the circular hymn-form are satisfied. The language conveys a vivid sense of place and in the first and last antistrophes especially, the sights, sounds, and emotions of Bacchic worship. Though constructed on the pattern of a cult hymn and marked by ritualistic turns of phrase, the song from beginning to end is alive, vigorous, and astonishing in its poetic intensity. Nothing in it is fossilized, artificial, or ornamental purely for ornament's sake. Two points may be emphasized in conclusion. First, in addition to the splendour of its poetry, it breathes a deep religious feeling, communicable from the chorus who sing it to the audience who hear it. A prayer addressed by Theban citizens to the Theban god would awake a quick response from the Athenians who sat in the theatre of this same god Dionysus to watch plays performed as part of the worship due to him and who saw his altar in the orchestra as a symbol of his presence. This god was as real to them as he was to the elders of Thebes, and the religious sense of the audience would be marvellously stirred by this hymn. Secondly, besides evoking this religious sympathy the ode reveals in a striking way how Sophocles has made a ritual prayer-hymn serve his immediate dramatic purpose. The chorus catch the mood of apprehension and urgent excitement from the end of the preceding scene and carry it over into their song, so that the actors' speeches and their own lyric are fused into one crescendo of emotion. Sophocles' surpassing skill as a dramatist is seen at its height in the handling of his choruses at such turning-points as these.[65]

In the iambic parts of the exodos which precedes the second commos the chorus learn from the messenger of the deaths of Haemon and Antigone, announce Eurydice's entry (1180), and comment briefly on the implications of her silent exit (1251 f.).

[65] Cf. e.g. *Aj.* 693; *O.T.* 1086.

The anapaests which herald Creon's appearance with Haemon's body (1257–60) proclaim his sole responsibility:

οὐκ ἀλλοτρίαν
ἄτην ἀλλ᾽ αὐτὸς ἁμαρτών.

The second commos is parallel in dramatic effect to the first, isolating Creon and the ruin of his life at the end of the play in the same way as the first isolated Antigone. In order however to allow him full expression to his grief, the chorus's part is confined to trimeters, two single lines at the central points in the first strophic system (1270 = 1293) and three pairs in the second (1326 f., 1334 f., and 1337 f.). The more formal tones of the coryphaeus's lines contrast strongly with the actor's lyrics. Creon is given a mixture of dochmiacs and iambics, which, especially in combination, are used in Greek tragedy to express extremes of emotion. The actor thus dominates the commos. His passionate cries, with words repeated and exclamations echoing one another at corresponding places in strophe and antistrophe, give his utterances the effect of a ritual lament (θρῆνος), as he holds in his arms the body of his son and then sees his dead wife. Communication between Creon and the chorus is complete in the first strophic pair: at 1271 he takes the point of the remark

οἴμ᾽ ὡς ἔοικας ὀψὲ τὴν δίκην ἰδεῖν

and answers

οἴμοι,
ἔχω μαθὼν δείλαιος

and at 1294 his eyes are turned to his wife's body when the coryphaeus points out to him that it is no longer concealed from view. In the second strophic system the first pair of trimeters (1326 f.) is more remote from the actor's lyrics, serving to divide strophe from antistrophe, instead of being an integral part, while the second and third pair occur in a five-line spoken conversation (1334–8). At each stage these trimeters are kept formal and rather prosaic in order to set the actor's words in higher relief.

The anapaests that conclude the play sum up Creon's tragedy in general terms. Wisdom is the chief element in happiness, and there is an absolute sanction against impiety towards the gods.

Boastful words pay a terrible penalty which teaches wisdom in old age. The repetition of τὸ φρονεῖν emphasizes to what an extent *Antigone* is for Creon a tragedy of ἄνοια, folly, failure of intelligence. An ancient scholar did well to annotate the last sentence of the play with the old maxim ῥεχθὲν δέ τε νήπιος ἔγνω, 'the fool learns after the deed is done'.[66] Creon has learnt the lesson too late and is left to rue his folly in anguish and loneliness.

Surveying the chorus's songs in *Antigone* one is struck by their abundance and by the range and diversity of their form and content. Including the parodos there are six odes, each of surpassing poetic merit and each revealing Sophocles' astonishing versatility as a poet and a dramatist. The parodos expresses the feelings of a whole community on the morning of victory in a song that begins with a greeting to the sunrise and ends as a call to worship and thanksgiving. Between, in contrasting styles and moods, as sung lyrics and recited anapaests alternate, we see and hear the sights and sounds of battle and in the signal punishment of the braggart Capaneus recall the lesson that Zeus hates the boastful tongue. The first and second stasima develop single great themes suggested by the scenes that precede them, the former acclaiming the δεινότης of man and owing much of its thought to contemporary ideas, the latter returning to an ancient theme, the destruction of a house by an inherited curse, and developing it in Aeschylean imagery and modes of thought. Both these odes, while arising directly from the dramatic context, range far beyond it and illuminate for us who read, just as they must have done for the spectators who watched, something of deep and enduring significance that lies beneath the surface of the action. Further, they suggest certain ideal standards, political and religious, by which the actions of the characters may be judged and with which they are at the moment in conflict; and they are, moreover, powerful instruments of dramatic irony. The hymn to Ἔρως is altogether different in tone. Unlike the first two odes, it ignores the deeper implications of the preceding scene and suggests a motive that could not have been expressed during the quarrel without weakening the foundation on which the son bases his case against his father. Its main purpose is thus not only to provide a moment of relaxation between a scene of

---

[66] *Il.* 17. 32; Hes. *Op.* 218, with παθὼν for ῥεχθέν.

anger and a scene of pathos but also to form a contrast to the gravity of the earlier odes. The next song is the chorus's answer to Antigone's last appeal and acts as a coda to her story with its three examples from myth of the inevitability of fate addressed solely to her as she is taken away. Alone of all the lyrics in the play it contributes little or nothing to our understanding of the action and thus constitutes almost an intermezzo, revealing Sophocles' gift for vivid and evocative description of three contrasting scenes. The last ode, the hymn to Bacchus, is the most immediately relevant and dramatic of all, both in its close connection with the context and in its impact on the emotions of the audience. There is thus in these songs a gradual movement away from the deeper issues that lie beneath the action, so that generalized reflection gives way to the exploitation of particular moments. The chorus's task as a dramatic instrument is to bring out, where necessary, the irony implicit in different stages of the play, to keep alive the tension of the tragedy until events resolve it, to stress the isolation in which Sophocles has set his heroine (these two tasks they perform especially in the commos), and to move the thoughts and feelings of the audience as required by the demands of the action. No less important than their dramatic function is the contribution the odes make to our understanding of the intellectual and moral problems raised by the play and to the enhancement of our delight in it by the power and varied beauty of their poetry.

IV

OEDIPUS TYRANNUS

As in *Antigone*, the chorus in *Oedipus Tyrannus* are representative citizens of their community, ἄνδρες πολῖται (512), χώρας ἄνακτες (911), held in high honour, γῆς μέγιστα τῆςδ' ἀεὶ τιμώμενοι (1223). Oedipus has been, unlike Creon, long established on the throne, and the city is more settled, more at one with itself than the Thebes of *Antigone*, released just before the opening of the play from hostile attack and the threat of anarchy. Oedipus' Thebes is however faced with a disaster within and united by the common danger of plague. The chorus know, love, and trust their king. They have a horror of any attack upon him, and their complete loyalty to him is an outstanding characteristic. He too trusts them, enlisting their aid and laying upon them a solemn charge to help him find the murderer of Laius. This charge they willingly accept, so that in the first epeisodion we are assured that the whole community will be working together for the sake of their city. In this connexion their practical advice that Teiresias should be consulted has already been anticipated by Oedipus (284ff.). They display a balanced reaction to the first wave of the quarrel between king and prophet, reminding them both of the main task in hand, which is to arrive at the best solution of Apollo's oracle (404–7).

We may note here another important feature of the chorus's attitude in the play. Besides their loyalty to Oedipus and their devotion to their community, they emphasize and maintain the strong religious tone which is established in the prologue. This is apparent in the parodos, which is constructed as a doublet of the priest's appeal to the king in the prologue (14–57); in their reminder to him at 278 f. of the need to rely on Phoebus' assistance in searching for the culprit, and above all in the second stasimon (863 ff.). No explanation of this difficult ode is satisfactory unless it takes into account the fundamental fact of the chorus's belief in the truth of oracles, the power of prayer, and the importance of observing established religious practices. This attitude of mind is no less an essential part of their character than their devotion to Oedipus. It accounts for the dilemma expressed with such intensity of emotion in the first stasimon (463 ff.), as well as for the tone and content of the second, in which they stress their fears that religious beliefs are menaced by Jocasta's attacks on oracles.

As the play progresses and Oedipus' personal tragedy tends increasingly to overshadow the disaster of plague that threatens to doom the city, so does the interest of the chorus become more and more concentrated upon the king and his fortunes. The common danger is forgotten in the threatened ruin of the individual, though in the lyric dialogue at a highly dramatic moment (660 ff.) the chorus express both points of view: their affection for the king and their concern for the suffering of Thebes. In this section of the play the Theban elders make their most significant intervention in the action, first calming Oedipus at the height of his anger, so that he remits the death sentence on Creon, and then turning to Iocasta and asking her not to pursue further the matter of the quarrel, in view of the city's plight. In the last stasimon (1186), the king's fate is universalized as a symbol of man's vulnerability, so that we contemplate his tragedy in a context that transcends both the individual and the community over which he ruled.

We may observe, in addition to these points, that Creon appeals to the chorus as ἄνδρες πολῖται for support after hearing about Oedipus' accusations (512). They ascribe these to anger:

> ἀλλ' ἦλθε μὲν δὴ τοῦτο τοὔνειδος τάχ' ἂν
> ὀργῇ βιασθὲν μᾶλλον ἢ γνώμῃ φρενῶν

'This reproach came from the violence perhaps of anger rather than from sound judgement' (523), and they silence Creon's further enquiries by displaying their complete discretion: ἃ δρῶς' οἱ κρατοῦντες οὐχ ὁρῶ, 'I turn a blind eye to the actions of my ruler' (530). Later in the same scene (616 f.), they commend to Oedipus Creon's judicious sentiments together with a warning of the danger of hasty judgement. They reveal here their tact and good sense together with a considerable insight into the king's character, crystallizing the impression he has created by his accusations against Creon and making explicit the contrast in character of the two men who were quarrelling.

Two further noteworthy interventions from the chorus occur towards the end of the tense scene between Oedipus and the messenger from Corinth, the first at 1051 where attention is drawn to Iocasta, who has been listening in silence to the long stichomythia and has guessed the truth somewhere about 1025 ff. The coryphaeus's remark brings her back into the orbit of the action so that attention is concentrated upon her final agony. Then, after the anguished cry that marks her exit (1071),[1] the coryphaeus points out to the king the manner of her departure and expresses the chorus's fears that evil may break forth from her silence, incidentally providing him with the verb that opens his speech:

$$\delta\acute{\epsilon}\delta o\iota\chi' \ \H{o}\pi\omega c$$
$$\mu\grave{\eta} \ '\kappa \ \tau\hat{\eta}c \ c\iota\omega\pi\hat{\eta}c \ \tau\hat{\eta}c\delta' \ \mathring{\alpha}\nu\alpha\rho\rho\acute{\eta}\xi\epsilon\iota \ \kappa\alpha\kappa\acute{\alpha}$$

followed immediately by Oedipus' ὁποῖα χρῄζει ῥηγνύτω (1074 ff.)

In the final scene, the messenger addresses the chorus as

$$\mathring{\omega} \ \gamma\hat{\eta}c \ \mu\acute{\epsilon}\gamma\iota c\tau\alpha \ \tau\hat{\eta}c\delta' \ \mathring{\alpha}\epsilon\grave{\iota} \ \tau\iota\mu\acute{\omega}\mu\epsilon\nu o\iota \qquad (1223)$$

whose solicitude for the House of Labdacus is part of their heritage, εἴπερ ἐγγενῶc . . . ἐντρέπεcθε. As a matter of technique, their two remarks at 1232 f. and 1236 help him into his speech after the emotion of his opening words. Their reaction to the sight of the blinded king in the anapaests at 1297–1306 is that of the average man, and they attribute his act to madness (μανία) and the drive of a δαίμων as they shrink from the spectacle with a shudder of horror. Their failure to understand the reasons for his action and their belief that death would have been preferable to a life of blindness (1367 f.) lead him naturally to explain his motives in a carefully argued speech. They give no clue however whether they are convinced; and in their closing lines at the end of the play he is the supreme example of man's vulnerability, just as he is in the last stasimon.

The character and status of the chorus in this play, while similar to that of *Antigone*, do not present so many problems. Less

---

[1] For the exit of a wife to suicide, cp. Deianira at *Trach.* 813 and Eurydice at *Ant.* 1243.

detached and objective about the chief character, the Theban elders are far more deeply involved with Oedipus in affection and loyalty. So much is apparent from a brief survey of the non-lyric parts of the play, and we may conclude when we have studied the odes in detail that they too do not, with one conspicuous exception, raise the same difficulties of dramatic relevance. We may notice also the skilful and unobtrusive way in which Sophocles has used the remarks of the coryphaeus as a link between the actors, so that the chorus's representative makes suggestions at appropriate moments, draws attention to reactions that might otherwise pass unobserved, and brings a character back into focus after a period of silence.

It was said above that the parodos is a doublet of the priest's speech in the prologue in which certain information is given, the two essentials being an account of the plague and the report brought back by Creon from the Delphic oracle. At 144 f. Oedipus, after dismissing the suppliants, says

ἄλλος δὲ Κάδμου λαὸν ὧδ' ἀθροιζέτω,
ὡς πᾶν ἐμοῦ δράσοντος

'let someone else summon together Cadmus' people, for there is nothing I will not do.' This prepares us for the entry of the chorus. They too must be informed of what audience and actors have already been told, and this is done by Oedipus after the parodos. The same technique is employed in *Ajax, Trachiniae,* and *Antigone*. The parodos derives the whole of its content and much of its form from the prologue.[2] The opening strophe, with its excited question about the report from Delphi, echoes the suspense of Oedipus and the suppliants as they await Creon's arrival. The link of mood and subject-matter between parodos and prologue is thus forged with perfect dramatic propriety in the first words of the song:

ὦ Διὸς ἀδυεπὲς φάτι, τίς ποτε ...
Θήβας;

a lyric expansion of Oedipus' question to Creon at 85 f., when he entered crowned with laurel as the bringer of good news.

---

[2] See W. Ax, *Hermes* 67 (1932), 413; Kranz, *Stasimon*, 185 ff.

The ode is an elaborate paean, as is clear from the address ἰήιε Δάλιε Παιάν (154)[3] to the Delian Apollo, reflected in the epithet ἰηίων for the pangs (καμάτων) in which the women cry ἰή (172) and in the phrase παιὰν δὲ λάμπει, 'the paean blazes forth' (186). In order to establish the function of the type of song to which this parodos belongs it is worth quoting in full the definition in the scholia to Aristophanes' *Plutus*, 636: 'A paean is a hymn to Apollo sung for the stopping of plague, but also for the stopping of war; and often too when danger is expected.' This note explains the mood of the Theban people when the play opens: suspense, apprehension, and fervent hope as they pray for deliverance in the person of the elders who form the chorus. Apollo, to whom in the first instance they address their prayer, is the god who dominates the tragedy and indeed Oedipus' whole story from the moment when he first consulted the Delphic oracle, as he relates at 787–93, until his bitter cry in the final commos (1329).

Before undertaking a detailed analysis of the parodos, we may note a few general features which mark its development out of the prologue. First, the description of the plague in the second strophe and antistrophe is a recapitulation of the priest's account at 15–30, recalling it in the choice of symptoms and incidents, notably, the blight on crops (25 = 171 f.), the death of embryos in the womb (26 f. = 172 ff.), the parallel pictures of the suppliants grouped round the altars, and the sound of lamentation and cries for help, the latter echoed from Oedipus' opening speech (5 = 182–86). Over both the iambics of the speeches and the lyrics of the parodos broods the god of pestilence, ὁ πυρφόρος θεός (27), who brings the fire of destruction; and in the song fire is a predominant image.

Secondly, the form of the main part of the parodos matches that of the priest's appeal to Oedipus (31–53), though the former is addressed to a trinity of deities and the latter to the mortal king, who, as the priest is careful to explain, must not be equated with a god (31 ff.). Nevertheless in his speech to Oedipus, he uses the formulae of ritual supplication to gods: repeated imperatives of appeal (46 f.), grounds for the prayer (47 f.), and most striking of all, a reminder to the king of his past services as an earnest of

---

[3] Cp. the echo Ἰήιε Φοῖβε in the third stasimon, 1096; and for this cry as a feature of Paeans, cf. Pindar's *Paeans* 2, 4, 5, 6. *Paean* 9 well illustrates the threat of peril in its address to the sun in eclipse.

his present power to help, ending with the emphatic καὶ τανῦν ἴϲοϲ γένου (53), a variant of the familiar εἴ ποτε ... καὶ νῦν formula which appears in the closing lines of the first antistrophe of the parodos (164 f.). In content, form, and mood the chorus's first song thus closely echoes the prologue and intensifies the atmosphere of menace there created. The description of pestilence and death in the iambics gains in pathos from the emotive power of song as we hear the chorus reflect in their prayer for divine aid the priest's appeal to the father-figure Oedipus. At the outset of this great tragedy our thoughts and sympathies are concentrated on a whole community united in supplication to their king and their gods in time of trouble.

A final point may be noted in the parallel structure of prologue and parodos. While the two prayers, the priest's to the king and the chorus's to the three deities, occupy the central position of both sections, the description of the suppliants and of the symptoms of plague, which appears first in the prologue, comes after the prayer in the lyric, as is natural because it gives the grounds of the prayer; and the lyric opens with the message from Delphi with which the prologue closed. This reversal of order, besides providing stylistic variation, is a fine stroke of dramatic technique, for when the chorus appear they must at once communicate to the audience their excitement at the rumour of Creon's message. There is thus a sharp contrast between the quiet, solemn note of the tableau-like opening and the heightened emotion of the parodos.

The parodos of *Oedipus Tyrannus* is the longest ode sung by the chorus alone in Sophocles' extant plays. Extending over three strophic pairs, it displays a remarkably lucid rhythmic pattern. The first pair is wholly dactylic, except for a single iambic dimeter (152 = 160), with its metrical structure exactly balanced by identity of the opening and closing dactylic runs enhanced by the echo of ἄμβροτε Φάμα at the end of the strophe in ἄμβροτ' Ἀθάνα at the beginning of the antistrophe. The second begins and ends with iambics, and there are single iambic dimeters at 173 and 174 = 184 and 186. The rest is dactylic, so that the increased use of iambics varies the rhythmic effect and points forward to the almost wholly iambic character of the third pair, apart from the single dactylic line in the middle (196 = 209), which recalls in its metrical form the invocation ἰήιε Δάλιε Παιάν at the centre of the first strophe. Further word-echoes are to be noted in ἀνάριθμα and ἀνάριθμος in the first lines of strophe and antistrophe of the second pair and more distant ones in θύγατερ Διός at the ends of identical dactylic lines at the opening and close of the first and second antistrophe and in χρυσέας = χρυσέα in 158 and 188. The combination of dactyls and iambics over a long stream of utterance recalls the parodos of *Agamemnon* 104–39 and the last stasimon of *Hippolytus* (1102–50). This rhythm is a splendid vehicle for sustained prayer; the effect is indeed liturgical, and content and form are exactly matched.

In the first strophe, which establishes a link with the prologue, Sophocles stresses the chorus's emotion by his choice and placing of words. Notable are the repeated phrases for tension and fear with their alliterative sound and the physical effect they suggest:

> ἐκτέταμαι φοβερὰν φρένα
> δείματι πάλλων

and immediately after πάλλων comes the ritual cry in the centre of the stanza, a natural release for the chorus's feelings. The strophe is rounded off by a repetition of the vocative with which it began, and is thus complete in itself.

The prayer begins in the first antistrophe (159) with an appeal to the three deities Athena, Artemis, and Phoebus. There is no connecting particle, as is natural in view of the break with the content of the strophe. Once started however, the paean streams in an unbroken flow over the remaining stanzas, reaching its climax in the fifth, where the banishment or exorcism of Ares is proclaimed as the purpose of the song; and in the final stanza the appeal for a divine presence is renewed in the return to the phraseology of ritual, κικλήσκω ... πελασθῆναι (209–13), addressed to Bacchus, the god of Thebes, and recalling κεκλόμενος ... προφάνητε in the first antistrophe.[4] Like the first stanza, the other five are thus composed together in circular form.

The separate sections of the prayer are carefully divided by the stanzas into a logical order. The first (159–67) consists of a single sentence opening with a pendent nominative participle κεκλόμενος which should not be emended away in spite of the following προφάνητε (164). The three deities are each distin-

---

[4] Compare the appeals to Bacchus by the Theban chorus at *Ant.* 153 ff. and 1115 ff.

guished by epithets which enhance their power, and for Artemis there is a relative clause localizing her cult in the market-place where she is worshipped by the Boeotians as Εὔκλεια, the Glorious One.[5] They are summoned to be visibly present in order to ward off doom (ἀλεξίμοροι, 162). This presence of the god or gods is regularly demanded as an essential part of such prayers, so that the powers addressed may see what is to be done and be themselves seen by those who summon them. The word ἀλεξίμοροι is explained in the last clause of the stanza, and the particular kind of doom and the power responsible for it are specified in the subsequent strophic pairs. The εἴ ποτε . . . καὶ νῦν formula which closes the opening prayer reminds the gods of a former successful ἀποπομπή, possibly, as the Scholiast suggests, of the Sphinx, and assures them of the praying subject's confidence in their abiding power to help. This invocation springs from the heart of the Theban elders and no doubt from the heart of the poet, for though there is no evidence to date the play, it was probably performed during the earlier years of the Peloponnesian War when the crops of Attica were being ravaged yearly by invasion, and war and pestilence took their toll of Athenian lives.

The first words of the second strophic pair (168),

$$\text{ὦ πόποι, ἀνάριθμα γὰρ φέρω}$$
$$\text{πήματα}$$

'Woe, for countless are the pains I suffer', introduce a description of the plague. The gods require a statement of the grounds for their summoning, and the details are given in the next two stanzas in a series of short paratactic clauses joined by the simplest of particles, thus providing a notable contrast in style to the flowing period of the preceding invocation. It is dangerous to assert that Sophocles must have based his account of the Theban pestilence on his experience of the plague at Athens, reinforcing the argument by searching the pages of Thucydides ii. 47–50 for parallel symptoms in the historian's prose and the poet's lyrics and using the very few parallels that can be found in order to fix a date for the play's composition. Apart from the difference in mood and purpose, one being a record of historical fact, the other a song in inspired poetry, there are in the two accounts considerable differences of content. For instance the two most

[5] See Nilsson, *Griechische Feste*, 237.

important symptoms in the song, blighted crops and premature births, do not appear in Thucydides. Further, in ii. 53 the historian points to the decay in morality and religious faith that resulted from the plague, whereas the dramatist emphasizes the need of the gods and the faith of the Thebans in the reality of their power. This sincere and deeply felt belief in the gods is apparent throughout the whole of the parodos. It does not however mean that Sophocles is preaching a sermon to his contemporaries on the need for faith in time of trouble but merely that it is not irrelevant to remember contemporary conditions when trying to interpret plays meant for public performance; and in the case of this play, we should not ignore the effect these two stanzas must have had on an Athenian audience at the probable time of its production.

To return to the details of Sophocles' account, we may note the clarity and realism with which he depicts his chosen scenes and the pathetic impact of this part of the song. The pathos is of course inherent in the subject, but it is enhanced by the opening cry of woe ὦ πόποι, an exclamation rare in tragedy, by the ethic dative μοι, by the apparent despair of finding a remedy, by the echo ἀνάριθμα = ἀνάριθμος, which has more than merely external rhythmic significance, and by the repetition and accumulation of ideas in the words νηλέα, ἀνοίκτως, λυγρῶν, ἐπιστενάχουσι, στονόεσσα in the antistrophe (179 ff.). Special, in fact sole, emphasis is laid upon the blighted crops and the failure of the women to bring forth live children: the sources of sustenance and the future of the race are threatened. These are the effects of plague traditionally selected by Greek poets, as may be seen in the great apotropaic prayers against pestilence in Aeschylus' *Supplices* 656–96 and *Eumenides* 928–87. After a scene depicting the wives and older mothers in supplication at the altar's edge while the paean rings clear and the flute accompanies the voice of lamentation, this section of the ode ends with a second appeal to Athena, reinforcing the first at the beginning of the prayer.

With the last strophic pair (190 ff.) comes the essential part of the whole parodos, because not until then are the trinity of deities told exactly what to do when they have appeared in answer to the invocations. They are to combine against Ares, the destroyer of men (βροτολοιγός)[6] not only by war but by

---

[6] His Homeric epithet, found in tragedy only here and at Aesch. *Supp.* 665.

pestilence, as in the present instance, where his usual function as god of war is denied him by the epithet ἄχαλκος ἀσπίδων, 'without brazen shields' (191). The artillery of Apollo Lycaeus and Artemis is to be reinforced by the thunderbolt of Zeus and Bacchus' gleaming torch in order to accomplish the banishment of the god who is without honour among the gods, τὸν ἀπότιμον ἐν θεοῖς θεόν (215). There are conventional elements in the strophe, as is pointed out by Ax,[7] who draws attention to the antiquity of the imperatival accusative and infinitive, "Αρεα . . . νωτίσαι (190 ff.), which appears in Homeric prayers and archaic inscriptions.[8] No alteration of ἀντιάζων to ἀντιάζω should thus be countenanced. Another feature of the formal ἀποπομπή is that Ares is offered a choice of abodes as alternatives to Thebes, either the great chambers of Amphitrite or the inhospitable Black Sea, where he haunts the perilous shores of Salmydessus.[9]

After its introductory strophe, the whole ode presents a remarkable unity of structure. The language is direct and vivid, with a predominance of words and expressions which convey a sense of impending doom in its most concrete form. In particular, we may observe the persistence of imagery from fire as an instrument of destruction, violent and irresistible, apparent both in the forces against which the chorus are praying, φλόγα πήματος (166), "Αρεα τὸν μαλερόν (μαλερός in Homer is a stock epithet of fire), ὃς φλέγει με περιβόατος (190 ff.), κρεῖσσον ἀμαιμακέτου πυρός (176), and in the weapons which they summon to their aid, τᾶν πυρφόρων ἀστραπᾶν κράτη wielded by Zeus (200), Artemis' πυρφόροι αἶγλαι (206), and Bacchus' blazing torch, φλέγοντ᾽ ἀγλαῶπι πεύκᾳ (214). These phrases suggest the fires of destruction and the rage of battle, the more so when we recall the important part played by fire similes in the descriptions of war and warriors in the *Iliad*. We may finally draw attention to the evocative simile at 175 ff.:

> ἅπερ εὔπτερον ὄρνιν
> κρεῖσσον ἀμαιμακέτου πυρὸς ὄρμενον
> ἀκτὰν πρὸς ἑσπέρου θεοῦ.

One after another the victims of the plague speed like a winged bird faster than irresistible fire to the shore of the western god.

---

[7] *Hermes*, loc. cit. 420.   [8] Cf. e.g. *Il.* 7. 179; *Od.* 17. 354.   [9] Cf. *Ant.* 970.

These lines display a rich concentration of ideas within a short compass. The ghosts of the dead are like birds: the comparison calls to mind the migrating cranes in the simile at the beginning of *Iliad* 3; and in ἑσπέρου θεοῦ there is perhaps an echo of Theoclymenus' vision at *Odyssey* 20. 356, where he sees the suitors' ghosts hurrying to Erebus below the dark West, ἱεμένων Ἐρεβόσδε ὑπὸ ζόφον.[10]

The link with the following scene is close and dramatic. The appearance of Oedipus with his single word αἰτεῖc as an answer to the prayer invests the king with an almost divine significance. It is likely that he enters during the last few lines of the parodos, in time to hear the chorus's final appeal at 209. In his first speech to the elders he informs them of the practical steps he is taking to comply with the instructions of the oracle about which they asked at the beginning of the song. It is important to emphasize again that in this scene, up to the moment of Oedipus' accusation against Teiresias (345 ff.), the uppermost thought is the danger to the community against which all must unite. The danger to Oedipus supervenes at 353, grows more and more menacing as the scene progresses, and finally becomes the dominant interest of the play.

It is the emergence of this menace to the king that sets the tone of the first stasimon (463), which consists of two songs each arising out of the preceding scene and closely connected with the dramatic context.[11] The first strophic pair speculates on the identity of the unknown murderer. Objective in mood, it describes in vivid imagery the flight of the criminal as he endeavours to escape the pursuit and punishment ordained by the oracle and proclaimed by Oedipus. It thus reflects the earlier part of the scene. The second song is subjective and personal to the chorus, full of doubts, fears, and conflicting emotions as they formulate the dilemma in which Teiresias' revelations have placed them. They are firm believers in the validity of Apollo's sacred oracle whose mouthpiece is the mortal seer, and they voice their agitation in emphatic terms at the beginning of the second strophe (483 f.). At the same time they are passionately loyal to Oedipus, who has given evidence of his qualities plain for all to see,

---

[10] For a further discussion, see Norden on *Aen.* 6. 309–12.

[11] See Kranz, *Stasimon*, 201 and 215.

coφὸc ὤφθη βαcάνῳ θ' ἀδύπολιc

his wisdom and his popularity (509),[12] and without proof of
Teiresias' accusations they will never believe him guilty. They
seek comfort in the thought expressed at the beginning of the
second antistrophe, that while the gods, Zeus and Apollo, have
full knowledge of the affairs of men, a mortal seer may be fallible,
because one man may surpass another in prophetic skill.

The question has sometimes been raised why the two themes
of the ode are presented in this order.[13] Some critics have felt that
the chorus might have expressed their thoughts about Oedipus
first and then passed on to the description of the escaping
criminal. The reasons for Sophocles' order are however fairly
clear. In the first place, it follows the succession of events in the
preceding scene where the command 'Hunt the murderer!',
which concerns the whole community, comes first and is at this
stage of the play of prime importance and urgency. Secondly,
Teiresias' last speech (447–62), with its account of the fate
awaiting the criminal, is the final utterance that the chorus hear
before their song, so that the transition from iambics to lyrics is
more immediate if the first strophe picks up what they have last
heard. Further, the seer's last speech, unlike the preceding one
(especially 413–23), refers to the murderer in the third person,

> τὸν ἄνδρα τοῦτον, ὃν πάλαι
> ζητεῖc . . .
>   οὗτόc ἐcτιν ἐνθάδε   (449 ff.)

and continues in an allusive style calculated to obscure the
specific references to Oedipus earlier in the scene. Accordingly,
the opening question of the ode and the words τὸν ἄδηλον ἄνδρα
πάντ' ἰχνεύειν (475 f.) spring directly from the studied ambiguity
of Teiresias' speech. Finally, though this is only a formal point,
the song opens with an urgent question recalling the opening of
the parodos and contains parallel references to the Φάτιc or
Φάμα which has flashed from Parnassus above the Delphic peak.
A certain symmetry of structure is thus achieved in the opening
of both odes.

---

[12] The meaning of ἀδύπολιc is best explained by Pindar's phrase ἀcτοῖc ἀδών, *N*. 8. 38,
'pleasing to his citizens', 'popular'.
[13] See Jebb's note ad loc.

The first two stanzas are composed in iambo-choriambic metres with an arresting effect gained by two anapaestic dimeters at 469–70 = 479–80, and though of course the chorus do not realize it, they describe the career of Oedipus himself, not only his future as an outcast fleeing human contact, but also his past as he fled from Corinth in fear of the oracle and found a haven at Thebes before becoming an outcast again. Some of the lyric description is derived from Teiresias' denunciation, notably the pursuit of the κῆρες (471 f = 418) and the vision of the fugitive in flight through the wilderness of wood and mountain. Most of the first strophic system is however a vague echo of what the chorus have heard. They mask the seer's explicit charges at 362 and 366 ff. beneath the phrase

$$\text{ἄρρητ' ἀρρήτων τελέσαν-}$$
$$\text{τα φοινίαισι χερσίν ...} \qquad \text{(465 f.)}$$

Such deeds, done with hands of blood, are too horrible to be named, too horrible perhaps for the chorus's comprehension. There is a terrible irony in this, as the Theban elders allow their imaginations to envisage the outcast's fate without knowing what the audience know, that this outcast is their king.

The most remarkable feature in the first half of the ode is the gradual emergence of a single concrete image. Suggested tentatively in the opening stanza with its impression of flight swifter than storm-horses, of assault (ἐπενθρῴσκει, 469) by the fires of Apollo, of pursuit by the dread κῆρες, it acquires vivid form at 478 in the phrase ὁ ταῦρος, placed emphatically at the end of a clause and coming with all the force of a revelation of identity, *ecce ille taurus*, 'Look! there he goes, the bull!' The transformation of the object of pursuit from τὸν ἄνδρα in 475 to the bull in the following sentence is an astonishing *lumen ingenii* whose brilliance should not be dimmed by attempts to turn it into a simile, a process which began in antiquity with the ruin of metre by the insertion of ὡς and ended in modern times with the specious ἰσόταυρος accepted by Jebb.[14] The bull is moreover an outcast from the herd as he wanders in the wilderness (ὑπ' ἀγρίαν ὕλαν ἀνά τ' ἄντρα), pathetic in his loneliness (μέλεος μελέῳ ποδί

---

[14] See p. 93, n. 10 on *Ant.* 113; and for πετραῖος = ἀνὰ πέτρας Fr. 518.3 P., πετραῖον ὄρνιν of the hoopoe among the rocks. J. F. Martin's ἰσόταυρος is brilliant but unnecessary: Oedipus *is* the bull.

χηρεύων, 479), trying to elude the oracles that buzz round him, living, like gadflies: for so must we interpret ζῶντα περιποτᾶται at the end of the stanza.

The second strophic pair is a strong contrast in mood, rhythm, and content. The flight of imagination has given way to the reality of shock as the Theban elders turn in upon themselves and face the implications of Teiresias' charges. The change of mood is marked by a peculiar rhythmic effect: choriambic tetrameters are followed by ionics and the two appear to intermingle throughout. An impression is created of disturbed and breathless movement which reflects the chorus's bewilderment. At the beginning they state the agony of doubt natural in those who believe in the truth of oracles and acknowledge the skill of their interpreters, and who yet cannot accept without proof the accusations made against their king: ὅ τι λέξω δ' ἀπορῶ, 'I know not what to say' (486). It is interesting to note here that they ignore, probably through lack of comprehension, Teiresias' hints about Oedipus' parentage and Theban origin (435 ff. and 452 ff.). To them he is a stranger from Corinth. What concerns them above all is the charge of murder so that his prestige as king has been assailed: without good grounds, based upon some past feud between Thebes and Corinth which they could use as a test, they will never join in an attack upon his fame among the people in their attempts to find the culprit.

The antistrophe provides a temporary answer to the chorus's perplexed state of mind in the fallibility of human prophets contrasted with the omniscience of Zeus and Apollo. It is, so runs the argument, open to anyone to prophesy,[15] and one man may surpass another in skill. The point is legitimate and well argued. The same word cοφός is applied to Oedipus himself in 509: his skill in interpreting riddles was proved at the time of the Sphinx's assault. In the absence of similarly manifest proof of Teiresias' superior cοφία, the Theban elders will never believe that their king is guilty.

This ode, like the parodos, is closely woven into the dramatic context, and its purpose is to set side by side two moods created by the preceding scene. First is the urgency of the hunt for the unknown murderer felt by Oedipus and the citizens of Thebes and prescribed by the Delphic oracle. This is communicated to

---

15 Cf. 1086; also *El.* 743 and *O.C.* 1080 for choruses in the role of μάντεις.

the audience in two stanzas which convey the utmost fervour of poetic imagination. The second mood is one of bewilderment aroused in the elders by Teiresias. This is conveyed in a pair of strophes that reflect the chorus's emotions emphatically at the beginning in the repeated δεινὰ μὲν οὖν, δεινὰ ταράccει answered with a rhyme-echo of particles in the antistrophe, ἀλλ' ὁ μὲν οὖν, so that the openings of both stanzas are similar in grammatical structure, a μὲν-clause followed by a δὲ-clause, expressing verbally the felt dilemma; and the ends of both stanzas are parallel in stating the Thebans' loyalty to Oedipus.

The contrast in mood between the two halves of this ode is intensely dramatic. There is a similar change of mood between the strophic pair and the epode in the first stasimon of *Electra*,[16] but what makes this song of *Oedipus Tyrannus* unique is that it presents in lyric form a chorus arguing with itself as though it were a single character and trying to extricate itself from an acute dilemma arising from the tension between the Theban elders' acceptance of Apollo's command, their shock at Teiresias' revelations, and their affection for their king. In addition, their terrified doubt and their desperate search for some clue foreshadow the dilemma that confronts Oedipus and Iocasta after the lyric dialogue (697 ff.); and the opening of the second antistrophe prepares us for her attempt to draw a distinction between Apollo himself and the mortal seers who interpret his oracles (709 ff.). Iocasta's solution is to reject utterly the prophetic art when she has heard Oedipus' account of his killing of the travellers, while the chorus's immediate answer is to emphasize their loyalty, though ultimately, in the powerful second stasimon, they affirm their absolute confidence in the validity of oracles. A link is thus forged between the two odes and between the reactions of chorus and actors across the 'development' section of the play.

The lyric dialogue (649–96) marks a break in the central scene, coming after Iocasta, announced by the coryphaeus, has entered at the height of the quarrel between Oedipus and Creon (633). The process of persuading the king, begun by her in the conversation between the three actors at 634–48, is continued by the chorus, who develop some of her arguments, so that the transition to lyric dialogue is smooth and natural. The chorus

[16] *El.* 473–515.

succeed in imposing their will on the king in one specific respect:
they persuade him to cancel the death sentence on Creon.
Incidentally, too, they restore him to a calmer state of mind from
a pitch of almost ecstatic anger (ὦ πόλις, πόλις, 629), so that the
subsequent conversation with Iocasta can begin at a quieter and
more rational level. Finally the passage from 649–96 plays an
important part in the revelation of his character.

Structurally, the dialogue consists of a strophe and antistrophe
separated by nine spoken trimeters for Oedipus and Creon (669–
77). Opening with a conversation in lyric iambics with a single
trimeter (655) divided between chorus and actor, the rhythm
then changes to dochmiacs for two lines indicating a rise in
emotional intensity as the chorus answer Oedipus' question φράζε
δὴ τί φῄς. After his two trimeters there is a lyric utterance from
the chorus in a mixture of iambics and dochmiacs with a single
cretic line (660–7). We may note the speed and flexibility of the
interchange between sung and spoken metres and the quick
response between actor and chorus, especially in the trimeter
with double ἀντιλαβή and the carrying over of the sense from one
participant to the other. The antistrophe, in which the chorus
turn from Oedipus to Iocasta, is exactly symmetrical with the
strophe in its division of lines between actor and chorus. The
language of the sung parts of this scene differs hardly at all from
that of the spoken, so that there is a homogeneity of mood and
style which lends great naturalness to the whole. As so often, we
can only regret our lack of evidence about the manner of
delivery and musical accompaniment in the shifts between
speech, recitative, and song. Analogies from opera are indeed
dangerous, but perhaps we may bear in mind the effect of
recitativo secco, the quick and flexible interchange of voices half
way between speaking and singing.

In imposing their will upon Oedipus,

$$τοὐμὸν παριεὶς καὶ καταμβλύνων κέαρ$$

'weakening and blunting my zeal', as he puts it (688), the chorus
are faced with a difficult task. They use the following arguments.
First they refer to 644–8 where Creon puts himself under a curse
of destruction if he is guilty of the charges against him: ἀραῖος
... ὀλοίμην, and Iocasta appeals to Oedipus first of all to respect
this oath,

μάλιστα μὲν τόνδ᾽ ὅρκον αἰδεcθεὶc θεῶν   (647)

before respecting herself and the chorus. The chorus repeat this appeal in similar words at 652 f.,

τὸν οὔτε πρὶν
νήπιον νῦν τ᾽ ἐν ὅρκῳ μέγαν καταιδέcαι

'Respect him who was no fool before and is now strong in his oath', and they amplify the point in answer to his question in the dochmiacs at 656 f.:

τὸν ἐναγῆ φίλον μήποτ᾽ ἐν αἰτίᾳ
cὺν ἀφανεῖ λόγῳ ‹c᾽› ἄτιμον βαλεῖν[17]

'Never dishonour a kinsman (or friend) who has put himself under a curse, by accusing him on an unproved rumour.' After making this powerful point,[18] the chorus move on to their second argument, recalling Iocasta's words at 635 f.: after affirming their loyalty to him with the strongest of oaths they remind Oedipus of the city's suffering and urge both him and Creon not to increase them by their own troubles. Moved by these arguments, Oedipus changes his decision to have Creon put to death. There is however no change of heart, as the contemptuous dismissal shows (ὁ δ᾽ οὖν ἴτω, 669): Creon will always be his hated enemy.

This highly dramatic scene, in which the chorus take part on the same terms as the three actors, is important for its revelation of certain developments in the king's character. Oedipus is of course obsessed with the idea of cτάcιc as we have seen already in his confrontations with Teiresias and Creon; and with this obsession comes a tendency to misunderstand motives and suspect friends. This is exactly what we see happening to him here. Creon's remarks at 609–12 about the injustice of confusing good with bad when judging men and the folly of rejecting a true friend are obviously in the chorus's mind during the dialogue, but they have made little impression on Oedipus who is revealed in this scene as ἀγνώc, as Creon says of him in 677. Used by Sophocles here in an unusual active sense, it may well, like

---

[17] Thus Jebb, and Dain's text in the Budé edition (1958). For a discussion see R. D. Dawe, *Studies on the Text of Sophocles* i. 238 f.

[18] On the legal aspects of this argument, see Gottfried Greiffenhagen, *Der Prozess des Oedipus* in *Hermes* 94 (1966), 158 ff.

ἀγνώμων, have a moral as well as an intellectual force and convey the idea of moral blindness, a state of mind in which normal judgements are perverted.[19] For Oedipus believes, wrongly, that the chorus in persuading him to drop his charge against Creon must be seeking his own death or exile (658 f.), in other words that they are siding with the party he suspects of plotting against himself; and he believes that Creon, who is really his friend, can never be anything but his enemy. Finally, when in response to Iocasta's request for details of the quarrel the chorus suggest that the matter should be allowed to drop (685 f.), he intervenes with a remark that reveals a further misunderstanding of their motives: instead of suggesting that the matter should drop, the chorus should have, so he implies, joined him in condemning Creon. As it is, in blunting his purpose, they have, for all their good intentions, merely succeeded in convincing him that they still support his supposed enemies. Hence their passionate and emphatic statement that they would be mad to abandon him (689 ff.), a remark which is especially poignant as it awakes no response in him. From this point in the play Oedipus and Iocasta are alone. In his delusion he has isolated himself from all but his wife, misjudging his friends, suspecting their motives, rejecting their support. A mind thus deluded contains within itself the seeds of ruin (ἄτη). The king's isolation increases as the play moves on. What began as a common enterprise now becomes a lone task as he drives himself ruthlessly towards the fatal discovery.

At the end of this scene, Oedipus, Iocasta, and the chorus are faced with a dilemma about the oracle: if it speaks the truth, Laius must have been killed by his son, i.e. the exposed baby who, as is apparent at this stage of the play, cannot be Oedipus; and if it was Oedipus who killed Laius, the oracle is false. Iocasta's solution is to reject utterly the art of prophecy, the chorus's is the second stasimon. Her famous attack on μαντεία develops early in the scene. Directed first against human prophets (707 ff.), it turns into a general assault on the whole mantic art just before she and Oedipus go into the palace at 862,

> ὥcτ᾽ οὐχὶ μαντείαc γ᾽ ἂν οὔτε τῇδ᾽ ἐγὼ
> βλέψαιμ᾽ ἂν οὕνεκ᾽ οὔτε τῇδ᾽ ἂν ὕcτερον

---

[19] See on *Ant.* 620–5, p. 109 above.

'And so henceforth, as for the art of prophecy, I would not look either here or there' (857 ff.). In the state of her knowledge at this stage and in her concern to calm Oedipus' anxieties, her sentiments are natural and appropriate dramatically, though shocking to conventional Greek susceptibility, as is clear from the last stanza of the song (897–910). How far Oedipus is himself involved in her scepticism it is hard to say, because his answer, καλῶc νομίζειc (859), gives very little away. Clearly enough he is full of dreadful imaginings when he leaves the stage. This is apparent both from the end of the speech in which he describes the killing of the party of travellers, especially 813–33, and from Iocasta's account of his state of mind when she reenters after the ode (914–17). He has however not uttered a single word of scepticism, let alone blasphemy, so far in the play, nor does he do so until he has heard from the Corinthian messenger of the death of Polybus whom he supposes to be his father (964 ff.). It follows then that the immediate cause of the ode lies in Iocasta's attack on the art of the prophecy; and the last stanza, as so often in the songs of Greek tragedy, especially those which range over wide issues, clarifies the precise point of contact with the preceding scene by referring to the very oracles about Laius which have been disregarded.

The conclusion of the ode should occasion no surprise. Many of Sophocles' generation believed in the inevitability of oracular truth, so that an attack on its validity could well be taken by these Theban elders as a symptom of the collapse of established religion. There is striking evidence of the prevalence of Iocasta's ideas and of the shock they caused at Athens some twenty years before this play was produced in an inscription on the fallen at Coronea (447 B.C.),[20] which insists that henceforth all oracles must be trusted; and the whole of the last stanza with its final words ἔρρει δὲ τὰ θεῖα reveals how deeply the chorus are disturbed by her impiety. The conclusion 'when oracles are disregarded, religion decays' would be accepted as reasonable by a contemporary audience. Further, oracles play a vital part in most of Sophocles' extant plays with plots turning upon the statements of oracles whose purport is misapprehended by mortal ignorance, so that to him the inevitability of oracular truth is an important

[20] First published by W. Peek, *Ath. Mitt.* 57. 142 ff.; 59. 252 ff.; *Hermes* 68 (1933), 353 ff. For discussion, see Bowra, *Problems in Greek Poetry*, ch. 6.

instrument of tragedy. This ode then of *Oedipus Tyrannus* springs immediately from the dramatic context, reveals an essential element in the thought of the play, and is absolutely consistent with the character and status of the chorus who sing it.

While however Iocasta's attack is the immediate cause of the song, there is far more than this behind it at a remoter distance both in the play itself and in the inherited beliefs that find expression in Greek poetry from early times well into the fifth century. Unlike the parodos and the first stasimon, which are confined to the context, this ode ranges far. The chorus, as in the first two stasima of *Antigone*, reflect upon some deeper issues raised by the progress of the whole play so far, thus enlarging the field in which thought and imagination can extend themselves. They retire to some distance from the action, especially in the central stanzas, so that in their state of apprehension they may remind themselves and the audience of the laws of heaven, the majesty of god, and the facts of sin and punishment. They are trying to re-establish confidence in traditional beliefs and principles which have been threatened within the play, and they are also seeking a solution to the agony of doubt expressed in the last two stanzas of the previous ode. In this respect then the song provides a pause for reflection within the gathering menace of the tragedy.

Many features in the play, apart from Iocasta's impiety, contribute to this atmosphere of menace. We may recall the descriptions of the plague and the pollution of Thebes by the presence of an unknown murderer, the search for whom was initially presented as a joint enterprise led with unsparing energy by the great Oedipus whom all love as the father of his people. It is probably the spirit of co-operation in the fight to rescue the city that the chorus are thinking of in the first antistrophe of the song when they beseech the god never to bring to an end τὸ καλῶς ἔχον πόλει πάλαιϲμα (879). They have seen 'the struggle that is honourable for the city', symbolized by Oedipus' efforts on Thebes' behalf throughout his reign, change into a struggle that is dishonourable, for it appears that the public interest has been lost sight of in two scenes of quarrel in which the king, provoked by Teiresias' accusations, imagines that he is engaged in a grapple for power with a rival party plotting to seize his throne: an example of τὸ κακῶϲ ἔχον πόλει πάλαιϲμα.[21] In

[21] See Oedipus' speech 380-9; and for the political implications of this stanza,

addition, with the emergence in him of this cτάcιc-complex which
threatens the unity of the city, there emerge also traits of
character which arouse misgivings, although they do nothing to
diminish his essential greatness or the devotion he inspires in the
Theban elders: suspicion and quickness to anger, hastiness in
judgement, over-confidence in the superiority of his intellect.
There are also the signs of delusion, revealed, as we have seen, in
the lyric dialogue (649–88). None of these defects however make
him a hybristic king. We must always remember that Oedipus
has saved Thebes once before, at the time of the Sphinx's assault,
and believes he can save it again. Therein lies his claim to
greatness in the eyes of his people.

Finally, in assessing the chorus's state of mind at this stage of
the play, we should take into account the menace of unmention-
able deeds (ἄρρητ᾽ ἀρρήτων, 465) and their consequences alluded
to in the earlier scenes and conveyed with extraordinary
vividness by Oedipus at 818–33, when he sees himself, if guilty,
as a polluted outcast: ἆρ᾽ οὐχὶ πᾶc ἄναγνοc; 'Am I not utterly
unclean?' (823), and at 830–3:

> μὴ δῆτα, μὴ δῆτ᾽, ὦ θεῶν ἁγνὸν cέβαc,
> ἴδοιμι ταύτην ἡμέραν, ἀλλ᾽ ἐκ βροτῶν
> βαίην ἄφαντοc πρόcθεν ἢ τοιάνδ᾽ ἰδεῖν
> κηλῖδ᾽ ἐμαυτῷ cυμφορᾶc ἀφιγμένην

'May I never, pure and holy gods, see this day, but be banished
from the sight of men before I see the defilement of such a fate
come upon myself!' The coryphaeus's reply to this, ἡμῖν μέν,
ὦναξ, ταῦτ᾽ ὀκνηρά, epitomizes the mood in which the chorus
begin their ode. It is this ὄκνοc, an almost physical shrinking from
threatened pollution suggested by Oedipus' words χραίνω (822),
ἄναγνοc (823), and κηλίc (833), that prompts them to preface the
song with a prayer for ἁγνεία, that purity which he fears he may
have himself defiled. This mood of dread requires not only the
opening prayer; it requires also, as a refuge from doubt and fear,
a statement of the validity of heaven's laws and a reaffirmation

---

Winnington-Ingram's important article in *JHS* 91 (1971), 119. A. A. Long's note on
879–81 (*Liverpool Classical Monthly* 3 (1978)) came my way too late for me to consider it
in my chapter on O.T. His suggestion that in this stanza the chorus are thinking of
Oedipus' violent quarrel with Creon is attractive.

in traditional language of traditional belief in the certainty of punishment for sin. It demands finally as precise an account as possible of the consequences of disbelief and the grounds for present fears. The ode indeed ranges widely, far beyond its immediate context, but nowhere beyond the limits of general reference to the subject of the play.

The song opens with a prayer for τὰν εὔcεπτον ἁγνείαν λόγων ἔργων τε πάντων, 'that holy purity in all words and deeds . . .'. In this phrase the epithet εὔcεπτος with ἁγνεία recalls Oedipus' θεῶν ἁγνὸν cέβας in 830, and the noun must be given its precise meaning, purity from physical defilement, for only then will the close connection of the first lines of the stanza with the king's speech 815–30 become fully apparent. The θεῶν ἁγνὸν cέβας is here defined in depth and range. The chorus regard it as a very real protection in time of trouble, guaranteed by laws eternally valid and fathered by Olympus alone with no human interference. Further, we may, if we understand correctly the meaning of the first clause (863 f.), observe that the chorus regard this ἁγνεία as a necessary condition of their portion of life. μοῖρα here means the share of life allotted by the gods to mortal men, and εἴ μοι ξυνείη μοῖρα implies a wish that without ἁγνεία this share of life may no longer accompany them. Like χρόνος ξυνών, πότμος ξυνηθής and similar expressions with words of time, destiny, and fate, μοῖρα is a companion of man throughout his life (μοῖρα ξυνοῦσα), granted to him at birth and removed at death. Accordingly, the meaning of εἴ μοι ξυνείη φέροντι μοῖρα should not be weakened by a paraphrase such as 'may it be my destiny to win or possess . . .' for this would require φέρειν not φέροντι. The participle in fact expresses a condition: 'may a share of life be my companion provided that I win or possess purity'.[22]

The prayer for ἁγνεία is followed by a statement of its sanctions. The νόμοι ὑψίποδες, 'the laws which move on high' (865), are identical with Antigone's ἄγραπτα κἀσφαλῆ θεῶν νόμιμα which she opposes to man-made laws and which alone she obeys.[23] In both passages there is the same polarity of expression designed to convey the idea of everlastingness and the mystery of a transcendental origin: in *Antigone*

---

[22] So Kamerbeek, ad loc. See also his article on the second stasimon of *O.T.*, *Wiener Studien* 79 (1966), 80 ff.

[23] *Ant.* 450–7.

οὐ γάρ τι νῦν γε κἀχθές, ἀλλ᾽ ἀεί ποτε
ζῇ ταῦτα, κοὐδεὶc οἶδεν ἐξ ὅτου᾽ φάνη,

'not today or yesterday, but for ever they live, and no one knows
from what source they came to light', in *Oedipus Tyrannus*, in the
more metaphorical language of lyric with a sustained image
from begetting and birth:

οὐρανίᾳ 'ν
αἰθέρι τεκνωθέντεc, ὧν "Ολυμποc
πατὴρ μόνοc, οὐδέ νιν
θνατὰ φύcιc ἀνέρων
ἔτικτεν, οὐδὲ μήποτε λά-
θα κατακοιμάcῃ

'begotten in the air of heaven, their father Olympus alone, and
no mortal being was their parent, nor shall oblivion ever put
them to sleep'. The climax is reached in the single sentence of the
last line (872), proclaiming the immanence in these laws of a
great and ageless god:

μέγαc ἐν τούτοιc θεόc, οὐδὲ γηράcκει.[24]

The effect of this stanza is extraordinarily impressive. Sophocles
understands the need at this moment of his play for a statement
of deep religious significance, not only to provide a sense of
security for the Theban elders but also to remind his audience of
the strength of divine laws at a time when human ignorance and
passion have taken control of the action.[25]

The antistrophe opens with the enigmatic statement

ὕβριc φυτεύει τύραννον.

This theme, developed over this and the next stanza, is no doubt
suggested to the chorus by Oedipus' tone in his quarrel with
Creon, which occupies the earlier part of the preceding scene.
There is no connecting particle, so the asyndeton may be
explained either as marking off the remainder of the song from
the introductory strophe, as in the parodos (159), or as amplifying
what has just been said with examples of the νόμοι ὑψίποδεc,

---

[24] For the agelessness of Zeus and θεοί, cf. *Ant.* 606 and *O.C.* 608.

[25] Similar prayers in odes from choruses menaced by fear and in need of divine
protection may be found at Aesch. *Pr.* 526–35 and Eur. *Med.* 635.

because over the next two stanzas we have a statement of one of
the most important of these laws, the inevitable cycle of ὕβρις,
κόρος, ἄτη, elaborated by a classic definition of κόρος, satiety
(874 f.) and ending with a vivid glimpse of the sinner hurtling to
destruction (ἄτη). In the second strophe (883), there follows a list
of the traditional sins which signalize the hybristic man. The
conclusion is that if such practices are held in honour, acts of
worship are pointless: τί δεῖ με χορεύειν; (895 f.).

To return to the opening words, the translation 'insolence
begets a tyrant' raises serious problems. In the first place, it is
improbable that τύραννος and its related noun τυραννίς in Greek
of this and earlier periods can have the bad sense of our words
tyrant and tyranny. Archilochus in the seventh century uses
τυραννίς of Gyges' royal power, and in this and the next century
and a half poets and historians use it to designate the phenomenon
of Greek tyrannies in which rulers exercised absolute power.[26']
When not a political term in this special sense, it is used, together
with τύραννος, to mean kingship, king, or ruler, without any
derogatory sense. This is the meaning of the words in Sophocles'
two Theban plays[27] and elsewhere in his works: king and the
exercise or office of kingship, not tyrant and tyranny. Nor is it
helpful to adduce as evidence that in this one place alone he is
using τύραννος in a bad sense the two passages of Thucydides[28] in
which first Pericles and then Cleon tell the Athenians that they
have a τυραννὶς ἀρχή, for in both the phrase is a political
metaphor and means an empire which exercises absolute power.
If then Sophocles is giving τύραννος a bad name in this ode, the
usage will be unique to him, so far as the evidence from his own
plays and from earlier poets goes. The dilemma may be finally
set in sharp relief if we give what is apparently the correct
translation, 'insolence begets a king'. This is manifest nonsense.

In the second place, the context in which these three words are
set is a general reflection, and therefore τύραννον is unlikely to
refer to a particular person. This consideration excludes Oedipus,

---

[26] e.g. the τυραννίδες of Cleisthenes at Sicyon, the Cypselids at Corinth, the Pisistratids
at Athens, the Deinomenids in Sicily. Poets of the seventh to fifth centuries normally use
τύραννος and τυραννίς of rulers and their power, e.g. Archilochus Fr. 19 W., Theognis 823,
1181, 1204, Pindar *P.* 2. 87; 3. 85; 11. 53; and if they want to give the words a bad name,
they indicate it by an opprobrious epithet or setting, e.g. δημοφάγος in Thgn. 1181.

[27] *Ant.* 506, 1056, 1169; *O.T.* 380, 408, 514, 588, 592, 939, 1095.

[28] Th. ii. 36; iii. 37.

Iocasta, Teiresias, and Creon, all of whom have been suggested by different scholars, even though none of them has exhibited in the play any of the characteristics of the hybristic person. Oedipus himself, the most obvious candidate, could not, in spite of his behaviour to Teiresias and Creon, be called τύραννος in the bad sense (assuming for a moment that the word has this force) by a chorus who have earlier in the play described him in terms of deep affection as the saviour of his city. Sheppard's solution is to refer the words to the chorus's fears as to what he may become: his behaviour and his character bear within them the seeds of tyranny.[29] This is at first sight attractive but it fails to convince because it still particularizes the reference and it gives a bad sense to τύραννος. Also, if the chorus are thinking of Oedipus in the antistrophe they must be envisaging him consciously in the second strophe as capable of the sins there listed. It seems unlikely that they could do this after what they said of him in the second half of the first stasimon and in the lyric dialogue. Moreover any conscious reference to him at this stage of the play would destroy the terrible irony of the third stanza of the ode.[30] Other scholars have sought for the τύραννος outside the play in contemporary Athenian life. It is however hazardous to begin any interpretation by assuming contemporary references; and in any case their views are widely divergent. Of historical figures Pericles, Protagoras, Cleon, and Alcibiades have all been suggested, nor has there been any lack of abstract candidates such as the Athenian Empire, the unbelief of the times, and the concept of 'tyranny' in general. None of these is satisfactory because they have no relevance to the dramatic situation and they all give the 'tyrant' a bad name.

We may now, having thrown doubt on all attempts to identify the τύραννος as a person or group of persons either within the play or in the historical scene, return to the point that the sentence is a general maxim. Sophocles' words suggest at first sight that an abstract (ὕβρις) begets a concrete (τύραννον) instead of another abstract, as it does in Aeschylus' metaphor at *Agamemnon* 763 ff., φιλεῖ δὲ τίκτειν ὕβρις ... παλαιὰ νεάζουσαν ... ὕβριν. We should then perhaps look for our elusive τύραννος not in an individual or group but in an abstract of which ὕβρις can

[29] J. T. Sheppard's edition of the play, 150 ff.
[30] Cf. Gerhard Müller, *Hermes* 95 (1976), 269.

be described as the parent. In writing of the cycle ὄλβος, κόρος, ὕβρις, ἄτη, Greek poets habitually use the metaphor of parentage. Solon and Theognis have variations of the same lines, which may express ideas from an earlier age:

τίκτει γὰρ κόρος ὕβριν ὅταν πολὺς ὄλβος ἔπηται
ἀνθρώποισιν ὅσοις μὴ νόος ἄρτιος ᾖ

'Satiety begets insolence when abundant wealth attends men whose mind is unsound.'[31] The parentage is reversed in the oracle quoted at Herodotus, viii. 77,

δῖα Δίκη cβέccει κρατερὸν Κόρον, Ὕβριος υἱόν

'Divine Justice will quench mighty Satiety, son of Insolence', and in Pindar's *Olympian* 13. 10,

Ὕβριν, Κόρου ματέρα θρασύμυθον

'Insolence, bold-speaking mother of Satiety'. The image reaches its most elaborate development in certain passages of Aeschylus, notably *Agamemnon* 750–71, where it is sustained over two lyric stanzas describing the begetting, birth, and growth of sin. This metaphor appears to be canonical in such contexts[32] from early times and probably springs from Hesiod's way of expressing the growth and relationship of abstract concepts in genealogical terms. It should therefore be exploited fully in interpreting Sophocles' phrase: he has indeed established it himself in the first strophe with τεκνωθέντες ... πατὴρ μόνος and θνατὰ φύcιc ... ἔτικτεν, though of course the reference is different.

Three solutions based upon this genealogical metaphor have been suggested. The first, which does not involve an alteration of the text, is due to Lloyd-Jones, who takes τύραννον as a 'kenning' for κόρον.[33] The connection of this κόρος, satiety, with ὕβρις is further defined in the protasis εἰ ... cυμφέροντα, and the translation will run 'insolence begets a tyrant, satiety: insolence if it be over-sated with abundance which respects neither due measure nor advantage ... plunges to its doom' (873–7). The cycle beginning with ὕβρις/κόρος ends with ἄτη. This interpre-

---

[31] Solon Fr. 5. 9; Thgn. 153.
[32] Cf. e.g. Aesch. *A.* 386 (Πειθώ ... παῖς ... Ἄτας); *Ch.* 648; *Eu.* 534; Eur. Frs. 10 and 438.
[33] *The Justice of Zeus*, 193 nn. 23 and 24.

tation has the great advantage of preserving the necessary generality of this part of the ode and of giving the abstract ὕβρις an abstract offspring in accordance with a traditional image from begetting and birth. It raises however a slight misgiving in that κόρος, which is essentially a state of mind rather than an active force, might not appropriately be described as a τύραννος; and we may feel that this word, in spite of the epithet κρατερός given to it in the oracle, is not active or powerful enough to exercise the control expected of a τύραννος.[34]

The other two solutions involve a change in the text. Eduard Fraenkel, with *Agamemnon* 763 ff. especially in mind, proposed

$$ὕβρις \ φυτεύει \ τύραννον \ ὕβριν$$

with a stop at ὕβριν, 'insolence begets an insolence which is a tyrant'.[35] ὕβρις in Greek is a mighty force which could well be called a tyrant that takes control. The other involves a more drastic alteration. Many years ago a philosopher friend suggested to me that one would expect Sophocles to have written

$$ὕβριν \ φυτεύει \ τυραννίς$$

'Royal power begets, or breeds, insolence'. This is indeed Blaydes's conjecture in his edition of Sophocles' plays, 1859. Strong arguments for it may be found in Winnington-Ingram's article,[36] and it is printed in Dawe's Teubner text of 1975. If scruples about altering so drastically a unanimous manuscript tradition can be overcome, the resulting sense is admirable. The train of thought develops as follows. τυραννίς, royal power, kingship, is attended by material prosperity, ὄλβος, which may produce κόρος, a feeling of satiety, and the ultimate offspring is ὕβρις. The cycle ends in ruin.[37] Discussion of these enigmatic words will probably never reach a conclusion, but it seems certain that the choice must lie between the last three solutions proposed because they alone preserve the required generality of the context, avoid applying τύραννον in a pejorative sense to a

---

[34] τύραννος is applied to Ἔρως in Eur. *Hipp.* 538 and Fr. 136. 1, and to Πειθώ in *Hec.* 816. Both of these are overmastering powers.

[35] Lloyd-Jones, op. cit. 193 n. 23.

[36] *JHS* 91 (1971), 132 f., where the irony is stressed by Winnington-Ingram.

[37] Besides the Aeschylean passages quoted above, the process is well illustrated by Pindar, *O.* 1. 55 f., of Tantalus and *P.* 2. 25–9, of Ixion. See also Solon Fr. 3. 7–9 and 34.

mortal, and make full use of the genealogical metaphor found in similar contexts from early times.

The second strophe (883) lists examples of acts likely to be committed by the hybristic man. As noted already, the chorus are probably not consciously thinking of Oedipus: they have in mind the processes of ὕβρις and its consequences in a general sense. Nor need we search the contemporary Athenian scene for examples of these offences in the speculations of sophists, the moral decay resulting from war and pestilence, and the distrust of the Delphic oracle for its undoubted support of Sparta during the Archidamian War. These circumstances may be borne in mind but they do not account for what is contained in the stanza, for the ode is no more a parabasis, in which the dramatist addresses his audience, than the first stasimon of *Antigone*. The sins listed, pride of word and deed, contempt for Δίκη, failure to reverence the images of the gods, acquisition of gains unjustly, and acts of sacrilege, all appear in Greek poetry, especially in Aeschylus' choruses,[38] and have a long ancestry; and they all receive condign punishment according to Zeus' laws of Justice. Some scholars have tried to find in certain of these sins a particular application to Oedipus and Iocasta, notably in the opening lines referring to pride in deed and word and contempt for Justice, and in

> τῶν ἀσέπτων ἔρξεται,
> ἢ τῶν ἀθίκτων ἕξεται ματάζων   (890 f.)

impious acts, such as Iocasta's attitude to oracles and the hint of incest in the last phrase. On the face of it these lines have a general reference, like the law stated in the closing lines of *Antigone*, χρὴ δὲ τά γ᾽ ἐς θεοὺς μηδὲν ἀσεπτεῖν, and in Aeschylus' ὅσοις ἀθίκτων χάρις πατοῖτο (*Agam.* 371), a comprehensive term for offences against things sacrosanct. Nevertheless, there is in this stanza an ambiguity of language probably intentional, which is essential to its irony, for when the truth comes out at the end of the play, it will be seen that Oedipus has, although unwittingly, in fact committed some of the sins here listed, above all parricide and incest which are so faintly suggested in 890 f. that the reference only becomes apparent in retrospect. These

[38] e.g. *Pers.* 811; *A.* 342, 371, 462–70, 527; *Eu.* 539.

two lines together, coming at the end of the list, sum up the series of conditional clauses divided by the central wish

κακά νιν ἔλοιτο μοῖρα
δυσπότμου χάριν χλιδᾶς

'may an evil destiny seize him for his ill-starred arrogance', so that we have a perfect example of the ABA type of period. Moreover they describe offences against the εὔσεπτος ἁγνεία for which the chorus prayed at the beginning of the ode and prepare the way for the personal statements

τί δεῖ με χορεύειν;

at the end of the strophe and in the first sentence of the antistrophe.

The meaning of 892 ff. is obscured by doubts about the text. The best manuscripts give

τίς ἔτι ποτ' ἐν τοῖσδ' ἀνὴρ θυμῷ βέλη
ἔρξεται ψυχᾶς ἀμύνειν;

Kamerbeek attempts the translation 'who will abstain from warding off (from the πόλις) with passion (θυμῷ) the shafts which wound his soul?' but this forces too much out of the Greek and the meaning is obscure. The only significant variant is θυμοῦ for θυμῷ. In some manuscripts τὴν θείαν δίκην is written above θυμῷ βέλη, and an ancient scholium on 892 has the paraphrase τὴν τιμωρίαν: these glosses give a pointer to the meaning but they fail to indicate what Sophocles wrote. The first problem is raised by ἔρξεται, and we may with little misgiving accept Jebb's arguments against it. Nor does the alteration of ἀμύνειν to ἀμύνων (Erfurdt) make it any easier to retain ἔρξεται in the Homeric sense of the active of this verb (*Iliad* 4. 130), of avoiding a weapon aimed, because it fails to remove the tautology with ἀμύνειν or ἀμύνων. Accordingly it is best to accept Musgrave's εὔξεται and assume a corruption from ἔρξεται in 890. The meaning will then be 'what man shall claim to ward off . . . ?'

Secondly, as to θυμῷ βέλη ψυχᾶς ἀμύνειν, the βέλη can only be weapons aimed at the man from outside and not the anguish or feelings of conscience that rise within his own soul, because ἀμύνειν implies defence against hostile attack. τίς ἐν τοῖσδ' ἀνήρ is then the sinner: 'what man involved in these deeds shall claim any more to ward off weapons directed against himself?'[39] Further, it seems that we must reject the dative θυμῷ as an error due perhaps to a reminiscence of the similar metaphor at *Antigone* 1085,

$$\text{ἀφῆκα θυμῷ καρδίας τοξεύματα}$$

'I have discharged in anger arrows aimed at your heart'.[40] We are left with two solutions. We may either read θυμοῦ as a defining genitive with βέλη, the shafts of wrath, both divine wrath, the κῆλα θεοῖο aimed at the wicked man, and the wrath also of the community outraged by his wickedness; or if we feel that θυμοῦ cannot stand without closer definition, we may accept Hermann's θεῶν βέλη.[41] γὰρ in the closing sentence, as often, gives the reason for the preceding remark: '[I say this] because if these practices are held in honour, i.e. if they go unvisited with wrath or punishment, why should I continue to celebrate the gods in acts of public worship?' The associations of χορεύειν are made clear by the gloss πανηγυρίζειν which appears in a few manuscripts. Dancing is singled out as the most conspicuous manifestation of religious feeling, and the conclusion of this stanza emphasizes both the significance of Greek Tragedy as an act of worship and the chorus's concern for the maintenance of belief in the certainty of justice.

The final antistrophe (897), opening with asyndeton, introduces an amplification of the chorus's own feelings and brings the ode into touch with the particular case at issue, Iocasta's attack on the veracity of the oracle about Laius, Λαΐου θέσφατα (906), which foretold that he would be killed by his son. The gods, especially Zeus and Apollo, reveal through oracles what is going to happen in particular cases, and if these revelations (τάδε, 902) are not going to come right so that all men may point to them as proofs of oracular truth (χειρόδεικτα . . . ἁρμόσει), there will no longer be any reason to consult oracles. In the following appeal to Zeus and his almighty power there is a renewal of the fervour of prayer that marked the opening strophe: 'if you are to justify your titles of κρατύνων and πάντ' ἀνάσσων,

---

[39] For ἀμύνειν with accus. and gen. cf. *Il.* 4. 11; 12. 402; 15. 731.

[40] See Denniston's note *CR* 47 (1933), 165.

[41] Both θυμοῦ βέλη and θεῶν βέλη require παλαίφατα in 906 for metrical reasons; see Dawe, op. cit. 246 f.

μὴ λάθοι

ϲε τάν τε ϲὰν ἀθάνατον αἰὲν ἀρχάν.᾽

The subject of λάθοι is not expressed, but it probably includes the proofs of oracular truth and also the content of the whole stanza if not the whole ode with its statements about eternal laws and the processes of sin and its punishment, 'may these things not escape your notice'. Zeus is here invoked as the supreme god who must exercise eternal vigilance. At the end of the play, when Oedipus is revealed as having committed incest and parricide and therefore as πᾶϲ ἄναγνοϲ, the irony of this last stanza will become apparent, for the Theban elders will be shown to have uttered a prayer to Zeus which was destined to be fulfilled in the ruin of their king.

The importance of this ode in the development of the tragedy is that it expresses at a critical stage certain permanent truths rooted in Greek belief: the necessity of purity in word and deed as a condition of life; the power of θεόϲ manifest in eternal laws; the cycle of ὄλβοϲ, κόροϲ, ὕβριϲ, ἄτη, and the consequent need for θεόϲ as a protector and champion; the belief that worship of the gods is conditional upon the certainty of punishment for sin; and the conviction that unless oracles are to be proved true, religion is in peril. These strong certainties are stated at a moment of apprehension in the chorus and of particular vulnerability for the two main characters in the play, when their behaviour and the march of events appear to be denying them, and delusion and ignorance are driving mortal beings to destruction. For all his greatness, Oedipus lives in a world of delusion and unreality, and this ode states what is true and real. The insecurity and illusoriness of man's greatness by contrast with the power of Zeus' law is the very core of this tragedy. The point is made in all its poignancy in the final song

ἰὼ γενεαὶ βροτῶν (1186)

but the foundation is laid and the audience prepared in the ode we have been discussing.

In spite of its difficulties of interpretation this is undoubtedly one of Sophocles' most impressive songs. There breathes throughout it a fervour and passion which we may feel comes from the heart of the dramatist no less than from that of the chorus as participants in the play, so that we are here vouchsafed a glimpse, as in the second stasimon of *Antigone*, of what Sophocles himself thought about the great issues of religion and morality. He has here expressed his thoughts in sublime language which while it owes much to traditional imagery and the organ-voice of Aeschylus, nevertheless has a chiselled clarity all his own. Each stanza concludes in a single emphatic statement about θεός and τὰ θεῖα, not a particularized god, but god, worship, and religious values in their most comprehensive sense. In the first two stanzas these statements are confident; in the second two, as the thought moves gradually to the individual case, they are full of foreboding and suggest despair. The stanzas are each self-contained in thought and structure, and the second strophe in particular (883–96), with its imprecation in the middle of the list of sins and its desperate question at the end, rises to an astonishing intensity of personal feeling. Apart from the rhyme-echo μήποτε λάθα, μήποτε λῦσαι (870 = 880) and the recurrence of θεός and τὰ θεῖα (872, 881 f., and 910), there are no special technical devices of language, and the metre is a conventional mixture of iambic and choriambic. A most dramatic effect is achieved at the transition from the ode to the next scene. Immediately upon the conclusion

> οὐδαμοῦ τιμαῖς Ἀπόλλων ἐμφανής·
> ἔρρει δὲ τὰ θεῖα

'nowhere is Apollo made manifest in honours; the worship of the gods is perishing', Iocasta enters with garlands and offerings of incense and turns to this same Apollo with a prayer for release from trouble, thus appearing to contradict the last words of the song and her own rejection of his oracles.

The flexibility with which Sophocles uses his choruses is well illustrated by the contrast between the second and third stasimon. In the third (1086), the elders of Thebes sing with a different voice and mood. They ignore what they have experienced and listened to in the play; they have shed away their forebodings; and they make no reference to the information brought by the messenger from Corinth which must have given them at least an inkling of the truth. Stripped bare of the character they have hitherto presented in the play and are to present again in the next stasimon and the final scene, they have become an immediate instrument of dramatic technique. The sudden change may perhaps seem disturbing if we think that a Sophoclean chorus should display in each ode the same kind of consistency with itself as is displayed in each scene by the characters who act on the stage. His choruses however possess a group personality rather than a completely coherent individual character, and besides sharing in the action with the actors they have the important function of influencing the audience as the dramatist requires, whether by reflecting at a distance on the deeper issues or providing a sharp stimulus of emotion. Consequently, while none of Sophocles' choruses sings odes inappropriate to its general role and status, the poet is nevertheless free to suppress and ignore attitudes acquired and expressed by his singers during his play in order to serve a particular purpose at the moment when each ode is sung.

In the third stasimon the chorus are a projection of the king's mood of exaltation which is thus continued in an unbroken sweep from his speech (1076–85) right through to the end of the song.[42] It is mainly from his last six lines that it springs. The foreboding of evil at Iocasta's exit, expressed in 1074 f., is banished by his words, and he imposes his mood so completely on the chorus that nothing impedes the transition from the actor's speech to the lyric. Everything is omitted from the ode that might check the excitement generated in the theatre at this climax of delusion, and in order to achieve its greatest effect this delusion must be shared by actor and chorus. The effect on the audience, as it is on the reader, must have been striking not only in its immediate emotional impact, but also in the overwhelming irony of the situation and in the mounting suspense as we wonder how long the delusion will last. This is one of the supreme moments in European Tragedy. Iocasta has perceived the truth and gone to her death, the reason for her agony misunderstood by the king. He himself, raised in his imaginings to a more than mortal sphere of being, stands poised above the precipice, a living illustration of the chorus's metaphor at 876 ff. of the second stasimon; and this ecstatic mood is caught and sustained in excited song before being swiftly shattered by the revelation of the truth in the following scene.

The ode consists of a single strophic pair in dactylo-epitrite

---

[42] For an analysis of this ode, see D. Sansome, *CPh* 70 (1975), 110.

rhythm. In the first stanza the elders envisage themselves as possessed of prophetic insight, an echo perhaps of what they had said in the first stasimon, that one man might surpass another in the mantic art (499–503). The turn of phrase, however natural in a context in which an event is imagined,[43] has in this song an additional point in view of the attacks made on the art of prophecy which so dismayed the chorus in the previous ode. In the address to Cithaeron (1089 ff.) as Oedipus' native country, nurse, and mother, there is an echo of the messenger's statement,

$$εὑρὼν ναπαίαις ἐν Κιθαιρῶνος πτυχαῖς \qquad (1026)$$

a line which also supplies the word εὕρημα, foundling, in 1106. This mountain is indeed the πατριώτης of Oedipus, the exile from Corinth, ξένος λόγῳ μέτοικος, an alien resident in Thebes, soon to be proved a native-born Theban, as Teiresias predicted in 452 f., and doomed to a second exile from the city over which he ruled and to a vagabond life on the mountain which he acclaims as truly his own after he has discovered his origin:

$$ἀλλ᾽ ἔα με ναίειν ὄρεσιν, ἔνθα κλῄζεται$$
$$οὑμὸς Κιθαίρων οὗτος \qquad (1451 f.)$$

'but let me dwell among the mountains, where is Cithaeron, renowned as my own'. The irony lies in the chorus's confidence that Cithaeron will be the scene of celebration and rejoicing when in fact it will, as Teiresias said in 420 f., ring with his lamentations.

After the echo in 1096, ἰήιε Φοῖβε, of the ritual cry to Apollo in the parodos (154), the antistrophe picks up and attempts to clarify Oedipus' enigmatic statements about his parentage in 1080 ff. There, he had proclaimed τύχη as his mother and the months as his kinsmen, marking the waxing and the waning of his fortunes. He had also, twice in his speech, expressed his determination to discover his origin (1076 and 1085). The chorus, wondering at his meaning and familiar with stories about babies born to nymphs in wild places, endeavour to help him and sustain his hopes by attributing his paternity, or at any rate his finding, to some god, Pan, Apollo, Hermes, or Bacchus. The effect is to invest him, as he stands on the brink of doom, with an

---

[43] Cf. e.g. *El.* 473; *O.C.* 1080.

aura of transcendental mystery. For a brief moment, in his own and the chorus's eyes, he appears to owe his destiny to the processes of nature and to have drawn his origin, by the intervention of a god, from the wilderness where he was found and to which he is destined to return. This impression of a wild and elemental quality in the king at the height of his delusion, is well conveyed throughout the ode by the repetition of words describing mountainous places and the beings that haunt them. Cithaeron, his own mountain, is addressed at the beginning. In the antistrophe, we meet Πὰν ὀρεccιβάτηc, Pan who walks the mountains, a spirit of wild places, the upland pastures loved by Apollo, Hermes, lord of Mount Cyllene, and Bacchus dwelling among the peaks, where he sports with the nymphs. Mountainous places of course play an important part in Oedipus' story, as may be seen not only in the references to Cithaeron throughout the play but also in the sustained image of the bull roaming over the mountains in the first stasimon, a projected symbol of the king himself. The present ode constitutes a climax of these ideas.

Comparison with the similar ecstatic ode just before the catastrophe at *Ajax* 693 suggests that this song too may have been accompanied by accelerated dance movements to match its emotion. Although there is no mention of dancing as an accompaniment, as in *Ajax* 701, we have in χορεύεcθαι πρὸc ἡμῶν (1093) a promise of dances at the all-night celebration in the light of the full moon. The present tenses of the infinitives in this passage, instead of the future, indicate the immediacy of the chorus's feeling and intention. The language of the song, free from striking flights of imagination, is simple, concrete, and precise, conveying its effect by the general tone. Two invocations, to Cithaeron and Phoebus, are followed in the antistrophe by urgent questions marked at the beginning by repeated interrogatives. This urgency is continued into the following brief scene in which after relentless cross-examination Oedipus' original question τίc δέ μ᾽ ἐκφύει βροτῶν; (437) and the chorus's own speculations in their song are finally answered. The king rushes from the stage and the Theban elders universalize the tragedy in the last stasimon.

The opening words of the ode ἰὼ γενεαὶ βροτῶν (1186) set its tone and explain its function, which is to present Oedipus and his fate as a symbol of the tragedy of mankind. The lament thus begins as a lament for the whole race of men. The theme is stated in the first strophe in language of exceptional clarity and precision with the key word βροτῶν repeated in the last clause. There are three rhythmic periods of the simplest and most formally lucid type of choriambic metre, each marking a stage in the thought. The first two acknowledge the nothingness of man in his life and the illusoriness of all human happiness, and the third adduces the fate of Oedipus as a warrant for the pessimistic conclusion βροτῶν οὐδὲν μακαρίζω, 'I call no mortal being happy'. The pity of this stanza is inexpressibly tragic. The view that the lives of men are as nothing and their happiness a mere seeming is deeply woven into the fabric of Greek thought from Homer's

$$οἵη περ φύλλων γενεή, τοίη δὲ καὶ ἀνδρῶν$$
$$(Iliad 6. 146)$$

through the speculations of early philosophers into some of the most sublime poetry of the fifth century, such as Pindar's

$$ἐπάμεροι· τί δέ τις; τί δ' οὔ τις; σκιᾶς ὄναρ$$
$$ἄνθρωπος$$

'Creatures of a day: what is a man? what is he not? a dream of a shadow'.[44] In Sophocles himself Odysseus states it at the end of the prologue to *Ajax* after Athena has displayed the distraught hero to him:

$$ὁρῶ γὰρ ἡμᾶς οὐδὲν ὄντας ἄλλο πλὴν$$
$$εἴδωλ' ὅσοιπερ ζῶμεν ἢ κούφην σκιάν$$

'I see that we are nothing but phantoms, all of us who live, or a fleeting shadow.'[45] This passage and Athena's concluding words form indeed the best commentary on the meaning of the first strophe of ἰὼ γενεαὶ βροτῶν. Man's whole existence is illusory, insubstantial, and subject to changing fortune as indeed Oedipus proclaimed at the height of his excitement:

$$οἱ δὲ συγγενεῖς$$
$$μῆνές με μικρὸν καὶ μέγαν διώρισαν$$

'the months, my kinsmen, marked me sometimes lowly, sometimes great' (1082 f.).

---

[44] *P.* 8. 95.   [45] *Aj.* 125 f.

We must be as precise as possible about the meaning of the
central period of the first strophe (1189–92). The definite article
with εὐδαιμονία suggests that the word has a well defined
significance in the currency of men's thought: 'what we call
happiness', almost a personification, when we remember the
Greek habit of prefixing the article to abstract nouns which
denote established concepts. Next, δοκεῖν and δόξαντα are
personal, as is shown by the masculine participle. δοκεῖν signifies
both what man imagines himself to be and what he seems to be
to others. Thus when the chorus state that no man wins more of
Happiness than the seeming and after the seeming, decline, they
mean that this stage is illusory not only for the possessor but also
for those whose lives are influenced by him.[46] Finally, ἀποκλῖναι
is taken by most commentators as a metaphor from the waning
of the heavenly bodies: the simple verb is used transitively with
the same meaning in the similar context at *Ajax* 131:

$$\text{ὡς ἡμέρα κλίνει τε κἀνάγει πάλιν}$$
$$\text{ἅπαντα τἀνθρώπεια}$$

'A day puts to rest and causes to rise again all mortal things'.

In the last period of the stanza the chorus turn directly to
Oedipus' δαίμων with the emphatic threefold repetition of τὸν
cόν to enhance the pathos. The word παράδειγμα, rare in poetry,[47]
means an example for instruction, whether by way of warning
or exhortation: instruction not only for the particular occasion
but also in truths of universal validity. The use of myths as
παραδείγματα and the gradual creation out of them of a body of
moral doctrine can be seen throughout Greek literature from
Homer onwards, and especially in lyric, both choral and
dramatic. So at the conclusion of the strophe we have a
considered judgement stated in such a way as to give it relevance
to the whole human predicament: βροτῶν οὐδὲν μακαρίζω. This
judgement is based upon a παράδειγμα drawn not from a remote
myth but from the fate of the living Oedipus who has moved
among the Thebans as their king and whose change from
happiness to misery has been presented on the stage before an
audience.

The antistrophe, introduced by the explanatory relative ὅστις,

---

[46] The point is well put by Musurillo, *AJPh* 82 (1961), 183 ff.
[47] Eur. *El.* 1085, the only other example in extant tragedy.

lists the qualities and achievements wherein Oedipus has shown his greatness: the high stroke of ingenuity whereby he became master of τοῦ πάντ᾽ εὐδαίμονος ὄλβου (an echo of τᾶς εὐδαιμονίας in the strophe), defeating the Sphinx and saving Thebes; and the kingship and high honours bestowed upon him. The fact that at 1193, 1202 f., 1207 ff., and throughout the last antistrophe, Oedipus is addressed in the second person should warn us to accept ἐκράτησας and ἀνέστας in 1197 and 1201. A shifting to and fro from second to third person in this passage would be intolerable. Throughout the stanza there are references to phrases and scenes earlier in the play. The king's fame was recognized by himself in his first speech at the beginning,

$$\text{ὁ πᾶσι κλεινὸς Οἰδίπους καλούμενος} \qquad (8)$$

and the affection in which he is held and his subjects' reliance on him as a saviour were emphasized by the priest in the prologue and throughout the play by the chorus. Such has been his impact upon the Thebans, τοιοῦτος ἐδόκει τοῖς Θηβαίοις and such he seemed to himself, τοιοῦτος ἐδόκει ἑαυτῷ, if we may bring out the force of δοκεῖν and δόξαντα in the strophe.

With the emphatic τανῦν δέ at the beginning of the second strophe (1204), the chorus turn from Oedipus' past greatness to the utter misery of his present condition, the stark *peripeteia* (ἀλλαγᾷ βίου, 1206). For this misery, as for the εὐδαιμονία in the first strophic pair, the evidence is given: incestuous marriage and the begetting of children on his mother. Of the two metaphors in which these facts are clothed, the first was used by Teiresias at 422 ff., τὸν ὑμέναιον ὃν δόμοις ἄνορμον εἰσέπλευσας, and is here repeated more explicitly with the word λιμήν,[48] the haven of wedlock in which he found refuge after his exile from Corinth. The haven is called great, μέγας (1208), because it meant marriage with a queen and succession to the throne of a great city,

$$\text{ταῖς μεγάλαισιν ἐν}$$
$$\text{Θήβαισιν ἀνάσσων.}$$

The second metaphor, in 1210 ff., is taken up in the final scene (1257, 1485, 1497), but is of too frequent occurrence throughout

[48] For the sexual overtones of λιμήν, cf. Empedocles Fr. 98.3 DK, Κύπριδος ὁρμισθεῖσα τελείοις ἐν λιμένεσσι.

Greek literature to have any special significance here. It is noteworthy that in this and the following stanza there is no mention of Oedipus' parricide. All the emphasis is concentrated upon the fact of incest. The reason is that in the preceding two scenes the king's whole effort has been directed to discovering the secret of his birth, and the search for Laius' murderer has been subordinated to the burning desire to find the answer to the question τίς δέ μ' ἐκφύει βροτῶν; Ever since then we have seen the gradual movement of his interest away from the murder-hunt towards the mystery of his origin, the solution to which has become the focus of his intellectual passion and his search for it more and more obsessive as the play moves towards the disclosure. It is as if he were being driven onwards by an inexorable 'Ερινύc.[49] When the answer is elicited by the tense interrogation in the preceding scene, the chorus in their last ode are naturally concerned solely with the supreme horror of incest. This concern is stressed by the realism of the accumulated terms in which the act and its consequences are described in 1207–15.

After the interrogative form of the second strophe, the antistrophe (1213) follows as a statement as if in answer to the question. Time, χρόνος, not a fixed point but a process inevitable in its movement, has found out the truth.[50] Χρόνος personified is often the revealer, the recorder, the preserver, and the shatterer in Greek poetry, a power that accompanies and controls the lives of men.[51] Here it is also a δικαστής, restoring δίκη, justice or right,[52] to a situation of unnatural horror, for such is the meaning of δικάζει τὸν ἄγαμον γάμον . . . τεκνοῦντα καὶ τεκνούμενον, a phrase in which the resources of language are strained to the utmost. Kamerbeek, following Hermann and Bruhn, may perhaps be right in taking πάλαι with δικάζει: the present tense will then suggest that χρόνος has been at work for a long time in the task of redressing the wrong until the moment of discovery, marked by the emphatically placed aorist ἐφῆυρε which refers to the final disclosure at the end of the previous scene.

---

[49] See Dawe, *HSPh* 72 (1967), 89–123 on the connection between ἄτη, 'Ερινύc, and ἁμαρτία.

[50] For the meaning of χρόνος see H. Fränkel, *Wege und Formen Fruhgriechisches Denken*, ch. 1.

[51] Pi. *O.* 6. 97; 10. 53 f.; Fr. 145B.; Soph. *Aj.* 646; Fr. 301 P.

[52] Cf. ἐν δίκη χρόνου, Solon Fr. 24D; and *O. T.* 614, χρόνος δίκαιον ἄνδρα δείκνυσιν μόνος.

The chorus conclude the ode with a personal statement, so that what began as a lament for mankind ends by reminding us of the close relationship which we have seen established between themselves and Oedipus throughout the play. The intensity of their sorrow is apparent especially in the second half of the stanza. They wish they had never seen him, and their grief is beyond all other men's. In this connection it seems best to read at 1218 ff.

$$\text{ὡς ὀδύρομαι}$$
$$\text{περίαλλ' ἰὰν χέων}$$
$$\text{ἐκ στομάτων}$$

with ὡς as an exclamation: 'How I lament, pouring from my lips a cry of woe beyond all other men!'[53] περίαλλα, so far from being 'utterly unsuitable', as Jebb says, makes the point that the chorus's lament is especially personal and poignant because of their closeness to Oedipus. The final words of the song recall the priest's appeal in the prologue (49 f.),

$$\text{ἀρχῆς δὲ τῆς σῆς μηδαμῶς μεμνώμεθα}$$
$$\text{στάντες τ' ἐς ὀρθὸν καὶ πεσόντες ὕστερον}$$

'let it never be our memory of your reign that we were first raised up and later cast down'. The second of these two lines suggests the correct interpretation of the last phrase in the ode, that ἀνέπνευσα ἐκ σέθεν looks back to the revival of life at Thebes after Oedipus' defeat of the Sphinx and that κατεκοίμησα τοὐμὸν ὄμμα signifies its eclipse in the darkness of his ruin.

The structure of this ode is straightforward and lucid, its sections carefully paragraphed by the stanzas and matched in the first strophic pair by simplicity and uniformity of the choriambic metre. In the second, when the thought moves from reflection on the past to the misery of the present, the rhythms are more varied: iambics followed at 1208 by hypodochmiacs[54] and closing with a reappearance of choriambics. Helped perhaps by the greater rhythmic variety, we may sense in the despairing questions of the second strophe a quickening of emotion and an increase in bewilderment in the repeated interrogations, τίς three

---

[53] So Lloyd-Jones, *JHS* 85 (1965), 168.
[54] See A. M. Dale, *The Lyric Metres of Greek Drama*[2], 114.

times in 1240 ff., πῶc ποτε twice in 1210, and in the intense pathos of the apostrophe

ἰὼ κλεινὸν Οἰδίπου κάρα

immediately after the stark presentation of the ἀλλαγὰ βίου in the opening period. This pathos is renewed by the corresponding

ἰὼ Λάϊειον ὦ τέκνον

at a similar place in the antistrophe, by the repeated εἴθε ... εἴθε introducing the wish at 1217, and by the exclamatory form of the next sentence marking the poignancy of personal grief. The emotion subsides in the final summing up introduced by the formal, even prosaic τὸ δ' ὀρθὸν εἰπεῖν.

The effect on audience and reader of ἰὼ γενεαὶ βροτῶν is twofold. In the first place it relaxes the tension and excitement aroused by the previous ode and the scenes on either side of it, and by universalizing Oedipus' tragedy in the opening words and thus enlarging the scope of pity, it induces a mood of acceptance which could not have been created by an outburst of particularized grief at the beginning. Accordingly, the movement of thought and emotion is from the general to the particular, so that his fate is seen in the context of accepted views about the creature, man. As the lament draws to its close, we who watch or read, warned in the first strophe of the frailty of all human happiness and filled with an all-embracing compassion, are prepared to listen with some measure of calm to the messenger's account of Iocasta's suicide and Oedipus' self-blinding. Sophocles has thus elicited the exact emotional response and created the exact mood required at this stage of the play.

Secondly, on a more intellectual level, in the light of the first strophe and its judgement on the nothingness of man and the illusory nature of happiness (εὐδαιμονία), the song is bound to raise in the mind the question 'What is, by contrast, real?' The answer may be found in the second stasimon: purity in word and deed guaranteed by laws eternally valid; the great god who grows not old; the inevitable processes of crime and punishment, even though the crimes may have been committed in ignorance; the necessity of belief in established religion; and the maintenance of worship and service to the gods. For parallel statements of what is real we may recall *Antigone* 450–57 and 604–25. In ἰὼ γενεαὶ βροτῶν the contrasts to these realities emerge with extraordinary power in the repetition δοκεῖν ... δόξαντα in 1191, followed by the description of the 'seeming' in the second stanza, the return at τανῦν δ᾽ ἀκούειν τίc ... to the fact of present misery in the third, and the final restoration of δίκη by χρόνος δικαcτήc in the last. Just as in the second stasimon of *Antigone*, especially the last two stanzas, we feel very close to the heart of Sophoclean tragedy, so do we feel in these two odes of *Oedipus Tyrannus*. The generations of mankind are vulnerable to the operations of an ageless god whose laws are eternal, worthy of respect, and in the eyes of many of Sophocles' contemporaries probably just; and these laws are the realities with which man the εἴδωλον, especially in the hour of his greatness, has to reckon. Both the seeming and the reality are stated in juxtaposition in the conversation between Odysseus and Athena that closes the prologue of *Ajax*.

After the speech of the ἐξάγγελοc, the commos naturally follows as the king reappears on the stage. It is introduced by a system of recited anapaests (1297–1306), which express the chorus's shock at the spectacle of physical suffering. In chapter 11 of the *Poetics*[55] Aristotle lists πάθοc, after περιπέτεια and ἀναγνώριcιc, as the third element of plot, defining it as πρᾶξιc φθαρτικὴ ἢ ὀδυνηρά, 'an action destructive or painful', and giving as examples deaths on the stage (ἐν τῷ φανερῷ)[56] and scenes of agony and wounding (περιωδυνίαι καὶ τρώcειc).[57] We need to lay stress on the technique of presenting such scenes in Greek tragedy. Normally it is only the result not the performance of the deed that is shown on the stage; and the physical shock at seeing the result comes as a climax of the agonized suspense created by a messenger's speech and is all the more powerful because it is received through the immediacy of eyesight after the mind has been gradually prepared. This impact of shock prevents quiet and rational utterance, so that lyrics in the form of a commos or a song from the stage between actors (μέλοc ἀπὸ cκήνηc)[58] precede

---

[55] *Po.* 1452[b] 9–12.
[56] In extant Greek Tragedy, Ajax kills himself on the stage, Evadne leaps from a rock on to Capaneus' pyre at Eur. *Supp.* 1070, and Menoeceus jumps into the dragon's lair at *Phoen.* 1018. Aristotle's use of the plural θάνατοι suggests that there may have been more deaths on the stage in plays no longer extant.
[57] For such scenes, see esp. the appearance of Heracles at *Trach.* 983, of Hippolytus at *Hipp.* 1347 and Philoctetes at *Phil.* 732 ff.
[58] For Soph. cf. *Trach.* 1004–42 and *El.* 1232–87, though here, Orestes does not sing.

the calmer tones of spoken trimeters. So here in the first words of
the coryphaeus, bewildered questions are followed by a turning
away from the sight (οὐδ' ἐcιδεῖν δύναμαί cε, 1303), as desire to
learn details, to ask questions, and to gaze longer on the spectacle
is overcome by a shudder of horror,

$$τοίαν φρίκην παρέχεις μοι.$$

The situation at this moment of *Oedipus Tyrannus* is similar to
the one at the beginning of the first commos of *Ajax* (346 ff.)
where the sailors are confronted with a sight equally horrible,
the hero amid the slaughtered cattle. Similarity of scene has
generated similarity of metrical form and structure, for when the
commos proper begins after Oedipus' opening anapaests and the
answering iambic trimeter (1307–12), the actor sings a mixture
of dochmiacs and iambics, and the utterances of the chorus are
confined to iambic trimeters, flat, dull, and at times banal. This
technique provides a foil to the actor's lyrics, ensuring that
attention is concentrated upon Oedipus and that there is no
distraction from his anguish. Even the banality of the chorus's
remarks may be a studied effect, for it is not the content of what
they say but merely the sound of their voice (τήν γε cὴν αὐδὴν
ὅμωc, 1326) that is required in order to establish communication
between the king and the chorus. This result is well achieved at
1321 when having heard the two flat lines 1319 f. he responds
with the poignant words

$$ἰὼ φίλος,$$
$$cὺ μὲν ἐμὸς ἐπίπολος ἔτι μόνιμος$$

'you are still my steadfast companion', thus recalling the elders'
loyalty and affection towards him affirmed throughout the play.
At the end of the antistrophe their two trimeters (1327 f.) repeat
the questions they asked in the anapaests 1299–1302, and
Oedipus' answer at the beginning of the second strophe prepares
us for the long speech that follows the commos. He lays upon
Apollo the responsibility for bringing about his sufferings,
repeating the words in order to stress his anguish:

$$Ἀπόλλων τάδ' ἦν, Ἀπόλλων, φίλοι,$$
$$ὁ κακὰ κακὰ τελῶν ἐμὰ τάδ' ἐμὰ πάθεα \quad (1329 f.)$$

and adds that the hand that destroyed his eyes was his alone. The precision of his answers to the chorus's two questions marks the extent to which actor and chorus are in touch with each other during the central part of the commos. This contact is sustained throughout the strophe until in the antistrophe (1349–66) he withdraws into the same tone of agonized soliloquy with which he opened the dialogue at 1307.

Apart from their question at 1327 f., there is perhaps one other exception to flatness and dullness in the chorus's trimeters, though unfortunately corruption of the text has put the interpretation of the words in doubt. Oedipus' appeal to the elders (1340 ff.) to cast him out of Thebes as accursed among men and loathed by the gods is followed by a pair of trimeters,

δείλαιε τοῦ νοῦ τῆς τε cυμφορᾶc ἴcον,
ὡc c᾽ ἠθέλησα μηδ᾽ ἀναγνῶναί ποτ᾽ ἄν   (1347 f.)

Thus the second line is given in the manuscript L, while A has ποτε at the end. ἄν is, of course, necessary. On the main textual point, μηδέ, 'not even' is unnatural, and ἀναγνῶναι, apart from an isolated example of the aorist passive in Euripides' *Helen* 290, never means to know, discover, or recognize in Attic Greek.[59] The simplest solution is to accept Dobree's μηδαμὰ γνῶναι. Before taking the discussion of this line any further, we may return to the first of the pair. νοῦc is here usually explained by reference to the immediate context and understood either as the king's decision to blind himself or as his realization of what he has done. It is however more likely that the chorus are lamenting the terrible result (cυμφορά) of the intellectual gifts which Oedipus employed with all his passion to discover the secret of his birth. This force of intellect (νοῦc) enabled him to solve the riddle of the Sphinx, as he himself recalled with pride at 396 ff., and within the play it is manifest at every stage that leads him to the truth about himself. He has now won through to complete knowledge by the exercise of νοῦc, and the result is bewailed with all its tragic consequences: 'wretched for your gift of mind and for the disaster it has brought'. This interpretation would support R. D. Dawe's theory[60] that Oedipus' ἁμαρτία consists in his

---

[59] The word means 'know' or 'recognize' in Homer (e.g. *Od.* 4. 250); also in Pindar *I.* 2. 23 and Hdt. ii. 91. The lines in Eur. *Hel.* may be interpolated; see A. M. Dale's note ad loc.

[60] See Dawe *HSPh*, loc. cit. 116–21.

passionate obsession to find out the truth about himself, and if correct, suggests that we should take ϲε in 1348 as subject of the infinitive γνῶναι, 'how I could have wished that you had never known the truth!'[61] The absence of an expressed object[62] for γνῶναι may perhaps be justified by recalling Iocasta's last fully articulate words to Oedipus at 1068

$$ ὦ \ δύϲποτμ' \ εἴθε \ μήποτε \ γνοίηϲ \ ὃϲ \ εἶ $$

'may you never know who you are!' The chorus's wish may be an echo of her cry instead of a repetition of 1217 f. in the final stasimon, εἴθε ϲε ... μήποτ' εἰδόμαν.

The commos is fully integrated into the dramatic structure both as a natural result of the events described by the messenger and as a preparation for Oedipus' reasoned speech explaining why he blinded instead of killing himself. This question is raised in general terms in the anapaestic introduction at 1299 ff., and explicitly at 1327 ff.; and in the concluding trimeters at 1367 f., there is an implied invitation to the king to explain his reasons for coming to what the chorus feel is a wrong decision. This is the final challenge in the play to his powers of intellect; and the technique is conventional in Greek tragedy where a character moves from impassioned lyrics to spoken trimeters in order to explain motives.

A last problem is presented by the closing seven lines of the play (1524–30). These are given to the chorus in the medieval manuscripts and to Oedipus in a note by an ancient scholiast on 1523 which suggests that the play should end with that line: αὐταρκῶϲ ἔχει τὸ δρᾶμα· τὰ γὰρ ἑξῆϲ ἀνοίκεια γνωμολογοῦντοϲ Οἰδίπου, 'the play is sufficiently concluded at this point, for what follows is inappropriate, with Oedipus indulging in gnomic comment.' The last phrase is a literary or aesthetic judgement with which we may be disposed to agree, for to our taste the concluding lines may indeed seem 'platitudinous and inadequate'[63] to the great tragedy we have read or witnessed. They also contain insoluble corruptions in 1526–29.[64] They enshrine

---

[61] So Dain–Mazon, Budé edition, followed by Kamerbeek.

[62] μηδαμά, originally a neuter plural used adverbially, may perhaps be felt as an object of γνῶναι.

[63] R. W. Livingstone in *Greek Poetry and Life*, 163 n.

[64] See the discussion in Dawe, *Studies*, i. 266–73.

a τόπος which appears at Euripides' *Andromache* 110 ff. and *Phoenissae* 1758–63, as well as commonly throughout Greek literature, 'call no man happy until he is dead'.[65] The passage in *Phoenissae* is probably spurious,[66] and its striking similarity to the ending of our play has led to the suggestion that this may be spurious also. Some scholars have accordingly bracketed 1524–30, leaving the play to close with a conversation between Oedipus and Creon; others, more convincingly, have realized that when plays ceased to be produced as connected trilogies, the coryphaeus, so far as our evidence goes, ended a play with a recited utterance,[67] and have assumed that this must always be composed in anapaests. They have therefore concluded that the suspected lines were interpolated to replace a lost anapaestic coda;[68] if however it is felt that even though similar to the spurious passage in *Phoenissae* and in part hopelessly corrupt they are not for those reasons necessarily spurious themselves, a case for their authenticity may be stated as follows. It is possible that Sophocles may have desired a special effect at the end of this play and that after the trochaic tetrameters in which the actors hold their final conversation (1515–23) he may have purposely continued the same metre into the coda. There is a parallel for this in Euripides' *Ion* which ends with four trochaic tetrameters from the coryphaeus following a conversation between the actors in the same metre. We may note that these are the only extant plays of either dramatist in which the actors' final lines are trochaic tetrameters, and they both, according to the medieval manuscripts, conclude with a trochaic coda.

These considerations strongly suggest that the last seven lines of *Oedipus Tyrannus*, if not rejected as spurious, should be given to the coryphaeus and not to Oedipus, though scholars are divided on this issue. An analogy has been drawn from the ending of *Agamemnon*, in which after a conversation in trochaic tetrameters between Aegisthus and the coryphaeus, Clytaemnestra closes the play with a couple of lines in the same metre. This should however not be used to prove that it is Oedipus who recites the closing lines of our play.[69] In the first place *Agamemnon* is the

---

[65] e.g. *Trach.* 1 ff.; Hdt. i. 32 and Dionys. Fr. 3. Nauck[2] 794.
[66] As is shown by E. Fraenkel, *S B Bayr. Akad.* (1963).
[67] Eur. *Tr.* ends with a *sung* utterance from the chorus.
[68] So Bruhn's edition (1913), followed by Pearson in OCT.
[69] So E. Fraenkel in his edition of Aesch. *A.* ii. 804n.

opening play of a connected trilogy, whereas *Oedipus* is complete in itself. Secondly, Clytaemnestra's lines are different in type and function, being the concluding part of a preceding conversation, and not a gnomic comment on the whole. Finally, due weight must be given to the fact that all Euripides' extant plays and the other six of Sophocles' end with an utterance from the coryphaeus.[70] Hence there is a strong probability that the closing lines of *Oedipus Tyrannus* were recited by the coryphaeus who addresses the Theban elders as their spokesman and delivers an objective summing up while the actors leave the stage.

The charge of inappropriateness levelled against the passage in the ancient scholium has been echoed by many scholars, some of whom have used stronger terms of condemnation.[71] Any judgement on this point is likely to be subjective. Granted that to modern taste the lines may appear dull in content, mediocre in expression, and unsatisfactory as an ending to one of the world's greatest tragedies, we may note that few of these codas in Sophocles and almost none in Euripides are remarkable either for their poetry or their thought. Exceptions are the endings of *Trachiniae*, *Antigone*, and possibly *Electra*, all of which comment effectively on the main issues of these plays. The final lines of *Ajax* are indeed commonplace and uninspired, while *Philoctetes* and *Oedipus at Colonus* close with brief sentences of dismissal. As to the gnomic comment in the last three lines of this passage, we should bear in mind that general maxims drawing lessons from myth and legend are an essential feature of Greek literature throughout the archaic and classical periods. Often, especially in choral lyric, their triteness is alchemized or concealed by the magic of language; sometimes, even in the highest poetry, it is left unadorned and starkly apparent. There is however little evidence that sentiments which modern taste is inclined to consider banal and inadequate to the context were so regarded by contemporary readers and audiences. Thus at the end of this play we have the final presentation of the παράδειγμα Oedipus as he has been depicted passing from happiness to misery; and the παράδειγμα is followed by gnomic comment, traditional and expected. Within these seven lines are compressed not only the thought of the first three stanzas of the last stasimon but also the

---

[70] Of Aesch.'s seven extant plays, only *A.* and *Pr.* end with actors' lines.
[71] 'A miserable ending', Friis Johansen, *Lustrum* 7 (1962), 247.

lesson for mankind in the reversal of the king's fortunes from his first appearance, renowned in the sight of all (ὁ πᾶϲι κλεινὸϲ Οἰδίπουϲ καλούμενοϲ), to his final ruin.

V

ELECTRA

According to the second ancient hypothesis and to the dramatis personae in the mediaeval manuscripts, the chorus of *Electra* consist of local maidens, ἐπιχώριοι παρθένοι. This statement however needs qualification. The scholiast's description of them as γυναῖκες τῇ Ἠλέκτρᾳ cυναχθόμεναι, 'women who sympathize with Electra's grief', is nearer the mark, for throughout the play they are referred to as γυναῖκες. They are evidently older than Electra, whom they address as παῖ and τέκνον; they advise her μάτηρ ὡcεί τιc πιcτά (234), a sufficient indication of age gap; they may well be married women;[1] and they are of noble birth, γενέθλα γενναίων 129, unlike Aeschylus' Choephoroe, who are captives of war and therefore household slaves. Clearly enough they hold a position of consequence in their city (πολίτιδεc 1227). These facts are important for their relationship with Electra, whom they are able to advise and exhort with some appearance of authority. She on her side is assured of their sympathy and friendship (133 f.). In addition, as they make clear in the first utterance (127), they hate the rule of Aegisthus. They are also aware of its oppressive nature, for they express relief that his absence from the city makes free conversation with Electra possible (314 f.). This suggests that if married they may well be the wives of citizens who form a party in opposition. The fact that they are free-born women of Argos and not members of the household living in the palace gives a wider background to the play and suggests that there are political undertones. These should not however be overstressed, though they are heard unmistakably in the chorus's exclamation ὦ πόλιc at Clytaemnestra's death (1413). Whereas Aeschylus had emphasized the ruin of a household with all its members from high to low,[2] Sophocles has by his choice of chorus both widened

---

[1] Kranz, *Stasimon*, 221 f.
[2] The point is well made by John Jones, *Aristotle and Greek Tragedy*, 142 f.

the scope of tyranny to cover a whole city and at the same time focused attention on Electra's isolation as she stands alone against ill treatment and oppression, unable to share her sorrows with other members of a household, her sister Chrysothemis having acquiesced in the authority of Aegisthus and Clytaemnestra.

The status and age of the chorus also allow them with perfect propriety to be the mouthpiece of a fundamental theme of the play, the certainty of justice operating through the Ἐρινύς of the murdered Agamemnon; to urge at fitting moments the need for εὐσέβεια and προμηθία; to hold the balance between contestants in passionate debate; and to act as a bridge between characters in the grip of intense emotion. These latter functions are well seen in the two debates between the sisters, at 369 ff. and 464 f. in the first, and 990 f. and 1015 f. in the second, and also in the great conflict between Electra and Clytaemnestra at 610 f. In this last passage it is probably impossible to decide to which of the two the words ὁρῶ μένος πνέουσαν, 'I see her breathing forth anger', refer.[3] In such cases, the coryphaeus usually comments on the preceding speech, which is here Electra's, but it seems difficult to imagine that the chorus's representative could have doubts about the justice of her remarks. Perhaps δίκη may here mean propriety and refer in a limited sense to the progress of Electra's speech from reasoned argument to passionate invective exceeding the normal rules of debate; and if so, the sole purpose of the two lines will be to correct the balance and remind the speakers to observe δίκη, or καιρός. They certainly allow Clytaemnestra time to gather her thoughts after her daughter's onslaught, even providing her with a word (φροντίδα) to help her into her reply.

Sophocles has chosen exactly the right sort of chorus for a play of intrigue. Their sympathy with Electra ensures that no embarrassment is felt at the presence of a neutral or disinterested body of people throughout the development of the action: all that is needed is an appeal for secrecy which comes quite naturally from the subordinate character Chrysothemis (468 ff.). In spite however of their support for Electra and their conviction

---

[3] See D. B. Gregor, *CR* 64 (1950), 87 f. D. J. Lilley, *CQ* n.s. 25 (1975) 309 ff., gives 610 f. to Clytaemnestra. See further R. D. Dawe's review of Kamerbeek's edition in *Gnomon* 48 (1976), 228–34.

that Orestes is an instrument of just vengeance, these women of Argos are far more than a mere projection of her personality. In the parodos (122) and the lyric dialogue at 823–71 they urge her to moderation in grief and thus attempt, as older women, to restrain her excesses. This gives the first two strophic pairs of the parodos the quality of an ἀγών, a contest, as we shall see later, in which actor and chorus conflict in the exchange of lyric dialogue. Sung dialogues of this type are a notable development in Sophocles' last three plays. They bring the chorus into the immediate orbit of the action, establish a close relationship between them and the actor, reveal facets of character and states of mind by the interchange of conversation, and enhance emotional effects at moments of crisis and tension.

Before discussing the parodos in detail we must devote some attention to the prologue and in particular to Electra's monody. In the four plays so far examined the prologues are complete unities in themselves. Even though,. apart from *Trachiniae*, the entry of the chorus has been prepared by an actor's remark, and the parodoi have taken up and developed themes already established in the prologue, nevertheless the impression of a double start remains. In *Electra* however the prologue merges into the parodos, the link being forged by Electra's solo, 86–120. This use of a linking solo is a significant advance on the technique of *Trachiniae*, whose chorus form a close parallel with that of *Electra*. In both plays a group of women who do not belong to the household of the principal actor enter the orchestra, drawn by a natural sympathy of sex, and comment on the heroine's predicament. Whereas the women of Trachis appear as it were out of the blue to sing the parodos, their entrance unprepared in the prologue so that the break between these two sections of the play is conspicuous, in *Electra* Sophocles, whose plot excludes any preparation in the prologue for the chorus's appearance, has provided his heroine with a monody which echoes themes from the prologue and suggests themes for the parodos, so that the transition from one to the other is smooth and natural. Her laments are first heard off stage at the end of Orestes' speech (77), which closes with a prayer to his native land and his country's gods after he has outlined his plan for vengeance in accordance with Apollo's oracle. The paedagogus prevents him from staying to hear what she says, and the stage is left empty for her entrance.[4] She is given thirty-four lines of sung anapaests in which she laments her condition, stating the facts of her father's murder, expressing her determination never to cease from mourning, and closing, like Orestes in the prologue, with a prayer for vengeance and for her brother's return, for alone, she no longer has the strength to bear the burden of her pain:

$$μούνη γὰρ ἄγειν οὐκέτι cωκῶ$$
$$λύπηc ἀντίρροπον ἄχθοc \qquad \text{(119 f.)}$$

This is the only extant play of Sophocles which introduces the principal actor with a monody before the entry of the chorus. This technique appears first in Aeschylus' *Prometheus* where Prometheus' first utterance[5] is a mixture of spoken iambics and recited anapaests with a burst of lyric as he hears the chorus's approach; and it is fully established in some of Euripides' plays which are almost certainly earlier than Sophocles' *Electra*.[6] The use of song or a mixture of song, recitation, and speech for the principal actor's first utterance in a play isolates his personality, increases the pathos of his situation, and evokes a heightened emotional response from audience and reader. Thus in Sophocles' play, Electra dominates the tragedy from the end of the prologue. Her loneliness and the physical misery of her condition are established by her solo before the chorus enters at 122, and during the parodos (121–250) she plays the leading part. In addition to isolating her personality at the beginning of his play, Sophocles has secured a further advantage by his chosen structure. Electra's cry

$$ἰώ μοί μοι δύcτηνοc$$

off stage (77) breaks into the prosaic trimeters of the prologue in which the precise details of the plan have been unfolded as the three men survey Orestes' heritage and plot its recovery in the bright dawn. Her first utterance on stage and her first communications with the chorus are in lyric. There is thus a highly effective contrast between the practical tones of the prologue and the emotional intensity of the parodos.[7]

---

[4] See Tycho Wilamowitz, *Dramatische Technik des Sophokles*, 168, on *El.* 77–85 and Sophocles' innovation in relation to *Choephoroe*.

[5] *Pr.* 88–127.

[6] e.g. *Hec. Tr.* and *El.*, if indeed Eur.'s play precedes Soph.'s.

[7] See J. H. Kells's perceptive note in his commentary ad loc.

The ensuing dialogue between Electra and the chorus is the first example of this type of parodos in Sophocles' extant plays. Aeschylus used it in his *Prometheus*, though there the actor recites anapaests between the lyric stanzas of the chorus; and the same technique appears in some of Euripides' plays earlier than Sophocles' *Electra*.[8] Apart therefore from those parodoi, probably the original type, which are confined to the chorus and are still found in some of Euripides' latest plays,[9] we have a different type whose development may be traced from an epirrhematic form, in which the actor speaks trimeters or recites anapaests and the chorus sing, into a complete lyric form, in which the actor also sings. The fully lyric parodos may have been inspired by a desire to integrate more closely the parts played by both chorus and actor in the scene that follows the prologue. On their first entry the chorus must be given information known already through the prologue to some of the actors and the audience. In Sophocles' earlier plays, in which the parodos is confined to the chorus, this information is imparted in the first epeisodion by an actor,[10] but in *Electra* a striking change occurs: chorus and actor are brought into contact with each other through the medium of sung dialogue. Further, the use of song for both reduces the emotional gap between them that might have been felt had the actor spoken trimeters or recited anapaests. In the parodos of this play Electra and the chorus together explore the pathos of her predicament through what is in the strict sense a commos, a shared lyric of lament. *Philoctetes* and *Oedipus at Colonus* reveal a further development: the parodos is no longer confined to lament but embraces a variety of feelings, excitement, curiosity, suspense, and shock. Thus did Sophocles, no less than Euripides, continue up to the end of his life to experiment with new methods of handling the relations between actor and chorus.

The parodos of *Electra* consists formally of three strophic pairs and an epode, each stanza being divided between actor and chorus with the chorus opening and Electra closing. In the epode she has by far the major part after three lines from the chorus. The strophes and antistrophes are longer than is usual in Sophocles' purely choral lyrics, so that the parts of both actor

---

[8] e.g. *Med.* (431 B.C.) and *Heracl.* (?424).   [9] *Ph., Ba.,* and *I.A.*

[10] C.f. e.g. Creon's speech, *Ant.* 163–210; Oedipus', *O.T.* 216–75; Deianira's, *Trach.* 141–77.

and chorus are given space to expand and make their full emotional impact. The formalized, evenly balanced distribution of these parts serves admirably to sustain and regulate the emotions of the participants throughout the long lyric interchange, the outlines of which can be traced from the chorus's opening question to Electra at 121, through her reactions at each stage to their attempts to comfort and exhort her, until the moment at 229, just before the epode, when she finally rejects their advice with the words

$$\text{ἄνετέ μ' ἄνετε παράγοροι}$$

'Leave me alone, leave me alone, my comforters'.

During the first two strophic pairs the chorus argue strongly with conventional commonplaces found throughout Greek literature from earliest times: weeping will not raise the dead (137–44); Electra's suffering is not unique (153–63); she should have courage and trust in the power of Zeus for time is a healer (173–9). Throughout the delivery of these platitudes runs a tone of rebuke, audible especially at 137 (οὔτοι), 140 ff., and 153 ff. (οὔτοι again), and resumed with added emphasis in the final antistrophe (213–20). In order to adapt their exhortations to Electra's case the chorus refer to the hope of Orestes' return (159–63 and 180 ff.) and of support from the dead Agamemnon (184). To all these words of comfort she has her answer: she must be allowed to weep for ever for her dead father, and for her brother's return she has no hope. She reveals how deep into sorrow she is plunged by comparing herself to the nightingale that weeps evermore for Itys and to Niobe (145–52), whom she accounts a goddess precisely because she weeps eternally in her tomb of rock. It is this remark more than anything else that prompts the chorus later (215 and 235) to use of her the word ἄτη, indicating that she is so obsessed with her sorrow that she has forgotten the proper norms of judgement and behaviour. During their attempts to win her from being in love with grief to a more balanced state of mind they elicit remarks from her which reveal the excesses to which sorrow has driven her: her admission that she is distraught (ἀλύειν 135); her outburst at 145

$$\text{νήπιος ὃς τῶν οἰκτρῶς}$$
$$\text{οἰχομένων γονέων ἐπιλάθεται,}$$

a glance no doubt at Orestes who she thinks has forgotten his family; her warped equation of eternal weeping with a god-like state (150); her acceptance of the infatuation which she herself acknowledges (221–5); and her utter rejection of all comfort (226–32). Against this, the women of the chorus represent a norm of balance, and the contest between them and Electra consists precisely in the conflict of their conventional standards of judgement with her obsession.

At the beginning of the third strophic pair (193) the chorus abandon for a moment their attempts to influence her and recall in impressionistic language the night of Agamemnon's murder. The passage is remarkable and demands some discussion. In the first place it picks up and amplifies Electra's description in her monody of Agamemnon's death (95–102) and employs the same rhythm of lamenting anapaests marked in the first few lines by heavy spondees. Thus at this moment in the parodos the chorus change their hortatory mood and heighten the emotional tone. Secondly, Sophocles reverts to the Homeric account of the murder,[11] in which the king was struck down at a feast and not in his bath by Clytaemnestra alone, as in Aeschylus. The words

$$\text{οἰκτρὰ μὲν νόστοιϲ αὐδά,}$$
$$\text{οἰκτρὰ δ' ἐν κοίταιϲ πατρῴαιϲ}$$

'Pitiful was the voice at his return, and pitiful on your father's couch' (193 f.), are mysterious and infinitely moving: they suggest that the crime was committed at a banquet celebrating Agamemnon's return (Electra's ὦ δείπνων ἀρρήτων ἔκπαγλ' ἄχθη (203 f.) appears to confirm this), and that there were cries of woe piteously repeated, but whether the deed took place at a feast in Aegisthus' house, as in Homer, or in Agamemnon's palace, as is suggested by πατρῴαιϲ, and whether κοίταιϲ refers to the couches on which the guests reclined, or to the bedrooms in the palace, we cannot tell precisely from the chorus's words. The only clear statement in this allusive sentence is that the weapon was a double-headed axe, and not, as in Homer and probably Aeschylus, a sword.[12] This lack of precision is surely intentional:

[11] *Od.* 11. 411 and 418 f. Cf. for the cry (193 f.) *Od.* 11. 421 οἰκτροτάτην … ὄπα … Καϲϲάνδρηϲ.

[12] On the weapon used by Clytaemnestra, see Fraenkel's edition of *Agam.* iii, app. B, 806.

the chorus recall the echoing cry of woe, its pathos emphasized by the repetition of οἰκτρά. They draw on their imagination under the stimulus of Electra's grief and evoke the full pity and horror of the scene at the moment of the axe's blow. We shall meet the axe again in the first stasimon (405 ff.). Finally, after this vivid image, the writing again becomes impressionistic:

$$\text{δόλος ἦν ὁ φράσας, ἔρος ὁ κτείνας}$$
$$\text{δεινὰν δεινῶς προφυτεύσαντες}$$
$$\text{μορφάν· εἴτ' οὖν θεὸς εἴτε βροτῶν}$$
$$\text{ἦν ὁ ταῦτα πράσσων.} \qquad \text{(197–200)}$$

These words conjure up the shape of the murderers, monstrously begotten of guile and lust, but whether the deed was done by a god or by human agency they leave in doubt. Sophocles may well be concentrating into one concise and mysterious phrase those passages in *Agamemnon* where the chorus invoke the δαίμων of the House of Atreus, and Clytemnaestra, seizing upon this idea in her defence, envisages herself in its shape.

These imaginings of the chorus arouse Electra to further heights of emotion in the second half of the strophe. In impassioned exclamations she apostrophizes the day of horror and the night of murder and prays for vengeance on those who ruined her life, thus repeating themes from her monody. The chorus in their reply (213–20) renew their earlier exhortations and urge her to moderate her grief. After the previous strophe in which she and the women of Argos were for a moment united in the visualization of Agamemnon's death, they now resume their conflict, and for the first time the chorus use the word ἄται to describe her state of mind:

$$\text{οἰκείας εἰς ἄτας}$$
$$\text{ἐμπίπτεις οὕτως αἰκῶς.}^{13}$$

Then in 217–20 they forecast the main argument that Chryso-themis will use against her sister in the following scene,

$$\text{τὰ δὲ τοῖς δυνατοῖς}$$
$$\text{οὐκ ἐριστὰ πλάθειν}$$

---

[13] Pearson's punctuation in OCT of 215 has much in its favour ... τὰ παρόντ'; οἰκείας εἰς ἄτας ἐμπίπτεις, 'don't you see the reasons for your present predicament? Your moods of obsessive grief are your *own* doing'. The asyndeton is explanatory and οἰκείας emphatic by position.

—one should not come into conflict with those in power—with which we may compare Chrysothemis' words in 339 f.,

$$\epsilon\mathgrm{i} \delta' \grelevθέραν \mu\epsilon \delta\epsilon\hat{i}$$
$$ζ\hat{η}ν, τ\hat{ω}ν κρατούντων \grestci πάντ' \grakουcτέα$$

'But if I must live in freedom, our rulers are to be obeyed in all things.'

Electra's reaction to this is important for the understanding of her condition. She admits full knowledge of her passion, ascribing it to the dire compulsion of her circumstances; she accepts the chorus's word ἆται and says she will never check her obsessive laments as long as she lives (221–5). Thus towards the end of the parodos the chorus elicit from her the poignant kernel of her tragedy: she is infatuated, even warped by her sorrows, and she is bitterly aware of it. She repeats the point in her speech immediately after the lyrics are at an end where she reasons carefully in defence of her attitude (254–7):

$$αἰcχύνομαι μέν, \hat{ω} γυναῖκες, εἰ δοκ\hat{ω}$$
$$πολλοῖcι θρήνοιc δυcφορεῖν ὑμῖν ἄγαν.$$
$$ἀλλ' ἡ βία γὰρ ταῦτ' ἀναγκάζει με δρᾶν,$$
$$cυγγνῶτε$$

'I am ashamed if my many lamentations make me seem to you to take my troubles too hard, but since dire constraint forces me to do this, forgive me.'; and at the end of her speech (307–9):

$$ἐν οὖν τοιούτοιc οὔτε cωφρονεῖν, φίλαι,$$
$$οὔτ' εὐcεβεῖν πάρεcτιν· ἀλλ' ἐν τοῖc κακοῖc$$
$$πολλή 'cτ' ἀνάγκη κἀπιτηδεύειν κακά$$

'And so in conditions such as these, my friends, I can show neither restraint nor reverence; but in the midst of evil I am forced to practise evil'. She repeats it again towards the end of her scene with Clytaemnestra (616–21) emphasizing especially the shame she feels at her behaviour,

$$εὖ νῦν ἐπίcτω τῶνδέ μ' αἰcχύνην ἔχειν,$$
$$κεἰ μὴ δοκῶ cοι· μανθάνω δ' ὁθούνεκα$$
$$ἔξωρα πράccω κοὐκ ἐμοὶ προcεικότα$$

'Be sure that I do feel shame for this, even if you do not think so:

I know that my behaviour is unseemly and unlike my true self.'

In such a state of mind she finds it impossible to listen to the voice of reason and moderation. From this moment the chorus realize that further attempts at persuasion are in vain. At the beginning of the epode (233) they use the familiar collocation of particles ἀλλ' οὖν ... γε, 'well, at any rate', to denote resignation, and they break off the argument with an assurance of goodwill and a final exhortation

$$\mu\grave{\eta} \ \tau\acute{\iota}\kappa\tau\epsilon\iota\nu \ c' \ \ddot{a}\tau a\nu \ \ddot{a}\tau a\iota c$$

leaving us in no doubt about their prognosis of Electra's condition: obsession tends to breed obsession. At the end of the parodos, after appealing to the custom of never forgetting the dead or ceasing to honour them with lamentations, she proclaims that if the victim is to lie unregarded and the murderers are to go unpunished, respect and piety will perish among mankind. It has been pointed out[14] that while here she bases her attitude on the foundation of αἰδώc and εὐcέβεια, shame or respect, and reverence, at the end of her long speech (307 ff.) she disclaims these virtues as impossible for her in the conditions under which she lives, thus reverting to the bleak feelings she expressed in the parodos 221–5. It is as if she were regarding herself from two points of view, both as the just avenger of her father and therefore εὐcεβήc, and also as a woman whose natural instincts are so warped that she feels incapable of either cωφροcύνη or εὐcέβεια in her daily conduct. A psychological 'split' of this type indicates that the mind is obsessed and the judgement confused. It is precisely in this condition that we should seek for the meaning of the word ἄτη, used of Electra three times in the plural and once in the singular, in the last two stanzas of the parodos. If a distinction is to be drawn between the singular and the plural, we might say that the former refers to the state of mind and the latter gives a more concrete sense, acts or instances of obsessed behaviour.

Looking back over this parodos, we may observe first that it is a contest in which one participant tries, and fails, to persuade another. Such scenes of persuasion, whether successful or not, possess an inherent power to create excitement whenever they occur in drama, whether they are long or short, composed in speech or song, or in a mixture of both. Secondly, Sophocles has

[14] See A. A. Long, *Language and Thought in Sophocles*, 151.

so constructed the parodos of this play that the tragic depths of Electra's heart and mind are gradually disclosed before our eyes by her own answers to the chorus's questions and admonitions, the disclosure culminating in the self-revelation of the final antistrophe. None of the effects of this process in creating tension, awaking compassion, and revealing character could have been so powerfully achieved by a conventional ode for the chorus alone. Further, certain devices of style and language in the dialogue regulate its development and its changes of emotional tone. We are able to trace easily the form which it takes: opening and closing with the chorus's attempts to urge moderation, it has as its centre-piece the vision of murder and thus displays a circular structure that can be found in poetry of every genre from Homer onwards. The arguments moreover are carefully paragraphed. After the introductory question and answer in the first strophe the three τόποι with which the chorus seek to comfort Electra are presented to her in the first antistrophe, second strophe, and second antistrophe. A significant change of mood occurs in the last strophe, when the attempt at persuasion is suspended during an exchange in which Electra and the chorus are united for a few moments of shared emotion as they conjure up the vision of Agamemnon's murder. The emotional intensity of this stanza (193–212) is marked by repeated words (οἰκτρὰ μὲν ... οἰκτρὰ δέ, δεινὰν δεινῶς), the threefold appeal at the beginning of Electra's piece, the fourfold alliteration of π at 210 where she asks Zeus to punish the guilty, and the use of heavy spondaic anapaests which recall the rhythms of her opening monody. Her emotion is carried over into the antistrophe, where the chorus resume their efforts to persuade her, and she makes further use of repetition and alliteration (221–9) to mark the passion with which she reveals her state of mind in answer to the chorus's final admonitions. For all its novelty in producing dramatic and emotional effects not hitherto apparent in Sophocles' parodoi, this lyric dialogue is still formal and stylized: neither the language nor the sentence-structure has yet achieved the naturalism and the flexibility which are such a striking feature of the parodoi of *Philoctetes* and above all *Oedipus at Colonus*.

The connection between the parodos and the first epeisodion is smooth and natural, with the coryphaeus giving the reason for the presence of the chorus, almost as if aware that they had interrupted Electra's monody, and emphasizing their sympathy with her interests. She follows with a reasoned statement of the position which she had outlined in her previous lyrics and reaffirms at the beginning and the end of her speech the points brought out in the third system of the parodos about her behaviour. The purpose of the brief conversation between Electra and the coryphaeus (310–27) is to provide a glimpse of the tyranny of Aegisthus, confirm his absence, and reveal the chorus's concern for the whereabouts of Orestes and their confidence that he will return. There follows the dispute between Electra and Chrysothemis which elicits, after the former has had the last word, the chorus's warning against anger and an injunction to each to learn from the other (369 ff.). At 404, in the course of the stichomythia, comes a turning-point, when Electra's attention is incidentally drawn to the offerings carried by her sister. This leads to the description of Clytaemnestra's dream (417–23), which completely alters the mood of the two sisters, so that Chrysothemis is persuaded to abandon her mission and participate in Electra's own offerings at their father's tomb (466–71). More important for a study of the chorus is the fact that the dream supplies the motive and subject-matter of the first stasimon (472–515) and also suggests the word μάντις in the first line and the theme of μαντεία which frames the strophe and antistrophe. In the epeisodion, Clytaemnestra's dream was merely recounted, not interpreted. Dreams need interpretation and supply an obvious field for the exercise of the mantic art both professional and amateur. The interpreter of this dream is no professional, no Calchas or Teiresias, but the chorus, who interpret it in the first two stanzas of their song. The point was made in the ancient scholium on 472: ὁ χορὸς ἐκ τοῦ ὀνείρου προμαντευόμενος θαρρεῖν παραινεῖ τὴν Ἠλέκτραν, 'the chorus foretell the future from the dream and exhort Electra to take courage.' The stasimon thus springs immediately from the action of the play and is completely relevant to the dramatic context. It is addressed to Electra (ὦ τέκνον, 478) who is alone on the stage, Chrysothemis having departed to place the new offerings on Agamemnon's tomb.

The opening words,

$$\text{εἰ μὴ 'γὼ παράφρων μάντις ἔφυν καὶ}$$
$$\text{γνώμας λειπομένα σοφᾶς}$$

'If I am not a crazy prophet and one lacking in skill', recall the similar clause at the beginning of the third stasimon of *Oedipus Tyrannus*

$$\epsilon \H{\iota}\pi\epsilon\rho \ \epsilon\gamma\grave{\omega} \ \mu\acute{\alpha}\nu\tau\iota c \ \epsilon\grave{\iota}\mu\grave{\iota}$$
$$\kappa\alpha\grave{\iota} \ \kappa\alpha\tau\grave{\alpha} \ \gamma\nu\acute{\omega}\mu\alpha\nu \ \H{\iota}\delta\rho\iota c. \qquad (1086)$$

The dramatic situation and effect are much the same in both plays. The chorus catch a mood of hope from the words of an actor in the preceding scene and communicate their confidence to both actor and audience. In the following scene this confidence is shattered, in *Electra* by the paedagogus's speech reporting the supposed death of Orestes (680–763), in *Oedipus* by the final revelation of the truth. In both odes we have the chorus prophesying in the role of μάντιc, though in *Electra* the prophecy will be fulfilled. Electra herself has acquired assurance from the dream (469 ff.), but it is left to the chorus to give form to what is in her mind and to affirm the justice of her hopes for vengeance. This they do in their ode by the confident future tenses εἶcιν, μετεῖcιν, ἥξει, πελᾶν, καταcχήcει, the repeated θάρcοc[15] at identical places (479 = 495) emphasized by the weighty spondaic ending to the iambic dimeters, and above all by the introduction of Δίκα, here entitled πρόμαντιc the prophetess (475), winning a just victory, and of 'Ερινύc as her instrument (491). The chorus here begin to visualize Orestes, whose homecoming is the central hope of Electra's life, as Justice and the Fury personified, just as they do in the last stasimon when they describe Orestes and Pylades entering the house to kill Clytaemnestra as

$$\mu\epsilon\tau\acute{\alpha}\delta\rho\rho\mu\rho\iota \ \kappa\alpha\kappa\^{\omega}\nu \ \pi\alpha\nu\rho\nu\rho\gamma\eta\mu\acute{\alpha}\tau\omega\nu$$
$$\H{\alpha}\phi\nu\kappa\tau\rho\iota \ \kappa\acute{\nu}\nu\epsilon c \qquad (1387 \ f.)$$

'pursuers of wicked crimes, hounds that none can escape'. The association of Δίκα with 'Ερινύc is established in several passages of Aeschylus,[16] and here it amounts almost to an identification if we pay due regard to the parallelism in structure and meaning of the opening sentences of the strophe and antistrophe (475 ff. and 489 ff.). Moreover the astonishing physical features with which both Δίκα and 'Ερινύc are endowed, χεροῖν, πολύπουc,

---

[15] 495 is corrupt, but θάρcοc, with μ'ἔχει omitted, is probable.

[16] C.f. e.g. *A.* 1432; *Ch.* 646–51; *Eu.* 551 f. See further, for the 'Ερινύεc in *El.*, Winnington-Ingram, *PCPhS* 183 (1954), 20–26.

πολύχειρ, χαλκόπους, help their identification with the human avengers.

At the beginning of the antistrophe (489), the Fury is imagined as a monstrous mixture of human and animal attributes described in alliterative and repetitive epithets which convey by their sound and associations a powerful impression of speed and relentless energy in pursuit. Her task is to punish the adulterous lovers, and we are reminded of Electra's words in her monody where she prays to the Ἐρινύες who take note of those who betray the marriage bed, τοὺς εὐνὰς ὑποκλεπτομένους (114). To match the Fury's energy, the adulterer's passion is portrayed as similarly violent:

$$\text{ἄλεκτρ' ἄνυμφα γὰρ ἐπέβα μιαιφόνων}$$
$$\text{γάμων ἁμιλλήμαθ' οἷσιν οὐ θέμις} \qquad \text{(493 f.)}$$

a collocation of words which almost defies translation, but which emphasizes the struggles of the lovers to gain their wicked ends by murder most foul. One inclines to take Ἐρινύς as subject of ἐπέβα,[17] a timeless aorist suggesting that the Fury's onslaught upon the adulterers is seen as imminent if not already accomplished.[18] Alternatively, if it is felt that the tense of ἐπέβα consorts ill with the futures ἥξει and πελᾶν (489 and 496), we may consider the plural ἐπέβαν, found in R and conjectured by Blaydes, with the lovers as subject and γάμων as object, ἄλεκτρ' ἄνυμφα as adverbial neuter plurals, and ἁμιλλήμαθ' οἷσιν οὐ θέμις, with a comma at γάμων, as an apposition to the whole sentence.[19] It would however be difficult to understand the evildoers as subject when they are not mentioned until the end of the following sentence. Again, in 495–8 the text is in doubt. The temptation to accept θάρcoc is strong owing to the word echo from the corresponding place in the strophe (479), and the need to stress the idea of confidence throughout the first two stanzas of the song. The concrete imagery of the first half of the antistrophe suggests that the τέρας of 497 is not Clytaemnestra's dream but the Fury herself, the nightmare monster of the chorus's interpretation, which they are confident will draw near to the

---

[17] So Kells ad loc.

[18] Jebb takes ἁμιλλήματα as subject of ἐπέβα, 'striving lust for marriage came upon those who had no θέμις'.

[19] See Dawe, *Gnomon*, loc. cit. 231.

guilty pair μήποτε ... ἀψεγές: the sinister double negative, never blameless or innocent, means in effect positively harmful. The difficulty of the dative ἡμῖν however remains, especially with the following τοῖc δρῶcι καὶ cυνδρῶcι with a different reference, and we should perhaps give attention to Bergk's ἄψεφεc and for ἡμῖν write ἡμῶν dependent on it. ἄψεφεc· ἀφρόντιcτον is recorded by Hesychius from Sophocles' *Phaedra* (Fr. 692 P.) and also in Bekker's *Anecd. Graeca* 476. 1, but without the name of the play. If it is allowed into the text here the translation would run: 'Confident am I that never never heedless of us will the τέραc draw near to them.'[20]

It is important to note how Sophocles has in the first two stanzas of this ode concentrated much that is Aeschylean in thought and language. The statement about Δίκα in the strophe reminds us of certain phrases in the last stasimon of *Choephoroe* (935–71), sung after the slaying of Clytaemnestra and Aegisthus, so that the chorus are there regarding their deaths as a fulfilment. Sophocles' emphasis on Δίκα recalls Aeschylus'

> ἔμολε μὲν Δίκα ...
> βαρύδικοc ποινά

at the beginning of his first strophe, echoed in the opening lines of the antistrophe

> ἔμολε δ᾽ ᾇ μέλει ...
> δολιόφρων ποινά   (946)

followed by

> ἔθιγε δ᾽ ἐν μαχᾷ χερὸc ἐτήτυμοc
> Διὸc κόρα, Δίκαν δέ νιν
> προcαγορεύομεν ...

Both thought and language in this ode of *Electra* are distilled from Aeschylus' more abundant phraseology. There is however an important difference: nowhere in the stasimon of *Choephoroe* is Δίκα actually identified with the Ἐρινύc. It is Sophocles who has affirmed this identity and stressed the united assistance of these powers to Orestes in accomplishing a just vengeance upon his father's murderers. Indeed, in Aeschylus the Ἐρινύεc are in the main μητρὸc ἔγκοτοι κύνεc, 'the *mother's* angry hounds'

---

[20] See the app. crit. to Dawe's Teubner text (1975), 79.

(*Choeph.* 924 and 1054) as is required by the structure and thought of the whole trilogy.

The first two stanzas of this song have an exhilarating effect upon actor and audience. Economy of language, powerful imagery, concrete visualization of nightmare forces at work in the interests of justice, and a strong confidence in ultimate success all contribute to this exhilaration. In addition, not only are Electra's thoughts clarified by the chorus's interpretation of the dream, but the hopes and prayers which she has uttered since her first appearance in the play (110–16, 209–12, 453–8) are thereby provided with a moral basis. She is thus inspired by their encouragement to face Clytaemnestra's onslaught in the following scene from a position of strength.

The epode forms a striking contrast of content, mood, and rhythm. It stands in isolation from the strophe and antistrophe, themselves a rounded whole, as is shown by the theme of μάντις, πρόμαντις, and μαντεῖαι which opens and closes them. The chorus turn from their vision of the 'Ερινύς and in an outburst of emotion recall the ancient sorrows of the house, going back, right out of the orbit of the immediate action, to a remote past, further back indeed than Aeschylus ever went in his *Oresteia*, in order to seek the origin of the πολύπονος αἰκεία.[21] This they find in the fatal charioteering of Pelops, who persuaded Myrtilus, the driver of Oenomaus, Hippodameia's father, to interfere with the linchpin of his master's chariot, so that Pelops won the race and the bride. Oenomaus however had his revenge when Myrtilus assaulted Hippodameia and was thrown into the sea by Pelops whose house he cursed as he drowned. The complicated story is merely hinted at in Sophocles's words, and the manner of its telling is yet another indication of the knowledge of myths presumed by Greek poets in their audiences.[22]

Some explanation must be sought for the altered tone of the epode. It has been suggested[23] that the chorus see Clytaemnestra approaching and thus end their song with a theme which could not give her offence, and also that the πολύπονος ἱππεία of Pelops foreshadows Orestes' disastrous ἱππεία described in the following

---

[21] αἰκεία is a very strong word, suggesting violence and outrage.

[22] Sophocles wrote an *Oenomaus*; cf. Pearson, Frs. ii. 121–31. Pelops' charioteering is described as the origin of the Atreidae's woes at Eur. *Or.* 988–94. Cf. also *Hel.* 386 f.

[23] By Errandonea, *LÉC* 23 (1955), 367 ff.

scene. There may be something in the latter point, but the former explanation is too external to satisfy, as it does not take sufficient account of Sophocles' habit of following Aeschylus in tracing the woes of a house back to an ancient origin in previous generations; and it ignores completely the tragic implications of the stanza. Just as in the second stasimon of *Antigone* with its reference to ἀρχαῖα τὰ Λαβδακιδᾶν οἴκων πήματα and to the ἄτη which gives no release to the house from a remote past up to the action of the play, so here Sophocles reveals himself as an adherent of the traditional doctrine of inherited sin arising from a single act and potent throughout each generation. The epode moreover, after the confidence and exhilaration of the first two stanzas, forces our attention again on the tragedy of Electra and of the house to which she belongs. The shift from strong certainty and optimism to the theme of continuing woe within a single short lyric reflects the changes in the heroine's own state of mind as waves of hope alternating with waves of despair break over her. For instance in the scene before the ode, acquiescence in lamentation has given place in her mind to a desire for action, and in the scene after it the confidence inspired in her by the first two stanzas and sustained throughout her conflict with Clytaemnestra is changed to deepest anguish by the account of Orestes' death. The last sentence of the epode reminds us that the πολύπονος αἰκεία, the misery and violence which began with Pelops and continued with the murder of Agamemnon αἰσχίσταις ἐν αἰκείαις (the repetition of the word in 487, 511, and 515 is significant) has a considerable course to run, for Clytaemnestra and Aegisthus have still to be slain, and Electra has still to be subjected to further misery before her final release in the recognition scene.

Nor must we forget the emotion[24] with which this last stanza is charged, apparent in the opening apostrophe

ὦ Πέλοπος ἁ πρόσθεν
πολύπονος ἱππεία

with the exclamatory ὡς and the strangely emotive word αἰανής suggesting woe protracted over a long and weary time; and apparent also in the frequent alliteration of π and in the striking rhythmic effect of the echo πολύπονος ἱππεία and πολύπονος αἰκεία (505 and 515). The unusual rhythm sustained over the

[24] For a similar emotional effect, cf. the apostrophe ὦ πόνος ἐγγενής at Aesch. *Ch.* 466 ff.

whole stanza is unique in Sophocles, though isolated cola of the type ⏒ ⏑ ⏑ ⏑ – – – occur from time to time in his plays:[25] here however it is dominant throughout, varied by cretics and a series of long syllables. The metres are difficult to analyse, but the effect is arresting after the more conventional choriambics and iambics of the strophe and antistrophe and serves to emphasize the difference in mood and content.

Within the brief compass of this song Sophocles has, as we have seen, not only concentrated a good deal of Aeschylean thought, but has in particular preserved much of what is the essence of his predecessor's treatment of this tragic theme: the working out of a pattern of vengeance by means of formidable powers whose constraint is all-compelling in its influence upon their human instruments and necessarily productive of tragedy in that it forces noble as well as ignoble natures to commit violent deeds from generation to generation. As for Electra, in the first two stanzas of this ode she is encouraged to believe in the justice and ultimate success of her cause, while in the epode she is reminded of the violence which has never left the House of Atreus since Pelops' original sin and which for all that is known at this stage of the play may continue after the next act of vengeance has been accomplished.

As if to mark the continuance of the πολύπονος αἰκεία from a remote past into the present situation of the play, Clytaemnestra, evil symbol of violence, appears unannounced at the close of the epode:

ἀνειμένη μέν, ὡς ἔοικας, αὖ στρέφῃ   (516)

'You are wandering at large once more, it seems.' The following long episode is divided into two sections, the first a conflict between mother and daughter, in which the former defends herself for murdering Agamemnon, and the latter demolishes her arguments; and the second containing the brilliant 'messenger's speech' of the paedagogus reporting, falsely, the death of Orestes in the chariot race at the Pythian Games. In this scene Sophocles reduces the role of the chorus to a bare minimum, two lines at the end of the long speeches of Clytaemnestra and Electra in order to provide a pause before the tense stichomythic climax

---

[25] e.g. *Trach.* 827 f. = 837 f. and 846 f. = 857 f. See A. M. Dale, *The Lyric Metres of Greek Drama*[2], 103.

and draw attention to the rising tides of anger (610 f.); two lines
to introduce the paedogogus to Clytaemnestra in a natural way
(662 and 665); and two lines summing up the effect of his speech:

φεῦ φεῦ· τὸ πᾶν δὴ δεσπόταισι τοῖς πάλαι
πρόρριζον, ὡς ἔοικεν, ἔφθαρται γένος   (764 f.)

'Alas, alas! now it seems, the stock of our ancient masters is
utterly destroyed, root and branch.' The hopes that were present
before the first stasimon are now completely shattered.

At this moment of Electra's desperate loneliness comes a lyric
dialogue (823–70) instead of a stasimon. The task of the chorus
here is similar to their task in the parodos though far more
difficult owing to the apparent finality of the preceding scene.
Nevertheless, as their opening questions show (823 ff.), they are
convinced of the reality of avenging powers[26] and again urge
restraint upon Electra as she utters cries of lament for her
brother. Moreover, they use the myth of Amphiaraus, Alcmaeon,
and Eriphyle to suggest hope. In the conversation leading up to
the story μηδὲν μέγ᾿ ἀΰσῃς (830) is a warning to Electra to restrain
her cries[27] and not to deny the existence of Zeus' thunderbolts
and the all-seeing sun. The writer of the note on 823 in the
ancient scholia indeed says that the actor should at the cry φεῦ
look up to heaven and raise a hand, presumably to accuse the
gods, and that this protest is stopped by the chorus's μηδὲν μέγ᾿
ἀΰσῃς. Electra's rejoinder ἀπολεῖς (831) startles the chorus into
the question πῶς; and she then reveals exactly what she cannot
bear: any suggestion that the dead may still be alive. In the
allusive plural τῶν φανερῶς οἰχομένων no doubt she has Orestes
primarily in her mind, but the chorus probably think of
Agamemnon as well, for they introduce the myth with
Amphiaraus, who must represent Agamemnon. The psychology
of the first strophe of this dialogue is very subtle: after the
paedagogus's speech Electra had gradually schooled herself into
an acceptance of Orestes' death, and had finally (817–22) made
up her mind how to end her days. A reversal of this resolve by a
glimmer of hope, however faint, she feels would kill her,
convinced as she is that he is dead; and she closes the strophe
with a final statement of this conviction after the ones in the

[26] Cf. 173 ff.
[27] Cp. the use of μηδὲν μέγ᾿ εἴπῃς, *Aj*. 386.

preceding scene (cf. 788 ff. and 804–22). We shall find the same psychological barrier at work in the following scene with Chrysothemis, when she is confronted by her sister with the evidence of the lock of hair left on Agamemnon's tomb.

The story of Amphiaraus is a good example of the allusive use of myth to instruct and exhort in lyric dialogue. Amphiaraus here represents Agamemnon, Eriphyle, who betrayed him, Clytaemnestra, and Alcmaeon, who avenged his father by slaying his mother, stands for Orestes. Neither Eriphyle or Alcmaeon are mentioned by name, but the story was familiar enough for the details to be grasped immediately by the audience[28] and by Electra to whom it is addressed: she catches the allusions at once and points out the essential difference, that Alcmaeon was alive to avenge his father, whereas Orestes has just been reported dead (841–9). The speed of interchange and the quickness with which she picks up the chorus's remarks are well marked in the first antistrophe by her interruptions of their sentences, first by the exclamations at 840 and then by her completion of the chorus's ὀλοὰ γὰρ by ἐδάμη at 845. The exclamations at 840, as a matter of technique, are necessary to balance those at 826, but they may serve also to give special emphasis to the triumphant

$$\pi\acute{\alpha}\mu\psi\upsilon\chi o c\ \mathring{\alpha}\nu\acute{\alpha}cc\epsilon\iota^{29}$$

by separating these two words from ὑπὸ γαίας, the associations of which wring a cry from Electra.

In the second strophic pair the chorus can do nothing but offer her trite commonplaces, which she rejects, just as she rejected them in the parodos.[30] We note her complete surrender to despair in 854–9 and also the bitter retort with which she reacts in 861 ff. to the cliché,

$$\pi\hat{\alpha}c\iota\ \theta\nu\alpha\tauo\hat{\iota}c\ \mathring{\epsilon}\varphi\upsilon\ \mu\acute{o}\rho oc$$

'Death is appointed for all men.' Such remarks are little more than sounds that complete the rhythmic and musical pattern of the stanza and indicate that Electra has again in this brief ἀγών,

---

[28] Sophocles wrote an *Alcmaeon* and an *Epigoni*, the latter especially famous. See Pearson, Frs. i. 68 ff. and 129 ff.

[29] πάμψυχος only here: a king on earth and therefore also a king among the souls of the dead and a prophet as well, cf. Pi. *P.* 8. 44.

[30] Cp. 854 ff. with 229.

just as she did in the longer one of the parodos, imposed her personality upon the chorus and effectively silenced any further attempt to argue with her. Thus, after the tension and argumentative exchanges in the first strophic pair, a mood of resigned pathos is established at the end of the commos, so that we are left with the picture of Orestes dead without due tribute of lament or burial from his sister. The point is resumed by Electra in her speech over the urn during which she utters the sounds of ritual mourning.[31]

An important technical feature of this commos (823–70), apparent for the first time[32] in Sophocles' extant plays, is the division of metrical and grammatical units between actor and chorus. This lyric ἀντιλαβή gives a lively impression of quick reaction between the participants and is to be noted at 844 f., 855 f., and 866 f. The technique is further developed in *Oedipus at Colonus*, notably at 529–35. Unfortunately we have no evidence to indicate whether the remarks of the chorus were sung by the whole chorus or by one member alone. It would indeed sound strange if fifteen people together sang πῶc at 831 or ναί at 845, so it seems a reasonable assumption that utterances of one or two words were confined to individual singers.

Structurally the function of this commos is to bridge the gap between two contrasting scenes, the first a scene of anger followed by despair, the second depicting a transition from despair to a new and terrible resolve. No doubt this could have been done by a stasimon, but lyrics shared between Electra and the chorus are more dramatic in themselves and more revealing of her character. By composing another dialogue more tense and more impassioned than the parodos, Sophocles has further enhanced what is one of the most important interests of the play: the revelation through the quick exchanges of conversation of Electra's state of mind at different stages of the plot. As a link with the following scene, the main feature of this dialogue is that it makes explicit the psychological barrier against the merest hint that Orestes may be alive, so that when Chrysothemis enters immediately afterwards and states that he is indeed alive, we are prepared for Electra's reception of the news. Her reaction is

---

[31] Cf. esp. 1160–4.

[32] *O.T.* 649 ff. = 678 ff. are not strictly parallel, because Oedipus and Iocasta do not sing.

complete disbelief, and she has no difficulty in convincing her sister that Orestes is in fact dead. Out of her despair however arises a new resolve, to kill Aegisthus herself. Perhaps the chorus's sketch of Amphiaraus' story has taught her the lesson that Agamemnon must be avenged and that with her brother supposedly dead she alone is left to be the instrument. As one would expect after the previous conflict between the sisters (328–404), Chrysothemis refuses to help from motives of prudence, and the scene ends in anger (1057). At this stage of the play Electra has been shown in three scenes of conflict with contrasting characters, each of which provides a fresh insight into her personality. There is the first conflict with Chrysothemis, modelled on the scenes between the two sisters in *Antigone*, in which the strength of one character is displayed against the foil of a weaker and more prudent type. In the middle comes the great ἀγών between Electra and Clytaemnestra, and finally there is the second conflict with Chrysothemis parallel with the first. These three scenes cover the central portion of the play, and their effect is assisted by the dialogues between Electra and the chorus in the parodos and in the commos at 823–70. She never leaves the stage from her first appearance at 86 until 1383, where she is off stage for fourteen lines, so that we can gauge exactly the impact upon her of each conflict and each report.

Before discussing the second stasimon, a few remarks may be made about the coryphaeus's two interventions in the scene between Electra and Chrysothemis (871–1057). After the former has stated her intention to kill Aegisthus and appealed with impassioned arguments for her sister's help, there is a two-line warning that in such circumstances prudence is an ally to both speaker and listener:

> ἐν τοῖς τοιούτοις ἐςτὶν ἡ προμηθία
> καὶ τῷ λέγοντι καὶ κλύοντι ςύμμαχος. (990 f.)

The masculine participles show the gnomic nature of this remark, which expresses a general truth and is neutral between the two sisters. It should not be taken as a rebuke to Electra for her plan, which indeed if it is to be successful requires a high degree of forethought from both of them. Chrysothemis in her opening sentence (992–4), as one would expect from her character, takes it as a warning to Electra, who she says has thrown caution (εὐλάβεια) to the winds. Balancing maxims of this type from the coryphaeus are a convention of Greek Tragedy during arguments between persons with opposed views. After Chrysothemis' speech urging her sister to restrain her passion (κατάσχες ὀργήν, 1011) and learn sense (αὐτὴ δὲ νοῦν σχές, 1013) the coryphaeus turns to Electra with the words

> πείθου. προνοίας οὐδὲν ἀνθρώποις ἔφυ
> κέρδος λαβεῖν ἄμεινον οὐδὲ νοῦ σοφοῦ.   (1015 f.)

The present imperative, addressed directly to her, 'be persuaded', is followed by another generalized remark, as is shown by the gnomic aorist ἔφυ. This couplet should not be taken as downright approval of Chrysothemis' attitude,[33] implying that she has a νοῦς σοφός and Electra has not and is therefore ἄνους not σοφή, because in the following ode the chorus say that if she succeeds in her act of vengeance she will be praised as σοφά τ' ἀρίστα τε παῖς, 'wise and bravest'. What we have after the opening word πείθου is another balancing maxim repeating the need for prudence, here called πρόνοια, a synonym of προμηθία, and for a νοῦς σοφός, both of them highly necessary to a young woman who contemplates taking on Aegisthus single-handed. We may also recall that much of the chorus's role, especially in the parodos and the commos, is to urge moderation and restraint upon Electra, so that these two lines are in keeping with their attitude to her at crucial moments in the play.

The second stasimon, 1058–97, is noteworthy for the difficulty of its language, some of which eludes precise interpretation;[34] and in addition it contains a major textual crux at 1087. It is however set firmly within the dramatic context. The first stanza comments upon the quarrel between the two sisters which closed the preceding scene and begins with an analogy from the observed behaviour of certain birds, probably storks,[35] in order to make the point that duty to parents is a natural instinct and imposes obligations upon the children to repay in equal measure the benefits they have received in birth and nurture. This duty is indeed an ancient prescription of morality, found in the so-

---

[33] So Kells 180 ff. of his edition. Further, he interprets the ode 1059 ff. as a criticism not of Chrysothemis but of Electra. In spite of its ingenuity, his argument does not convince me.

[34] e.g. 1063–5 and 1085–9.   [35] Cf. Ar. *Av.* 1355 f.

called Χείρωνος ὑποθῆκαί quoted by Pindar in *Pythian* 6. 26 f., as well as in the Decalogue; and the offence of γονέων κάκωσις was punishable by loss of citizenship under contemporary Athenian law. The traditional interpretation of the opening sentence of the first strophe is probably correct: the chorus are suggesting a reproof of Chrysothemis for her failure to support Electra in her act of vengeance as a return for benefits received from their father. She is not, as they imply, reciprocating on the same terms as her sister (ἐπ' ἴσας, 1062); and it is worth noting the remark in the ancient scholium on this line that the chorus tactfully use the first person plural ἵνα μὴ δοκῇ φορτικὸς εἶναι τούτοις καθ' ὧν τὸν λόγον πεποίηται, 'so that those against whom the remark is directed may not think that the chorus are lacking in good manners.'

There follows a powerful oath by Zeus' lightning and Themis in heaven in which there is no subject, only the predicate ἀπόνητοι. At first sight it appears that the subject should be the same as that of τελοῦμεν, those of us who do not repay their parents equally; and the oath would be appropriate in a reference to the fate of those who neglect the ancient duty alluded to in the first sentence. The scholiast however identifies the subject as οἱ περὶ τὸν Αἴγισθον and interprets ἀπόνητοι as ἀθῷοι, but this would be obscure in the context, as there is no mention of Agamemnon's murderers until the end of the antistrophe (1080) and it is doubtful if ἀπόνητοι, free from πόνος, could mean ἀθῷοι, immune from punishment. Kells, assuming that the chorus have aligned themselves with Chrysothemis, sees a reference to Agamemnon, who has failed to help his children by coming to their rescue.[36] These divergences of view indicate that Sophocles is here being ambiguous, perhaps deliberately. If, as seems most probable, the oath refers to those who neglect their parents, it must be Chrysothemis who is uppermost in the minds of the chorus, though they express themselves in the generalizing first person plural; and οὐ ... δαρὸν οὐκ ἀπόνητοι[37] may suggest that she will not for long continue to enjoy the ἄπονος βίος, the trouble-free life which has hitherto been hers and for which Electra reproached her so bitterly in the first act (359–62). If however

---

[36] See his edition 179–81.

[37] ἀπόνητοι, only here in extant tragedy, is probably a metrical equivalent of ἄπονοι, 'free from care or trouble', like the Latin 'securus'.

we assume that the wording of the passage is intentionally vague, we sense in it a menace of πόνοι, reinforced by a powerful oath; and how shall one define these πόνοι more precisely than by saying that they are the very stuff of the tragedy which is being enacted, and involve all the characters, good, bad, or merely weak?

In the last sentence of the strophe, there is again an echo from Aeschylus' *Choephoroe*. Sophocles has here concentrated into four lines the great scene in that play (315–509), in which Orestes, Electra, and the chorus appeal to the dead Agamemnon and endeavour to arouse his spirit to help them in the deed of vengeance. He does not however employ the same technique as his predecessor because there is no ritual summoning of the dead but only a message sent below the earth (χθονία φάμα, 1066) to report in summary form the impressions gained by the chorus from the preceding scene. The idea of the dead receiving messages from the living is familiar from a few passages in Pindar,[38] but in these instances the news is good, a victory in the games reported to dead ancestors, a fit subject for celebration by a chorus. In Sophocles' play on the other hand, the message is one of shame, and there is nothing to celebrate: ἀχόρευτα φέρουϲ' ὀνείδη. These words may well echo *Choephoroe* 495, where Orestes asks

$$ἆρ' ἐξεγείρῃ τοῖϲδ' ὀνείδεϲιν, πάτερ;$$

The ὀνείδη are the report of the shameful deeds listed in the previous few lines, which should awake Agamemnon from the dead.

The antistrophe (1070) gives the contents of the message: there is νόϲοϲ in the house, the sisters have quarrelled, and Electra is betrayed and alone with her tears on a sea of troubles, not anxious at the prospect of death but ready and willing to leave the light of day once she has destroyed the twin Ἐρινύϲ. The stanza ends by affirming her supremacy as εὔπατριϲ, to be translated, with Jebb, 'noble child of noble father'. This word was applied by the chorus to Orestes in the parodos (162) and used by Electra of her brother in the commos (858). Now that he is presumed dead, his sister inherits the epithet. There is no doubt here of the chorus's attitude: in using the word of Electra in this

---

[38] Cf. *O.* 8. 77–84; *O.* 14. 20 ff.; *P.* 5. 100 f.

emphatic position at the end of the message to the dead, they are commending wholeheartedly her resolve to avenge her father.

There is a remarkable use of language in the first sentence of the antistrophe where the epic word φύλοπις (1073), occurring only here in extant tragedy, is used of the quarrels between the two sisters. Normally it brings to mind the uproar of Homeric battle and might be thought too strong an expression for the scenes of argument between Electra and Chrysothemis. We may recall the use of πόλεμοι in the parodos (219) to describe the conflicts between Electra and the δυνατοί who rule the house. φύλοπις however stresses the violent impact of the sisters' quarrels on the mind of the chorus. The metaphor in ἐξιϲοῦται is no doubt derived from the equalizing of a balance, and the subject, διπλῆ φύλοπις, is an example of abstract for concrete: the two sisters quarrelling are no longer at harmony with each other in friendly life together.

At 1080 the chorus refer to Clytaemnestra and Aegisthus as διδύμαν Ἐρινύν. This is noteworthy in view of the other contexts in the play where the word is used of the powers to whom Electra herself prays in her opening monologue and whom the chorus themselves in the first stasimon regard as righteous avengers. Moreover in the next ode (1384–97) they envisage Orestes and Pylades as ἄφυκτοι κύνες, i.e. Ἐρινύες, as they enter the palace to kill Clytaemnestra. The identification of both sides as Ἐρινύες is however explained if we remember that Sophocles held the same view of these powers as Aeschylus. To both dramatists they were spirits of vengeance at work in a family from the moment when the πρώταρχος ἄτη, the original deed of violence, set in motion the whole process of the family's destruction. Thus in the House of Atreus, the Ἐρινύς or Ἐρινύες have manifested themselves in successive generations since the first act of outrage which for Sophocles in this play was the charioteering of Pelops, described in the epode of the first stasimon (504–15). Some member or members of the doomed family are chosen by these powers as their instruments to avenge a deed committed by another member whether of the same or an earlier generation. So here, Aegisthus and Clytaemnestra have avenged upon Agamemnon crimes committed both by him (the sacrifice of Iphigeneia) and by his father Atreus; and Electra in her turn is chosen by the same powers to destroy Aegisthus and, so the chorus imply,

Clytaemnestra. As each member of the family forges a further link in the chain of doom, so each claims that the powers of vengeance working within him are the just instruments of the law δράσαντα παθεῖν, the τριγέρων μῦθος of *Choephoroe* 314. In Sophocles' play both Clytaemnestra and the chorus who support Electra use the word ἑλεῖν, perhaps with overtones of its legal sense 'to convict', when referring to an act of vengeance committed or contemplated. At 528, Clytaemnestra said of her slaying of Agamemnon

$$\text{ἡ γὰρ } \varDelta\text{ίκη νιν εἶλεν, οὐκ ἐγὼ μόνη}$$

'It was Justice that slew him, not I alone'. In this song (1080) the chorus use the same verb of Electra's intended deed, διδύμαν ἑλοῦς' Ἐρινύν; and both sides are convinced that their act is legally just. We may recall Clytaemnestra's defence of herself to the chorus at *Agamemnon* 1475–1504, where at 1500 ff. she imagines the avenger of Atreus (ὁ παλαιὸς δριμὺς ἀλάστωρ Ἀτρέως) taking her shape in order to exact payment for a crime long ago. Even so at *Electra* 1080 the chorus imagine her and Aegisthus as διδύμα Ἐρινύς.[39]

In the second strophic pair the chorus turn to Electra and address her directly, ὦ παῖ παῖ (1084). They develop the point made in the last sentence of the previous stanza, extolling her choice of a life of tears,[40] instead of a life of dishonour, her wisdom, and her courage (coφά τ' ἀρίστα τε παῖς, 1089). Aware now that she has decided to act alone and that she has proved her determination and her character in conflict with her sister, they no longer try to dissuade her from her tears or counsel prudence, but encourage her without reserve and close their song by commending her especially for her εὐςέβεια. The words ἃ δὲ μέγιστ' ἔβλαςτε νόμιμα recall the famous passages in *Antigone* 453 ff. and *O.T.* 863 ff. describing the ultimate sanctions of divine law which take precedence over all laws of man's devising. One of these νόμιμα is εὐςέβεια, and it is sanctioned by Zeus (1097). In the last words of the ode the chorus state their conclusion: they have found that Electra's εὐςέβεια entitles her

---

[39] See Winnington-Ingram, *PCPhS*, loc. cit. 20.

[40] ἄοικον (Lindner) or ἄνοικον (Pearson) may be preferred to κοινὸν of the manuscripts in 1086, because κοινὸς αἰών could hardly mean 'death', and κοινὸς with αἰών meaning 'life' is unlikely when Electra's isolation is so strongly stressed throughout the play.

to a place of supreme honour for observing these sanctions. The word here means her piety in accepting the duty, in spite of her predicament, to avenge her father, just as it did in her closing remark in the epode of the parodos that if the dead are not avenged, respect and piety among men would vanish,

$$\text{ἔρροι τ' ἂν αἰδὼс}$$
$$\text{ἁπάντων τ' εὐсέβεια θνατῶν.} \qquad \text{(249 f.)}$$

We may remember also that in the preceding scene she holds out to Chrysothemis, should she help her kill Aegisthus, the prospect of winning from the dead of their family a name for εὐсέβεια in this same sense:

$$\text{πρῶτον μὲν εὐсέβειαν ἐκ πατρὸс κάτω}$$
$$\text{θανόντοс οἴсῃ τοῦ καсιγνήτου θ' ἅμα} \qquad \text{(968 f.)}$$

'you will win praise for piety from our dead father below, and from our brother too'.

This is not the place for a lengthy discussion of the textual problem in 1087. In this context τὸ μὴ καλόν, if sound, must mean the dishonour of a shameful life which no ἀγαθόс or εὔπατριс will put up with. The point is made by the chorus in 1082–4 and by Electra in 989: to put it positively, τὸ μὴ καλόν is τὸ αἰсχρόν. Further, καθοπλίсαсα, if sound, can only mean to prepare or equip;[41] the clause will then be meaningless and must therefore contain a corruption. Two ways of dealing with the problem have been suggested: first, to alter the participle to a verb meaning rejecting or subduing—καθιππάсαсα, ἀπολακτίсαсα, but none of these is convincing. ὑπεροπλίсαсα (Heimsoeth), 'overpowering by force of arms' is the best suggestion, as it preserves the greater part of the manuscript reading and secures exact metrical corresponsion with 1095;[42] or, secondly, to attack τὸ μὴ καλόν. Lloyd-Jones has suggested[43] that τὸ μὴ represents the word τομή, a cut in surgery, as a gloss on the word ἄκοс, a remedy, comparing Aeschylus' *Supplices* 268 (ἄκη τομαῖα) and *Choephoroe*

---

[41] The gloss καταπολεμήсαсα in the scholium on 1087, 'having warred down' is hardly supported by the analogies of κατακοντίζειν, κατατοξεύειν, καταιχμάζειν, 'shoot down with javelin, arrow, etc.' because ὁπλίζειν does not mean 'to use a weapon', and καθοπλίζειν could not therefore mean 'to overcome by a weapon'. It always means 'equip, prepare'.

[42] Cf. *Od.* 17. 268, where ὑπεροπλίζειν occurs in the middle with the sense 'overpower'. Suidas and Hesychius record an aorist active of this verb.

[43] *CQ* N.s. 4 (1954), 95.

539 (ἄκος τομαῖον); and he suggests ἄκος καλὸν καθοπλίσασα, 'making ready an honourable remedy'. One has however doubts about getting rid of the phrase τὸ μὴ καλόν, dishonour, in view of its importance in the argument both of this ode and of the preceding scene.

The importance of this song in the structure of the play is that it reinforces the point made in the strophe and antistrophe of the first stasimon (473–502), that vengeance for the murder of Agamemnon is an act of justice based upon the law that children should honour their parents. It also gathers together the arguments about εὐςέβεια and εὔκλεια which Electra used in 968–85 when trying to win Chrysothemis' support, and thus makes the further point that the act of vengeance will bring honour and a name for piety. Finally, in the last words, it states that this piety is one of the μέγιςτα νόμιμα and is moreover sanctioned by Zeus. Such a reaffirmation of the moral basis of the deed that Electra contemplates is dramatically and psychologically necessary after the suffering and the extremes of emotional tension to which she has been subjected throughout the play. The chorus no longer express misgivings about the performance and consequences of the act of vengeance or reflect on the remoter woes of the House of Atreus as in the epode of the first stasimon: the expression of such feelings would weaken the effect of the ode on Electra's morale when she is about to face the final *bouleversement* of her emotions in passing during the next scene from the depth of sorrow and despair in the urn-speech to the uninhibited ecstasy of the recognition.

The connection of the ode with the following scene is brilliantly contrived. Orestes appears, disguised and unrecognized, as if in answer to the message to the dead, the χθονία φάμα of 1066. This *coup de théâtre* is of course immediately obvious to the audience, who know the details of the plot from the prologue (44–66), but for the chorus and Electra, the moment of truth must be delayed until the climax of the recognition-scene when after the almost unbearable tension of the extended stichomythia she presents Orestes to the women of Argos with a triumphant cry:

> ὦ φίλταται γυναῖκες, ὦ πολίτιδες,
> ὁρᾶτ' Ὀρέςτην τόνδε, μηχαναῖςι μὲν
> θανόντα, νῦν δὲ μηχαναῖς ςεςωμένον   (1227–9)

'My dearest friends, my fellow citizens, look upon Orestes here, dead by feigning, and now by feigning saved.' The full purpose and effect of the χθονία φάμα are now made clear to the people in the play: the message reporting ἀχόρευτα ὀνείδη to the Atreidae below has been answered by the epiphany of the living Orestes from the dead.

During the next scene (1098–1383) the role of the chorus is again minimal. At the beginning the coryphaeus introduces Orestes and his companions naturally into the action by answering his questions; and after Electra's long and moving lament over the urn he speaks three lines of conventional commonplace urging moderation in grief in order to provide a brief pause before the excitement of the stichomythia and to give Orestes time to collect his thoughts and consider how to cope with the situation (1171–3). Apart from an expression of joy at 1230 f., the chorus take no further part in the scene[44] when the ecstasy of discovery finds release in the partially sung dialogue between brother and sister, and the murder plan reaches its moment of fulfilment.

After her prayer to Apollo Lycaeus asking for his help in carrying out the plan, Electra leaves the stage at 1383 and follows Orestes and Pylades into the house: they have already gone in at 1375. Immediately after her exit the chorus sing a brief two-stanza ode in excited dochmiac and iambic metres, with a cretic-paeonic opening:[45]

ἴδεθ' ὅπου προνέμεται
τὸ δυσέριστον αἷμα φυσῶν "Αρης   (1384 f.)

'See where Ares advances, breathing the blood-lust for vengeance which none can fight against.' This song, in whose rhythms one can almost hear the sound of footsteps, accompanies the avenger's strides as they move towards their design. The same technique is apparent in the anapaests from the chorus that precede the murder of Aegisthus at *Choephoroe* 855–70, though there is in them not the same certainty about the issue as in Sophocles' play. At *Medea* 1251, just before the children's death-cry is heard, there is a similar type of ode accompanying Medea's entry into

---

[44] Unless 1322–5 are given to the coryphaeus as by Dawe, *Studies on the Text of Sophocles*, i. 198, and in the Teubner edition of 1975.

[45] Cp. the rhythm of the ἐφύμνια at Aesch. *Eu.* 328 ff. and 372 ff.

the house to kill them, though its tone is very different, for the
chorus pray to the Earth and the Sun to avert a deed of horror
which they are powerless to prevent; and at *Heracles* 735 before
the killing of Lycus by Heracles, the chorus lead up to the
tyrant's death-cry by a conversation between themselves in
which dochmiacs and spoken iambic trimeters mark the tension
of the scene. At moments such as these the conventions of the
Greek Theatre do not allow the chorus to satisfy a natural
instinct by leaving the orchestra in order to assist, prevent, or
witness deeds of violence that must take place off the stage. Such
songs and utterances, however, well illustrate the way in which
the dramatists have turned convention to good account by using
their choruses to create, maintain, and increase suspense as the
audience await the victim's cry.

The most striking feature of this ode is the identification of the
human avengers with the ἄφυκτοι κύνες, the hounds in whose
form Aeschylus envisages the Ἐρινύες in *Choephoroe* 924 and 1054
(ἔγκοτοι κύνες), and throughout the earlier part of *Eumenides*.
The vision here so objectively presented has no doubt been in the
minds of the chorus ever since their μαντεία in the strophe and
antistrophe of the first stasimon, 498–502, so that this song
constitutes a continuation and fulfilment of the earlier one. This
vision is now about to become a reality, no longer a dream
suspended as it were before the dreamer's eyes between certainty
and uncertainty:

> ὥϲτ᾽ οὐ μακρὰν ἔτ᾽ ἀμμενεῖ
> τοὐμὸν φρενῶν ὄνειρον αἰωρούμενον   (1389 f.)[46]

'therefore the vision in my mind will not for long wait in
suspense.' In the strophe Ares is the hunter advancing inexorably
as he tracks his prey, and the avengers are the hounds that assist
him. At the end of the antistrophe another figure appears,
Hermes, a canonical deity in this story,[47] in order to give divine
assistance in the execution of the cunning plot (δόλον ϲκότῳ
κρύψαϲ, 1396); and we may remember that he was invoked by
Electra in her monody (111) in his role as χθόνιοϲ.

The immediacy of the chorus's vision in this ode may help us
to understand the words

---

[46] Cf. Aesch. *A.* 975–8 for a similar image for fear hovering before the mind.

[47] Cf. Aesch. *Ch.* 1, 727, 812. Hermes is traditionally associated with ruses and
deceptions.

$$\nu\epsilon\alpha\kappa\acute{o}\nu\eta\tau o\nu \ \alpha\hat{\iota}\mu\alpha \ \chi\epsilon\iota\rho o\hat{\iota}\nu \ \check{\epsilon}\chi\omega\nu \qquad (1394).$$

The text is rightly suspect, but αἷμα is surely sound, as it is an echo of the same word in exactly the same place in the identical dochmiac 1385, though the meaning is different in the two places. In 1385 it denotes the blood lust[48] which Ares breathes as he advances, φυcῶν being an extension of the common use of πνεῖν with such words as φόνον, while in 1394 the chorus envisage the actual blood upon the avenging hands, shed by the weapon which is to kill Clytaemnestra: the vision is made real in 1422 (φοινία δὲ χεὶρ cτάζει θυηλῆc ῎Αρεοc). αἷμα is moreover attested in the ancient *lexica*, though the glosses μάχαιρα and ξίφοc are misconceived because αἷμα cannot possibly be the actual weapon, nor obviously does Orestes enter the house with a drawn sword. The phrase is in fact highly impressionistic: by a forward leap of the imagination the result of the deed is seen before it is done. νεακόνητον is probably corrupt, and is due to the misinterpretation of αἷμα as a weapon. The α should be long on the analogy of similarly formed words with νέοc,[49] at any rate in Greek of this period; and blood cannot be described as newly whetted. What is needed is a word meaning freshly shed, an equivalent of νεόρρυτον, but none of the suggestions is compelling.

The language and sentence structure assist the impression of energy and speed demanded by the tension of the plot at the moment when the ode is being sung. Apart from the echo of αἷμα in 1385 and 1394, the shift from future to present tense in the repeated ἀμμενεῖ ... ἀμμένει at 1389 and 1397 marks the transition from intention to imminent execution; δολιόπουc (1392) and δόλον (1396) remind us of the cunning stratagem outlined in the prologue;[50] and ἀρχαιόπλουτα echoes ἀρχέπλουτον from Orestes' prayer (71 f.) and recalls the ancient wealth of the heritage to which his deed will restore him. The sentences are short, simple in construction, and composed of weighty words, each of which adds something to the imagery; and there are only two particles in the predominantly paratactic structure of the whole. Particularly impressive rhythmically are the two pairs of complete iambic trimeters at the middle and end of the ode

---

[48] For this use of αἷμα cf. Eur. *Phoen.* 790.
[49] Cf. e.g. νεηκονής *Aj.* 820.
[50] δόλοιcι κλέψαι χειρὸc ἐνδίκουc cφαγάc (35). Cf. also 1228 f.

(1386 = 1393 and 1390 = 1397): in the middle they add solemnity
to the stamping dochmiacs that surround them and give weight
to the endings of the stanzas. As the song proceeds we follow the
movements, even the thoughts of the killers: first there is Ares
breathing bloody slaughter, then his hounds, then a comment
from the singers as they sense that their vision is about to be
realized. In the antistrophe we see Orestes stealing into the house
of his fathers, the blood of his victim already on his hands, and
finally Hermes in his function of δόλιος, the god of guile as well
as escort to the living and the dead, emphasising that intrigue is
the very stuff of the plot.

    Immediately upon the last words of the ode Electra reappears
(1398). As the note in the scholia on 1404 implies, Sophocles uses
her as an ἐξάγγελος, whose function is to relate deeds done within
a house. She does not however do this in a long speech like the
Nurse in *Trachiniae* who acts as an ἐξάγγελος to report Deianira's
suicide (899–946), but in a dialogue with the coryphaeus. In
dispensing at this point with a second messenger's speech and
using the principal actor, Sophocles combines economy with
great dramatic effect, so that nothing relaxes the tension created
by the ode as we await Clytaemnestra's expected cries. So far as
her role of 'messenger' is concerned, Electra confines herself to
the barest details. First, she sets the scene of the murder, with
Clytaemnestra preparing the urn for burial and Orestes and
Pylades standing close at hand: a grim travesty of a scene on a
grave-stele (1400 f.). Secondly, in answer to another question
from the coryphaeus she explains why she has come out of the
house (1402); and finally, at Clytaemnestra's first cries of horror
at discovering the identity of the two figures standing near, she
arrests and concentrates attention by the sinister remarks with
τις: βοᾷ τις ἔνδον (1406), and ἰδοὺ μάλ' αὖ θροεῖ τις (1410). At the
first of these, the chorus's utterances change from speech to song
as the excitement increases and remain lyrical for the rest of the
strophe. Throughout this part of the dialogue Electra cannot
remain inside the house to witness or participate in the deed, as
she almost certainly does in Euripides' *Electra*, 1165 ff., because
she must keep a look-out for Aegisthus, whose arrival from the
country is expected at any moment. She stays however at the
house door in order to be within earshot of Clytaemnestra and of
Orestes, to whom she addresses her remarks from 1411 onwards.

The point is made clear when he obeys her savage command:
'Strike a second blow if you can' (1415).

Two other examples[51] in extant Greek Tragedy of an actor on
stage reporting to the chorus what is going on behind the scenes
occur in Euripides. At *Hippolytus* 565–600, Phaedra listens at the
door to the violent altercation between Hippolytus and the Nurse
and reports what she hears to the chorus, whose remarks, as the
tension grows, change immediately from spoken trimeters to
sung dochmiacs;[52] and at *Orestes* 1297–1310 Helen's cries as she
is about to be killed are heard from inside the house, while
Electra reports to the chorus.[53] The similarities of situation
between this scene and this part of Sophocles' *Electra* are sufficient
to suggest that Euripides may have had it in mind: at 1297 of
Orestes, Electra's

$$\mathring{\eta}κούcαθ'; \mathring{α}νδρεc \ χεῖρ' \ \mathring{ε}χουcιν \ \mathring{ε}ν \ φόνῳ$$

recalls her

$$\mathring{α}νδρεc \ αὐτίκα$$
$$τελοῦcι \ τοὔργον \qquad (El. \ 1398).$$

All three scenes turn to effective advantage the convention which
forbids the chorus to rush from the orchestra to listen at doors or
try to get a sight of off-stage violence.

At this crisis in the plot of Sophocles' play the chorus clarify
beyond doubt their reaction to Clytaemnestra's murder at the
moment when it takes place. There is a shudder of horror (φρῖξαι
1408), when they hear her first shout, but no expression of pity
at her death-cry. It is important to interpret correctly their other
two sung utterances in the strophe, 1413 f. and 1417–21. Both
are cries of triumph and as such consistent with the chorus's
attitude throughout the play towards the deed of vengeance.
Hermann's coι should be accepted in 1413, ethic or possessive
dative with μοῖρα, because the present tense of φθίνειν is probably
never transitive. The exclamation

$$\mathring{ω} \ πόλιc, \ \mathring{ω} \ γενεὰ \ τάλαινα, \ νῦν \ coι$$
$$μοῖρα \ καθαμερία \ φθίνει \ φθίνει$$

---

[51] Three, if one includes *H.F.* 887 ff., but there, Amphitryon is not on the stage.
[52] See Barrett's edition ad loc.
[53] 1297 of Eur. *Or.* should be given to Electra.

'City and family that has suffered, now the fate that has been yours day by day is dying, dying!' covers the day-to-day lot of the city over a long period of time under the usurpers as well as that of the individual members of Agamemnon's family. The adjective is formed directly from the prepositional phrase καθ' ἡμέραν: the μοῖρα has been present day by day without intermission, and with Clytaemnestra's death it too dies away. The second comment follows her death at 1417: reverting for the last time to the theme of the Ἐρινύες (ἀραί) which they have used throughout the play, the chorus announce that the curses are accomplishing their task of vengeance, and their function is therefore at an end. It is perhaps significant that the same word τελοῦσι is used of the human avengers at 1398 and of the powers whose instruments they are at 1417. The word moreover occurs at two other places in the scene;[54] there is in it a sense of finality.

Both these comments from the chorus in the strophe indicate the way in which Sophocles has chosen to treat the story: the killing of Clytaemnestra in his play alone precedes that of Aegisthus, and this novel variant to the usual story leads to the superb piece of melodrama which ends the tragedy. It is the matricide which breaks the chain of doom, and there is no aftermath of misgivings, no menace of future terrors to plague the conscience. This deed releases the family from its bondage of suffering: thus do the chorus deliver their summary in the anapaests which conclude the play. The contrast with both Aeschylus and Euripides is absolute. At *Choephoroe* 1007 ff. and 1019 f. the chorus express a presentiment of future woe in spite of their celebration of the triumph of justice and the return of light to the house in the ode 935–71; and their final words, though structurally a lead into the last piece of the trilogy, are a perplexed question full of foreboding:

> ποῖ δῆτα κρανεῖ, ποῖ καταλήξει
> μετακοιμισθὲν μένος ἄτης;

'At what point will it work its accomplishment, at what point will the power of ἄτη be lulled to rest and cease?' In Euripides' *Electra* (1176–1232) the chorus reflect Orestes' doubts and the turmoil in their own minds raised by the matricide, though their last significant comment is in keeping with Sophocles' treatment:

[54] 1435, 1464.

$$\tau\acute{\epsilon}\rho\mu\alpha\ \kappa\alpha\kappa\hat{\omega}\nu\ \mu\epsilon\gamma\acute{\alpha}\lambda\omega\nu\ \delta\acute{o}\mu o\iota\sigma\iota \qquad (1232)^{55}$$

'the end of great evils for the house'.

At the opening of the antistrophe (1422), the chorus announce with conventional formality the entrance of Orestes and Pylades with Clytaemnestra's blood dripping from their hands, a sight which they welcome with the masterly understatement οὐδ' ἔχω ψέγειν. Their vision in 1394 is now made real. After this formal opening tension mounts again over the expected arrival of Aegisthus, for during the conversation between Orestes and Electra (1424 ff.) the chorus have no doubt taken over the task of watching for him which had been performed by her in the strophe, so that their announcement of his approach interrupts their talk with the increased urgency of song (1427 f.). At this point there is an unfortunate lacuna in the text, proved by the need for symmetry and exact correspondence in line division, at any rate for Sophocles, with the strophe, so that we miss Electra's comment on hearing that her mother is dead. I can find no doubts or misgivings in Orestes' lines, 1424 f. The contrasting δὲ clause to τὰν δόμοισι μὲν καλῶς is not expressed, but he obviously has in mind τἄξωθεν δέ, the arrival of Aegisthus. There is no place for regret here; it is probably the recollection of Aeschylus, *Choeph.* 1016 and of Euripides' treatment of this phase of the plot in his *Electra* that has led some scholars[56] to see an expression of doubt in Orestes'

$$Ἀπόλλων\ εἰ\ καλῶς\ ἐθέσπισεν$$

'if Apollo prophesied rightly.' Nor does Electra's question τέθνηκεν ἡ τάλαινα; (1426) necessarily imply pity, because pity at this moment would be out of character, and τάλας like τλήμων can express detestation.[57] We can only guess at the substance of her reaction to the news of Clytaemnestra's death: taking a cue from the exclamation

$$αἰαῖ.\ ἰὼ\ στέγαι$$

in the corresponding line in the strophe, we may surmise that her remarks began with the release of emotion in a cry of triumph

---

[55] See Denniston's edition of Eur. *El.*, pp. 190 f. and 202.
[56] e.g. Kaibel in his edition ad loc.
[57] Cf. *Trach.* 1084 and *El.* 273.

followed by a brief thanksgiving to the gods to whom she has
prayed for vengeance or by a reminder that the last enemy
remains to be overcome. The lyric interventions of the chorus in
the antistrophe are strictly practical and directed to the actors:
they warn them of Aegisthus' approach, tell Orestes and Pylades
to get back into the vestibule (1433),[58] and advise Electra on the
tone to adopt in speaking to Aegisthus. These remarks are in
mood and function strongly contrasted with the corresponding
lines of the strophe: there, the chorus reflected upon the
significance of the matricide for the fortunes of the city and the
family; here, they arouse a more immediate excitement as they
participate in the action and help the actors to prepare for the
magnificent piece of theatre which closes the play.

To match the difference in mood between the lyrics of the
chorus in the two halves of this dialogue, there is a contrast also
in the language. The shudder of horror expressed in the assonance
of

$$\text{ἤκους' ἀνήκουστα δύ-}$$
$$\text{cτανος, ὥcτε φρῖξαι} \qquad (1407 \text{ f.})$$

is answered by the abrupt cutting off of the actors' conversation
(1428) as Aegisthus is seen approaching; in place of the
passionate exclamations ὦ πόλις, ὦ γενεά and the striking
repetition φθίνει φθίνει (1413 f.) followed at once by Clytaemnestra's cry as the first blow is struck, there is in the corresponding
place in the antistrophe (1433 f.) the matter-of-fact command to
Orestes and Pylades; and the conversational style of the advice
which closes the dialogue contrasts well with the majestic
simplicity of the language at the end of the strophe with its
strongly emphasized antitheses, its subtle rhymes, and its
evocative echo in παλίρρυτον αἷμα of the ancient doctrine that
blood will have blood:

$$\text{τελοῦc' ἀραί· ζῶcιν οἱ}$$
$$\text{γᾶc ὑπαὶ κείμενοι.}$$
$$\text{παλίρρυτον γὰρ αἷμ' ὑπεξαιροῦcι τῶν}$$
$$\text{κτανόντων οἱ πάλαι θανόντεc} \qquad (1417\text{–}21)$$

'The curses are finishing their work: the buried live: blood flows
for blood, drained from the killers by those who died of old.' This

[58] Though the text is in doubt, the sense is clear.

is indeed a fitting coda to the theme of vengeance which runs through the play.

A noteworthy feature in the formal structure of this passage 1398–1441 is the skill with which Sophocles has concentrated so much movement and excitement within the limits of strophic discipline. At a moment of high suspense created by the stasimon one actor rushes out of the house (cὺ δ' ἐκτὸc ἦξαc, 1402) and describes the setting for the murder of another soon to be accomplished off stage, while the need to watch for Aegisthus adds urgency to the execution of the deed. The tension increases with each appeal and cry of the victim, each sung utterance of the chorus, and each remark of the actor and then subsides for a moment with the summing-up at the end of the strophe. At the third line of the antistrophe after the formal announcement (1422 f.), the killers reappear and report success; the chorus catch sight of Aegisthus, and Electra obviously tries to push Orestes and Pylades back into the house out of sight (ὦ παῖδεc, οὐκ ἄψορρον; 1430). Five lines later, in response to urgent appeals from both Electra and the chorus, the killers re-enter the house before the end of the antistrophe (καὶ δὴ βέβηκα, 1436). All these comings and goings, cries 'off', alarms, and quick exchanges between speakers and singers are controlled by the laws of rhythmical symmetry and exact responsion in the division of lines. The control is however exercised with such unobtrusive skill, and the tone and style are so flexible in their changes to suit the action that there is no impression of a rigid and unnatural schematism.

The use of strophic discipline in the organization of dialogue scenes of this type seems to be Sophocles' general habit, so far as we can judge from the meagre evidence of seven plays. Apart from the astrophic dialogue between the Nurse (who does not sing) and the chorus at *Trachiniae* 871–95, we do not meet 'free' lyric conversation until the last two plays, *Philoctetes* and *Oedipus at Colonus*, and then it is used sparingly and only after a preceding strophic system, like an extended epode.[59] This is perhaps surprising at a time when Euripides had been experimenting with 'free' dialogue ever since *Hippolytus* (428 B.C.), both wholly sung and in a combination of speech and song; and in his later plays he increased its use more and more. The fact that Sophocles

[59] *Phil.* 1169–1217; *O.C.* 208–36.

did not, so far as the evidence goes, develop these experiments to the same extent as his younger contemporary, suggests that he had a more conservative approach to his art, and that he did not yield in the same way to the metrical any more than to the linguistic influences of the new dithyramb as Euripides undoubtedly did, notably in the Phrygian eunuch's aria at *Orestes* 1369–1502.

Perhaps the most important feature of the choral odes in *Electra* is the stress they lay on the theme of vengeance and justice; and the identification of these two, especially in the first stasimon, provides a moral basis for the plot. In addition, they enhance the psychological interest of Electra's character by revealing the dark forces that fashion her behaviour, and they make us continually aware of the tragic issues that lie beneath the excitement of the play, concentrating and summarizing much of what Aeschylus wrote in the lyrics of his *Oresteia*. The planning of the vengeance and the theatrical brilliance of its execution, the tragic figure of Electra, the self-indulgence of Chrysothemis, and the villainy of Clytaemnestra are all presented against this constant and unifying ground-base of 'Fury-justice' which is audible throughout.[60] Heard first in Orestes' prayer at the end of the prologue, its tones increase in power especially in the first and third stasima where they reach their fullest resonance as the avengers speed to kill their victim. They then cease with the triumphant τελοῦς' ἀραί as she falls beneath Orestes' sword.

The odes which the chorus sing are in consequence strictly relevant to the dramatic situation at each stage in the progress of the plot; and when the singers range afar, as they do in the epode of the first stasimon, the limit of their range is within the theme of the inherited curse which was sounded by Aeschylus in the *Oresteia*. Compared with *Antigone* and *Oedipus Tyrannus*, the songs of *Electra* have not the same variety of reference, the same diversity of poetic feeling, or the same power to lead mind and emotions over widely different areas of experience: their function is rather to concentrate attention on the single issue of Δίκη and Ἐρινύς, using it to give Electra moral support and inspire her with confidence at moments of despair, resolve, and exaltation. The language, imagery, and rhythms of these odes all serve the purpose of the plot, which is to accomplish an act of vengeance.

[60] Winnington-Ingram *PCPhS* loc. cit. 22.

There is in the first and third of these songs an astonishing use of vivid concrete imagery to suggest an inexorable movement towards this design. The words are chosen with great economy, the rhythms reflect in their sound the urgency of the language and the drive of the action, and the structure of the sentences is uncomplicated by involved periods.

In the lyric dialogues and in their interventions in the iambic scenes, particularly in the latter part of the play, the chorus perform a function that contrasts with that of the odes, for they urge upon Electra the need for self-control in grief and for forethought (προμηθία, πρόνοια) when she has declared her intention of killing Aegisthus herself. Their attitude, especially in the parodos and in parts of the dialogue at 823–70, gives these scenes an air of conflict so that the heroine's obsessive grief is set against a norm of restraint and moderation. Further, as the chorus persist in their questionings and their attempts to persuade, we can observe how they elicit from Electra the tragic nature of her predicament and reveal the effect upon her character of years of ill treatment and lonely brooding, as she mourns for her father and yearns for the return of her brother. As to technique, while the parodos is constructed on the more formal pattern of a conventional commos, there appear in the other two dialogues a quickness of interchange and a flexibility of style and language which mark an advance on Sophocles' earlier plays and foreshadow further developments in the same direction to be found in *Philoctetes* and *Oedipus at Colonus*.

VI

PHILOCTETES

Dio Chrysostom, when comparing the treatments of Philoctetes' story by Aeschylus, Sophocles, and Euripides, makes two important statements about the chorus in the only surviving play on this theme: first,[1] that Sophocles composed his chorus not of the natives of Lemnos like the other two dramatists but of the sailors who accompanied Odysseus and Neoptolemus; and second,[2] that his lyrics do not contain much gnomic element or incentive to virtue, such as are found in Euripides, but display a marvellous sweetness and magnificence. The literary judgement at the end of the second statement is perhaps disputable, but the rest of it is broadly true. The rarity of gnomic and hortatory comment[3] is to be explained by the care which Sophocles always takes in adapting the sentiments of his choruses to their role and status: τὸ γνωμικὸν καὶ πρὸς ἀρετὴν παράκλησις, in Dio's words, would sound strange on the lips of a crew of Greek sailors whose task is to help their captain kidnap the hero but would come fittingly from a group of locals urging endurance in suffering. It is however from the first statement that the most important consequences flow. In changing his predecessors'[4] choruses from native Lemnians to Neoptolemus' sailors, Sophocles has not only made it possible for his chorus to take part in the action but has also emphasized the utter desolation of Philoctetes, thus adding infinitely to the pathos of his ten years' existence on an uninhabited island with no companions except disease and the wild creatures that provide him with food. Loneliness is thus central to his predicament and central also to the tragic quality of the play, as indeed it is to most of Sophocles' extant tragedies. No human association, except rarely and fleetingly with the stray traveller in haste to be on his way, ten years' brooding over the wrongs done to him by the Greeks, the agony of his wounded

---

[1] Dio lii. 15.   [2] Ibid. 17.   [3] For an example cf. *Phil.* 1140–5.
[4] Euripides' play 431 B.C., Sophocles' 409 B.C.

foot, the weary struggle for food and drink, all this might have dehumanized him, but such is Sophocles' art that he has succeeded in making him a figure of tragic dimensions who commands respect and compassion. This compassion is maintained in the play by the utterances of the chorus as they reflect upon his desolation.

In addition, by making Neoptolemus bring the chorus with him, Sophocles has ensured that there is no illogicality (τὸ ἄλογον) in his treatment of the story. The question why nobody has visited Philoctetes in ten years does not arise, and we know from Dio[5] that this caused embarrassment to Euripides' chorus of local Lemnians, though not apparently to Aeschylus'. Further, there is no need for the entry of Sophocles' chorus to be prepared for in the prologue of his play, because it is natural that Neoptolemus should bring a landing-party with him to help in the search for Philoctetes' cave. Finally, in a play of intrigue the presence of the chorus tends to cause problems for the dramatist, who has to arrange, sometimes artificially, for them to be sworn to secrecy. The difficulty is obviated in this play, as Neoptolemus' crew are evidently in the know from the start.[6] Nor do they require a detailed description of the scenery, but merely a few directions in the parodos, as they will have had time to familiarize themselves with it during the prologue, if, as is probable, they disembarked with the actors. There is no means of telling whether they became visible to the audience before the prologue is over: it would be more effective dramatically if they did not appear until their first urgent question at 135:

$$\text{τί χρὴ τί χρή με, δέσποτ', ἐν ξένᾳ ξένον}$$
$$\text{cτέγειν, ἢ τί λέγειν πρὸc ἄνδρ' ὑπόπταν;}$$

'What am I, a stranger in a strange land, to hide, what to speak when I face a man who must be suspicious?' Sophocles has thus removed every obstacle to a smooth transition from prologue to parodos. The action is continuous from the opening lines of the play, and when the chorus utter their first words they immediately take part as one of the actors and share in the plan outlined by Odysseus.

[5] Dio lii. 7.
[6] See Jens-Uwe Schmidt, *Sophokles. Philoktet*, 46. Taplin, *The Stagecraft of Aeschylus*, 370 argues against the chorus's entry at the beginning of the play.

This technique marks a considerable advance on that of Sophocles' previous extant plays. We have seen that in the earlier ones there is a break after the prologue, so that the parodos constitutes a fresh start. While *Electra*, with its actor's lyric anapaests at the end of the prologue and its parodos in the form of a sung lament shared between actor and chorus, points the way towards fusing the two opening sections, the really significant change comes in *Philoctetes*, where both prologue and parodos are essential parts of the action. The same technique is further developed in *Oedipus at Colonus*, where the interchanges of conversation between chorus and actors are quickened, with a consequent gain in liveliness and flexibility.

In form the parodos of this play is epirrhematic: the chorus ask questions in lyric, and Neoptolemus answers in matter-of-fact tones, his anapaests giving the briefest directions. For instance at 144 ff. there is a vivid impression of the young leader in front signalling to his men and inviting them to take a look at the cave; and at 163 ff. a sensible inference is drawn from what the trained eye has observed at its entrance. The contrast in metres, lyrics from the chorus, recited anapaests from the actor, reflect a difference in mood: the sailors are tense, they feel that the man they seek is suspicious (136), and they are uncertain of his reactions. They are completely dependent on their young leader, whom they address as δέσποτα and τέκνον in the first strophe; and they describe their relationship with him in stilted terms of respect, notably in 138 f., with its sententious way of saying that kings have superior wisdom. Neoptolemus on the other hand is strictly practical: his mood, for all the excitement he may be feeling, is restrained and unemotional, as befits an enterprise conducted with the precision of a naval commando raid.

Besides sharing in the action, the chorus also have the vital task of conveying to the audience the pathos of Philoctetes' predicament and engaging their sympathies on his behalf. This they do in the second strophic system (169–90) by an imaginative description of his way of life. In the opening words, οἰκτίρω νιν ἔγωγε, the emotion of pity essential to tragedy is evoked before he himself appears; and in the succeeding lines the chorus depict his isolation from human contact and his physical suffering. They express their wonder how he copes with the business of living, recalling Neoptolemus' words at 162 f., and in the last few lines of the antistrophe, they suggest his cries of pain echoing from the cave:

> ἁ δ' ἀθυρόστομος
> ἀχὼ τηλεφανὴς πικρᾶς
> οἰμωγᾶς ὕπο χεῖται.[7]　　　　　　(188 ff.)

The themes of these two stanzas, lyrical expansions of some of the statements in the prologue, appear again and again in speech and song throughout the play. They mark a notable difference in mood from what precedes and follows: action yields place to reflection, so that within the parodos as a whole we experience the tension in the chorus's mind between the excitement of the search and their feelings of pity, just as in the parodos of *Oedipus at Colonus* we sense the conflict between compassion, horror, and curiosity in the old men who guard the sacred grove. The change from absorption in the plot to contemplation and then back again to alert suspense when Philoctetes' cry is heard at the beginning of the third strophic pair is hinted at in the parodos of *Electra* when the chorus and Electra recall the night of Agamemnon's murder in an impressionistic stanza[8] that interrupts the conflict which is its main theme. In both plays therefore we find the same circular or ABA construction in the parodos, but in the earlier one the extremes of mood are not in such sharp contrast, and the exchanges between chorus and actor lack the urgency and the dynamic shifts between action and emotion which give the parodos of *Philoctetes* its dramatic power.

By the end of the second strophic pair the build-up to the hero's entry is complete. Neoptolemus' anapaests 191–200, explaining the reasons for the castaway's predicament and mentioning incidentally that Philoctetes himself is to take part in the capture of Troy, are interrupted by the chorus at 201, a line with double ἀντιλαβή which marks the renewal of suspense as the cry, imagined at 188 ff., is made real:

> Χο. εὔστομ' ἔχε, παῖ. Νε. τί τόδε; Χο. προὐφάνη κτύπος
> 　　　　　　　　　　　　　　　　　　　　　　　　(201)

---

[7] Thus Erfurdt, followed by Pearson, OCT. The text is uncertain, see Jebb's edition ad loc., and appendix, 235 f. πικραῖς οἰμωγαῖς (Brunck), ὑπακούει (Auratus) is attractive: 'answers his bitter laments'.　　　　[8] *El.* 193–212.

'*Ch.* Silence, my son! *Ne.* What now? *Ch.* A sudden sound.' The crescendo of excitement gathers speed at the beginning of the antistrophe when the chorus announce that Philoctetes is close at hand,

$$οὐκ ἔξεδρος, ἀλλ' ἔντοπος ἀνήρ.\qquad(211)$$

We are to imagine perhaps that the shout, first heard as a vague noise, κτύπος . . . ἤ που τῇδ' ἢ τῇδε τόπων (201 ff.), becomes more distinct and localized as he approaches the cave from the back entrance, limping slowly in his pain.[9] The cry at 216 (βοᾷ τηλωπὸν ἰωάν) may, in the sailors' view, be due to a stumble (ἤ που πταίων) or to the sight of their ship at anchor in one of the island's inhospitable coves. His greeting to the party,

$$ἰὼ ξένοι\qquad(219)$$

picks up ἰωάν in 216, and the echo of ἰωάν in ἰώ forms a natural vocal link between parodos and epeisodion, suggesting that the cry was not a moan of pain but a hail, as he saw first the ship, and then, a few moments later, Neoptolemus and his crew.

Attention may be drawn to a few points of style and rhythm. One notices the word echoes κατ' ἀνάγκαν and ὑπ' ἀνάγκας at 206 = 215, emphasizing the difficulty of Philoctetes' progress, the repeated questions and words (157 and 205) to stress excitement, and the exclamations at the end of the second strophe (177 ff.) as the chorus reflect with heightened emotion on his way of life and set it in a general context of human suffering:

$$ὦ παλάμαι θνητῶν$$
$$ὦ δύστανα γένη βροτῶν$$
$$οἷς μὴ μέτριος αἰών$$

'Alas! the designs of mortals, alas! the ill-starred generations of men, doomed to extremes of fate.' In this central strophic pair of the parodos the language is more highly wrought and allusive in its use of words, as imagination is given free play, especially in the antistrophe 180–90. The opening and closing pairs display less poetic intensity, and the style, apart from the rather stilted first strophe, is simple and natural as befits the action and the status of the chorus. The most striking effect occurs in the first

[9] See D. B. Robinson, *CQ* n.s. 19 (1969), 34 ff. for a discussion of scenery and presentation; also T. B. L. Webster's edition ad loc.

lines of the last strophe and antistrophe (201 = 210), with the lyric ἀντιλαβή used for the first time in Sophocles' extant plays in his *Electra*.[10] We should note finally how the lyric metres correspond to the varying moods in the parodos: a mixture of iambic, aeolic, dactylic, and possibly ionic rhythms helps to convey the excitement of the first and third systems, while a uniformly aeolic rhythm, consisting largely of glyconics, well suits the sustained pathos of the two central stanzas.

In order to appreciate fully the effect of this parodos, a considerable exercise of imagination is required. We know little about the capabilities of the contemporary theatre in depicting scenery, but there is enough 'verbal scene-painting'[11] in the prologue to suggest the main aspect of the terrain. Philoctetes' cave is on a higher level than the stage upon which Neoptolemus and Odysseus have been conversing, and the chorus in the orchestra are probably only a very little way below the stage, otherwise their captain's invitation at 146 to inspect the cave would be implausible. We may envisage a rocky scene with sparse scrub vegetation represented by the dramatist who invented σκηνογραφία.[12] Against this background much activity takes place: movements upwards and forwards, gestures, sudden stops, alerts as the excitement of the search increases, and then, after the retardation of the central strophic pair, the sudden cry, at first indistinct, then gradually growing louder as it accompanies Philoctetes' painful steps, and finally his long-awaited appearance as a climax to the movement of the play, which has continued virtually unchecked from the opening of the prologue. Perhaps the most impressive feature of this parodos is its fusion of action and emotion into an intensely dramatic whole to which chorus and actor together make their contribution.

In the following long epeisodion (219–675) Sophocles uses his chorus sparingly. They are given only three iambic interventions, first at 317, where the coryphaeus comments on Philoctetes' speech with an expression of pity; secondly at 522, in pained rebuttal of Neoptolemus' remark that his crew will change their tone when they have Philoctetes with his gangrened foot at close quarters with them on board ship; and finally at 539, for the conventional announcement of a new character. These spoken interventions are economical and natural, the middle one introducing a note of realism into the play just after the lyric appeal (507–18) which may appear overdone in its urgency.

Special interest is aroused by the two lyric strophes in corresponsion at an interval of 104 lines of spoken trimeters (391–402 = 507–18).[13] This is an effect unique in extant Sophocles[14] and is found elsewhere only in Euripides' *Orestes* 1353 ff. = 1537 ff. and *Hippolytus* 362 ff. = 669 ff., a much longer interval; and there, the antistrophe to the chorus's strophe is sung by an actor. In *Philoctetes* Sophocles replaces the normal two-line spoken comment after a long actor's speech by a ten-line sung strophe at 391 in order to enhance the effect of Neoptolemus' lying speech and convince Philoctetes that it is genuine. The chorus are thus brought into the central intrigue of the plot. The emotional tone of this and the answering stanza is heightened by a mixture of iambics and dochmiacs, and in the first also by the use of appeals, interjections, and a curiously interlocked word order in the last few lines. Its opening address to

$$ὀρεστέρα \ παμβῶτι \ Γᾶ \qquad (391)$$

recalls the solemn invocation of $Γαῖα$ in Homeric oaths.[15] She appears here under the aspects of Cybele and of Rhea, mother of Zeus himself,

$$μᾶτερ \ αὐτοῦ \ Διός$$

and $μᾶτερ \ πότνια$; she haunts Pactolus flowing with gold; she sits on a throne decorated with carvings of bull-slaying lions;[16] and as a climax in the last words she is majesty most high. Her influence pervades the whole stanza, which with its accumulated apostrophes distributed throughout and its relative clause describing a region of her power, contains some features of the hymn-style. Moreover the terms in which she is addressed call to mind, in their fusion of different cult-titles, the riches and religions of Asia Minor, background to the Trojan War. The single main verb in the middle ($ἐπηνδώμαν$, 395) recalls how the

---

[13] See Reinhardt, *Sophokles*, 283 nn. 2 and 3.
[14] *O.C.* 833–43 = 876–86 is not parallel as the stanzas involve actors as well.
[15] e.g. *Il.* 3. 278 ff.; 19. 259; *Od.* 5. 184.
[16] For Pheidias' statute of Cybele in Athens, see *Hesperia* 23 (1954), 169.

sailors appealed to this ancient and impressive deity at Troy when the arms of Achilles were handed to Odysseus, as described by Neoptolemus at 363 ff. After hearing this somewhat overwrought utterance from the chorus Philoctetes cannot fail to accept Neoptolemus' lies as the truth. The sailors here play their part with great effect, following the instructions given them in the parodos,

$$\pi\epsilon\iota\rho\hat{\omega}\ \tau\grave{o}\ \pi\alpha\rho\grave{o}\nu\ \theta\epsilon\rho\alpha\pi\epsilon\acute{v}\epsilon\iota\nu \qquad (149)$$

'try to help as the moment requires', which in addition to their immediate purpose in the context of the search suggest that they are to do their captain's bidding at crucial moments throughout the play.

The answering antistrophe at 507 follows upon Philoctetes' moving appeal to be taken on the ship either to his homeland or to a place from which he can make his way there (485–506). In its opening words, οἴκτιρ' ἄναξ, the theme of pity, echoed from the central section of the parodos, is heard again. It has now become an essential element in the duping of Philoctetes, and before the epeisodion is over, we sense that Neoptolemus himself will eventually succumb to this emotion and put the whole enterprise at risk. As it is, the young man has won Philoctetes' confidence, so that he is convinced that he is to be taken home (530–8). The chorus conclude with an appeal to expediency: if Neoptolemus hates the Atreidae, he should turn their evil deeds to Philoctetes' profit and escape the wrath of the gods by taking him home. This advice is given, as the words ἐγὼ μέν (511) show, in the form 'I should if I were you', so that the sailors leave the final decision to their captain. Both men are about to go into the cave to prepare for the voyage when their departure is delayed by the entry (540 f.) of one of Odysseus' men disguised as a merchant, together with the scout whom we met in the prologue. The purpose of the ensuing dialogue is two-fold: first, to hasten the voyage by warning Neoptolemus that the Greek chieftains are about to intervene; secondly, to report Helenus' prophecy that the capture of Troy requires Philoctetes' presence; and if he cannot be persuaded to go of his own free will, Odysseus will take him by force (593 f. and 610–19).

Although the details of the kidnapping enterprise have been carefully worked out, by the end of the scene (675) human

emotions begin to put the issue in doubt. We are becoming aware
that the whole scheme is being endangered by the very emotion
which is essential to its success. Neoptolemus must be moved by
compassion for Philoctetes in order to win his confidence, and
this compassion is leading to a conflict in the young man's mind
between his human feelings and his loyalty to the commands of
his superiors. Suspense grows as we wonder what the effect of
Philoctetes' appeals is likely to be on Neoptolemus now that a
bond of friendship has been forged between them (671–4). We
also ask whether the sailors' compassion is genuine or whether it
has been assumed for the sake of the plot, for we know that they
are fully involved in it. Further, there is a fine irony in the
situation: Philoctetes is about to embark on a voyage to what he
thinks is his homeland but what the plot requires shall be Troy;
and after hearing the account of Helenus' prophecy, the audience
knows that Troy must eventually be his destination.

At this moment of doubt and suspense in the middle of the
play, when psychological and moral issues are beginning to
predominate, Sophocles has placed the only stasimon (676–729).
It is sung to an empty stage and therefore directed to the
audience, for Philoctetes and Neoptolemus have gone into the
cave to collect a few items for the voyage. Prominent among
these is the bow: Philoctetes must make sure that he has the full
complement of arrows, so that none may be left behind to fall
into hostile hands (652 ff.). There have been many references to
the bow in the earlier part of the play as a weapon vital for the
capture of Troy. Whether with or without its owner is at first
intentionally left vague by the dramatist in order to mystify the
audience. It is not until the merchant's report (610 f.) of Helenus'
prophecy that Sophocles makes clear beyond all doubt that
Philoctetes as well as the bow is needed. This speech (610–19) is
of course heard by Neoptolemus' sailors, and the problem of the
last stanza of the stasimon (719–29) can be stated quite simply:
how, knowing the prophecy and being accomplices in the plot,
can they proclaim that Philoctetes is to be taken home? Before
discussing this problem, we may note some points in the last part
of the conversation which closes the epeisodion and consider
some features in the content and structure of the ode.

At 652–4, Neoptolemus for the first time in the play has his
attention drawn to the bow as a physical object. Hitherto it has

been mentioned frequently in speech and song, but it must now be displayed to view because from now onwards it plays an increasingly important part. Moreover, the sight of it has a striking effect upon him: he regards it as an object of reverence to which obeisance is due as to a god:

> ἆρ᾽ ἔστιν ὥστε κἀγγύθεν θέαν λαβεῖν,
> καὶ βαστάσαι με προσκύσαι θ᾽ ὥσπερ θεόν;   (656 f.)

'is it lawful for me to have a closer look at it, to handle it and worship it as a god?' Philoctetes agrees to this request, and we feel that Neoptolemus is about to gain possession of it. Not only does he agree, but, at 667 ff., uses the familiar language for an exchange of gifts:

> θάρςει, πάρεςται ταῦτά ςοι καὶ θιγγάνειν
> καὶ δόντι δοῦναι.

The bow shall be passed from one to the other and back again as a symbol of reciprocal friendship. Neoptolemus takes the point immediately in his lines 671–3:

> οὐκ ἄχθομαί ς᾽ ἰδών τε καὶ λαβὼν φίλον.
> ὅςτις γὰρ εὖ δρᾶν εὖ παθὼν ἐπίςταται,
> παντὸς γένοιτ᾽ ἂν κτήματος κρείςςων φίλος

'I rejoice to have seen you and to have you as a friend, for the man who knows how to give and to receive benefits in return must be a friend beyond all price.' The two then go into the cave. A powerful mystique now surrounds the bow as a visible pledge of their friendship. Although Neoptolemus has not at this stage of the play abandoned the plan to take Philoctetes and the bow to Troy, the bond of sympathy forged between them strongly suggests that the young man may not be able to maintain the deception much longer. There is no good reason to doubt the sincerity of the feelings he expresses in conversation with Philoctetes at 656 f. and 671 ff. These latter lines (671–4 χωροῖς ἂν εἴςω) are genuine and must be given to Neoptolemus. They indicate an important development in the relations between the two, so that we sense the imminence of a change of heart and wonder how and when the truth will be revealed to Philoctetes.

The first three stanzas of the stasimon reflect upon the hero's sufferings and amplify themes from earlier parts of the play, especially the middle strophic pair of the parodos. There is a piteous picture of his life on Lemnos as the chorus describe his efforts to find relief from his pain and food and drink for his needs. At 710 f. the reference to the bow and arrows reminds us that in addition to their importance in the capture of Troy and the symbolic meaning suggested at the end of the epeisodion they are also essential to Philoctetes' existence. The pathos of these stanzas is enhanced by various devices of style. After an opening illustration from the fate of Ixion on his wheel the chorus express their amazement at his survival in the repeated πῶc ποτε πῶc ποτε ... πῶc (687), which stresses the emotion they feel. The second stanza elaborates the theme of loneliness suggested in the last lines of the first strophe and the pain and difficulty of movement, and closes with a moving simile, παῖc ἄτερ ὡc φίλαc τιθήναc (702), 'like a child without its dear nurse'. At the beginning of the third the thought shifts to his efforts to obtain food and drink, and ends with a cry of compassion in the vocative,

$$\mathring{ω} \ \mu ελέα \ ψυχά. \tag{713}$$

These stanzas are continuous in grammatical structure:[17] linked by ἵνα (where) in 691 and the participle αἴρων (709), they form a single flowing period which creates a powerful impression of desolation, pain, and ceaseless struggle. The sufferer is innocent of all crime, a man like other men, the victim of ruin undeserved:

$$ὃc \ οὔτ' \ ἔρξαc \ τιν', \ οὔτι \ νοcφίcαc,$$
$$ἀλλ' \ ἴcοc \ ὢν \ ἴcοιc \ ἀνήρ,$$
$$ὤλλυθ' \ ὧδ' \ ἀναξίωc. \tag{683–5}$$

Most of the main verbs describing Philoctetes' troubles are in the imperfect tense (ὤλλυτο, 685; ἦν, 691; εἷρπε, 701; προcενώμα, 717), as is natural for a narrative of experiences repeated over ten long years. There is thus conveyed not only the essential emotion of pity but a mood also of hopelessness throughout a period of protracted strain.

The contrast of mood and emotion in the final antistrophe is striking. The opening νῦν δέ cancels the effect of the earlier part of the song as the chorus look forward with certainty to a complete reversal in Philoctetes' fortunes:

[17] See Kranz, *Stasimon*, 178; Jens-Uwe Schmidt, op. cit. 132.

νῦν δ' ἀνδρῶν ἀγαθῶν παιδὶ cυναντήcαc

εὐδαίμων ἀνύcει καὶ μέγαc ἐκ κείνων   (719 f.)

'but now, having met the son of noble ancestors (Peleus and Achilles), he will at last be happy and mighty.' He is to be taken by Neoptolemus to his ancestral home by the banks of Spercheius, scene of Heracles' apotheosis on the heights of Mount Oeta. This reference to Heracles reminds us that he was the original owner of the bow and looks ahead to his appearance as a *deus ex machina* at the end of the play; and in the last words of the song,

Οἴταc ὑπὲρ ὄχθων   (729)

we catch an echo of Philoctetes' own words χθόν' Οἰταίαν (664).[18] The emotion aroused by the thought of νόcτοc, the return after years of absence to a longed for home, informs the whole of the last stanza and contributes much to its effect. Important also is the passing reference to Neoptolemus' εὐγένεια: he is ἀνδρῶν ἀγαθῶν παῖc, and from such a person ἀρετή may be expected. This theme has indeed been heard in the play before, especially in the prologue,[19] where Odysseus persuaded Neoptolemus to act against his better nature, and again in Philoctetes' impassioned speech before the song (ἀρετῆc ἕκατι in 669).

There have been many attempts to solve the problem of this stanza. Some may be easily dismissed, for instance the suggestion that Philoctetes and Neoptolemus reappear at the end of the third stanza, and the chorus hastily change their tone in order to maintain the deception.[20] This would destroy the intensely dramatic effect of the attack of agony following immediately upon the exalted optimism of the end of the song. To be considered more seriously is Müller's theory[21] that the sailors are misled by the last part of the previous scene from 628 into believing that Philoctetes and Neoptolemus have reached a compromise whereby the former will be taken home and the latter will go to Troy with the bow. The virtues of this theory are that it preserves the inherent irony of the situation, takes into account the effect on the chorus of the developing

---

[18] Cf. also 479 and 490.

[19] 79; 88.

[20] So Jebb ad loc., refuted by Tycho Wilamowitz, *Die dramatische Technik des Sophokles*, 286 f., and Kranz, *Stasimon*, 221.

[21] *Wege der Forschung, Sophokles*, 212–38.

relationship between the two men, and treats them as a character in the play subject to the limited insight of the average man and therefore liable to make a wrong diagnosis of the future course of the plot. These are all important points. One difficulty however is that the theory leaves unexplained the sailors' behaviour in the Sleep Scene (827–64), where they urge Neoptolemus to act without delay when Philoctetes is sleeping off the effects of his paroxysm (835 f.). If, according to Müller, they seriously believe at the end of the song that the hero is to be taken home, and then, resuming a role of deceit, urge 100 lines later that he should be abandoned while asleep, we might expect Sophocles to have given a reason for their change of attitude. Further, the theory does not sufficiently recognize Sophocles' habit of using his choruses as an instrument with which to guide the mind and emotions of his audiences in any direction required by the immediate dramatic context; and when, as here, emotions and interests are in conflict on the stage and the issue is in suspense, this role of the chorus leads on occasion to inconsistencies between parts of the same song and between one song and another which can only be explained if we always remember the presence of an audience whose thoughts and feelings have to be engaged and directed.

With this function of Sophocles' choral odes in mind we may develop Tycho Wilamowitz's view[22] and hazard an interpretation of the dramatic purpose of the song as a whole. Its structure and content suggest that the first three stanzas, reviewing in a long flowing period the pathos of Philoctetes' sufferings, are a preparation for a contrasting climax in the last. The imperfect tenses indeed hint at this:[23] the years of misery are seen as something which may be coming to an end, so that with νῦν δέ at 719 we are not unprepared for a *peripeteia* of emotions, a change from pity for the past to hope for the future. Sophocles has here used his chorus as an instrument to heighten the impact of this contrast of emotions upon his audience. The mood generated by the last stanza echoes that of the impassioned words in which Philoctetes lists the benefits he expects from Neoptolemus as if

[22] Op. cit. 293. See also Lloyd-Jones's review of this book, *CQ* N.S. 22 (1972), 226 f.

[23] The point is well made by Jens-Uwe Schmidt, op. cit. 132. His view that the sailors intend Philoctetes to hear the last stanza from inside his cave seems to me unlikely though it would mean that they are still playing their part in the trickery, as at 391 f., 507 f., and 836 f.

they were something he has already received, so great is his trust in the young man:

ὅϲ γ' ἡλίου τόδ' εἰϲορᾶν ἐμοὶ φάοϲ
μόνοϲ δέδωκαϲ, ὅϲ χθόν' Οἰταίαν ἰδεῖν,
ὅϲ πατέρα πρέϲβυν, ὅϲ φίλουϲ, ὅϲ τῶν ἐμῶν
ἐχθρῶν ἔνερθεν ὄντ' ἀνέϲτηϲάϲ μ' ὕπερ   (663–6)

'for you alone have granted me to look upon this sunlight of hope, to see the land of Oeta, to see my aged father and my friends—you have raised me above my foes beneath whom I lay prostrate.' In these lines his delusion is at its height, and he is exalted by the belief that his νόϲτιμον ἦμαρ is assured. This exaltation must be crystallized in lyric utterance so that the feeling is shared alike by actor, chorus, and audience. By a peculiarly Sophoclean stroke all hope of a voyage home, or indeed anywhere, is shattered by the cry of pain that follows swiftly on the last words of the song. A similar effect is achieved by the third stasimon of *Oedipus Tyrannus* (1086–1109), where Sophocles uses his chorus to communicate to the audience Oedipus' almost manic exaltation at the height of his delusion just before the truth is revealed to him. Further, we meet with conflicts between one emotion and another in the same song notably in the first stasimon of that play (*O.T.* 463–571), in which the excitement of the hunt for the murderer gives way to doubt and dismay at Teiresias' denunciation of Oedipus; and in *Electra* 473–515, where supreme confidence in the inevitable punishment of Agamemnon's murderers is followed by a moving lament for the continuing sorrows of the House of Atreus. This stasimon however of *Philoctetes*, unlike the other instances just mentioned, is remarkable for the way in which it depicts the transition from one emotion to another, so that the whole song is a unity directed towards the single purpose of creating in the audience a mood of hope at a moment of crisis in the play. Immediately after the song is over, hope is cancelled, and pity and horror return with the following scene of agony.

It is interesting to note that in his last extant play but one Sophocles has restricted himself to a single stasimon. There are pointers in this direction in his *Electra*, which contains only three stasima in contrast to the rich and varied songs of *Antigone* (five) and *Oedipus Tyrannus* (four); and in these two plays the parodoi are choral. During the later part of the fifth century Euripides in some of his plays and to a greater extent Agathon were tending to use stasima as interval songs with a tenuous or even non-existent connexion with the dramatic context.[24] This suggests that they already felt the choral ode to be superfluous as an integral part of a play but were unwilling to abandon a long established convention. Sophocles, however, so far as the limited evidence of seven plays can take us, had no such inhibitions. He simply reduced the number of stasima and brought the chorus into closer relationship with the action and the actor by an increasing use of lyric dialogue, following the contemporary trend of Euripides, where however we find no compensating reduction in the number of stasima. This feature of *Electra* and *Philoctetes* is also due in some measure to the nature of the two plays. Both are dramas of intrigue. Curiosity, tension, and excitement are aroused in the former by a murder plan and its execution, and in the latter by a more subtle conflict of character and psychology. In neither case must there be too much interruption from elaborate choral odes, and the suspense-curve must proceed to its climax unbroken by far-reaching comment and reflection. In his last play, *Oedipus at Colonus*, which is more like an oratorio than any of his others, Sophocles to a large extent restores to the chorus their role as singers, giving them four stasima, while at the same time developing still further the technique of lyric dialogue.

The ensuing scene of agony, during which Neoptolemus gets the bow (776), brings the action to a temporary stop, and the retardation is similar to the one produced by the entry of the merchant at 542. These unexpected delays to the fulfilment of Odysseus' plan are vital in sustaining the suspense which is such an important element in the play. Sleep overcomes Philoctetes (826) as a natural relief from intolerable pain, and the chorus at once resume their role in the plot. We might have expected a stasimon at this point but a lyric comment on Philoctetes' agony would have been far less effective dramatically. Sophocles accordingly brings his actor into the lyric system in order to emphasize the participation of the chorus in a critical situation on the stage: an opportunity for action has been created by the hero's falling asleep, and the moment is seized by the sailors to

[24] Arist. *Po.* 1456[a] 28 f. See also the scholia on Ar. *Ach.* 443 and Eur. *Phoen.* 1019.

press home the point upon an already reluctant and worried Neoptolemus. No formal ode could have so successfully maintained the necessary tension and suspense as the audience wait to see what action, if any, will be taken before Philoctetes wakes up. The period of his sleep is thus filled by a sung triad from the chorus with four hexameter lines recited by Neoptolemus between the strophe and antistrophe.

The strophe (827–38) is remarkable for the perfection of its rhythm and language in the opening address to Sleep.[25] Sophocles has here exploited the utmost possibilities of euphonious sound by the use of long vowels and diphthongs in echoed sequence:

$$\text{Ὕπν' ὀδύνας ἀδαής, Ὕπνε δ' ἀλγέων}$$
$$\text{εὐαὲς ἡμῖν}$$
$$\text{ἔλθοις, εὐαίων εὐαίων, ὦναξ}^{26}$$

'Sleep that knows not anguish, painless Sleep, breathing gently, come, as we pray, with blessing, with blessing.' The same effects are repeated in the antistrophe (βαιάν μοι, βαιάν, ὦ τέκνον, (845)) and in the opening words of the epode (οὖρός τοι, τέκνον, οὖρος, (855). In form the first five lines of the strophe are a ὕμνος κλητικός to Sleep: so much is suggested by the epithets of the vocative Ὕπνε, the verbs ἔλθοις and ἴθι ἴθι, and the ethic datives ἡμῖν and μοι which stress the personal interest of the person praying. The power addressed is asked to be present in order to perform the requested act,

$$\text{ὄμμασι δ' ἀντίσχοις}$$
$$\text{τάνδ' αἴγλαν} \ldots \qquad (830)$$

The interpretation of τάνδ' αἴγλαν has been much disputed in the past, but is now probably settled.[27] The request 'keep before his eyes this light which is now spread over them', followed by an appeal to παιών, a title of Asclepius the healer, shows that αἴγλα here is metaphorical. Starting from the familiar use of φάος to mean a light of comfort, we may refer to Aristophanes, *Plutus* 634–40, much of which is probably a parody of a fragment of

---

[25] For an account of 'the subtle and exquisite metrical art of this ode' see A. M. Dale, *The Lyric Metres of Greek Drama*[2], 117 ff.; and on the ode as a Paean to Sleep, see J. A. Haldane in *CQ* N.S. 13 (1963), 53.

[26] For a similar sound cf. Eur. *Ion* 125 ff. = 141 ff.

[27] See Pearson's note on Fr. 710 (Frs. ii. 317); also his article in *CR* 35 (1911), 246, and Haldane, loc. cit.

Sophocles' *Phineus* (710 P), and note especially the words Ἀσκληπίου παιῶνος (636) and ἀναβοάσομαι ... μέγα βροτοῖσι φέγγος Ἀσκλήπιον (640), 'I shall summon up Asclepius, a great light for mortal men'. So in this passage of *Philoctetes* the chorus call upon Sleep with Asclepius' powers of healing and bringing the light of comfort to the sick, and ask him to keep this light before Philoctetes' eyes. The use of αἴγλα instead of the more usual φάος or φέγγος is to be explained by the mythical association of Αἴγλη with Asclepius.[28]

A host of associations crowd about the god Sleep on Lemnos.[29] In *Iliad* 14. 230 he is summoned from this island by Hera to assist her by putting Zeus to sleep, and if we are meant by Sophocles to recall the celebrated Διὸς ἀπάτη, the chorus may be summoning Sleep in a double capacity, both as a healer and as a deceiver. The first role is apparent in the word παιών (832); the second is strongly suggested by the latter half of the strophe, in which the chorus, now once again a participant in the plot, urge the need for quick action:

πρὸς τί μένομεν πράσσειν;
καιρός τοι πάντων γνώμαν ἴσχων
πολύ τι πολὺ παρὰ πόδα κράτος ἄρνυται   (836–8)

'Why do we delay to act? Opportunity which decides all actions wins a great victory by a quick stroke.' The word πράσσειν, in itself vague, is interpreted by Neoptolemus to mean that they should make off with the bow while its owner is asleep. In the hexameters (839–42)[30] he states in authoritative terms and in the metre of oracular utterance that the bow is useless without Philoctetes and points out the shame involved in a fruitless deception of the kind suggested by the chorus:

κομπεῖν δ' ἔστ' ἀτελῆ σὺν ψεύδεσιν αἰσχρὸν ὄνειδος.

These four hexameters mark the contrast between the sententious tone of the young man and the excited conspiratorial whispering of the sailors. In spite of his recapitulation of what they should have gathered from the merchant's account of Helenus' prophecy (610–19), they continue to urge departure while Philoctetes lies

---

[28] On Sophocles' connection with Asclepius' cult in Athens, see J. A. Oliver, *Hesperia* 5 (1936), 91–122 and the texts there cited.

[29] See D. M. Jones, *CR* 63 (1949), 83.

[30] See Winnington-Ingram, *BICS* 16 (1969), 48 f. on these hexameters.

helplessly asleep and the wind is favourable. This process of persuasion occupies the last two stanzas of the lyric, and he wakes up at the very moment when the audience may be wondering whether Neoptolemus will yield to it.

The scene (730–867) from the end of the stasimon until Philoctetes awakes is one of the most powerful in extant Greek Tragedy for its portrayal of extreme physical agony. Moreover, in addition to the pity and horror aroused by the sight and sound of the hero's suffering, doubt and suspense must be created and sustained in the audience: what will Neoptolemus do after listening to his sailors? Will he obey the oracle, yield to the persuasions of his crew, or reveal the plot to Philoctetes? To raise these questions and keep tension alive is the principal function of the chorus in this scene.[31] The doubts are still unresolved when Philoctetes' awakening delays whatever action may have been contemplated as a result of the lyrics. However after a further appeal, based upon the young man's nobility of character (874–81), Neoptolemus at length resolves them by revealing the purpose of his expedition to Lemnos because he realizes that in sustaining the deception any longer he is acting against his true nature:

> ἅπαντα δυσχέρεια, τὴν αὑτοῦ φύσιν
> ὅταν λιπών τις δρᾷ τὰ μὴ προσεικότα   (902 f.)

'All is offence when a man abandons his true nature and acts unlike himself.' Sophocles has again in the sailors' lyrics, no less than in the stasimon, used his chorus as an instrument for working on the emotions of his audience so that they react in the way he requires at this stage of the play. The feeling that their behaviour in this scene is absurd, irrational, or inconsistent is somewhat lessened if we remember not to expect the same consistency in a flexible instrument of technique as we do in an individual character.

Between the sleep-scene and the commos at 1081, Philoctetes, though relieved from physical pain, experiences a climax of mental anguish. Neoptolemus discloses the trick to get him and the bow to Troy, and moved by the great speech 927–63, is on the point of handing the weapon back when Odysseus appears from an ambush and prevents him (974 ff.).[32] One of the three

---

[31] See D. B. Robinson, *CQ* 19, loc. cit., for a good discussion.

[32] On this scene see Oliver Taplin's article in *GRBS* 12 (1971), 25 ff.

interventions of the coryphaeus in this part of the play occurs at
the end of Philoctetes' speech at 963 f., and is significant in the
closely knit dramatic structure. First, the opening words τί
δρῶμεν; foreshadow Neoptolemus' τί δρῶμεν, ἄνδρες; in 974
when at the crisis of his dilemma he is about to give back the
bow. The sailors' remark prepares us for this moment. Secondly,
we are assured in 964 of their complete dependence upon their
commander: it is he who must decide whether to sail away or
yield to Philoctetes' entreaties. The agony of indecision is at its
height over the following ten lines, with the cry οἴμοι, τί δράcω;
at 969, followed at 974 by τί δρῶμεν, ἄνδρες; where, ironically,
after 964, he appeals to his men for help in making up his mind.
In their next intervention, 1045 ff., they express what they think
of Philoctetes' character after listening to his second long speech:

> βαρύc τε καὶ βαρεῖαν ὁ ξένος φάτιν
> τήνδ' εἶπ', 'Οδυccεῦ, κοὐχ ὑπείκουcαν κακοῖc

'The stranger is bitter, Odysseus, and bitter are his words: he
does not give way before his troubles.' This judgement may
explain the tone of remonstrance they adopt in parts of the
ensuing commos. Finally, at 1072, when Philoctetes has appealed
to the sailors to have pity on him in his desolation, the coryphaeus
repeats the point made in 963, that the issue rests with their
commander, who has been silent since 974.

At 1081 begins the long lyric dialogue between Philoctetes
and the chorus. The way to it has been prepared throughout the
preceding iambic scene from 865, and it is a natural continuation
in song of the last twenty or thirty lines of that scene. No doubt
in Sophocles' earlier period we might have had a stasimon at this
point, closely related in mood to the hero's emotion at the end of
the actors' conversation and reflecting on the pathos of his
loneliness, but a stasimon, however closely connected with the
dramatic context, would have made too much of a break at this
moment in the play. Philoctetes' desolation must be given
heightened expression from his own lips in lyric form so that
there may be no interruption in the crescendo of emotion.
Sophocles accordingly makes his principal character sing for the
first and only time in the play. Much of what he sings is a lyric
expansion of what he has already said.

In form this commos consists of two long strophic systems

divided between actor and chorus with the actor's part predominant, followed at 1169 by an extended epode, with faster exchanges between the participants marked by ἀντιλαβή at 1184 f. and 1204–11. This is the first occasion on which Sophocles in his extant plays employs a long passage of astrophic dialogue with both actor and chorus singing. His previous experiments with sung dialogue have all been rigidly antistrophic from *Ajax* onwards. Astrophic lyric conversation occurs increasingly in Euripides' plays of his middle and later periods and is parallel with his growing use of ἀπολελυμένα, which are by nature astrophic, in actors' solos. In his last three plays Sophocles has however not to any great extent followed this fashion: Electra's monody after the prologue in her play and Antigone's at the end of the parodos of *Oedipus at Colonus* are the only examples of actors' solos in his extant tragedies.

Just before the commos begins, Philoctetes appeals first to Neoptolemus not to desert him (1067), but the young man's answer is forestalled curtly by Odysseus; and secondly to the chorus (1070 f.) who again, as in 963 f., state their absolute obedience to their captain. He himself, evidently under Odysseus' control, acknowledges that his compassion may have been excessive and bids his sailors remain while preparations are made for the voyage. He also hints that Philoctetes may be brought to a better state of mind:

$$\chi o \tilde{v} \tau o \varsigma \ \tau \acute{a} \chi' \ \grave{a} \nu \ \varphi \rho \acute{o} \nu \eta \sigma \iota \nu \ \grave{e} \nu \ \tau o \acute{v} \tau \psi \ \lambda \acute{a} \beta o \iota$$
$$\lambda \acute{\psi} \omega \ \tau \iota \nu' \ \acute{\eta} \mu \tilde{\iota} \nu. \qquad \qquad (1078 \ \text{f.})$$

He and Odysseus then leave the stage. The tone and subject-matter of what follows arise immediately from what has just been said: acting upon Neoptolemus' hint the sailors in their part of the commos make an attempt at persuasion which however fails.

Philoctetes' utterances begin (1081) with a lyric concentration of much of his previous speeches, especially 952–60. He appeals first to the cave which has been his home for so long, and here we recall what he said in the early speeches after his first appearance in the play. Uppermost in his mind is his dependence on the bow for food, and he is struck by the ironical thought that without it he will be at the mercy of the birds which he once shot to keep him alive.[33] At the end of the first antistrophe (1111 ff.) his thoughts move to the trick played upon him and to Odysseus who planned it. This occupies him throughout the second strophe, during which he appeals to the bow as a sentient being to observe the wickedness of his enemy. In the antistrophe (1146) he returns to his opening theme and dwells with the mounting passion of despair on the irony of himself as victim of the birds who were once his victims (1155 ff.). A distinct pattern may be observed in these utterances: Odysseus' treachery forms the centre-piece, framed by the apostrophes to his cave and to the wild creatures that inhabit his island. Irony and desolation dominate his laments, and during the strophic sections of the commos he is deaf to the interventions of the chorus.

For their part, the sailors adopt a tone of remonstrance and remind him first that his predicament is due to his own bad choice,

$$\text{cύ τοι cύ τοι κατηξίω-}$$
$$\text{cαc, ὦ βαρύποτμε} \qquad (1095)$$

where the repeated pronoun and the particle mark the reproof, and in the phrase

$$\text{παρὸν φρονῆcαι}$$
$$\text{λῴονοc ἐκ δαίμονοc} \qquad (1098)$$

they virtually repeat Neoptolemus' words at 1078 f. Next, keeping up the same tone in their two following utterances (1116–22 and 1140–5), they rebuke him for his attack on Odysseus, disingenuously denying that they have themselves been guilty of deception and urging him not to reject their friendship. They also present a sententious maxim (1140 ff.) as they remind him of Odysseus' situation working in the interests of his superiors. Trite and banal as their appeals are, they form a calm and tolerably rational foil to Philoctetes' passion. On the other hand, the chorus have no conception of the overwhelming tragedy of his fate, no understanding of the turmoil in his mind and the alternating pressures of hope and despair to which he has been subjected. The reason they give for his predicament, that he chose the worse course when he could have chosen the better,

---

[33] Thus Pearson's text at 1093 f., but the passage is corrupt, perhaps insolubly.

their own self-exculpation, and their reminder of Odysseus' rank
and station fail to make any impression on him, and it is not until
the last lines of the second antistrophe (1163–8), which return to
the plea of friendship heard at 1122, that their remarks penetrate
his mind, so that communication is eventually established in the
first words of the epode addressed to

$$ὦ λῷϲτε τῶν πρὶν ἐντόπων \qquad (1170 f.)$$

'kindest of those who have been in this place before'.

The epode thus grows naturally out of the last six lines of the
formal lament. Its shifting rhythms and rapid interchanges of
dialogue mark a renewal of excitement and suspense after the
more static part of the commos and reveal the terrible tensions
and cross-currents in Philoctetes' mind as he first of all tells the
chorus to leave him when they advise him to come to Troy and
then when they make a move to depart (ἴωμεν, ἴωμεν, 1179)
implores them to stay. Distracted by exposure to physical pain
and consumed with hatred for the Greeks at Troy, he is now
beyond the reach of reason. His utterances become more frantic,
and at last (1202 ff.) his despair culminates in a prayer for a
sword to end his miserable life. After a final apostrophe to his
homeland

$$ὦ πόλιϲ, ὦ πόλιϲ πατρία \qquad (1213)$$

he goes into his cave, and the scene ends with words which recall
what he said in 951, οὐδέν εἰμ᾽ ὁ δύϲμοροϲ: here, more starkly, ἔτ᾽
οὐδέν εἰμι, suggesting a closure in death or fainting.[34]

The rhythms of this commos well reflect the progress of
emotion. Beginning with straightforward choriambics for Philoctetes' address to his cave, it introduces two dactylic tetrameters
with a dochmiac intervening (1091 f.). The chorus's reply is
delivered in a mixture of iambics, dochmiacs, and a single dactyl,
with a choriambic clausula. In the second strophic pair (1123–
68), we find a similar mixture but without dochmiacs, and
dactyls are more in evidence. Choriambic metres are used to
close the utterances of both actor and chorus. A greater variety
of rhythms is introduced at 1169[35] where the long and
increasingly impassioned dialogue begins, and here we find, in
addition to the metres already used, a run of ionics for the

[34] Cf. e.g. Soph. *El.* 677; Eur. *Alc.* 390.   [35] See A. M. Dale, op. cit. 41n.

exchanges at 1175–8. Dactylic lines are more frequent, especially in the latter part, 1196–1208, where Philoctetes reaches the climax of his despair. Iambic and aeolic rhythms form the close as he withdraws into his cave. The organization of the metres throughout the whole commos suggest a careful control in the development of thought, emotion, and action. After a comparatively formalized lament for two strophic pairs, communication is established between actor and chorus at the end of the second antistrophe; and in the epode, with its rapid conversation and quickened emotion, there is a corresponding variety of rhythms: ionics appear, and dactyls, heard sparingly in the earlier sections of the commos, are used more insistently as Philoctetes' passion increases, until the apparently hopeless ending restores the iambics and choriambics which dominate the strophic stanzas.

So ends the powerful scene which began with the awakening of Philoctetes after his attack of agony (866). There is no break in dramatic tension between that moment and his exit at 1217, and in order to evoke the sharpest emotional response from the audience as his mental anguish drives him to wish for death,

$$\varphi o \nu \tilde{\alpha} \; \varphi o \nu \tilde{\alpha} \; \nu \acute{o} o c \; \mathring{\eta} \delta \eta \qquad\qquad (1209)$$

Sophocles has concluded the scene in lyric form. The commos is therefore an integral part of the movement of the play from the sleep scene until the hero disappears into his cave to perish of starvation, and the chorus by their participation in the lyrics which mark the closing minutes have played an essential part in increasing the emotion required as the play reaches 'a real, though morbid end'.[36] At this point the sailors' part is done, and we hear no more of them until the conventional anapaestic coda.[37]

Looking back over the choral sections of this play, and allowing for the reduction in the number of formal odes, we may note the importance of the chorus in creating and sustaining compassion for the hero in the first half of the play until Neoptolemus' pity is aroused. Further, they are instrumental in exciting a mood of hope followed by a feeling of doubt and suspense at the centre of

[36] Taplin, op. cit. 36.

[37] Taplin (op. cit. 39 ff.) has convinced me that the four lines 1218–21 announcing the approach of Odysseus and Neoptolemus are spurious. Unannounced entries are a feature of this play, cf. 974, 1293.

the play. Throughout they also perform the part assigned to them as fellow-conspirators with their captain in an enterprise involving trickery and mental cruelty. We thus detect a certain inconsistency in their behaviour which some critics have attributed to lack of imagination or stupidity on the part of the sailors but which is better explained by Sophocles' use of them, as of most of his choruses from time to time, both as an instrument to move his audience and as an actor assisting in a plot. At the same time we may feel that there is in the utterances of the chorus in *Philoctetes* a lack of the poetic intensity which is apparent in the songs of the sailors in *Ajax*, who afford a close parallel in rank to Neoptolemus' crew. In the early play the yearning for home after weary years at Troy provides a theme which runs throughout and issues at intervals, especially in the final stasimon, in poetry of the highest quality. *Philoctetes* however contains no such natural source of song, and apart from a few passages in the review of the hero's life in the parodos and the stasimon, and the marvellous exploitation of verbal music in the sleep scene, there is not much to stir the imagination. Nor are the minds of audience and reader stretched and taxed by wide-ranging reflection in song on the deep issues raised by the conflicts of the play: these are allowed to speak for themselves through the mouths of the actors. As a result of this, the problem presented by the single stasimon is not one of relevance to its dramatic setting, as it is in some of the odes of *Antigone* and *Oedipus Tyrannus*. This lack of high poetry and moral and intellectual comment in the writing for the chorus is explained by the nature of the plot and the status and role of Neoptolemus' commandos who take part in the raid on Lemnos. It must on no account be ascribed to a weakening of the dramatist's powers in the closing years of his life, for in *Oedipus at Colonus* the songs display an unsurpassed quality of feeling and expression, and there is no sign that the fires of his inspiration are dimmed.

The most important feature in the use of the chorus in *Philoctetes* is the great advance in lyric dialogue between chorus and actor. From the first rather stilted attempts at this technique in the second parodos of *Ajax* where Tecmessa (who however does not sing) and the chorus search for the hero's body (864 ff.) until its perfection in *Oedipus at Colonus*, we may trace its gradual development. Fundamental to it is the use of chorus and actor on the same level of quick and close communication, and its consummation is a kind of lyric stichomythia, a continuation into song of the rapid give and take of spoken conversation, marked by frequent ἀντιλαβαί and interruptions of grammatical structure. We have therefore to exclude from consideration the more formal set pieces such as epirrhematic scenes, static commoi, and antiphonal laments which persist throughout Greek Tragedy from the earliest extant play to the latest.[38] Signposts along the path of this development in Sophocles' plays before *Philoctetes* are the passage of *Ajax* noted above; *Trachiniae* 875–95; *Oedipus Tyrannus* 649–96; *Electra* 823–70 and 1398–1441. Only in the last passage but one does the actor sing, yet a striking impression of a growing flexibility and rapidity of communication is created by all of them after the first; and they all occur at moments of exciting action and deep emotion, the search for a corpse, the discovery of a suicide, the climax of a quarrel, the depth of an overwhelming despair, the perpetration of a murder. In *Philoctetes* the process is carried a stage further. The dramatic impact of the parodos, after an epirrhematic opening and a central strophic pair for reflection, is suddenly intensified at 201 = 210 by the breathless exchanges between actor and chorus as the hero is heard approaching; and again in the commos, after a formal lament, actor and chorus are brought more closely together in rapid communication by a long epode which displays all the stylistic devices of fully perfected sung dialogue. This technique reaches the highest pitch of dramatic and emotional intensity in the parodos and first sung dialogue of *Oedipus at Colonus*. There are parallels for these developments in Euripides, who had for the last twenty years of the fifth century been experimenting with lyric conversation between actors, and actors and chorus. An important tendency in the choral technique of tragedy during this period is thus apparent. Successful attempts were being made to bridge the gap between chorus and actor and to make their relationship less formal, so that both might together contribute an equal share, in the heightened tones of song, to moments of crisis in action and emotion.

[38] Cf. Aesch. *Pers.* (472 B.C.) 931–1007 and Soph. *O.C.* (406 B.C.), 1724–50.

VII

OEDIPUS AT COLONUS

It is appropriate that this play should have a chorus of old men. Written by Sophocles at the age of ninety when Athens faced defeat after a quarter of a century of war and produced posthumously by his grandson in 401 when defeat had come, it portrays the last hours of Oedipus, once a great king, now a vagabond in exile, old and blind yet full of passion and still a potent instrument of the ancient curse on the Labdacid house which he uses with shattering effect upon his son;[1] and it closes with his transfiguration into a semi-divine being reconciled at death with the Eumenides who inhabit the sacred grove at Colonus which forms the scene of the play. This grove, hallowed by a mystical sanctity peculiar to the powers that haunt it, is the special charge of the old men of the chorus, guardians of this place (τῆcδ' ἔφοροι χώρας, 145). They are moreover given an identity as οἱ ἐνθάδ' αὐτοῦ μὴ κατ' ἄcτυ δημόται, 'the demesmen on the spot, not in the town' (78): the technical term distinguishes them from the people of the metropolis and marks them as members of the deme or district of Colonus, the birth-place of Sophocles himself. Their age and their function as guardians of the holy place lend a special interest and importance to their role both as singers and as participants in the action, and in both roles the dramatist uses them with consummate skill to guide emotions and thoughts as required by the movement of the play without once abandoning consistency in his depiction of their status.

In the first place, as χρόνῳ παλαιοί (112), the chorus are able to sing with perfect propriety the three great odes in the central section of the play: the praises of Colonus and Attica (668); the battle-song (1044); and the lament for lost youth and the pains of old age (1211). The meaning of these odes is much enhanced if we remember that they are sung by old men, for in the first the singers emphasize what in their land has resisted destruction and

[1] Cf. 1370–92; also for the first imprecation, on both his sons, 421–30.

therefore provides a sense of permanence and a promise of comfort to the old and weary as well as a challenge to the young and vigorous; in the second they visualize a violent action in which their years prevent them from joining, so that we are made aware of the pathos in the repeated wishes to be present at the fight (1044 and 1081–4), the longing to escape from the situation on the stage to a scene of battle appropriate to youth; and in the last they sing of the sorrows of old age from which death is the only saviour, pointing to Oedipus as well as themselves to illustrate their theme and including both in an all-embracing pity:

$$ἐν ᾧ τλάμων ὅδ', οὐκ ἐγὼ μόνος \qquad (1239)$$

'In this state is this unhappy man, not I alone'. γῆρας thus makes an essential contribution to the emotions stirred by these songs.

Secondly, in Oedipus' scene with Creon (728–886), where the two old men confront each other with ever increasing passion, and violence is committed and further violence threatened, we are again reminded of the pathos of old age:

$$καὶ γὰρ εἰ γέρων κυρῶ,$$
$$τὸ τῆσδε χώρας οὐ γεγήρακε σθένος \qquad (726 \text{ f.})$$

'for even if I am old, this country's strength has not grown old', say the chorus as Creon approaches, but all they can do is to gesture unavailingly and shout for help when he seizes Antigone. A parallel climax occurs when Creon is about to lay hands on Oedipus himself (874), but again the old men of Colonus in whose charge Theseus has left him (653) can do nothing but make a show of action and shout until Theseus bursts in upon this scene of violence and noise and quells the frustrated and angry passions.

As to the status of the chorus as guardians of the grove, we are made aware of their intense local patriotism, their feeling for the place, its natural features and religious associations, their precise knowledge of the details of ritual, their holy dread of the holy goddesses (σεμναὶ θεαί) who inhabit it, and their anxious and excited search for the trespasser who profanes it. From these feelings arise the tensions of the parodos with its conflict between their awe of the Eumenides and their natural compassion: the point is made clear in the four lines spoken to Antigone by the coryphaeus at the close of her lyric solo:

ἀλλ' ἴσθι, τέκνον Οἰδίπου, σέ τ' ἐξ ἴσου
οἰκτίρομεν καὶ τόνδε συμφορᾶς χάριν·
τὰ δ' ἐκ θεῶν τρέμοντες οὐ σθένοιμεν ἂν
φωνεῖν πέρα τῶν πρὸς σὲ νῦν εἰρημένων   (254–7)

'But know this, child of Oedipus: we pity you and him alike for
your misfortune, but since we tremble at what may come from
the gods, we could not speak beyond what we have now said to
you.' Other characteristics of the chorus may be briefly noted: a
natural curiosity which compels them to press Oedipus with
further questions about himself in the second lyric dialogue (510–
48); a conventional view of morality apparent in the argument
they use in support of their refusal to keep their promise to
Oedipus when they learn who he is (229–33); a complete
dependence on Theseus the King, who alone must decide the
suppliant's fate (294 f.); and a willingness to accept with courage
the responsibility for protecting him from those who would drag
him from his sanctuary.

In the following pages we shall examine first the role of the
chorus as actors, both in iambic scenes and in sung dialogues, and
secondly their role as singers of the four odes. This division
underlines a very real difference between their dramatic function
and their poetic function and also enables us the better to observe
Sophocles at work both as playwright and as lyric poet. In the
sung dialogues of *Oedipus at Colonus* Sophocles displays in perfected
form a technique used intermittently in most of his plays and
exploited with increasing skill in his last three. The main features
of its final perfection are a closer and more sustained participation
of actor and chorus together in the action; an increasing use by
both of song in passages where information and instruction are
imparted and received; the interruption of metrical and
grammatical units by the rapid exchanges of sung stichomythia
which reveal in heightened form the tensions between chorus
and actor; a complete absence of stilted and formal phraseology
in sung conversation, and a new flexibility and naturalness of
style and language. Lack of evidence prevents us from deciding
whether the chorus's parts in these rapid exchanges were all sung
by the whole chorus together or by small groups or by single
members. It may perhaps be straining credulity to assume for
instance that the instruction ἔτι βαῖνε πόρσω in 178 of the parodos

or the question ἀλλ' ἐϲ τί; in 524 was sung by fifteen voices rather than by one, but the problem must remain unsolved, and speculation is useless.

The entry of the chorus in this play is prepared for during the prologue. At 36 perhaps a gardener, or at any rate a local, appears and warns Oedipus and Antigone to move from where they are as the place is sacred to the dread goddesses, daughters of Earth and Darkness (ἔμφοβοι θεαί, Γῆϲ τε καὶ Ϲκότου κόραι, 39 f.). At 47 he admits he has no authority to remove the trespassers until he has made a report. Then at 64 ff. he reveals that the place is inhabited and that the inhabitants are called after Colonus, the hero of the spot; and finally he departs to make his report to οἱ ἐνθάδ' αὐτοῦ μὴ κατ' ἄϲτυ δημόται who shall decide whether he can stay or go on his journey (78–80). This gradual preparation for the entry of the chorus ensures in a perfectly natural way that both audience and actors know quite a lot about them before they appear. Further, the conversation between Oedipus and the local man (36–80) is a preview in miniature of the parodos and indicates the course it will take. After the man's departure Oedipus speaks a long and impressive prayer to the goddesses who inhabit the grove (ὦ πότνιαι δεινῶπεϲ, 84) to receive him with compassion, and in answer to this appeal to divine beings the old men of Colonus appear, alert and agitated at the report of trespassers within the sacred precinct. Oedipus and Antigone have retired from view into the grove at 113–15. The chorus enter the orchestra to an empty stage and the parodos begins with a scene of search. A natural excitement is thus created at once by the situation[2] and is reflected in the short eager questions at the opening of the strophe:

$$\text{ὅρα· τίϲ ἄρ' ἦν; ποῦ ναίει;} \qquad (118)$$

'Look! who was he? Where is he?' We are in a different dramatic world from that of *Ajax* with its marching anapaests at the entry of the chorus or *Trachiniae*, *Antigone*, and *Oedipus Tyrannus* with their flow of song.

The formal structure of the parodos of *Oedipus at Colonus* is easy to grasp. It consists of two strophic pairs, the first confined to the chorus, followed by an extended epode and closed by a lyric solo from Antigone (237–53). Oedipus and Antigone appear at the

[2] Cp. *Aj.* 866 ff., *Phil.* 135 ff.; Eur. *Heracl.* 73 ff.

end of the first strophe (137), and there is a conversation between
him and the coryphaeus in recited anapaests before the purely
choral antistrophe (150–69). A further conversation in anapaests,
this time between father and daughter, precedes the second
strophic pair which opens at 176 and is completely in the form
of a lyric exchange between the chorus and the actors: in both
strophe and antistrophe (176–87 = 192–206) the parts are
divided in exact responsion between the singers, ensuring a
strictly formal structure for what is an extended passage of
excited movement. Between the two stanzas of the second pair
Oedipus recites four lines of anapaests giving instructions to his
daughter (188–91). The lyric conversation 207–36, which forms
the long epode, is divided between Oedipus and the chorus, with
the possible exception of 217

$$\lambda\acute{\epsilon}\gamma', \ \acute{\epsilon}\pi\epsilon\acute{\iota}\pi\epsilon\rho \ \acute{\epsilon}c \ \acute{\epsilon}c\chi\alpha\tau\alpha \ \beta\alpha\acute{\iota}\nu\epsilon\iota c$$

'Speak, since you are coming to the brink', assigned in the
manuscripts to Antigone.[3] A close parallel to this use of an
extended epode as a climax to sung dialogue is provided by
Philoctetes 1169–1217. To conclude the parodos, Antigone sings
an astrophic solo (237–53), which arises immediately from the
preceding dialogue and is therefore an essential part of it instead
of being an isolated *cri de coeur* like Electra's monody in her play
and so many of the actors' solos in Euripides. As a transition to
the first epeisodion four spoken trimeters are given to the
coryphaeus (254–7).

The scholia record that Antigone's solo and the closing
trimeters were regarded as spurious by certain ancient scholars
but were not however obelized by Didymus in the first century
B.C. The reason given was that it was better for Oedipus to begin
his speech of justification immediately after the chorus's closing
words at 236. Antigone's role is however to represent humanity
and mercy, as she does with great effect before and during the
scene with Polyneices (1181 ff.; 1414 ff.); and her appeal for
compassion at the end of the parodos establishes her character
early in the play.[4] This point is indeed made in a perceptive note
in the ancient scholia. In addition, the four trimeters 254–7 with
their formal summary of the chorus's attitude lower the tensions

[3] Raanana Meridor, *CQ* N.S. 22 (1972), 229 ff., gives strong reasons for assigning 217
to the chorus.

[4] On Ant.'s role see Winnington-Ingram, *JHS* 74 (1954), 24.

of the parodos so that Oedipus may begin his closely reasoned speech in a calmer atmosphere.

In the first strophe the chorus voice the shock they have experienced at the intrusion of trespassers into the holy precinct. Their agitation is conveyed by various devices of metre, style, and language: urgent questions and commands; adverbs in asyndeton (130 f.); repetition of words, ὁ πάντων, ὁ πάντων (119 f.), πλανάτας, πλανάτας (123) marked by the bacchiacs; alliteration, especially of π. The lines from 125–33 in particular express the religious awe felt by the old men for the Eumenides, here called ἀμαιμάκεται κόραι. The epithet, familiar in Epic, sounds strange in a passage whose choice of words is otherwise simple and naturalistic. The chorus tremble to utter the name of the goddesses and pass by with averted eyes, in silent meditation, without audible prayers: ἀδέρκτως, ἀφώνως, ἀλόγως ... ἱέντες where the bacchiacs again produce a striking effect (130 ff.). For all its excitement and its depiction of conflicting emotions, the whole stanza is perfectly shaped, opening and closing with the same question phrased in the same language, ποῦ ναίει; (118) and ποῦ μοί ποτε ναίει (137),[5] with the ethic dative emphasizing the chorus's personal interest. At this moment Oedipus is led out of the grove by Antigone, and the anapaestic rhythm of the last clause of the chorus's lyrics prepares for the conversation between him and the coryphaeus. The antistrophe (150) begins with an exclamation of horror at Oedipus' appearance, blind, old, bedraggled, unkempt, and in worn and dirty clothes,[6] and continues with instructions to the intruder giving precise details about the grove and its furniture and warning him to leave the precinct which he profanes.

With the second strophic pair (176–206) the dialogue, hitherto conducted in recited anapaests, is completely sung by both actors and chorus except for Oedipus' four lines of anapaests separating strophe from antistrophe (188–91). It is essential to visualize the movements that accompany the exchanges from 176 onwards:

> Οι. ἔτ'οὖν; Χο. ἔτι βαῖνε πόρcω.
> Οι. ἔτι; Χο. προβίβαζε, κούρα,
> πόρcω· cὺ γὰρ ἀίεις.

---

[5] ναίει here means 'is' rather than 'dwells', cf. *Trach.* 99.
[6] See Polyneices' description of him, 1258–61.

'*Oed.* Still further? *Ch.* Come still further.
Oed. Further? *Ch.* Lead him onwards, maiden, for *you* understand.'
In obedience to these instructions Oedipus is led out of the grove
to the exact spot where the chorus are satisfied that he may sit.
He reaches it at the opening of the antistrophe (192 f.), and not
until then do the movements cease, so that conversation proper
can begin with the conventional question so familiar in Homer,
τίς πόθεν εἰς ἀνδρῶν;, here modified into lyric form at the end of
the stanza:

$$αὔδασον, τίς ἔφυς βροτῶν;$$
$$τίς ὁ πολύπονος ἄγῃ; τίν' ἂν$$
$$coῦ πατρίδ' ἐκπυθοίμαν;$$ (204-6)

'tell us, from whom were you born? Who are you, thus led on
your weary way? What is your country?' The answer is dragged
out of Oedipus in the epode (207 ff.), in which the ruthless
questioning culminates in a cry of horror at 220, ἰού, wrung from
the old men as they hear the words Λαΐου ἴστε τιν' ἔκγονον; 'do
you know of a son of Laius?', and Oedipus' confirmation of his
identity in 221 f. The exclamations ὦ Ζεῦ ... ἰὼ ὣ ὣ ... ὣ ὣ
vividly suggest their revulsion as they shrink from his presence;
and before Antigone can answer her father's question,

$$θύγατερ, τί ποτ' αὐτίκα κύρcει;$$

'My daughter, what will happen now?', they order the trespassers
out of the place,

$$ἔξω πόρcω βαίνετε χώρας$$

thus breaking the promise they gave at the beginning of the
second strophe:

$$οὔ τοι μήποτέ c' ἐκ τῶνδ' ἑδράνων, ὦ$$
$$γέρον, ἄκοντά τις ἄξει$$ (176 f.)

'Never, never shall anyone drag you from this resting-place
against your will.' To excuse their action they resort to the
conventional precept that deceit may be requited in its own coin
(229-33). Antigone closes this powerful scene by appealing to
the chorus' compassion, successfully, as the coryphaeus acknowledges in his four trimeters (254-7). The increasing tension of this

epode is conveyed by changing rhythms, first aeolics, which have indeed dominated the strophic sections of the parodos, then ionics for three lines beginning with ἀντιλαβή at 212, and finally the gradual emergence of dactyls ending in a dactylic run delivered probably as a πνῖγος in one breath before it slows up into an iambic clausula.[7] To match this, Antigone's solo begins with aeolic elements and settles into dactyls at 243, also with an iambic clausula.

This parodos gives the impression of a masterly recognition scene in lyric form with a revelation as its inevitable climax. Here however there are no tears of joy to conclude it, but a shock of revulsion. During its course the chorus are gripped by a variety of conflicting feelings, outrage, religious awe, curiosity, compassion, horror. Entreaties are made and instructions given with appropriate gestures and physical movements so that emotion is reflected in action; and truth is at last elicited by remorseless questioning until at the moment of revelation horror dominates all other feelings, and the wanderers are ordered from their sanctuary. At this crisis calm is restored by Antigone, and the parodos closes with compassion and religious awe in even balance. We may thus detect the rhythm of the whole scene: the tension, already high at its opening, increases gradually from the appearance of Oedipus and Antigone at the end of the first strophe. Both chorus and actors contribute to the action on equal levels of intensity as the exchanges between them grow in urgency and rapidity. An actor's song quells the passions that have been aroused and secures a comparatively quiet ending. There is moreover no check in the development of the scene although it is divided formally into two strophic pairs, an extended epode, and an actor's solo. This division has however not resulted in any schematism of movement or thought. For instance, the instructions given to Oedipus in the first antistrophe are continued in the second strophe, and he does not reach the precisely right position until the beginning of the antistrophe. Similarly the question about his identity is asked at the end of the second antistrophe and answered during the formally distinct epode. This is sung dialogue at its full perfection, dramatic and intensely exciting.

At the beginning of the first epeisodion (254), the coryphaeus

[7] On the metres, see A. M. Dale, *The Lyric Metres of Greek Drama*,[2] 39 ff. and 138 n. 3.

summarizes the chorus's mood in four spoken trimeters. The words τὰ δ' ἐκ θεῶν τρέμοντες are an echo from the first strophe of the parodos, ἃς τρέμομεν λέγειν (128), and this awe of the goddesses prevents the old men from committing themselves beyond what they have already said. It is therefore necessary for Oedipus to continue in a reasoned speech the process of persuasion begun by Antigone in her appeal for compassion. He makes two points. First, in reviewing his past experiences he puts the emphasis on what he has suffered, not upon what he has done:

$$τά γ' ἔργα μου$$
$$πεπονθότ' ἐστι μᾶλλον ἢ δεδρακότα. \qquad (267)$$

Here, though he mentions the incest (τὰ μητρός, 268), he is thinking especially of the killing of his father, an act committed in retaliation for acts done to him.[8] In amplifying this point he is using the plea of justifiable homicide, allowable in Attic Law as in our own, and he can therefore argue that even if he had acted in full knowledge of Laius' identity, he would not have been κακὸς φύσιν, wicked in his nature. In contrast, the acts of his parents were, unlike his own, done in full knowledge of all the facts (270–74). He is therefore innocent, both legally and morally,

$$νόμῳ δὲ καθαρός, ἄιδρις ἐς τόδ' ἦλθον$$

as he puts it in 548. The argument is powerful and recurs at significant intervals in the play, notably in the second lyric dialogue 522–48 and in the scene with Creon at 974–99. Oedipus himself did not use it in the parodos, though Antigone hinted at it in her appeal (ἔργων ἀκόντων, 240), so that he must himself justify his behaviour in front of the chorus.

In the second place, he informs them that his presence in the grove, as a sanctified being, will bring benefit to the people of the place:

$$ἥκω γὰρ ἱερὸς εὐσεβής τε καὶ φέρων$$
$$ὄνησιν ἀστοῖς τοῖσδε \qquad (287 f.)$$

'For I have come, sacred and pious, and the bringer of benefit to

---

[8] See the account of the killing, *O. T.* 804–13.

these people'. His warrant for this statement, though he does not say so here, is the oracle he received at Delphi in his youth when fleeing from Corinth,[9] mentioned in the prologue 86–95, especially 92,

$$\kappa\acute{\epsilon}\rho\delta\eta\ \mu\grave{\epsilon}\nu\ o\grave{\iota}\kappa\acute{\eta}\sigma\alpha\nu\tau\alpha\ \tau o\hat{\iota}c\ \delta\epsilon\delta\epsilon\gamma\mu\acute{\epsilon}\nu o\iota c$$

'with blessings for those who received me, because I lived there'. The chorus's comment at the end of his speech is non-committal (292 ff.), though we know that the second point has impressed them (cf. 463 f., and 629 f.). The first, to which they do not refer, must be made clear to them beyond all doubt, and this is done in the lyric dialogue 510–48: in fact the need for this clarification is probably the main reason why Sophocles has there substituted a dialogue for a stasimon, which we might have expected at this stage of the play. In the meantime, the natural decision of the guardians of the grove is to refer the whole question to Theseus (294–309).

At this moment Ismene arrives and announces the impending attack of Polyneices on Thebes to recover his throne from his brother Eteocles (377–81). She also reports Creon's proposed mission to fetch Oedipus nearer Thebes so that the defenders of the city may have control of him (396–400). Neither of these announcements, important as they are in the movement of the plot, is of immediate concern to the chorus, so they take no part in what is purely a family matter. It is however obvious from the coryphaeus's remarks when they re-enter the discussion at 461 that they have listened with attention to what has been said; and when they are brought naturally into the conversation by Oedipus at 457 ff., their compassion for him and his two daughters is confirmed. Further, they accept his claim to save their land as a μέγας cωτήρ (459 and 463), as is shown by their instructing him to perform certain ritual acts to atone for his trespass. They here re-enter the action as actors and make an important contribution to the religious atmosphere of the play.

The passage 465–92 is reminiscent of the scene in Aeschylus' *Choephoroe*[10] in which the coryphaeus, representing the chorus, instructs Electra in the forms of prayer she is to use at Agamemnon's tomb. In both plays the passages are stichomythic, with the coryphaeus predominant in that he gives answers to the

[9] Cf. *O. T.* 788–93.   [10] *Ch.* 106–23.

actor's questions. In *Choephoroe* the emphasis is on prayers and their content, while in *Oedipus at Colonus* what is stressed is the exact detail of ritual acts and the need for their scrupulous performance as a preliminary to the prayer dictated at the end (486 ff.). In prescribing the acts which the trespasser must perform the coryphaeus reveals the precise functions of the chorus as guardians of the Eumenides' grove, their attitude of reverence to the goddesses of whom they spoke in the parodos in mystical tones of awe, and their acceptance of the suppliant provided he obeys their instructions:

$$\text{καὶ ταῦτά coι}$$
$$\text{δράcαντι θαρcῶν ἂν παραcταίην ἐγώ,}$$
$$\text{ἄλλωc δὲ δειμαίνοιμ' ἄν, ὦ ξέν', ἀμφὶ coί} \quad \text{(490 ff.)}$$

'If you do this, I would stand by you with courage; otherwise, I would fear for you.' At the end of this scene a decisive stage is reached in the fortunes of Oedipus at Colonus. Accepted there after due lustration and prayer, he is left with Antigone, fearful indeed of being alone, old and physically weak as he is, but assured of the chorus's support and the forgiveness of the Eumenides for his trespass. When Ismene withdraws to perform the prescribed ritual, we experience a sense of quietness and religious fulfilment as Oedipus and Antigone await the arrival of Theseus with the more practical guarantees of security which he is to offer. At this resting-place in the action of the play we might expect a choral ode in tune with the mood of calm. Instead, we have a lyric dialogue which shatters this mood with astonishing effect.

The arresting change of tone and atmosphere is apparent at the beginning, as Sophocles resumes the technique he used in the parodos. Quick exchanges in lyric between chorus and actor, appeals, refusals to answer, shocked interjections of incredulity, and relentless cross-examination[11] emphasize the horrors inherent in Oedipus' past life and awake in audience and reader a powerful emotional response. Thus in the first antistrophe and second strophe the precise implications of the incestuous marriage are laid bare in the repetition of the word ἄτα (526 and 532 f.) and the explicit description of the act of incest and its consequences at 534 f. The chorus's curiosity on this point was

[11] See Winnington-Ingram *JHS*, loc. cit. 18.

naturally aroused by the conversations between Oedipus and his daughters in the preceding scene, and here it is satisfied to the fullest extent. As if this were not enough, the chorus raise again in the final antistrophe the subject of Laius' killing. It is important to stress the *ad horrorem* effect of this dialogue. No doubt Sophocles aimed at it for its own sake and also to mark a strong contrast with the mood both of the preceding scene and the following scene which reveals the practical kindness and tact of Theseus.

Apart from what we may call the purely emotional function of this dialogue, two points emerge from its content which help to explain further Oedipus' attitude towards his past. First, he must impress on the chorus that his actions were not done of his own choice. Although he argued to this effect in his speech to them, 266–74, they did not comment upon it subsequently, so that he must be assured that they have taken his point. Hence at the opening of the first antistrophe (521 ff.), before he begins to answer their questions, he states that his sufferings were involuntary:

$$\text{ἤνεγκ' οὖν κακότατ', ὦ ξένοι, ἤνεγκ'}$$
$$\text{ἀέκων μέν, θεὸς ἴστω,}$$
$$\text{τούτων δ' αὐθαίρετον οὐδέν.} \quad (521\text{-}4)$$

'I have suffered misery, strangers, I have suffered through no will of my own, god be my witness—none of these things was of my choosing.' Then in the second strophe and antistrophe he makes the point again in lines with double interruption (539 = 546) marking urgency and excitement, and he sums up his defence at the end of the dialogue:

$$\text{καὶ γὰρ ἄνους ἐφόνευς' ἀπό τ' ὤλεσα.}$$
$$\text{νόμῳ δὲ καθαρός, ἄιδρις ἐς τόδ' ἦλθον.} \quad (547 \text{ f.})$$

The first of these two lines is corrupt in the manuscripts, and Pearson's text, here printed, is a doubtful conflation of suggestions. In particular, Porson's ἄνους could not mean 'in ignorance', but only 'in folly', which is not here to the point. Jebb prints Mekler's

$$\text{καὶ γὰρ ἂν οὓς ἐφόνευς' ἔμ' ἀπώλεσαν}$$

'those whom I killed would have slain me', which has the advantage of making Oedipus repeat in full the plea that he

acted in self-defence, but is faulted on metrical grounds, because
the line is a dactylic tetrameter which must end with an open
dactyl – ᴗ ᴗ.[12] The corruption is probably confined to the word
before ἐφόνευς‘, given in the manuscripts as the unmetrical
ἄλλους. What is needed is either an object for the verbs or an
adverb:[13] 'Yes, I did indeed kill, but I am guiltless in law for I
acted in ignorance.' This seems to be the logic of the sentence,
and if so, it should be punctuated with a comma at ὤλεσα and a
colon at καθαρός, the resulting asyndeton being explanatory. It
is to be noted that the whole passage from 538–48 echoes both
the form and the content of the argument Oedipus used in the
earlier scene, especially in 267, with its juxtaposition of πεπονθότα
and δεδρακότα, resumed in ἔπαθες ... ἔπαθον ... ἔρεξας ... οὐκ
ἔρεξα (538 ff.), and 270–4. A close connexion is thus assured
between the preceding scene and the sung dialogue, and the
chorus are left in no doubt as to Oedipus' position as he sees it
himself. Further, the theme of requital for deeds done to himself
and of his moral innocence of acts done in ignorance forms an
essential part of the arguments used in his speech to Creon,
expressed with the same force of logic and intensity of emotion
(962–87).

The second point, closely connected with the plea of
involuntary action, is revealed by Oedipus' use, twice in the first
antistrophe, of the word ἄτη: γάμων ἄτᾳ (526) and παῖδε, δύο δ’
ἄτα (531).[14] Though no doubt he is thinking primarily of the
ruin of his own life by the marriage with his mother and of the
visible symbol of that ruin in his two daughters, we should
nevertheless bear in mind the ruin (ἄτη) inherent in the destiny
of the Labdacid house, hounded through the generations by
hostile gods. Antigone's final words in her solo at the end of the
parodos touched upon this theme:

> οὐ γὰρ ἴδοις ἂν ἀθρῶν βροτὸν ὅςτις ἄν,
> εἰ θεὸς ἄγοι,
> ἐκφυγεῖν δύναιτο. (252 f.)

'Look well and you will not see the mortal who could escape if a

---

[12] Cf. e.g. this play 243 ff., and *Ant.* 339 f. = 350 f.
[13] Mr T. C. W. Stinton tried ἐμούς, but admits that this probably needs the definite
article; also ἁπλῶς.
[14] Cp. Creon's use of ἄτα of Antigone and Ismene, *Ant.* 533.

god should hound him.' The feeling that the house is bound to inescapable doom recurs at significant places in the play.[15] Here in the lyric dialogue, the arguments Oedipus uses to establish his innocence are reinforced by the choice of the word ἄτη to describe his marriage and the children born of it. As far as Sophocles is concerned, the great ode at *Antigone* 583 depicting the ἄτη of the Labdacids at work over the generations is sufficient to bring out the overtones of the word in this passage of *Oedipus at Colonus*, and to remind us that here, no less than in the earlier play on this theme, we may recall the ancient doctrine of inherited doom in his view of the Oedipus story. Finally, there is a moving pathos in Oedipus' calling by the name of ἄτα the two daughters upon whom alone he relies for care and affection; and a powerful irony in that the Furies ('Ερινύες), who lurk beneath the ἄτη of his house and who use him as an instrument to ensure by his curse the destruction of his two sons and his devoted daughter, are the same Eumenides in whose grove he finds his resting-place.

This dialogue, to sum it up, creates by the use of contrast as a conscious effect aimed at by the dramatist, an intense excitement after a scene of religious calm; reawakens the emotions of audience and reader to the horror Oedipus feels and expresses at the ruin of his life; emphasizes the passion with which he strives to impress upon the chorus his legal and moral innocence; and tells us something more about the character of the chorus themselves, their curiosity and their relentless persistence in a cross-examination which elicits, step by step as though in a court of law, the pleas he makes in his defence. All this is achieved by further exploitation of the same techniques that were used with such effect in the parodos.

The coryphaeus formally announces Theseus' entry at 549 f. His attitude as revealed in his first speech and subsequent handling of the problem presents a contrast to that of the chorus. We are in the presence of a ruler, calm, confident, tactful, and practical, who welcomes Oedipus without fuss or curiosity and makes the necessary arrangements for his safety. From this point for a considerable stretch of the play, the interventions of the coryphaeus in the iambic scenes are all what may be called actors' interventions and therefore dramatically significant. In

[15] 369–73; 788; 964 ff.; 1299; 1434.

other words there are no balancing maxims between actors' speeches of the type so familiar in Greek tragedy; for the two lines at 937 f. after Theseus' speech and the two at 1014 f. after Oedipus' are not gnomic but strictly *ad hoc*: where we might have expected colourless neutral statements on the perils of anger, we have positive judgements on the characters and attitudes of the speakers. This diminution in the gnomic role of the coryphaeus in spoken parts, no less than the increase in sung dialogue, indicates that Sophocles was tending in his later plays to use the chorus more and more as an actor instead of a commentator. For instance, at 629 f. the coryphaeus brings to Theseus' attention the point made by Oedipus at 287 ff. and 459 f., that he has a benefit to confer on Athens, and he thus dispels any hesitation Theseus may have felt about accepting the suppliant. Again, at 638 (ϲέ νιν τάξω φυλάϲϲειν) and 653 (ἀλλὰ τοῖϲδ' ἔϲται μέλον) Theseus brings the chorus into the very centre of the action by assigning them a specific part in protecting Oedipus. This role they accept with confidence when Creon's approach is announced by Antigone at 722 after the ode to Colonus and Athens:

θάρϲει, παρέϲται· καὶ γὰρ εἰ γέρων κυρῶ,
τὸ τῆϲδε χώραϲ οὐ γεγήρακε ϲθένοϲ.   (726 f.)

and at 833–43 = 876–86, they endeavour to perform their task.

The scene from 820–90 is one of the most striking examples of violent action on stage in the whole of extant Greek Tragedy.[16] The build-up to it begins with the stichomythia following Oedipus' speech to Creon, who reveals at 818 f. that he has already seized Ismene and intends to seize Antigone as hostages in his attempt to force Oedipus to accompany him to the borders of Theban territory. Mounting passion and excitement are marked by the ἀντιλαβή beginning at 820, in which the coryphaeus eventually joins with two spoken trimeters 824 f., and then with urgent interventions in the middle of lines 829–32. At 832 Creon, or more probably his bodyguard, seizes Antigone (τοὺϲ ἐμοὺϲ ἄγω), and Oedipus appeals to the city for help, ἰὼ πόλιϲ.[17]

---

[16] Cp. e.g. Aesch. *Supp.* 825–902, where the Egyptians try to carry off Danaus' daughters.

[17] For the scene 831–90, see Oliver Taplin, *GRBS* 12 (1971), 31.

The scene is formalized as follows. A strophe opening with dochmiacs followed by iambic trimeters from Creon, Oedipus, and the coryphaeus, and closed by dochmiacs from the chorus, is separated from its antistrophe by thirty-two lines of spoken dialogue. The mixture of sung dochmiacs and spoken trimeters marks high emotional tension and here accompanies agitated movements as the chorus threaten violence,

$$τάχ' ἐς$$
$$βάϲανον εἶ χερῶν		(834 f.)$$

'You will soon come to the test of blows', and demand Antigone's release. At 840 Creon orders the captain of his bodyguard to be on his way with her (ϲοὶ δ' ἔγωγ' ὁδοιπορεῖν), and in the closing dochmiacs the chorus shout to the inhabitants of Colonus for help. The dialogue separating strophe from antistrophe is shared between Antigone, until she is carried off (846), Oedipus, Creon, and the coryphaeus, a wrangle between two angry old men, one blind and helpless, and the representative of the chorus, also an old man. It mounts to a climax in form closely parallel to the dialogue that preceded the strophe, when Creon, having announced at 860 that he will seize Oedipus, actually makes as if to seize him:

$$ἀλλ' ἄξω βίᾳ$$
$$κεἰ μοῦνόϲ εἰμι τόνδε καὶ χρόνῳ βραδύϲ.		(874 f.)$$

'I will carry you off by force, even though I am alone and slow with age.' This climax is exactly similar in point of action to 832 (τοὺϲ ἐμοὺϲ ἄγω), and is the signal for the antistrophe to begin, like the strophe, with a shout from Oedipus, ἰὼ τάλαϲ. The chorus's cry for help which closes the antistrophe (ἰὼ πᾶϲ λεώϲ, ἰὼ γᾶϲ πρόμοι), addressed to a wider and more powerful group than the ἔντοποι, the locals, at the end of the strophe, is answered by Theseus himself who rushes on stage θᾶϲϲον ἢ καθ' ἡδονὴν ποδόϲ (890). His opening four lines are recited in trochaic tetrameters, the only ones in this play, so that the excitement generated is carried over into the opening of the dialogue before settling down with iambic trimeters at 891. The movement of the whole scene from 833 is controlled by the discipline of its strophic form with identical line divisions between the participants, proving the existence of a lacuna at 881 f.; and the intervening thirty-two lines of spoken dialogue mark a lowering of tension between the climaxes of violence.

It is difficult to decide how far the chorus engage in physical acts in their attempts to restrain Creon. The evidence from the text is inconclusive, nor are we justified in inventing stage-directions. It is however clear that they advance threateningly towards Creon at 835 in view of his command 'Keep back' (εἶργου, 836), but they are powerless to prevent Antigone's abduction (μὴ 'πίτασσ' ἃ μὴ κρατεῖς, 839, 'do not give orders where you have no power'). In the dialogue after the strophe Creon's μὴ ψαύειν λέγω at 865 suggests that they make a movement to lay hands on him, now that he is alone. This is as far as we can go in visualizing what happens. The problem is indeed further complicated by the question of the presence or absence of a raised stage in the theatre of Dionysus at the end of the fifth century.[18] If the stage was raised above the orchestra on a platform a foot or two high, physical contact between actors and chorus was less likely than if both were on the same level, and we may acquiesce in a series of threatening movements accompanied by gestures. This may be thought more in keeping with the conventions of Greek Tragedy which seem to have required that actors and chorus should be kept apart. Those who do not believe in the existence of a raised stage have no difficulty in envisaging a violent display of physical action in this scene, even the manhandling of Creon by members of the chorus. It may however be thought that threats, movements forth and back, and gestures are as effective dramatically and more dignified than a general mêlée. True enough, there is in this chorus no paralysis of senility of the type that substitutes debate for action in the chorus of *Agamemnon* (1343–71) when the king's death cry is heard, but the pathos of the scene as well as its controlled excitement within the balanced pattern of strophic form are perhaps better served by the show than the reality of physical violence.

In the scenes following the second and third stasima, the interventions of the chorus are again strictly functional. The coryphaeus in their name announces Theseus' approach with

---

[18] For opposing views see Pickard-Cambridge, *The Theatre of Dionysus*, 69 ff., and P. D. Arnott, *Greek Scenic Conventions*, chs. 1 and 2. Taplin, *The Stagecraft of Aeschylus*, 441 f. points out that if there was a raised stage, it was only very slightly raised.

Antigone and Ismene, rescued from Creon's troops (1096 ff.), but they take no further part in this scene. In the Polyneices scene they are given a couplet (1346 f.) after his long speech, offering advice to Oedipus which echoes Antigone's at 1187 ff., that the suppliant should be heard for Theseus' sake (τοῦ πέμψαντος οὕνεκα); and after Oedipus' reply ending with the terrible curse they urge Polyneices to return whence he came as soon as possible (1397 f.). Again, there is no hint of a maxim. These interventions also serve to provide pauses after two long speeches, so that the actors may gather their thoughts for their replies. In this connection it may be noted that at 1348 Oedipus begins his reply by addressing the chorus directly in answer to the point made by τοῦ πέμψαντος οὕνεκα and referring to his son in the third person before turning on him with the full force of his anger at 1354.

After Polyneices' departure at 1446 there is an epirrhematic passage of a conventional type, consisting of two strophic pairs for the chorus with the stanzas separated by five lines of spoken trimeters divided in exact corresponsion between Oedipus and Antigone in the form AABAA. The structure is thus straightforward, and the rhythms of the sung parts are a mixture of dochmiacs and iambics. The first strophe opens in a reflective mood, though the repetition νέα ... νεόθεν ... νέα and the dative μοι indicate excitement. There has been some dispute as to the reference of νέα τάδε ... κακά in 1447f. Most probably the words refer to the immediately preceding scene and not to the thunder clap, as the elder Wilamowitz thought,[19] for the following reasons. First, the language of the opening lines does not indicate a spasm of terror, which is in fact expressed at the beginning of the antistrophe (1462 ff.), and the maxims which follow at 1451–5 would be inappropriate if the thunder had pealed before the strophe began. Secondly, we would miss the sudden change of mood from reflection to fear at the end of the strophe when the thunder breaks into the thought and the singers greet it with the instantaneous aorist ἔκτυπεν and the interjection ὦ Ζεῦ in a sentence with no connective. Thirdly, the words

> νέα τάδε ...
>
> κακὰ παρ' ἀλαοῦ ξένου

[19] In Tycho Wilamowitz, *Dramatische Technik des Sophokles*, 332 f. For the view I support, see Jebb's edition ad loc.

followed by

$$εἴ τι μοῖρα μὴ κιγχάνει$$

and the explanation in 1451 f., are the chorus's comment on the preceding scene, especially the curse on Polyneices and Antigone's vain appeal that he should abandon an expedition which he himself knows will be fatal (1432 f.). The terms of Oedipus' curse, with its invocation of τάϲδε δαίμονας (the Erinyes/Eumenides), Polyneices' explicit references to his father's Erinyes (1299 and 1435), and his words at 1443 f. (ταῦτα δ' ἐν τῷ δαίμονι καὶ τῇδε φῦναι χάτέρᾳ, 'these things rest with Fortune, whether they are thus or otherwise') all furnish the subject matter and some of the language of the chorus's reflections: εἴ τι μοῖρα ... ἀξίωμα δαιμόνων and ἐπεὶ μὲν ἕτερα.[20] In these lines they imply that what they have heard in the previous scene is the manifestation of a doom at work in Oedipus' family, decreed by powers (δαίμονες) whose ordinances never fail to be fulfilled:

$$μάταν γὰρ οὐδὲν ἀξίω-$$
$$μα δαιμόνων ἔχω φράϲαι.$$

They then continue with a conventional remark about all-seeing time observing the vicissitudes of men's fortunes. At this moment the first clap of thunder breaks their reflections. Oedipus, who knew from the oracle that he was to expect some such sign (95), recognizes that his hour has come and asks for Theseus to be summoned. The chorus are too panic stricken by the thunder to attend to his instructions and can do nothing but dilate upon their fears for the next two stanzas.

It is to be noted that the peals of thunder occur at unsymmetrical and therefore unexpected intervals during the chorus's lyrics, the first at the end of the first strophe (1456), the second during the antistrophe (1466 f.), the third at the beginning of the second strophe (1477 f.). Their irregularity enhances the effect of surprise as the chorus describe them in some detail with suitable exclamations of panic, notably the appeals to Zeus which close the first three stanzas like a refrain. Increasing excitement is marked by the predominance of dochmiacs over iambics in the second strophic pair. Oedipus' requests become more urgent in

[20] Though 1454 is hopelessly corrupt, the general sense is clear.

the third five-line exchange with Antigone (1486 ff.), and in the final stanza (1491–9) the chorus join in the cry for Theseus, having at last caught Oedipus' urgency and adding the significant point about the benefit which they have picked up from his line 1489

$$\text{ἀνθ' ὧν ἔπαςχον εὖ τελεςφόρον χάριν}$$

echoed in

$$\text{δικαίαν χάριν παραςχεῖν παθών}$$

'in return for his benefits, I will give him a return that fulfils my promise', and 'he should render a just return for benefits' (1497).

This whole epirrhematic passage vividly depicts a progression in the mood of the chorus from reflection, through fear, to a more rational state of mind so that they can enter the action by shouting for Theseus

$$\text{ἰὼ ἰώ, παῖ, βᾶθι βᾶθι}$$

just as they did in the Creon scene. The peals of thunder, expected since the prologue, which summon Oedipus to his death, produce an apocalyptic effect and sound a magnificent prelude to the mystery of his passing. The chorus's expressions of panic and doubt, their appeals to the gods, their vivid, often alliterative descriptions of the thunder, all contrast strikingly with the measured tones of the intervening trimeters in which Oedipus with a new found confidence and authority issues commands in the knowledge that he is being summoned to his death.

The long purely lyric commos which follows the messenger's account of Oedipus' last acts and death recalls in some respects the extended θρῆνος at the end of Aeschylus' *Septem* (875–1004) in which Antigone, Ismene, and the chorus lament the deaths of Polyneices and Eteocles. In both scenes two actors are involved and play a predominant part, and in both, the final stanzas display an increasingly passionate movement in the quicker interchanges of lyrics after a quieter opening. In *O.C.* the lament consists of two strophic pairs, the first very long drawn out, the second shorter. The messenger's speech was delivered to the chorus alone so that when Antigone and Ismene enter at 1669 they are not aware that the chorus have heard his story. This fact is important for the interpretation of 1675–78. In the first place

it confirms the manuscripts' reading παροίϲομεν at 1675. The two
sisters have themselves experienced what the messenger described
at 1598–1617 and 1638–47, and presuming that the chorus are
ignorant of what happened they prepare to give their own
account: ἀλόγιϲτα παροίϲομεν, 'we shall tell a tale which we
cannot explain'; the chorus's τί δ' ἔϲτιν; is an invitation to be
more explicit, and Antigone's answer brings us to the second
point. All the manuscripts give οὐκ ἔϲτι(ν) μὲν εἰκάϲαι, φίλοι at
1677, which is corrupt metrically by reference to the obviously
sound 1704, so that either οὐκ or μὲν must be ejected. Since both
the lemma and the paraphrase in the ancient scholia contain a
negative, one inclines to regard μὲν as the intruder,[21] and if so,
Antigone's reply 'we cannot guess' is an amplification of her
word ἀλόγιϲτα just above. Thirdly, the question mark at βέβηκεν
is unlikely, for the chorus cannot ask 'Is he gone?' just after
hearing the messenger's speech and in particular his clear
statements of fact at 1580 and 1583. βέβηκεν, without any
punctuation mark, will be the opening word of a line confirming
the one certain thing, the fact of Oedipus' death, which is
interrupted by Antigone's ὡϲ μάλιϲτ' ἂν ἐν πόθῳ λάβοιϲ, 'as one
might wish', a point she repeats and amplifies at the corresponding
place in the antistrophe 1704 ff., and again at 1713. She is
concerned to emphasize that for all the mystery of his death (ἐν
ἀφανεῖ τινι μόρῳ φερόμενον, 1682) he died, as he wished, in a
foreign land.

In the second strophic pair the tempo and intensity of emotion
are marked by a greater use of interrupted lines. Whereas in the
strophe, 1724–36, Antigone and Ismene share the exchanges, in
the antistrophe Ismene retires into the background, so that the
chorus take Antigone's place and she takes Ismene's. Antigone's
role as the dominant actor throughout the commos is thus
emphasized at the end. That she is dominant also in character is
made clear enough in the strophe by her determination to see
her father's grave and be killed upon it, and by Ismene's attempts
to restrain her, a recapitulation in miniature of the contrast
between the two sisters drawn with such skill in *Antigone*. The
chorus's part in the commos is subordinate to the actors', and
their main function, apart from a few questions to elicit
Antigone's attitude to her father's death and to the years of

[21] See Wilamowitz, *Griechische Verskunst*, 523.

tending him (1677, 1705, and 1741), is to offer commonplaces of comfort at the end of the first strophe and antistrophe.

This closing lament cancels the mood of calm induced by the messenger's account of Oedipus' passing and substitutes for it a sense of desolation and despair. Although the father has won reconciliation with the powers of the underworld and achieved the end he wished for, there remains for the daughters a life of mourning and deprivation as they leave Athens for Thebes, where further pain awaits them in the mutual slaughter of their brothers and where Antigone will perish for her beliefs. The contrast between Oedipus' fulfilment in death and the future for his sons and daughters imparts not only a tragic poignancy to the last scene of the play but also a terrible irony, in that his use of the family curse against Polyneices, besides ensuring the death of the sons he hates, ensures also the death of the daughter he loves.[22] Thus the Erinyes, converted as far as Oedipus and Theseus' Athens are concerned into the Eumenides, the kindly ones, have not yet finished their work with the house of Labdacus.

A few remarks may be made by way of summarizing the role of the chorus as actors. This play is initially concerned with a suppliant[23] who trespasses on a sacred grove guarded by a group of old men. The theme of supplication is found in some Greek Tragedies of an earlier date: Aeschylus' *Supplices* and *Eumenides* and Euripides' *Heracleidae, Supplices*, and *Hercules Furens*. Certain features are common to all of them.[24] The suppliants, whether actors or the chorus (as in Aeschylus' *Supplices*), disturb the life of a community and create almost intolerable dilemmas for those to whom they appeal. In addition, there is a persecutor, either the ruler of another state or his envoy, or a usurper from within, as in *Hercules Furens*, who demands their surrender, and a benevolent king who has the power to save them. The community that receives the suppliants is assured of benefits from their acceptance, so that self-interest and religious scruples are alike satisfied. In *Oedipus at Colonus* the suppliant's life-history and antecedents present special dangers to the community,

[22] The point is well put by T. C. W. Stinton, *Hamartia in Aristotle and Greek Tragedy*, *CQ* N.S. 25 (1975), 246. See also Lloyd-Jones, *The Justice of Zeus*, 117–19, and Winnington-Ingram, *JHS*, loc. cit. 24.

[23] Oedipus refers to himself or is referred to as ἱκέτης in 44, 284, 487, 634, 1008.

[24] For an extended account of 'Suppliant Plays' see A. P. Burnett, *Catastrophe Survived*; also J. P. Gould, 'Hiketeia', *JHS* 93 (1973), 90.

among them threats of sacrilege, pollution, and foreign war. Further, there are urgent appeals for compassion, promises given and retracted, painful conflicts of emotion, relentless interrogations, and long speeches of persuasion before the suppliant is accepted after acts of propitiation and assurances of protection. After his acceptance, the persecutor, Creon, arrives, kidnaps the suppliant's daughters, and threatens his person. The chorus, representing the community, are old and feeble; and the king, young, vigorous, and authoritative, appears in answer to the old men's shouts and saves the suppliant and the community from further immediate threats. In all these essentially dramatic happenings the chorus are intimately involved, and we need to emphasize their contribution to the excitement and tension of the play, at least until the end of the scene with Creon (1043). Moreover, the theme of supplication provides unity to the structure of the whole play, for it is not until Oedipus' mysterious death as reported by the messenger that all doubts as to his reconciliation with the gods are banished, and we know that there is divine sanction for the fulfilment of the promises made in the prologue and repeated at intervals to the chorus and Theseus as inducements to accept him. Finally, this theme affords a signal opportunity for yet another portrait of the enlightened and benevolent Theseus of Euripides' *Supplices* and *Hercules Furens* and above all for an encomium of his kingdom, Athens, which finds immortal expression in the first stasimon. The point is well made in the fragment of an ancient hypothesis to Euripides' *Supplices*, τὸ δὲ δρᾶμα ἐγκώμιον Ἀθηναίων, and is equally true of Sophocles' play.

We turn now to the role of the chorus as singers. In *Philoctetes* Sophocles developed the technique of lyric dialogue at the expense of stasima. In *Oedipus at Colonus* the balance is largely restored and there are four songs, remarkable for inspired poetry and intense feeling. We have to consider not only the precise context in which they are set but also their relevance to the play as a whole and the reactions which the dramatist wishes to elicit from his audience. This last point requires us to keep in mind also certain external influences, such as the age of the poet and his chorus and the contemporary atmosphere of the city before whose citizens his play was performed, for three of these songs have a relevance not only to the play as a piece for the theatre

but also to the circumstances of Athens during the closing years
of the fifth century.

The first stasimon (668–719) is one of Sophocles' most famous
odes. Its theme is the praise of Colonus developing into the
glorification of Attica and Athens, and it is addressed by the
chorus of old men to Oedipus, the stranger who after years of
wandering has been accepted as a suppliant in old age to dwell
in the grove which they guard as his final home. In the preceding
scene Theseus agreed to receive him and to protect him from the
threat of abduction (656 f.), thus relieving him of his fears about
Creon's intentions, foretold by Ismene (396 f.). The ritual acts
necessary to his acceptance have been duly performed (469–
506), and Theseus has at his first entrance displayed the quality
of his character, his serenity and firmness of temper in contrast
to Oedipus' irascibility and anxious dread, and his tact and calm
sympathy as a foil to the chorus' first reactions. All fears are
allayed by Theseus' speeches (631 ff. and 656 ff.), and there falls
on the play at this moment a mood of tranquillity which recalls
the atmosphere of the opening where Antigone and the gardener
describe the peace and beauty of the grove in terms which
anticipate the ode. This sense of calm, interrupted by the
excitement of the parodos and the earlier doubts about Oedipus'
acceptance, is now restored. It is therefore essential dramatically
to emphasize again the nature of the suppliant's place of refuge
at an obvious pause in the movement of the play just before the
calm is broken by a scene of violence which puts to the test the
confidence expressed in the song. The point is well made by
Antigone at 720, when she sees Creon and his troops approaching:

$$\mathring{\omega} \ \pi\lambda\epsilon\hat{\iota}\sigma\tau' \ \grave{\epsilon}\pi\alpha\acute{\iota}\nuοιc \ \epsilon\mathring{\upsilon}\lambdaογο\acute{\upsilon}μ\epsilonνον \ π\acute{\epsilon}δον,$$
$$ν\hat{\upsilon}ν \ c\grave{ο}ν \ τ\grave{α} \ \lambdaαμπρ\grave{α} \ τα\hat{\upsilon}τα \ δ\grave{η} \ φα\acute{\iota}ν\epsilonιν \ \acute{\epsilon}ππη.$$

'O land most highly praised, now it is your task to proclaim the
truth in these bright words', to which the coryphaeus replies that
in spite of the old age of the singers the strength of their land has
not grown old. These lines show how perfectly the ode is
integrated into the immediate context.

In addition to this precise relevance, the ode in glorifying
Colonus and Athens develops in lyric form a theme heard at
intervals throughout the play. Apart from the amplification of

certain features in the prologue, the olive, the vine, and the nightingales from Antigone's description (16 f.), the holiness of the place and the god Poseidon from the gardener's account (54 f.), the theme of Athens' praise is heard on Oedipus' lips in his prayer at 108, and again in his speech to the chorus at 260 ff. and 282. After the ode, Creon finds it politic to refer to the surpassing strength of Athens (734); Theseus in the same scene calls attention to his city's respect for justice and the law (913 f.); and Oedipus (1006 f. and 1125 f.) refers to the piety, justice, and integrity in which it excels all other cities. This theme of praise both leads up to and issues from the song, so that the heightened language of lyric and the more measured speech of the actors unite in creating an atmosphere of patriotic pride which pervades the whole play.

This last consideration justifies a reference to the contemporary background. Sophocles at the age of ninety here glorifies his native deme of Colonus, Attica, and its metropolis, through the mouths of a chorus of old men at a time when his country was on the brink of disaster, and the morale of the Athenians had been shaken by years of internal faction and the vicissitudes of war. The whole play, and this ode in particular, must have made an astonishing impression on the audience who first saw it in 401 after their city had been defeated; and when at the close of the song the coryphaeus proclaims his confidence in his country's strength, his words gain in power if we recall what had happened to Athens over the past ten years and note some significant phrases in the ode. For what Sophocles is concerned above all to emphasize are certain features of his native land which know not old age or defeat but give a promise of renewal and permanence, an assurance of inviolability and undisturbed calm. We may observe for instance the frequent occurrence of the word ἀεί to denote continuance,[25] whether it be of Dionysus haunting the grove where the nightingales sing (679), of the narcissus and the crocus ever flowering (681 ff.), of the streams of Cephisus ever irrigating the fields (685–91), or of Zeus and Athena ever watching over the olive trees (703–6). The theme of calm undisturbed is heard above all in the description of the grove at 674 ff.; and the olive itself occupies the whole of the second

---

[25] The ἀεί theme here should be seen against the background of 607–20, in which Oedipus develops the theme of impermanence.

strophe, a symbol of invincibility and self-renewal, the nourisher of each fresh generation of children:

$$\text{φύτευμ' ἀχείρωτον αὐτοποιόν,}$$
$$\text{ἐγχέων φόβημα δαΐων,}$$
$$\text{ὃ τᾷδε θάλλει μέγιστα χώρᾳ,}$$
$$\text{γλαυκᾶς παιδοτρόφου φύλλον ἐλαίας}$$

'tree unconquered, self-creating, terror of enemy spears, which flourishes greatly in this land, nourisher of young life, the grey-leafed olive' (698–701). Behind these lines lies the story recorded in Herodotus viii. 55 that after the burning of the acropolis by the Persians in 480 B.C. the sacred olive put forth new growth two days after the fire. This tale of miraculous renewal gives to Sophocles' words a meaning that would not be lost upon an audience who a few years before they saw the play had experienced total defeat, though Lysander did indeed spare their city from a second conflagration. Moreover, we are told in the *Atthis* of Androtion that Archidamus during his annual invasions of Attica in the early years of the Peloponnesian War refrained from destroying the sacred olives. Finally, vivid associations of worship and cult are suggested by the divine powers who appear in the song: Dionysus and his attendant nymphs haunting the inviolate ivy thickets, the goddesses Demeter and Persephone, the Muses and Aphrodite, Zeus and Athena, and in the last stanza Poseidon. Such a land is indeed a sure refuge in the midst of trouble, whether we think of the last decade of the fifth century or of the violence which Oedipus and the old men of the chorus are to face in the next scene of the play.

The clarity with which the song is paragraphed between its stanzas is matched by the lucidity of its sentence structure. The first stanza is periodic in design but straightforward and uninvolved. The second is composed in a series of clauses joined by the simplest of conjunctions, τε, οὐδέ, ἀλλά, as is the third, and the final antistrophe is enlivened in the middle by a note of religious fervour as the chorus address Poseidon in the tones of a hymn. Apart from the more obvious points of word order, such as the opening of the first two stanzas with εὐίππου and θάλλει, both important for the meaning of the ode, we may note that in the third and fourth stanzas the identification of the tree (φύτευμα 698) with its long list of attributes and of the gift (δῶρον 709) is postponed to the ends of the sentences in which they are described, and comes in each case as an effective climax.[26]

A further insight into the quality of Sophocles' poetry may be gained by glancing at a few more details of language and technique. The epithets, many of them unique or rare, are chosen with great economy and precision, and they specify not only the outward appearance of the features they describe but also the inner significance of what Sophocles selects for praise. These two functions of his epithets are interwoven, and examples occur in all the stanzas. For instance an important theme in the ode is suggested by its first word εὐίππου explained and expanded in the last stanza, especially in 711 and the subsequent lines to 715, so that there is a return at the end of the song to the opening lines. The rest of the strophe depicts the actual scene of the play with vividly descriptive epithets, the white hill of Colonus (τὸν ἀργῆτα Κολωνόν, 670), the piercing song of the nightingale from the green thickets, the ivy, οἰνωπός because of its dark leaves and its purplish black berries. Side by side with these descriptive words are others which convey the sanctity of the place, its fertility, and its peace amid the shade of its foliage, ἄβατον, μυριόκαρπον, ἀνάλιον, ἀνήνεμον πάντων χειμώνων, 'untrodden, thousand-fruited, unvisited by the sun, undisturbed by any storms of wind' (675 ff.); and the closing lines provide a glimpse of Dionysus who haunts the holy place, and whose altar is visible to the audience in the orchestra.

In the antistrophe (681) the epithets for the flowers are vivid and detailed: καλλίβοτρυς depicting a cluster like a bunch of grapes and χρυσαυγής the golden stamens of the crocus as its petals open in the sun. Holiness is again hinted at in the ancient association of the narcissus with Demeter and Persephone; and the ideas of refreshment and continual renewal of life and growth are inherent in the scene of irrigation with its attendant epithets ἄυπνοι, νομάδες, ὠκυτόκος, ἀκήρατος, ending with the unique adjective στερνοῦχος describing the hillocks in the plain of Attica and embodying the same metaphor as Pindar's μαστός (breast), of the hill of Cyrene in *Pythian* 4. 8. The stanza closes, like the first, with divine beings, the Muses in dancing chorus, and Aphrodite.

The second strophe (694) displays similar features. All the

26 See further Stinton, *GRBS* 17 (1976), 323–8, *The Riddle at Colonus*.

epithets of the olive except the colour word γλαυκᾶс (701) are suggestive of ideas essential to the meaning of the song, as has been explained already: αὐτοποιόν, self-creating or -created, found only here in a literary text; ἀχείρωτον (a rare word), invincible, as in Thucydides vi. 10, rather than 'not planted by the hand of man', which would be tautologous with αὐτοποιόν and is philologically improbable; παιδοτρόφου 'nourishing young life', a rare synonym for the more usual κουροτρόφοс. This stanza, like the two preceding ones, ends with divine beings; and in the word Μόριοс (705) Sophocles invents a new cult-title for Zeus to describe the function here assigned to him as guardian of the sacred olives, μορίαι.

In the final stanza our thoughts are led to Athens, the mother-city (ματρόπολιс, 707), and we feel that in the opening sentence we have reached the climax of the whole song. The three closing epithets εὔιππον, εὔπωλον, εὐθάλαссον, defining the αὔχημα μέγιстον, convey a sense of triumphant confidence in the supreme gift of Poseidon, the horse and the sea, or to put it more prosaically, cavalry and sea-power. The god himself is then acclaimed in a hymn as the inventor (πρῶτοс εὑρετής) of the bridle described in a striking metaphor as ἵπποιсιν τὸν ἀκεстῆρα, 'the healer of the wild temper of horses', which recalls Pindar's phrases, φίλτρον ἱππεῖον and φάρμακον πραΰ, 'a magic charm for the horse', 'a gentle drug', for the bridle with which Bellerophon tamed Pegasus.[27] The song ends with a brief scene of ships leaping over Poseidon's domain, and in the closing lines one can almost hear the splash of oars and the dancing feet of the Nereids, τῶν ἑκατομπόδων Νηρῄδων ἀκόλουθοс.

In its dramatic context this ode is a welcome to Oedipus the suppliant and a challenge in face of a threat from Creon the persecutor. Against its contemporary background it is a stirring exhortation (παραμύθιον) addressed by the dramatist to his fellow-citizens. Sophocles, sensing his own and his city's decline, looks for what is permanent at a time when Athenian strength on land and sea was gravely threatened; and when the play was produced, the mighty glory (αὔχημα μέγιстον) proclaimed in the last antistrophe had become little more than a dream of vanished pride. Finally, the celebration of Poseidon's gift of the horse to Athens helps to connect the song with the next stasimon (1044),

[27] *O.* 13. 68 and 85.

which imagines in brilliant detail the cavalry engagement between the forces of Theseus and Creon.

In reading this ode one naturally turns to another fine song in praise of Athens, the first two stanzas of Euripides' stasimon at *Medea* 824.[28] A brief discussion may serve to bring out the differences between the two. The contemporary circumstances of the time when *Medea* was first performed in 431 differed vastly from the scene at the end of the century. War, though threatening, had not yet come, Athens was still at the height of her glory, and her immortal longings were not yet quenched. Not only is the background of the two odes different, but they are distinct also in dramatic purpose, structure, and content. The chorus of *Medea* are describing in the first strophic pair the moral and intellectual qualities of a city renowned for perfection of climate and excellence in art, so that in the second pair they may turn to Medea with the argument that such a city, so holy and so civilized, will never receive a murderess; and the dramatic purpose of the ode is to dissuade her from killing her children. In structure therefore the song falls into two parts. On the other hand Sophocles' ode, with its different dramatic purpose of welcoming and reassuring a suppliant already accepted, sweeps from beginning to end in an unbroken stream of praise, widening its flow from its source in the white hill of Colonus, until in the last stanza it reaches Athens.

The features which the two poets select for praise are also different. Euripides concentrates on the intellectual and artistic life of his city, where the sons of Erectheus, whose food is knowledge, walk in a brilliant atmosphere where dwell the Muses who created Harmony; and he describes the clear sky, the gentle winds, and the roses mainly as a background to the cultured life of the citizens. In Sophocles' ode however the intellectual and artistic life plays no part except perhaps for the lines at the end of the first antistrophe, where the Muses and Aphrodite are associated. The hint is indeed very faint, unlike the emphasis given to this association by Euripides, who develops it in a whole stanza ending with the famous words in which intellectual and artistic skill (Σοφία) is united with the instincts of love in partnership to create every kind of excellence. Apart

---

[28] See Page's edition of Eur. *Med.*, vii ff. and the notes ad loc.; also Kranz, *Stasimon*, 200.

from the presence in both odes of the Muses and Aphrodite in company, a conventional union throughout Greek poetry, the only other themes they share are the inviolability of the land and the streams of Cephisus.[29] Both odes are however instinct with patriotic pride, though Sophocles does not appear to owe very much to his predecessor in the details of content and form. Perhaps we may go forward four centuries to Virgil, whose beloved Italian countryside, like Sophocles' Attica, had been ravaged by years of war when he wrote his inspired praise of Italy in the second book of the *Georgics* (136–76). These forty lines of Latin poetry affect the reader with emotions very like those aroused by Sophocles' song. Though Virgil's range is wider, both poets are writing against a similar background and have adopted the same principle in choosing what to praise: natural features for their own sake; and they both display the same intense love of their country, the same belief in its unique quality, and the same confidence in its survival.

The second stasimon (1044–95) follows the scene in which Creon's forces abduct Antigone, and Creon himself threatens Oedipus. The whole mood of the play has changed from the quiet confidence that preceded the ode in praise of Attica to the tension of imminent battle; and the song is placed at the moment when Theseus has despatched his men to rescue Antigone and Ismene from the Thebans. Oedipus and the chorus await the result of the challenge issued by Antigone at 721. The ode therefore has an immediate relevance to its dramatic setting and also reminds us of earlier references within the play to possible future hostilities between Athens and Thebes.[30] There may be no need to look for contemporary associations, but it has been suggested that Sophocles may have had in mind an engagement recorded by Diodorus among others[31] between a Peloponnesian force which included 1200 cavalry of whom the greater part were Boeotians, and a troop of Athenian horse, who were victorious. This skirmish took place very near Athens in the year 408 or 407, when Sophocles may have been pondering the subject of this play; and the song, which describes a fight between

---

[29] Cp. *O.C.* 702 f. and 687 with *Med.* 825 f. and 835.

[30] Cf. 396–400, 411, 605, 616–23, 1037.

[31] See Bowra, *Sophoclean Tragedy*, 300 and n. 1. The ancient authorities besides Diodorus xiii. 72, are Xen. *Hell.* i. i. 33; *Mem.* iii. v. 4; and the scholium on *O.C.* 92.

Athenian and Theban cavalry, may have stirred memories in an audience many of whom could have taken part in the engagement, for Diodorus records that the Athenians, hard pressed by a Peloponnesian force at the gates of their city, ordered all the older men and the strongest of the youth to present themselves under arms. It should be stressed however that there is no need to adduce contemporary events in order to interpret this ode. Regarded strictly in its context as part of the play, it has great poetic power in its manner of presenting to the blind Oedipus a scene of action expected from the moment his daughters were carried away.

In the economy of the play, the interval occupied by the pursuit, the fight, and rescue and return of the sisters is filled by a song which continues in strophic form the excited anticipation of battle aroused towards the end of the preceding scene. In the passage 833–86, the chorus's threats were frustrated by old age and stage convention, but as soon as the scene is at an end, their excitement expresses itself in lyric, and they imagine an engagement at which they wish they could be present. This wish is stated twice, in the opening words, and again at the end of the second strophe (1081 ff.). The repetition suggests that it is a leading motif which provides a clue to the mood and type of the lyric. The chorus long to get away from the present and participate in the activities of youth: old age prevented action at the moment of violence at 833 ff., but it does not inhibit song and the free flight of imagination. Moreover the optatives of wish (εἴην and κύρσαιμι 1083) that frame the description of the battle, together with the personal statements οἶμαι (1054), μοι (1075), and μάντις εἰμι (1080) and the concluding prayer (1085–95), suggest a strongly emotional mood that pervades the whole ode. As to its type, the wish with which it begins recalls those odes or parts of odes in Greek tragedies commonly known as 'escape lyrics', in which the chorus express a longing to get away from an intolerable situation on the stage.[32] Sophocles has however given a different turn to the convention, for the chorus here wish to escape to a scene of violent action, and it is this that they emphasize twice in the song.

---

[32] Cp. e.g. *Trach.* 953 ff.; Eur. *Hipp.* 723 ff.; *Andr.* 862 ff.; *Hel.* 1478 ff. On 'escape lyrics' in general see Shirley Barlow, *The Imagery of Euripides*, 37 ff. and Ruth Padel, *Imagery of the Elsewhere*, CQ N.S. 24 (1974), 227.

This ode also performs a further function in the structure of the play: it is a substitute for a messenger's speech. Instead of giving an extended set of variations on the escape theme like the first two stanzas of Euripides' stasimon at *Hippolytus* 732 and leaving the description of the fight to a messenger, the chorus themselves present the scene in visionary terms. Many of the conventional features of such speeches are indeed to be found in the song: detailed description of place and its associations of custom or cult (1047–53 and 1059–61), and of battle-manoeuvres and highlights in technical language (ἐπιστροφαί, 1045; πᾶς γὰρ ἀστράπτει . . . ἄμβασις, 1067–70),[33] but because the ode is a vision, not a factual account, the details are presented as alternatives, and the ambiguities about the precise locality of the fight, the kind of forces used, and the state of the conflict explain the frequent use of disjunctive words which contribute much to the required feeling of liveliness and suspense.

The visionary quality of the whole song is emphasized by the chorus themselves, especially in the second and third stanzas, where the vivid present tenses ἀστράπτει and ὁρμᾶται (1067 f.) after the futures μείξουσιν (1047), ἐμμείξειν (1057), and ἁλώσεται (1065) suggest that the singers are in fact acting the fight in emotion and imagination; and in the personal forms of expression,

προμνᾶταί τί μοι
γνώμα τάχ' ἐνδώσειν (1075 f.)

and

μάντις εἰμ' ἐσθλῶν ἀγώνων (1080)

they see themselves as prophets compelled by the wooings of their fancy to foretell a happy issue. The vision is moreover experienced with the passion of immediacy, as is clear not only in the selection of pictorial detail described in the present tense, itself a mark of prophetic utterance, but also in the short sentences, the urgent questions, the sparing use or total absence of connectives, and the repetition of words:

δεινὸς ὁ προσχώρων Ἄρης,
δεινὰ δὲ Θησειδᾶν ἀκμά.
πᾶς γὰρ ἀστράπτει χαλινός,
πᾶσα δ' ὁρμᾶται . . . (1065–7)

---

[33] See A. A. Long, *Language and Thought in Sophocles*, 144 ff.

τᾶν δεινὰ τλᾱcᾶν, δεινὰ δ' εὑ-
ρουcᾶν . . .
τελεῖ τελεῖ . . . (1077–9)[34]

The unique nature of this ode in Sophocles' extant tragedies is apparent when it is compared with two other songs of his which describe battle and combat. The parodos of *Antigone* tells of the repulse of the Argive invaders from Thebes, and the elders who form the chorus have experienced what they describe immediately before the play begins. For all its poetic intensity and pictorial detail the scene is presented with the objectivity of fact and without the visionary quality which marks the ode in *Oedipus at Colonus*. Again, the first stasimon of *Trachiniae* (479–530), in which the chorus sing of the wrestling match between Heracles and the river god Achelous, is primarily a ballad of battle long ago, a lyric narrative of great poetic brilliance depicting a mythical scene of violence. True enough, hints of a prophetic and visionary style may be detected elsewhere in Sophocles' lyrics. The bull roams through the woods and over the rocks in the first stasimon of *Oedipus Tyrannus* (463–82); Agamemnon's murder is visualised in the parodos of *Electra* (193–200), and in two songs of the same play (475 ff. and 1384 ff.) the chorus imagine Justice and the Furies, embodied in Orestes and Pylades, advancing to the slaughter of Clytaemnestra. The subject matter and dramatic purpose in each of these cases is however totally different, and it is in this stasimon of *Oedipus at Colonus* alone that a vision of a battle in progress is sustained throughout three stanzas of a long ode.

The fourth stanza is a prayer for victory, addressed to four deities, Zeus, Athena, Apollo, and Artemis, the last two of whom are asked to come in person to help 'this land and its citizens',

διπλᾶc ἀρωγὰc
μολεῖν γᾷ τᾷδε καὶ πολίταιc. (1094 f.)

That the prayer is in ritual form is apparent from the high-sounding epithets and titles attached to the powers concerned and from the 'epiphany' word μολεῖν in the last line. In answer to the prayer Theseus appears with Antigone and Ismene, a proof that the chorus's prophecy (1080) was true. In his

[34] 1065–8, 1077, 1079.

announcement to Oedipus, the coryphaeus refers to the phrase
μάντις εἰμι in the song (1080):

$$τῷ σκοπῷ μὲν οὐκ ἐρεῖς$$
ὡς ψευδόμαντις   (1096 f.)

'You will not say that your watcher is a false prophet'. The
connection of the ode with the following scene is made precise by
this verbal link as well as by the device of introducing a human
figure in answer to a request for the presence of a god.[35]

Apart from the three lines 1096–8, the chorus take no part in
the short scene that separates the second from the third stasimon.
Oedipus welcomes his daughters, thanks Theseus for rescuing
them, and learns from him of Polyneices' presence as a suppliant
at Poseidon's altar. To Theseus' advice that there is a compulsion
to receive suppliants based upon respect for the gods (1179 f.)
Antigone adds her appeal that Polyneices should be given an
audience, with the argument that the father should not requite
the son's wrongdoing with another wrong (1189–91). She also
warns him of the consequences of anger. In the event he agrees
to hear his son on condition that he remains safe from capture.
The prospect of a bitter and passionate interview between the
two is now assured, but first comes the song on the folly of
overstepping the reasonable limit in length of days, developing
into a recital of the woes that attend old age (1211–48).

In form the ode is simple: a strophe and antistrophe followed
by an epode. The strophe begins with a statement of the
traditional maxim μηδὲν ἄγαν applied especially to length of
days and taken as obvious in the singers' judgement: 'Whoever
desires length of life beyond τὸ μέτριον is in my opinion a fool',

σκαιοσύναν φυλάσ-
σων ἐν ἐμοὶ κατάδηλος ἔσται.

The reason for this opinion is then given: the things that give
delight vanish and in their place comes pain. There follows the
conclusion

ὁ δ' ἐπίκουρος ἰσοτέλεστος,
"Αιδος ὅτε μοῖρ' ἀνυμέναιος
ἄλυρος ἄχορος ἀναπέφηνε,
θάνατος ἐς τελευτάν.   (1220–3)

---

[35] Cf. e.g. *Ant.* 1155; *O.T.* 216; *El.* 660.

'but the helper comes, the fulfilment for all alike—when the doom of Hades is revealed, with no marriage-song, no lyre, no dance—death at the last.' Death, the end for all alike, is the helper who rescues us from the woes of old age. The adjective ἰςοτέλεςτος (1220), found only here in classical Greek, concentrates into one word the Homeric concept τέλος θανάτοιο and the many forms in which we find the commonplace that death comes to all alike. Simonides (15 P) combines them both:

$$\text{ὁ δ' ἄφυκτος ὁμῶς ἐπικρέμαται θάνατος·}$$
$$\text{κείνου γὰρ ἴςον λάχον μέρος οἵ τ' ἀγαθοὶ}$$
$$\text{ὅςτις τε κακός,}$$

'Inevitable death hangs over all alike: both good and bad share in it equally.' The words occur in a context similar to that in Sophocles' song after a few lines listing the troubles of life, and Plutarch quotes them to illustrate the view that death is preferable to life:

$$\text{κρεῖττόν ἐςτι τὸ τεθνάναι τοῦ ζῆν.}^{36}$$

The three epithets with Ἄιδος μοῖρα, ἀνυμέναιος, ἄλυρος, ἄχορος (1221 f.) represent the three delights relevant especially to youth which death interrupts, wedding songs, music, and dancing, amplifications indeed of τὰ τέρποντα in the previous sentence, the pleasures which old age cannot recover. The most interesting idea however in this clause is contained in the word ἐπίκουρος (1220).[37] Such a considered and explicit statement of the view of death as a positive ally is remarkable in Greek poetry of the Classical period, though there are many instances of appeals to death by intending suicides or by those in physical agony.[38] These are not strictly parallel, because they are delivered in moments of extreme passion or pain. The idea of θάνατος as a helper is singularly appropriate to this play, whether we consider Oedipus, about to find peace in death after the troubles of his life and an old age full of wrath, as depicted in the play, or the chorus, sharing old age with him, as they state at the beginning of the epode (1239), or Sophocles himself, ninety years old when he wrote this song.

[36] Plu. *Consol. Apoll.* 11. i. 220.

[37] Hermann's ὁ δ' ἐπίκουρος for the senseless and metreless οὐδ' ἐπὶ κοῦρος or κόρος of the manuscripts is generally accepted in 1220.

[38] e.g. *Aj.* 854; *Trach.* 1040; *Phil.* 797.

The antistrophe (1224) is composed in exactly the same way as the strophe. It opens likewise with a traditional maxim that can be traced back through Herodotus, Bacchylides, and Theognis to a mythical tale about Silenus' reply to Midas in answer to the question what was the best thing for man.[39] As in the strophe, the second sentence gives the reason for the maxim, expanding into a list what was stated in general terms as πολλὰ λύπας ἐγγυτέρω, 'many things nearer to pain than to joy' (1215 f.), and the stanza ends with a description of old age in a series of privative adjectives ἄκρατες, ἀπροσόμιλον, ἄφιλον (1236 f.), which echo the attributes of "Αϊδος μοῖρα in the strophe. There is thus in the two stanzas a perfect symmetry of structure: maxim, reason, and conclusion follow one another in both. Death forms the climax of the first, old age of the second. The thought proceeds from a pessimism confined, in the strophe, to the loss of youth as years advance, and lightened by the concept of death as deliverer, to a pessimism that in the antistrophe embraces the whole of adult life as the chorus identify the troubles (κάματοι) that beset it in a dismal list: φόνοι, cτάceιc, ἔρις, μάχαι καὶ φθόνος, murders, factions, strife, battles, and envy:[40] these are the experience of man as soon as he has let youth with its follies pass by,

> εὖτ' ἂν τὸ νέον παρῇ
> κούφας ἀφροσύνας φέρον.   (1229)

The view of old age here expressed has a long tradition in Greek poetry. In Homer, γῆρας is in the main something mournful and frightful (λυγρόν, cτυγερόν).[41] Hesiod calls it accursed (οὐλόμενον) and makes it the offspring of Night, along with Nemesis, Deception, Sex, and Strife, a formidable brood.[42] Mimnermus held it in peculiar horror for it made a man ugly, destroyed his delight in looking at the sun, and ruined his sex appeal; and according to him, Tithonus' immortal old age is more miserable than death (θανάτου ῥίγιον ἀργαλέου).[43] There is indeed another side to this gloomy picture, beginning with the *Odyssey*[44] where γῆρας is twice called λιπαρόν (comfortable), and

---

[39] *Hdt.* i. 131; Thgn. 425; B. 5. 160.

[40] This is the manuscripts' order of the list and should probably be kept, as φθόνος is different in type and constitutes the motive for the other items.

[41] *Il.* 19. 336; *Od.* 24. 250.

[42] *Th.* 225 ff.

[43] Frs. 1–5 D.

[44] *Od.* 11. 136; 19. 368.

followed by Pindar, who in addition to holding the usual view of it as hateful envisages a λιπαρὸν γῆρας with a prospect of peace and happiness.[45] Sophocles himself, as certain fragments show,[46] is well aware that old age can also bring wisdom, knowledge, and contentment; but although Oedipus says at the beginning of the play that his sufferings and length of days have taught him patience (cτέργειν), there is little sign within the play that his experiences have calmed his passionate temper. Nearer the mark is Creon's line at 954:

> θυμοῦ γὰρ οὐδὲν γῆράc ἐcτιν ἄλλο πλὴν
> θανεῖν.

'there is no old age for anger, only death'.

The attitude towards old age represented in these and many other passages in Greek literature forms a necessary background to the first two stanzas of Sophocles' song, but the three privative adjectives describing it at 1236 need some discussion. ἄκρατεc is immediately intelligible, however we translate it: 'powerless' or 'uncontrolled in passion'. The former is probably better, as the latter may require a defining noun in the genitive. Both meanings however suit certain passages in the play, especially the scene with Creon, where the anger of the two old men and the inability of both Oedipus and the chorus to resist violence add a note of tragic pathos to the whole scene. ἀπροcόμιλον, found only here,[47] and ἄφιλον are however surprising. Both express the isolation of old age from society and friends; and while it may be unwise to look for too specific a reference in a general statement, we may note that those epithets deny not only the concept of φιλία so important in the relations between Oedipus and Theseus and the ὁμιλία established with the chorus, but also the bond of love between Oedipus and his daughters. The denial of φιλία is however seen in the failure of both Eteocles and Polyneices to care for their father in old age[48] and in the quarrel between father and son in the following scene.

---

[45] *N.* 7. 99.

[46] Frs. 193, 260, 664, 950 P.

[47] This word is echoed in 1277 (δυcπρόcοιcτον κἀπροcήγορον). Though here used in a tragic context, epithets of this type, as Mr Stinton reminds me, are regular of angry, tetchy old men in Comedy. Cf. Phryn. com. fr. 18 (*C.A.F.* i. 375), ἀδιάλεκτοc, ἀπρόcοδοc, 'unconversible, unapproachable'; *C.A.F.* iii. 587, ὁ μονογέρων μονότροπον καὶ δύcκολον γέροντα cημαίνει, see J.-M. Jacques, Men. *Le Dyscolos* (Budé), 33 ff.

[48] For this theme in the play cf. 342 ff. and 1354–69.

The epode (1239) turns from general statements to the particular instance, presenting Oedipus and the old men of the chorus as examples; and the personal pronoun ἐγώ marks the conclusion of the song. Both alike find themselves in the predicament described at the end of the antistrophe, and this final stanza thus brings the ode into immediate connection with the dramatic context. The simile at 1242 ff. has a Homeric quality and may indeed echo the one at *Iliad* 15. 618–22, describing the Achaeans' resistance, like a rock based in the sea, to Hector's onslaught.[49] There is however a closer parallel in Sophocles himself. At *Antigone* 586 ff. the doom, ἄτη, that buffets a House which the gods wish to destroy is compared to the waves that roar and beat against the headland exposed to winds and sea. In this passage of *Oedipus at Colonus* and in *Antigone* 586–93 there are striking similarities: κυματοπλὴξ ἀκτά and ἀντιπλῆγες ἀκταί, the wave-beaten headlands; the same association of ἄτη and ἆται with the fury of the sea; the same sound of words chosen for alliterative effect, and the same accumulation of detail. The ἆται that beat upon Oedipus are themselves the waves, and he is the ἀκτὰ χειμερία, the headland that fronts the storms of winter.[50] The epode swells in a single period of overwhelming poetic power whose magnificence is enhanced by assonance, verbal echoes, and precise imagery. No translation can do justice to it, so it must be quoted just for the sound of the Greek:

> ἐν ᾧ τλάμων ὅδ', οὐκ ἐγὼ μόνος,
> πάντοθεν βόρειος ὥς τις ἀκτὰ
> κυματοπλὴξ χειμερία κλονεῖται,
> ὣς καὶ τόνδε κατ' ἄκρας
> δειναὶ κυματοαγεῖς
> ἆται κλονέουσιν ἀεὶ ξυνοῦσαι,
> αἱ μὲν ἀπ' ἀελίου δυςμᾶν,
>   αἱ δ' ἀνατέλλοντος,
> αἱ δ' ἀνὰ μέσσαν ἀκτῖν',
> αἱ δ' ἐννυχιᾶν ἀπὸ Ῥιπᾶν.

[49] See Bowra, op. cit. 354.
[50] 'I stand . . . as one upon a rock
  Environed by a wilderness of sea
  Who marks the waxing tide grow wave by wave'.
       Titus Andronicus, Act III, Sc. i.

This song has a relevance to the play which is both immediate and more remote. Just before it is sung the menace of the scene with Polyneices is made apparent in the conversation between Oedipus and Theseus (1156–80). The old man's obstinacy is contrasted with Theseus' reasonableness, his hatred with the other's final warning about the legitimate claim of a suppliant to audience. Then comes Antigone's moving appeal (1189–91 and 1201–3). Oedipus yields with a bad grace, and on condition that he shall retain full control over his own person (1204–7). The course of the coming interview is unpredictable but the situation is full of foreboding as the chorus wait to see what effect Theseus' and Antigone's words will have upon him. At any rate Polyneices' approach constitutes a further threat, after Creon, to Oedipus' safety, a final battering of the waves of doom that beat upon him, a threat also of further strife, battles, and violent deaths. The ode is sung as they await Polyneices' arrival, and the simile of the storm-beaten cape in the last stanza foreshadows the father's craggy immobility which confronts the son in the following episode:

> τί ϲιγᾷϲ;
> φώνηϲον, ὦ πάτερ, τι· μή μ' ἀποϲτραφῇϲ.
> οὐδ' ἀνταμείβῃ μ' οὐδέν; ἀλλ' ἀτιμάϲαϲ
> πέμψειϲ ἄναυδοϲ, οὐδ' ἃ μηνίειϲ φράϲαϲ; (1271–4)

'Why are you silent? . . . Say *something*, father; don't turn away from me . . . No answer at all? Will you reject me and send me away without a word, without explaining the reason for your anger?' A few lines later (1277), when Polyneices refers to his father's ϲτόμα as δυϲπρόϲοιϲτον κἀπροϲήγορον, 'unapproachable, unconversible', we are reminded of the chorus's epithet for old age in the ode, ἀπροϲόμιλον (1236).

In the wider context of the play the song is the comment of old men united in sympathy with the old king, Oedipus, as they make clear in the opening words of the epode. They have throughout become aware of his characteristics: his passionate temperament, his formidable stubbornness, his confidence in his innocence, the rock-like power of his personality. They know all about his story and the disasters which have been his constant companions throughout his adult life, parricide, incest, blindness, exile, vagrancy, strife between his sons, abduction of his daughters, and threats of personal violence. As he stands before them at the verge of death they express in this ode their verdict on old age, in particular an old age such as his with its burden of pain: φόνοι, cτάceιc, ἔρις, μάχαι καὶ φθόνος. It is difficult to give a precise reference to each item in this list, and an attempt to do so would perhaps be unwise, for the words, as in most great poetry, have a resonance beyond the immediate context. Violent deaths, factions, strife, and battles are all implicit in the story of the Labdacid house as well as apparent and foreshadowed in certain episodes of the play, manifestations of the doom that assails it from of old, as the chorus sing at *Antigone* 594 f.:

> ἀρχαῖα τὰ Λαβδακιδᾶν οἴκων ὁρῶμαι
> πήματα φθιμένων ἐπὶ πήμαcι πίπτοντα,

'Ancient are the woes of the Labdacid house: I see them falling on dead men's woes'. As to φθόνος, envy, this is a τόπος, especially in Pindar, who regards it as an abiding force in human actions. Here we may see in it the envy of Polyneices for the younger brother who usurped his throne, the envy of old age for the delights of youth, and in a more general sense the motivation behind the preceding items in the list.

The censure of old age in the antistrophe (κατάμεμπτον, 1235) recalls to some extent Euripides' great ode at *Hercules Furens* 637 in which the old men of the chorus contrast the burdens of age with the delights of youth. Their lyric is however essentially an encomium of youth and lacks the pessimism of Sophocles. Moreover they proclaim their confidence in the power of song as an abiding solace:

> οὐ παύcομαι τὰς Χάριτας
> Μούcαιc cυγκαταμειγνύς,
> ἁδίcταν cυζυγίαν·
> μὴ ζῴην μετ' ἀμουcίας
> ἀεὶ δ' ἐν cτεφάνοιcιν εἴ-
> ην· ἔτι τοι γέρων ἀοι-
> δὸς κελαδεῖ Μναμοcύναν.   (*H.F.* 673–9.)

'I shall not cease to link the Graces with the Muses, union most sweet. May I not live when music is silent but ever be found where garlands are. See, the old singer still hymns Mnemosyne.'

In Sophocles' ode the pessimism seems at first sight unrelieved:
it finds no solace during life, and death alone brings deliverance.
This view of death is important in the context of a play which
depicts the closing hours of a long and troubled life and moves,
towards its end, to a scene of unearthly calm in the account of
Oedipus' passing. We may note also that this aspect of death is
echoed in the final stasimon, the nucleus of which is a prayer to
the power that grants eternal sleep (τὸν αἰένυπνον, 1578). These
considerations may reveal a glimmer of light in the dark
pessimism of the song. Nevertheless, in contrast to the two
preceding odes it is profoundly tragic in its evocation of the
pathos of old age, and in this contrast of mood resides much of its
power, since it leads the mind and the emotions along paths as
yet unexplored in the lyrics of the play.

Up to this point we have confined discussion to the relevance
of the song as part of the Tragedy. This is the first task of
interpretation. Its impressiveness is however enhanced if we
remember Sophocles' great age at the time of its composition.
We may then perhaps regard it also as a judgement on the
experience of a long life protracted into the years of his city's
decline. This does not mean that he consciously composed it as an
envoi to his fellow citizens, using the chorus as his mouthpiece, but
only that he can hardly have been unaffected by the contemporary political scene. Further, we should try to imagine the
effect his words are likely to have had on his audience. There
may be political overtones in the list at 1234 f., as is suggested by
Herodotus' account of oligarchy as a type of government:[51] . . .
ἐς ἔχθεα μεγάλα ἀλλήλοισι ἀπικνέονται, ἐξ ὧν στάσιες ἐγγίγνονται,
ἐκ δὲ τῶν στασίων φόνος, 'men arrive at a state of strong mutual
enmity, from which arise factions, and from factions, murder.'
With this passage in mind we may feel that Sophocles' words
would recall to his audience the melancholy record of faction,
violence, and murder that darkened the final decade of the fifth
century: the oligarchic conspiracy of 411 B.C., the murder of
Phrynichus, the execution of Antiphon, and, after the poet's
death, the bloody reign of the Thirty Tyrants in 404–403. The
ode then becomes, not only for us who read it but also for the
Athenians who heard it sung, the epilogue of the γερὼν ἀοιδός
who had spent 60 years of his life in composing tragedies for

[51] Hdt. iii. 82.

performance at Athens and had witnessed both her glory and her decline. The temptation to see in parts of this song a reflection of its contemporary background and to imagine its effect upon an audience is indeed powerful and should perhaps not be resisted provided that we have first set it in its dramatic context.

The final stasimon (1556) follows the speech in which Oedipus, now assured by the three peals of thunder that he has reached the verge between life and death (ῥοπὴ βίου μου, 1508), assumes control of the play, speaking and acting as a being transformed. He gives the instructions which Theseus and his daughters must follow and closes with a farewell to the daylight, invisible to him (ὦ φῶc ἄφεγγεc, 1549), and a prayer for the future prosperity of Attica, its king, and its inhabitants. At the end of this speech, a sense of awe pervades the play as the ode is sung to an empty stage. The chorus themselves express this feeling in the propitiatory words with which they begin the song, εἰ θέμιc ἐcτι, 'if it is right . . .'.

The ode consists of a single strophe and antistrophe and is in the form of a ritual prayer. It must therefore be seen as an act of worship, instinct with religious solemnity as the singers await Oedipus' death. They address a series of powers, first the unseen goddess (Persephone, 1556) then Aidoneus (Hades), King of the realms of night, to grant him an easy and painless passage to the underworld. In the antistrophe they turn to the χθόνιαι θεαί, the goddesses who dwell below the earth, the Erinyes-Eumenides to whom Oedipus appealed in the prologue (84 f. and 106); and to Cerberus, the mythical guardian of Hades' kingdom, here vividly imagined in an extended description as he lies asleep or snarling at the gates. The assonance in εὐνᾶcθαι κνυζεῖcθαι recalls the repetition Ἀιδωνεῦ Ἀιδωνεῦ in the corresponding line of the strophe (1559 = 1571) and is a further example of Sophocles' exploitation of word and sound echoes. The final appeal is to Γᾶc παῖ καὶ Ταρτάρου, son of Earth and Tartarus, Death. This genealogy is elsewhere unattested and may therefore be the poet's invention.[52] The last line with its emphatic opening pronoun and ritual verb sums up the purpose of the ode as a ὕμνοc κλητικόc in which a power is summoned by prayer to perform a definite task:

cέ τοι κικλήcκω τὸν αἰένυπνον

[52] In Hesiod *Th.* 212, θάνατοc is the offspring of Night and has no father.

'on you I call, the giver of eternal sleep.' The epithet, found only here, is sufficient identification, for Death and Sleep are a well known pair of brothers. Apart from the two lines in corresponsion noted above we may observe the cumulative effect throughout this song of expressions describing the features of the underworld and its inhabitants. τὰν παγκευθῆ νεκύων πλάκα (1563 f.) is echoed at the end of the antistrophe in νερτέρας νεκρῶν πλάκας, the vast spaces which conceal the dead. παγκευθῆ and πολυξένοις (1563 and 1570) complement one another, as do ἀνικάτου and ἀδάματον of Cerberus (1568 and 1572); and over all broods the familiar metaphor of the underworld as a place where the dead are received as guests when Cerberus has allowed them a clear entry (ξένον, πολυξένοις, ἐν καθαρῷ βῆναι ὁρμωμένῳ ... τῷ ξένῳ 1562, 1570, 1575 f.).

For all its simplicity of structure the ode is extraordinarily impressive. It awakes in the audience a mood of religious awe appropriate to the mystery surrounding Oedipus' death, to be described in the next scene. In the form of a ritual prayer the chorus ask that the old king, reconciled with a just god, may soon be at peace after the troubles of his life and the storms of passion depicted in the play. This prayer for an easy passing is the final acknowledgement that Death, θάνατος ἐς τελευτάν, is the deliverer, and it stresses the importance of this idea in the closing moments of Oedipus' life. As for his reconciliation with the gods, the last sentence of the strophe (1565 ff.) echoes Ismene's line 394:

νῦν γὰρ θεοί σ' ὀρθοῦσι, πρόσθε δ' ὤλλυσαν

'Now are the gods raising you up; before, their purpose was to destroy you.' In this line the gods are not identified, so that we do not know whether they belong to the upper or the nether world. Likewise in the ode the chorus speak of an unidentified δαίμων δίκαιος (1567), a just power exalting Oedipus at the moment of his death, and in this exaltation lie his justification in the sight of the gods and the fulfilment of promises first heard in the prologue and repeated in his last speech, that possession of his body is a guarantee of Attica's safety, so that the inhabitants will accord him the worship due to a semi-divine benefactor.[53]

The text of 1565 ff. has been assailed,[54] but it appears that the

---

[53] See Farnell, *Hero Cults*, 332 ff.   [54] See Jebb's note ad loc.

chorus are making two points, first, that many woes came upon
Oedipus and to no purpose; in other words that throughout his
life his woes were intended by the gods to destroy him and that
the play shows the frustration of this purpose (μάταν ἱκνουμένων);
and secondly, that in death a just power may exalt him again.
One thinks here not only of Ismene's words at 394 but of the final
stasimon of the first Oedipus play,[55] in which the great king of
Thebes, in his subjects' eyes an almost god-like figure at the
beginning, is at the end revealed as nothing, an outcast from
among men, rejected by the gods and doomed to a vagabond life,
until in the later play he is received at Colonus and requited with
honour. In this sense perhaps more than in any other the later
play may be seen as a sequel to the earlier.[56] There is also in this
sentence, particularly in the implications of the word αὔξοι
(1567), a more immediate relevance to the dramatic context.
Oedipus' speech just before the song reveals a new found
ascendancy over those around him, a full knowledge of what
must be done, and a calm sense of control, so that we feel that he
has in a mysterious way increased in stature, all frailty shed
away, all passion spent; and in the following scene this impression
of knowledge and authority is enhanced by the messenger's
account of his last words and deeds. He is moreover summoned
to death by the voice of an unidentified and benevolent god:

> ἦν μὲν cιωπή, φθέγμα δ' ἐξαίφνης τινὸς
> θώυξεν αὐτόν, ὥcτε πάντας ὀρθίας
> cτῆcαι φόβῳ δείcαντας ἐξαίφνης τρίχας.
> καλεῖ γὰρ αὐτὸν πολλὰ πολλαχῇ θεόc·
> ὦ οὗτοc οὗτοc, Οἰδίπους, τί μέλλομεν
> χωρεῖν;   (1623–8)

'There was silence, and suddenly the voice of someone cried out
to him, so that our hair stood on end for dread. For a god called
him many times and in many ways: Oedipus, Oedipus, why do
we wait to go?' The first person plural, μέλλομεν, subtly indicates
the sympathy and friendliness of the god who summons him. His
raising up by a δαίμων δίκαιος is thus accomplished, and he goes
to his death a being sanctified.

[55] *O.T.* 1186–1222.

[56] On the relation between the two Oedipus plays, see Bernd Seidensticker, *Hermes* 100
(1972), 255–74.

As is usual with Sophocles, the songs of this play are completely consistent with the status and role of the chorus. They develop many themes suggested by the action: love of country and confidence in its survival, the desire to experience the excitement of battle, the pathos of old age, and the hope of an easy death at the end as a deliverance from the troubles of life. All these are fitting subjects for song on the lips of old men, and the lyrics in which they are explored constitute an astonishing monument to the undiminished vigour and inspiration of a man who was entering on his tenth decade when he wrote them. What we do not find in these songs, as we do in some of those in *Antigone*, *Oedipus Tyrannus*, and *Electra*, are any reflections on the moral and intellectual problems of the play: discussion of these is confined to actors' scenes with occasional maxims from the chorus, as in *Ajax*, *Trachiniae*, and *Philoctetes*. This absence of moral and intellectual comment from the songs of *Oedipus at Colonus* is indeed perfectly consistent with the type of chorus chosen by Sophocles for his last play, for they are essentially simple countrymen, not elders of a city, and they are moved above all by a heartfelt love of their deme and its wider setting, a deep sense of awe and duty as guardians of a sacred place, and the natural sympathy of old age for old age. Their odes therefore express reactions which are almost exclusively emotional. Finally, in the songs of this play, more perhaps than in any other of Sophocles' extant tragedies, we do well to keep in mind the contemporary background and to try by an effort of imagination to assess their effect on an Athenian audience at the end of the fifth century.

INDEXES

I. INDEX OF AUTHORS AND PASSAGES

3. INDEX OF GREEK WORDS